MACHIAVELLI'S *PRINCE*

Machiavelli's *Prince*

A New Reading

ERICA BENNER

OXFORD
UNIVERSITY PRESS

OXFORD
UNIVERSITY PRESS

Great Clarendon Street, Oxford, OX2 6DP,
United Kingdom

Oxford University Press is a department of the University of Oxford.
It furthers the University's objective of excellence in research, scholarship,
and education by publishing worldwide. Oxford is a registered trade mark of
Oxford University Press in the UK and in certain other countries

Published in the United States of America by Oxford University Press
198 Madison Avenue, New York, NY 10016, United States of America

British Library Cataloguing in Publication Data
Data available

Library of Congress Cataloging in Publication Data
Data available

ISBN 978-0-19-965363-8

Printed in Great Britain by
Clays Ltd, St Ives plc

Quanto piú mi è cresciuto la speranza, tanto mi è cresciuto el timore . . . Oimé, che io non truovo requie in alcuno loco! Talvolta io cerco di vincere me stesso, riprendomi di questo mio furore, e dico meco: Che fai tu? Se' tu impazzato? Quando tu l'ottenga, che fia? . . . Non sai tu quanto poco bene si truova nella cose che l'uomo desidera, rispetto a quello che l'uomo ha presupposto trovarvi?

The more my hope has grown, the more my fear has grown . . . Woe is me! I can't find rest anywhere! Sometimes I try to conquer myself, reproaching myself for this fury of mine, and say to myself: What are you doing? Are you crazy? When you get her, what'll it amount to? . . . Don't you know how little good a man finds in the things he has longed for, compared with what he expected to find?

(Mandragola, Act IV, scene 1)

Acknowledgements

I have been inspired and challenged by discussions with other scholars, some at early stages of writing and others when the manuscript was more or less complete. I regret that I had too little time and space to address all their suggestions in the text. *Nondimanco*, I thank the following for their contributions to my thinking on the *Prince*, and hope for future opportunities to continue our discussions: Adrian Blau, Guillaume Bogiaris, Dirk Brantl, Dallas Denery, Denis Fachard, Benedetto Fontana, Tankred Freiberger, Rolf Geiger, Michael Gillespie, Giovanni Giorgini, Anthony Grafton, Ruth Grant, Otfried Höffe, Andreas Kablitz, George Kateb, Daniel Stein Kokin, Robyn Marasco, John McCormick, David Miller, Cary Nederman, Luis Javier Orjuela, Giovanni Panno, Zbigniew Pelczynski, Mark Philp, Alessandro Pinzani, Emanuele Cutinelli Rendina, Jorge Andres López Rivera, Rodrigo Romero, Rahul Sagar, Peter Schröder, Quentin Skinner, Peter Stacey, Vickie Sullivan, Diego von Vacano, Ever Eduardo Velazco, Armando Villegas, Maurizio Viroli, Daniel Weinstock, Will Wittels, and Catherine Zuckert. Special thanks are due to John Najemy for his *prudentissimo* advice on my original book proposal.

Some of the ideas in this book were presented at the Groupe de Recherche Interuniversitaire en Philosophie Politique, Montreal; Philosophisches Seminar, Tübingen University; Oriel College, Oxford; the Center for Human Values, Princeton; Duke University; Universidad Javeriana, Cali, Colombia; and Renaissance Studies Association conferences in Montreal and Washington, D.C. I thank the organizers for their invitations, and the audiences and other participants for their comments.

I also thank Andrew Hurrell, Catherine Clarke, and the anonymous readers for OUP for their valuable suggestions; and Dominic Byatt, Aimee Wright, Carla Hodge, and Mandi Gomez at OUP for all their editorial support.

I am grateful above all to Patrick and to my mother, to whom I dedicate this book. Since words cannot express the depth of my gratitude, I shall leave them out.

Contents

Prudence and trust

Redemption

Detailed contents

Foundations

Abbreviations

Machiavelli's works

Ai Palleschi	Original in *Opere* vol. 1.
AW	*Art of War* [Dell' arte della guerra]. Original in *Opere* vol. 1.
Cagione	*Cagione della Ordinanza*. Original in *Opere* vol. 1.
CC	*The Life of Castruccio Castracani of Lucca* [La vita di Castruccio Castracani da Lucca]. Original in *Opere* vol. 3.
D	*Discourses on Livy* [Discorsi sopra la prima deca di Tito Livio]. Original in *Opere* vol. 1.
Decennale	Original in *Opere* vol. 1.
Dell' Ambizione	*Tercets on Ambition*. Original in *Opere* vol. 3.
Di Fortuna	*Tercets on Fortune*. Original in *Opere* vol. 3.
Discursus	*Discourse on Remodelling the Government of Florence* [Discursus florentinarum rerum]. Original in *Opere* vol. 1.
FH	*Florentine Histories* [Istorie fiorentine]. Original in *Opere* vol. 3.
GA	'A Portrait of German Affairs' [*Ritracto delle cose della Magna*]. Original in *Opere* vol. 1.
Legations	*Legazioni e Commissarie*. Original in *Opere* vol. 2.
MF	*Machiavelli and his Friends: Their Personal Correspondence*. Trans. and ed. James B. Atkinson and David Sices. Original in *Opere* vol. 2.
Provisione	*Provisione della Ordinanza*. Original in *Opere* vol. 1.3.

Other works

AP	Aristotle, *Politics*
AR	Aristotle, *Rhetoric*
ANE	Aristotle, *Nicomachean Ethics*
GD	Guicciardini, *Dialogues*
LH	Livy, *Histories* [Ab urbe condita]
ME	Benner, *Machiavelli's Ethics*
PolH	Polybius, *Histories*
PL	Plutarch, *Parallel Lives of Greeks and Romans*
PM	Plutarch, *Moralia*
SJW	Sallust, *Jugurthine War*

SWC	Sallust, *War with Catiline*
TA	Tacitus, *Agricola*
TH	Tacitus, *Histories*
TPW	Thucydides, *Peloponnesian War*
VA	Virgil, Aeneid
XC	Xenophon, *Cyropaedia*
XH	Xenophon, *Hiero*

Introduction

De' principi si parla sempre con mille paure e mille rispetti.

Princes are always spoken of with a thousand fears and a thousand hesitations.

(*Discourses*, I.58)

Niccolò Machiavelli's *Prince* is one of the most famous books in the world—and perhaps the least understood. Its author announced the existence of a first draft 500 years ago, in a December 1513 letter to his friend Francesco Vettori. The letter begins with a vivid description of how Machiavelli spent his days at his small family estate outside Florence, where he had gone in March after suffering a series of political and personal disasters. The Florentine republic he had served for 14 years had been overthrown in September of the previous year. In the ensuing months Machiavelli was dismissed from his political posts, accused of taking part in a conspiracy against the new rulers, imprisoned, and tortured. Recovering his spirits *post res perditas*, 'after these wretched affairs',[1] he tells Vettori that his greatest solace comes in the evenings when, retreating to his study:

> I step inside the antique courts of the ancients where, lovingly received by them... I nourish myself on that food that alone is mine and for which I was born.... And because Dante says that no one makes knowledge [*fa scienza*] without retaining what he has understood, I have jotted down what capital I have made from their conversation and composed a little work [*opusculo*], *De principatibus* ('Of principalities'), in which I delve as deeply as I can into the cogitations concerning this topic, disputing the definition of a principality, the categories of principalities, how they are acquired, how they are maintained, and why they are lost. And if ever any whimsy [*ghiribizo*] of mine has given you pleasure, this one should not displease you. It ought to be welcomed by a prince, and especially by a new prince; therefore I am dedicating it to His Magnificence Giuliano.[2]

In September 1512 the 33-year-old Giuliano de' Medici had led troops against Florence, backed by Pope Julius II and Spanish forces, and deposed the republican government that had employed Machiavelli. By late 1513 rumour had it that Giuliano's brother Giovanni, now Pope Leo X, might employ him

---

[1] As he inscribed on a copy of his 'Discourse on the reorganization of the Florentine state for arms'.

[2] Machiavelli to Vettori, 10 December 1513, *MF* 263–5.

to assert papal control over the Romagna,[3] as a decade earlier Pope Alexander VI had used his son Cesare Borgia—a key figure in the *Prince*—to further his political aims in the same turbulent region. These plans never materialized, and Giuliano died early in 1516. In the end Machiavelli dedicated his book to Giuliano's and the Pope's nephew Lorenzo II, who had been made *de facto* ruler of Florence in 1515.

We do not know when the dedication was changed, or whether Machiavelli ever presented his *De principatibus* to any Medici prince. It remained unpublished during his lifetime, but circulated among his friends and further afield. In 1523 an extensively rewritten version appeared under the name of Agostino Nifo, a philosopher and theologian with close ties to the Medici. Nifo's changes preserved many of the *Prince*'s themes and examples, but recast its basic analytic categories to make it more amenable to prevailing monarchical and Church doctrines.[4] Machiavelli's book was first published posthumously in 1532. But Church and other political authorities soon came to view it as a major troublemaker. Its author was denounced to the Inquisition in 1550. When the Church instituted its Index of Prohibited Books in 1559, all Machiavelli's works—not just the *Prince*—were put on the list. According to Lord Acton, 'he was more rigorously and implacably condemned than anybody else', and 'continued to be specially excepted when permission was given to read forbidden books'.[5]

What made this 'little work', the 'whimsy' of a disgraced Florentine civil servant, so threatening—and whom did it threaten most? The *Prince*'s early readers were sharply divided on these questions. Those loyal to the Papacy and Catholic monarchies were the first to denounce it as a godless handbook for tyrants. The English Cardinal Reginald Pole claimed that it attacked the foundations of civilization itself. 'I found this type of book', he declared, 'to be written by an enemy of the human race. It explains every means whereby religion, justice and any inclination toward virtue could be destroyed.'[6]

Readers with republican and anti-Papal sympathies thought the exact opposite. Behind its morality-subverting mask, they insisted, the *Prince*'s basic purposes were moral: it surreptitiously defended justice, virtue, and civility against the corrupt Popes and monarchs who were the real enemies of human decency. Henry Neville, an English republican who published translations of Machiavelli's works, agreed with critics like Pole that the *Prince* described the moral sickness of its author's times in terms that 'are almost able to nauseate

---

[3] Their father was Lorenzo 'il Magnifico' (1449–1492). Their elder brother, Piero, had been Florence's last Medici head of state, having been expelled from the city with his family in 1494.
[4] Nifo (2008/1523). See chap. 1.
[5] Acton (2005/1907), 215.   [6] Pole in Kraye, ed. (1997/1536), 274–85.

his Readers, and talk of such Ulcers, Boyls, Nodes, Botches, Cankers, etc. that are scarce fit to be repeated'. But rather than wanting to 'teach or exhort men to get this Disease', Machiavelli sets out the causes and symptoms of political disorder 'to the end that men may be bettered, and avoid being infected with it, and may discern and cure it, whenever their incontinence and folly shall procure it them'.[7] The Dutch-Jewish philosopher Benedict Spinoza argued that when Machiavelli 'describes at great length' the means used by 'a prince whose sole motive is lust for despotic power', his intention was to warn free peoples not to hand over their fate to such men, however desperately they longed for a saviour.[8] Alberico Gentili, an Italian Protestant who taught law at Oxford, claimed that the *Prince* sought to expose the corrupt maxims practised, but not openly admitted, by princes and popes. 'While appearing to instruct the prince', Machiavelli was actually 'stripping him bare' to reveal the tyrannical dispositions found in most new princes.[9] One of the last readers to endorse this republican and moral reading of the *Prince* was the Swiss philosopher Jean-Jacques Rousseau, who observed in 1762 that the Holy 'Court of Rome', as he called the Papacy, 'has severely prohibited [Machiavelli's] book, and I should think that it would: it is the Court he depicts most clearly'.[10]

Five centuries later, many readers might think that these early disputes over the *Prince*'s morality or immorality and its stance toward tyranny missed the book's profounder message: that traditional distinctions between moral and immoral, tyranny and freedom cannot help us to address all the complex issues that arise in political life. On this now widespread view, the *Prince* teaches us—perhaps quite reasonably—that those in power have no choice but to relax their moral standards if they want to stay safe and secure their parties' or countries' interests in the real world.[11] Even the book's most sympathetic readers find it hard to understand how Rousseau could hail the *Prince* wholeheartedly as 'the book of republicans'.[12] The political conflicts that inspired Machiavelli to write the *Prince* are remote from our own experiences; its examples and philosophical categories seem dated. When we don't engage too deeply with them, what we get from its pages is a bold defence of pragmatic amorality, which shocks few people today.

This book tries to bring some of those conflicts, examples, and categories back to life, so that we can better understand why some of the *Prince*'s most perceptive early readers—including many philosophers who, like Machiavelli, had great literary talents—saw it as a work aimed at restoring high moral standards in politics. Machiavelli's *Prince*, I suggest, is a masterwork of ironic writing with a

---

[7] Neville (1691), 5. [8] Spinoza (1958/1677), VI.4–5, VII.1, X.1.
[9] Gentili (1924/1594), III.9. [10] Rousseau (1964/1762), III.6.
[11] See Philp (2007), 37–54. [12] Rousseau (1964/1762), III.6.

moral purpose. On the one hand, it warns aspiring princes about the dangers of trying to assert absolute control over people who care about freedom. On the other, it teaches ordinary citizens to recognize early warning signs of control-hungry behaviour in their leaders, and to impress on them the need to establish political and military 'orders' (*ordini*) that can keep tyranny at bay. Machiavelli uses a range of ironic techniques to underscore the problematic character of many princely actions he seems to praise.[13] At the same time, he uses irony to exercise readers' capacities to see through misleading political spin.

At the *Prince*'s core is a biting *critique* of both ruthless *realpolitik* and amoral pragmatism, not a revolutionary new defence of these positions. Far from eroding ancient contrasts between good and evil, just and unjust, or tyranny and freedom, Machiavelli's book shows readers the dire consequences that ensue when our language and practices fail clearly to distinguish them.

If the *Prince*'s apparently amoral teachings were not meant in earnest, why has its irony eluded so many readers, especially in the past two centuries? Irony is by definition non-transparent. It seems to say one thing while hinting indirectly at another message, by means of signs, puzzles, or other provocations. The successful relaying of this message depends on an audience sufficiently attuned to the relevant clues to pick them up. Such clues may be created by a text itself, so that readers need no knowledge of referents outside the text to recognize or interpret its ironies. More often, ironic writings presuppose common understandings between writer and readers that the former play on to provoke recognition. If a writer lavishes praise on the achievements of a man whose projects famously collapsed before or shortly after his death, or describes a notorious villain as a model of virtue, readers familiar with the subject's reputation will suspect that the author is being ironic. While such understandings are evocative for readers immersed in a particular culture, the ironies may be lost on readers remote from that culture.[14] This book seeks to recover a small part of the background needed to understand the *Prince*, paying particular attention to ironic forms of writing that were well known to Machiavelli's contemporaries, but seem obscure today.

MACHIAVELLI'S LIFE AND TIMES

The year Niccolò Machiavelli (1469–1527) was born, the mantle of 'first citizen' in Florence was assumed by the 20-year-old Lorenzo de' Medici,

---

[13] I outline some of these in the section on 'Ironic Techniques' that follows this Introduction. There is a wide-ranging literature on irony, both in general and in specific writers or periods. For example, see Muecke (1982), Knox (1989), and others cited below.

[14] See Hutcheon (1995), 97.

later called *il Magnifico*. In theory, Florence was a republic, governed by a broadly based body of citizens through elected magistrates. In reality one family, the Medici, had dominated the city for 35 years as a *de facto* dynasty. They were immensely wealthy bankers who had risen to 'princely' rank—but without holding princely or noble titles—by funding popular wars and using their money and connections to secure loyal supporters.[15] Most Florentines acquiesced in the fiction that their city still lived as a free republic where the rich and powerful were subject to the same laws as everyone else—even while the Medici manipulated ballot boxes to put their supporters in public offices, intimidated opponents with questionably legal taxes, and whittled away at the popular council that gave less well-connected citizens a voice in government.

In 1494, 60 years of Medici rule ended, and broad-based republican institutions were restored.[16] In 1498, the 29-year-old Machiavelli was appointed to his first public posts as Second Chancellor of the republic and Secretary to the Ten of War. Both posts made him responsible for highly sensitive matters of diplomacy, intelligence gathering, and military security. For reasons that remain unclear, but probably due to his father's status as a tax debtor, Machiavelli was not eligible for elected magistracies or to sit on public councils, though he could work as a civil servant.

Nevertheless, within a few years the young Secretary developed a burning desire to overhaul Florence's sorry defences, an ambition that went well beyond his official brief. Florence was a merchant city run by tradesmen and bankers who relied for their military needs on foreign troops or hired mercenaries. The first of these dangerously increased the city's dependence on much stronger foreign powers, while the second—as Machiavelli would stress in the *Prince*—were even less trustworthy. This lesson was brought home to Florentines in 1499 when a prominent mercenary captain, Paolo Vitelli, was executed on suspicion of having been bought off by Florence's enemies. Machiavelli saw clearly that the trouble could have been avoided if Florence had captains drawn from among its own citizens, and a military subject to strict civilian control. Between various diplomatic missions and starting a family, he launched an energetic campaign to form a citizen militia. Despite intense opposition, Machiavelli's project was approved by 1506, and he was appointed as its head. Troops from his militia helped to win a celebrated victory over Pisa in May 1509.

Florence was not the only Italian state whose military defences needed reforming. Venice, Naples, Milan, and smaller city-states had long used foreign troops or mercenaries, a situation that forced them to depend heavily on external powers, chiefly the kingdoms of France and Spain and the German

---

[15] As described in Machiavelli's *Florentine Histories*, *FH* VII.
[16] See chaps 2 and 24. See Najemy (2006), 250–453 for an excellent account of Medici ascendancy and its opponents.

Empire. Italians paid a high price for such dependence. Both French and Spanish kings claimed dynastic rights over Naples, and brought vast armies in to the peninsula to fight over it. Milan was a veritable battleground for various foreign powers seeking a foothold in northern Italy. While recent popes in Rome claimed to exercise coherent leadership over Italy's several, mutually competitive states, in practice their policies tended to undermine prospects of forming any cooperative Italian defences, as Machiavelli argues in the *Prince*, chapter 11. Both his early and later writings show a strong interest in seeking to improve military collaboration among Italians to prevent the worst: the gradual 'acquisition' of all of Italy by large foreign monarchies with their formidable military forces. In the decades after Machiavelli's death, this did indeed come to pass.

Machiavelli's first lengthy work was a poem, *Decennale* (1504), that chronicled the depressing realities of recent Italian history and described the self-destructive power struggles among states, princes, and pontiffs. Machiavelli presents one ambitious new power after another seizing triumphant supremacy over the others—only to tumble ignominiously from its heights, bringing bloodshed and chaos in its train. Each new player throws himself into the game of power politics with more zeal and ingenuity than the last. Over and over, cities or princes adopt supposedly 'Machiavellian' measures: they break laws and promises, deceive friends, and show no scruples about taking what belongs to others. And over and over, after fleeting successes, their ambitions collapse. If lasting success eludes individual players, the collective results are far worse. Each new attempt further destroys chances of any stable order in Italy. By the poem's end,

> By no means is Fortune yet satisfied; she has not put an end to Italian wars, nor is the cause of so many ills wiped out;
> And the kingdoms and the powers are not united...[17]

Machiavelli does not treat this hyperactivity as natural or uncontrollable. It arose, he suggests, from an unhealthy craving to dominate others. Both Italians and foreign powers were to blame. Florentines too had their share of responsibility. Their bitter wars to control neighbouring Pisa made them rely far too heavily on French support, earning the Secretary-poet's reproach: 'and you [Florentines] for Pisa have too strong desire'.[18] In a later poem Machiavelli marvels that men don't check their political and military appetites, since their devastating results have been seen many times before:

> That which more than anything else throws kingdoms down from the highest hills is this: that the powerful with their power are never sated.

---

[17] *Decennale* I, lines 523–6.   [18] *Decennale* I, line 536. See chap. 5.

From this it results that they are discontented who have lost, and hatred is
stirred up to ruin the conquerors;
   Whence it comes about that one rises and the other dies; and the one who has
risen is ever tortured with new ambition and with fear.
   This appetite destroys our states; and the greater wonder is that all recognize
this transgression, but not one flees from it.[19]

Instead of wanting to teach princes and republics to play this power-political
game, Machiavelli depicts it as wantonly destructive of the most cherished
human values: safety, stable order, and freedom. 'From Ambition', he wrote in
another poem usually dated around 1509,

come those wounds that have killed the Italian provinces . . .
   If from others a man will deign to learn the ways of Ambition, the sad example
of these wretches can teach him.[20]

These recurring critical judgements of excessive ambition and competitive
power-politics should not be forgotten when we read the *Prince*.
   Another notable feature of Machiavelli's early writings is their irreverence
toward the arrogant powerful. His literary executor (and grandson) Giuliano
de' Ricci reported that Machiavelli's youthful works included a blisteringly
satirical play based on Aristophanes' *Clouds*, composed around 1504. Like its
Greek model, Machiavelli's play mocked high-profile contemporaries; sadly, it
has long been lost.[21] Machiavelli's correspondence shows that he and his
friends revelled in puncturing the pretensions of the 'great', and in mocking
those who mistook titles for quality. Unembarrassed by his relatively modest
background, in one of the first letters attributed to him the 28-year-old
Machiavelli stoutly defended his family's claims in a property dispute with
the powerful Pazzi clan. Here we get a taste of Machiavelli's lifelong fondness
for deflating anyone's claims to be superior because of mere birth and
connections—and of his sense of drama. 'If we, mere pygmies, are attacking
giants', the letter declares, we show our far greater '*virtù* of spirit' by taking
on 'a competitor at whose nod everything is done immediately.' Rather than
see the Pazzi 'bedecked with our spoils', the Machiavelli would 'strive by
every means available' to recover it, even if their hopes of winning were
slim: for 'whatever outcome Fortune may reserve for us, we shall not regret
having failed in such endeavours'.[22] In the event, Machiavelli's family won the
case, proving on a small scale a point Niccolò would often make in his
writings: that comparatively weak families, individuals, cities, and peoples
should always resist those who try to take what is theirs. Even if they lose

[19] Machiavelli, 'The Ass' (*Asino*), V.34–46.   [20] *Dell' Ambizione*, lines 122–3, 160–1.
[21] Radif (2010) has tried to reconstruct its main themes.
[22] Machiavelli to Cardinal Giovanni Lopez, 2 December 1497, *MF* 7–8.

some battles, their efforts make life harder for their oppressors; and their value is seen in the free-spirited quality of their actions, not in victory or defeat.[23]

When reading the *Prince*, it is essential to remember that Machiavelli was never only a practical political man or a political 'scientist'. From an early stage in his life he was also a poet, a writer of imaginative letters, and a brilliant satirical dramatist. Indeed, this last talent won him more fame among contemporaries than his political works. His comedies *Mandragola* and *Clizia*, both written after the *Prince*, were hugely popular in Machiavelli's lifetime, and even now the *Mandragola*—an excoriating send-up of moral and political corruption in Florence—is widely considered one of the greatest Italian plays.[24] It should not seem improbable that his more 'serious' political works include a large satirical or ironic element.[25] And many of the *Prince*'s chapters have a distinctly dramatic structure, imitating the rising ambitions and difficulties of 'new' princes.

MACHIAVELLI, THE MEDICI, AND THE *PRINCE*

In 1510 the hot-headed Pope Julius II launched a crusade to expel the French and other foreign 'barbarians', as he called them, from Italy—not long after he himself invited them in.[26] When Florentines refused to break ties with the republic's long-time ally France, Julius threatened to overthrow the government and restore the Medici by force. At the end of August 1512, with Julius' blessing, Spanish troops attacked Prato, a neighbouring city under Florentine control, and 'massacred the city's population in a pitiable spectre of calamity', as Machiavelli wrote a few weeks later.[27] Distraught Florentines agreed to Spanish and papal demands, and the Medici reclaimed their former standing as 'first citizens' in a republic ostensibly still based on widely shared power and the rule of law.

In fact, the newly installed leadership promptly dismantled many institutions that had protected public freedoms. Freedom of expression was sharply curtailed. Open or suspected critics of the new government were silenced in various ways—in a few cases through exile, in others through fear of being slapped with punitive taxes. Machiavelli's citizen militia was one of the first casualties of the new quasi-principality. In November 1512 he was stripped of both his posts and banished from the chancellery offices. His

---

[23] See *ME* chap. 5.   [24] See Martinez (2010), Fachard (2013).
[25] While both satire and irony often say what is not meant, irony is subtler: it is less transparent than satire, and thus more easily overlooked, and usually aims to provoke thought where satire aims more simply to ridicule or shame its subjects.
[26] See chap. 26.
[27] Machiavelli to a Noblewoman, circa 16 September 1512, *MF* 215–16.

case was exceptional: according to Ridolfi, no other chancellery officials except Machiavelli's loyal assistant Biagio Buonaccorsi were sacked.[28] Worse was to come in February 1513, when a conspiracy against the Medici was revealed and Machiavelli was suspected of involvement. Though no evidence was found against him, he was imprisoned for three weeks and subjected to several bouts of interrogation under torture. Even then he would not stay silent vis-à-vis the Medici, but wrote two sonnets to Giuliano, mocking his own pathetic situation and humorously protesting his innocence.[29] He was released in a general amnesty after Giovanni de' Medici was elected Pope Leo X.

Machiavelli's ensuing correspondence with Vettori, now Florence's ambassador in Rome—and deeply unhappy about the recent *coup d'état*, though his brother's friendship with the Medici shielded him from suspicions of disloyalty—gives us a vivid picture of Machiavelli's attempts to cope with his own harsher fate. Refusing to give up hope of returning to political life and his far-reaching projects for reforming Florentine defences, he implored Vettori to take up his case with the new Medici Pope and his cousin, Cardinal Giulio de' Medici, later Pope Clement VII. Then in December he announced the existence in draft of his work on principalities, which he had already shown to other close friends and was constantly revising: 'I am', he told Vettori, 'continually fattening and currying it.' He explained his reasons for wanting to present the book to Giuliano, though not his reasons for writing it: to escape poverty, and in 'the desire that these Medici princes should begin to engage my services, even if they should start out by having me roll along a stone'. For 'through this study of mine, were it to be read, it would be evident that during the fifteen years I have been studying the art of the state I have neither slept nor fooled around'.

To modern readers used to a more ideological style of politics, it might seem odd that Machiavelli longed to work for a government that had brought him to such a 'great and continuous malignity of fortune'.[30] This desire does not, however, necessarily indicate a pragmatic willingness to adapt his political loyalties or principles. Medici-led governments were seldom so autocratic as to force critics to choose between active opposition and wholehearted allegiance. This one allowed many men who were known supporters of the deposed republic, including a number of Machiavelli's friends, to continue working as diplomats and civil servants. It was not naïve for Machiavelli to hope that he might earn a living as they did, perhaps working in his old field of external defence, without getting entangled in partisan conflicts. It was even possible to imagine working from within some middle-level government post to gently prod the new leaders toward reform.[31]

[28] Ridolfi (1963). [29] Machiavelli, 'Two Sonnets to Giuliano'.
[30] *Prince*, Dedication. [31] See Conclusion.

Indeed, ancient and humanist precepts considered it the duty of good men to help their cities by getting close to rulers—especially unjust or tyrannical ones—and doing whatever they could to influence their conduct for the better.[32] In more oppressive times, they may only be able to restrain a ruler's excesses. But in the best case, they might persuade him to give up the tyranny or principality altogether, and voluntarily establish a republic. Machiavelli took a stab at the second, more radical kind of persuasion in 1520 when, after the death of the *Prince*'s eventual dedicatee Lorenzo II, he was among several known critics of the Medici who were asked to suggest improvements to the government. His response advises the Medici to give up their princely 'state' voluntarily, and suggests reforms that would take the city nearer to the form of a 'true republic'. The arguments are not idealistic. Machiavelli insists that it is in the Medicis' own interests to step down and give power back to 'the whole body of citizens' and their ancient laws. Otherwise their government would never be stable, and must soon turn toward full-blown tyranny or savage partisan warfare. Either way, Machiavelli implores his addressees to 'imagine how many deaths, how many exiles, how many acts of extortion will result' if matters remain as they are.[33]

In 1513 Machiavelli was in no position to offer similar advice—at least not directly. Despite Vettori's efforts, the Medici cold-shouldered Machiavelli's appeals to give him a chance to prove his good faith and usefulness to his fatherland. But if he was barred from serving it through active politics and unable freely to discuss his ideas for reform, he found indirect ways to express his political views when it was risky to state them outright. In his years of diplomacy and intelligence gathering, Machiavelli had become adept as a writer of coded and semi-cryptic dispatches. In private letters too, he often speaks of being constrained to convey messages by dropping hints or 'signs' (*cenni*) between the lines of innocently chatty text, due to the sensitive content of some exchanges.[34] When in 1520 he was commissioned by Cardinal Giulio de' Medici to write a new history of Florence—paid work under government auspices at last, though still not in active politics[35]—he told his friends that he had deep reservations about how and how far to express his true opinions. 'Here in the country I have been applying myself . . . to writing the history', he writes to Francesco Guicciardini:

> and I would pay ten *soldi*—but no more—to have you by my side so that I might show you where I am, because, since I am about to come to certain details,

[32] See Plutarch's 'That a Philosopher ought to Converse Especially with Men in Power', and 'To an Uneducated Ruler', *PM* X.28–71.

[33] *Discursus*, 115.

[34] See *MF* 51–3, 365, 393–5, 398; also *AW* VII.123–33.

[35] A few years later after completing the *Histories*, Machiavelli's well-connected friends finally persuaded Giulio—now Pope Clement II—to entrust him with minor diplomatic missions, and then to establish a new version of his civilian militia. In 1527 the Medici were expelled from Florence and a republic was restored. Machiavelli died soon afterward.

I would need to learn from you whether or not I am being too offensive in my exaggerating or understating of the facts [*le cose*]. Nevertheless, I shall continue to seek advice from myself, and I shall try to do my best to arrange it so that—still telling the truth—no one will have anything to complain about.[36]

But even when he did not have to dissimulate for political reasons, Machiavelli seems to have enjoyed writing in paradoxes that force readers to puzzle out his message. And the *Prince*, as we'll see, is packed with paradoxes and an ancient form of 'coded' language.

A PECULIAR KIND OF HANDBOOK

What kind of book is the *Prince*? In outward appearance, it resembles other 'mirrors for princes' (*specula principum*), a type of work common in the Middle Ages and Renaissance, with roots in ancient times.[37] These books sought to teach rulers how to do their job in an effective and just manner. They were typically dedicated to younger, less experienced rulers by older men who offered the benefit of their practical or philosophical wisdom. The manner of their teaching could be more or less direct. More direct ones took the form of handbooks that present straightforward rules or maxims, interspersed with examples from ancient history. Isocrates' letter 'To Nicocles' and Seneca's *De clementia*, dedicated to the emperor Nero, were famous exemplars. Their purpose was not simply to exhort rulers to act wisely and justly, but also to warn them of the dire consequences they must suffer if they fail to do so. Thus Isocrates tells the tyrant Nicocles that although kings are placed in authority over vast wealth and mighty affairs, and therefore imagined to be 'the equals of gods', the unpleasant truth is that 'because of their misuse of these advantages' they have brought it about that many consider the life of a ruler as a terrible burden. When people reflect on the great 'fears and dangers' so many monarchs have faced, their unhappy ends and 'instances where they have been constrained to injure those nearest and dearest to them', they 'conclude that it is better to live in any fashion whatsoever than, at the price of such misfortunes, to rule over all Asia'.[38]

Other 'mirrors for princes' were historical and literary works that taught similar lessons indirectly, by presenting images of rulers to be imitated—or avoided. In such works, the author keeps a lower profile than in openly didactic handbooks. Instead of making straightforward judgements about

---

[36] Machiavelli to Guicciardini, 30 August 1524, *MF* 351.

[37] For a comparison of the similarities and differences between the *Prince* and other 'mirrors for princes' that differs from my interpretation, see Skinner (1978), 113–38.

[38] Isocrates, 'To Nicocles', 4.

better and worse methods of rule, he offers a complex portrait of a ruler's life and deeds, and invites readers to evaluate them for themselves. Perhaps the greatest work of this type is Xenophon's *Cyropaedia*, meaning 'The Education of Cyrus'. Along with Virgil, Xenophon is one of only two writers whom Machiavelli names in the *Prince,* and the *Cyropaedia* is the only book he names.[39] His manifest interest in that work when writing the *Prince* and later the *Discourses*, where he refers six times to the *Cyropaedia*—more than to any other work except Livy's histories—suggests an essential starting-point, though a challenging one, for readers who seek to understand Machiavelli's message and puzzling methods of writing.[40]

There is one very notable difference between the *Prince* and more conventional 'mirrors for princes' composed nearer to Machiavelli's own times.[41] These sought to teach rulers how to be good monarchs, which meant above all how to avoid doing whatever leads to tyranny. The opposition between good monarchy and bad tyranny lies at their core. Machiavelli's little book seems to dispense with this opposition. The words 'tyrant' and 'tyranny' are altogether absent, an extraordinary omission in a book that appears to have the same educative purposes as other handbooks. Moreover, the *Prince* seems to recommend the most notorious methods and aims that had been associated with tyranny since ancient times: deception, the violation of oaths, the assassination of suspect or inconvenient allies, taking advantage of weaker foreign states that ask for your aid, and even the quest for 'absolute' power.[42]

Does Machiavelli's work thereby break with all traditional political morality, ancient as well as modern? This view gained a wide currency in the twentieth century. But the idea that the *Prince*'s teachings are uniquely 'modern' is a rather recent construction, which appears convincing only if we take the book's morality-subverting assertions at face value. There are very good reasons, however, not to do so.

IRONY AND POLITICAL CRITICISM

The word 'irony' comes from the Greek *eirôneia*, meaning dissimulation or feigned ignorance. An ironic statement or work appears to say one thing while conveying another meaning. The presence of irony is signalled by a tension between explicit statements or appearances and quite different, unstated implications of what the ironist presents. Since the impulse behind ironic writing is 'a pleasure in contrasting Appearance with Reality',[43] it has long

---

[39] Chap. 14.   [40] See chaps 6 and 14; Strauss (1958), 161–2, 291; *ME* 71–88.
[41] As well as the fact that Machiavelli wrote in the vernacular.
[42] The last in chap. 9.   [43] Sedgewick (1965), 5.

been used as a weapon of political criticism. When depicting political leaders who use decent words to cloak far less decent realities, the critical ironist mimics their skewed values as a mirror for all to see—excusing or praising what deserves to be condemned, omitting or belittling what should be commended. Irony is especially suited for political criticism in conditions where it is dangerous for writers to express their views openly. Ironic techniques play down or mask, but seldom completely hide, a writer's critical views of a subject: they use various clues or signals to alert readers to judgements that differ from those made explicitly.

Irony may have constructive as well as critical aims. Ancient writers such as Xenophon, Virgil, Tacitus, and Plutarch used ironic dissimulation as a tool of moral and political education.[44] Its aim was to train readers to distinguish mere appearances of virtue or wisdom from qualities that deserve those names. This philosophical exercise had important practical uses. By reading works that imitate the specious rhetoric and appearances encountered in public life, people learn how these phenomena are generated, and become better equipped to avoid harmful policies or traps set for them by ambitious leaders. Since in political reality both leaders and ordinary people are constantly bombarded with half-truths and debased moral standards, ironists present these standards—or behaviour that conforms to them—without openly critical comment, challenging readers to resist becoming infected by them.

Inspired by ancient ironists, many sixteenth- and seventeenth-century writers treated irony as 'a game with a deceptive surface which the reader is challenged to penetrate'. They used what Douglas Duncan calls the 'art of teasing' as a 'process of educative testing . . . whereby the moral intelligence of the public was to be trained by being subjected to attempts to undermine or confuse it'.[45] If readers, or viewers of an ironic play, are inclined to accept what is falsely presented as wisdom as truly wise, they fail the test. They either allow deceptive arguments and appearances to entrap them—as happens daily in political life, often with disastrous consequences—or their judgement was already corrupted.

Before Machiavelli, several Italian writers discussed these critical and educative uses of irony, in some cases admitting that they practised it themselves. Annabel Patterson has traced an important strand of critical dissimulation centred on Virgil's pastoral poem the *Eclogues*, where many readers detected a muffled yet distinct 'republican voice' behind louder declarations that praised or acquiesced in tyranny. The great poet Petrarch (1303–1374), whose *Italia mia* is quoted at the end of Machiavelli's *Prince*, wrote that he had been inspired by Virgil's example to write 'the *Bucolicum Carmen*, a kind of cryptic poem (*poematis genus ambigui*) which, though understood only by a few,

---

[44] On Xenophon and Plutarch, see *ME* 64–84; on Virgil, below; on Tacitus, O'Gorman (2000).
[45] Duncan (1978), 37, 2.

might possibly please many; for', he explains, 'some people have a taste for letters so corrupt that the well-known savour, no matter how sweet, offends them, while everything mysterious pleases them, no matter how harsh'. Petrarch adds mischievously that his cryptic poem had once fallen into the hands of 'some high-ranking personages' who were represented in them, but were unable to decipher those dangerous allusions. At the more obvious level, his poem aimed to 'please' the corrupt, particularly certain men of power; at a deeper level that remained opaque to them, it told the far less pleasing truth. For 'though truth has always been hated, it is now', the poet declares, 'a capital crime'.[46]

Virgil and Petrarch's critical ironic tradition was rekindled in Florence under the first Medici 'princes'. Writers here faced a glaring contradiction between the city's old republican ideals of shared power, free expression, and transparent justice, and the realities of Medici control. Patterson identifies subtly critical strategies in a number of apparently deferential writings, including a pastoral poem dedicated by Cristoforo Landino to the 'Magnificent' Lorenzo. By placing its dedicatee in a now lapsed 'phase of decency and innocence', the poem hinted at the gap between that golden age and present, deficient realities 'while permitting Landino to remain laudatory without'. In 1487, when Machiavelli was 18, Landino published a commentary on Virgil's *Eclogues* suggesting that the Roman poet adopted the mask or 'persona' of a character living happily under the empire. But he 'concealed beneath that vulgar surface another sense more excellent by far, so that the work was adorned with a double argument': the obvious one seeming to celebrate his times and the emperors, the 'hidden' one discussing 'greater matters'. Landino refrained from saying what these were, but managed to slip into his own scholarly commentary 'an extraordinary republican moment' discussing liberty, and other passages that 'counter, or at least complicate . . . expressions of unequivocal support for Medician politics that Landino inserted into his prefatory address'.[47] Given his contemporaries' familiarity with such strategies, it is hardly far-fetched to suspect that Machiavelli may have used them for similar purposes.

SIGNS OF IRONY IN THE *PRINCE*

Why suspect that the *Prince* is a thoroughly ironic work? Discrepancies between the overtly prince-friendly *Prince* and the *Discourses*' clear preference for republics are one ground for this suspicion. The discrepancies are still

---

[46] Patterson (1987), 12–13, 43–4.

[47] Patterson (1987), 67–8, 75–8. Also see O'Hara (2007) on ironic and other truth-seeking uses of inconsistency by Roman authors.

greater on a careful reading of the *Florentine Histories*.[48] Before and after he wrote the *Prince*, Machiavelli was critical of the methods used by 'new' princes, including the Medici, to make themselves rulers over their own or others' cities. The main theme of his early poems—the *Decennale*, *Di Fortuna* and *Dell' Ambizione*—is how the unscrupulous methods and ambitions of power-hungry popes, new princes, and *stati* were ruining Italy; while his 1520 *Discursus* directly urges the Medici to restore a *vera repubblica* in Florence or face inevitable disaster.[49] It is hard to believe that the same author whose early and late writings treat the phenomenon of self-aggrandizing, unprincipled new princes as a lethal civil disease would—in a bout of opportunistic job-seeking—purport to teach the same princes how to succeed in their business.

Secondly, the *Prince*'s often shocking content raises the question of whether Machiavelli could reasonably have expected political and Church authorities in his time to welcome his little work. How did he expect the Medici and other ecclesiastical 'princes'—so eager to cast themselves as legitimate champions of order, justice, and religion—to respond to his audacious suggestions that they should assassinate their rivals, break their oaths, and launch offensive wars without any pressing necessity? As Rousseau pointed out in 1762 and Garrett Mattingly in 1958, Machiavelli's choice of modern examples would have been seen as scandalously provocative in his times, and recognized as a sign of ironic purposes.[50] If Machiavelli's end was to please his city's new authorities so that they would let him return to public life, his means—laying bare and seeming to approve of the serpentine ways used by all new princes, especially recent popes—seem oddly chosen.

The *Prince*'s use of ancient examples raises further suspicions. Most modern readers see nothing problematic in Machiavelli's advice to imitate the Roman Empire's ceaseless struggles for ever-greater 'greatness'; or to pursue grandiose ambitions on the pattern of Theseus, Romulus, or Cyrus; or to use hunting as practice for war. But anyone who consults the *Prince*'s main ancient sources—Xenophon, Sallust, Polybius, Livy, and Plutarch—must be deeply puzzled, since they treat these themes in far more critical ways than Machiavelli appears to do. In some cases, his overt judgements of ancient figures clash so violently with those of his favourite authors that one cannot help but suspect irony. Perhaps not every reader in Machiavelli's times would have read enough Polybius or Livy to realize that the *Prince*'s praise of the despicable and buffoonish Philip V, king of Macedon, was as improbable as its praise

---

[48] Rousseau (1964/1762), III.6 claimed that 'the contradiction between the maxims of his book on the Prince and those of his discourses on Titus Livy and of his history of Florence proves that this profound politician has so far had only superficial or corrupt readers'.

[49] See *ME* 16–37.

[50] Mattingly (1958). In Rousseau's view, 'the choice of his execrable hero', the notoriously violent Cesare Borgia, 'suffices to exhibit [Machiavelli's] secret intention' to criticize corrupt political standards.

of Borgia. But a reader with even a little humanist education would surely have wondered whether, by urging modern princes to imitate the 'criminal' emperor Severus—as Machiavelli calls him in the *Discourses*—the author was being ironic. It is sometimes suggested that he sought to subvert all ancient judgements. A more likely purpose was to expose the corrupt thinking of princes in his 'times', when judgements were so perverted that the actions of devious and violent ancient rulers were widely imitated and admired.

But the best reasons to suspect that the *Prince* is ironic can be found in the style and content of the text itself. Leo Strauss has perceptively discussed its many stylistic peculiarities.[51] Overtones of bold certainty are mingled with doubtful, nervous, or ominous undertones, followed by long discussions of the difficulties—or impossibilities—of ever attaining the goals set out with such confidence. When such problems appear in Machiavelli's masterfully controlled writing, readers who appreciate his logical rigour and literary gifts may reasonably suspect the presence of irony.

As for content, there are serious problems of coherence among the *Prince*'s most general standards. If we try to identify a few basic criteria for evaluating the book's numerous maxims and examples, a text that at first blush seems to present its author's straightforward judgements soon starts to look slippery. Machiavelli, as everyone thinks they know, held that the 'ends justify the means'. But what, in the *Prince*, are the appropriate ends of prudent action? At times the personal greatness, reputation, and survival of the prince himself are all that seem to matter for Machiavelli. At other times, he implies that a prince's desires for power can only be satisfied if he gives priority to the stability, security, and well-being of the 'generality of people' (*universalità*) over his private ambitions. Nor do these two ends always converge in the *Prince*. In chapter 19, for example, one of the two 'happiest' Roman emperors, Severus, achieves great personal power and security by oppressing the people. On the other hand, chapter 12 suggests that princes are strongest who put military commands—including the prince's own command—under strict civilian and legal controls.

In chapters 3 and 4, again, Machiavelli describes—and seems to commend— republican Rome's ambition to dominate the 'free' province of Greece, although he also states that there was no pressing necessity for the conquest. Then in chapter 5 he sets out compelling reasons to respect people's desires to live in freedom from foreign occupation, and warns princes that they must face recurrent violent resistance if they remove that freedom. It is hard to see how Machiavelli, or anyone else, can give equal weight to both these ends—nonnecessary conquest for the sake of maximizing power on the one hand, desires for freedom on the other. And it seems inconsistent that the same book teaches princes and empires how to seize power, even 'absolute' power, over peoples who value self-government. Here and in other instances, the *Prince*'s morally

[51] Strauss (1958).

flexible 'Machiavellian' precepts appear to contradict the book's strongest, most consistently developed arguments. Many readers have perceived a contradiction between Machiavelli's strong preference for freedom and his apparent reluctance to criticize the Romans for depriving other peoples of their independence.[52] But there are, in fact, fiercely critical undertones in Machiavelli's discussions of Rome's imperial ambitions. In the *Discourses* he says that expansion became 'pernicious' to republican Rome during and after the wars with Carthage and Greece, shows the terrible costs of the city's penchant for constant military expansion, and says point-blank that Rome's imperial overreaching destroyed the republic's cherished liberty and security. His criticisms of decreasingly virtuous Roman 'modes' in the later republic are less direct in the *Prince*, but nonetheless audible.[53]

Machiavelli's basic standards become still harder to define when we ask what he considers the most effective means for pursuing princely ends. There is a deep, recurring tension between two 'modes' of action discussed throughout the *Prince*. One is associated with steadiness and trust, the other with changeability and deceptive appearances. At times Machiavelli insists that a prince's self-preservation depends on satisfying his subjects' desires for non-arbitrary rule, transparency, firm mutual obligations, and regular order. At other times, the most effective princely 'modes' are said to be non-transparent, variable in accordance with 'the times', and indifferent to stable expectations on the part of subjects or allies. Chapter 18 tells princes to break faith when this gives them an edge over rivals, or helps them rise to greatness. Yet in chapter 21 and before, Machiavelli says that it is *always* best to make and keep firm commitments to subjects and allies—even if this sometimes puts the prince on the losing side, and seriously limits what he can do to increase his own power. More generally, chapter 25 begins by advancing a cautious approach to dealing with fortune's caprices by patiently building 'dykes and dams' long before troubles strike. This approach is linked to the *Prince*'s most obvious practical aim: to teach readers how to construct a well-ordered, well-defended *stato* that has fair chances of lasting long after their deaths. But on the very next page, Machiavelli declares that it's better to handle fortune with youthful impetuosity than with an older man's caution, and to beat her into submission instead of patiently building firm orders to regulate her moods.

THE USES OF INCONSISTENCY

There are several easy solutions to the *Prince*'s apparent contradictions. The easiest is to say that they were inadvertent, products of a not very systematic

---

[52] Plamenatz (2012), 48; Hörnqvist (2004).   [53] See chap. 3.

mind or the author's volatile 'passions'. Such accounts will seem implausible to anyone who detects the logical structure, powers of clear judgement, and artistic care that permeate the *Prince*. Another solution sees Machiavelli's inconsistencies as a deliberate expression of scepticism, intended to unsettle readers' received notions of truth and reflect a world where no stable judgements are possible.[54] Sceptical readings are superficially plausible given Machiavelli's highly ambiguous style of discussion. Nonetheless, I find them hard to accept. The *Prince* and all Machiavelli's main writings appeal constantly to stable standards of truth against falsehoods and misleading appearances, and to reasonable judgements against unreasonable opinions. He doesn't tell readers straight out what constitutes a 'true knowledge of histories', but the *Discourses* state clearly that lack of such knowledge causes moral confusion and political disorders.[55] To speak as Machiavelli often does of the false and dangerous appearances that lead men to ruin, he must have in mind some truer qualities behind the appearances that, when recognized, help avert destruction. Without defining these qualities for readers, he invites them to consider for themselves what they might be, and to recognize their profound importance for any sustainable—and recognizably human—orders.

Among contemporary scholars, perhaps the most favoured solution treats the *Prince*'s inconsistencies as merely apparent: Machiavelli's different political standards are relative to circumstances. On this view, Machiavelli thought that some circumstances are friendly to freedom in republics, while in others principality or even tyranny 'has good effects and there is no alternative to it'.[56] At times one should work steadily and cautiously to forestall fortune's downturns, at other times strike and beat her; sometimes break faith, but also know how to glean the benefits of others' trust in your fidelity.

If one looks for a general statement of this circumstance-relative position in the *Prince*, the best candidate is the claim made near the end of chapter 18 that a prince 'needs to have a spirit disposed to change as the winds of fortune and variations [*variazione*] of things command him'. This claim is echoed in chapter 25, where we read that if one 'would change his nature with the times and with affairs, his fortune would not change'. If variability is Machiavelli's overarching criterion of political *virtú*, while careful ordering or stability or freedom are appropriate aims of *virtú* only in some conditions, then many of the *Prince*'s apparent inconsistencies can be explained away.

But if we follow the order of the *Prince*'s text and pay close attention to its language, we find many reasons to doubt that the ability to change one's 'spirit' or one's nature is part of *virtú* at all. Firstly, Machiavelli first commends this ability—or seems to commend it—very late in the book. Before chapter 18, the ability to order and command one's own forces regardless of fortune's

---

[54] For example, Kahn (1994).   [55] *D* I.Pref.
[56] For example, see Plamenatz (2012), 44, following Pasquale Villari; Berlin (1981/1958).

'variations' looked like the height of *virtù* in the *Prince*. The book's main practical proposals call for a *virtù* that builds firm orders to 'govern' (*governare*) fortune. This steady, self-directed kind of *virtù* is especially needed to build civilian militias as the foundation of renewed Italian strength. Such orders have to be founded on a self-imposed logic that makes one as independent of fortune's whims as possible—for although no one is immune to their effects, virtuous works can help one avoid being subject to fortune's 'commands'.

Secondly, even in chapter 18 and later, Machiavelli does not identify *virtù* with the ability to change at fortune's command. On the contrary, he frequently underscores the deficiencies of those who allow fortune to blow them hither and thither. Throughout the *Prince*, the word *variazione* is a byword for fortune's blind and destabilizing oscillations. In chapter 19, variability (*varia*) tops Machiavelli's list of qualities that win contempt, associating it with pusillanimity, effeminacy, and irresolution, 'from which a prince should guard himself as from a shoal'.[57]

Thirdly, just after declaring that men should change their modes with the 'times' in chapter 25, Machiavelli turns around and says that this kind of versatility is well-nigh impossible. 'No man', he writes, 'may be found so prudent as to know how to accommodate himself to this.' According to Machiavelli's strongly egalitarian anthropology, even the most prudent men are incapable of perfect foresight and self-control. The variation argument therefore rests on an unrealistic view of human capabilities. It reflects a longing for total control of circumstances that cannot be completely controlled—though they can be 'managed' or 'governed' by self-ordering *virtù*.

PRINCES OF *VIRTÙ* AND OF FORTUNE

A central argument of this book is that in the basic antithesis between *fortuna* and *virtù*, Machiavelli offers a solution to his own inconsistencies. Early on in the *Prince*, he sets out a general, reflective standard that serves as a touchstone for evaluating the book's particular precepts and examples: namely, that it is better to acquire and hold power by means of one's own *virtù* than by fortune and others' arms.[58] I argue that he uses the antithesis to signal indirect judgements about the prudence and praiseworthiness of actions or maxims. When he stresses the role played by fortune in an agent's actions, however successful, he implies some deficiency in the quality of those actions, even

---

[57] Chap. 19. For examples that show why this 'mode' weakens princes in the long run, see chap. 16 on varying one's spending patterns to court popularity, and chap. 21 on changing alliances to avoid defeat.

[58] See chap. 1.

when they are mixed with *virtù*—and even when he lavishes words of praise on them.[59] For fortune and *virtù* are not equally efficacious 'modes' of action, depending on circumstances. Machiavelli maintains that it is *always* better to rely on *virtù* than on fortune, both in principalities or republics, and in corrupt or virtuous political conditions. Some 'modes' of ordering human relations always tend to bring stability and safety, while others always tend toward their opposites. This, I'll suggest, should be our standard for judging the inconsistent policies discussed in the *Prince*, not particular conditions.

Some kinds of *virtù*, moreover, are more conducive to stability and safety than others. What Machiavelli calls '*virtù* of spirit' (*di animo*) is especially effective for acquiring power, winning battles, or making conquests. But his exemplars of exceedingly bold and spirited *virtù* tend to be less skilled at maintaining political power, or at founding a secure legacy for future generations. Since the *virtù* of great captains and conquerors is insufficient for great statesmanship, leaders who fail to develop the political and intellectual virtues needed to maintain what they acquire turn by default to fortune—hoping that something other than their own abilities might prop them up.

Machiavelli's *fortuna–virtù* antithesis is not freestanding. It forms the basis for a patterned, normatively coded language that signals Machiavelli's reflective judgements throughout the *Prince*, and is developed further in his later works. Some words, that is, always have a positive sense associated with *virtù*, while others are always associated with *fortuna* and its destabilizing, *virtù*-corroding effects. Some of these are listed in the section on 'Coded words' that follows this Introduction. Machiavelli's remarkably consistent use of these words stands in striking contrast to his inconsistent statements. This language embodies basic standards for judging the diverse policies described in the *Prince*.

The entire *Prince*, I'll suggest, can be read as a series of confrontations between two kinds of prince, or two 'modes' of princely action: one that depends on *virtù* and 'one's own arms', the other on fortune and 'the arms of others'. If we assume that these 'modes' can be fruitfully combined, or that in some circumstances princes need to rely on fortune more than on *virtù*, we may overlook Machiavelli's subtle criticisms of *any* policy that depends on the advantages he identifies with fortune. Machiavelli was a literary man as well as a political one, and the *Prince* is a carefully structured work of art as well as a work full of razor-sharp, profound political analysis. His use of the *virtù–fortuna* antithesis and its corresponding ironic language reflects his fondness for wickedly provocative wordplay. But it also embodies a philosopher's concern to analyse particular examples and actions in terms of more basic causes, general distinctions, and reflections on human capacities and limitations.[60]

---

[59] See 'Ironic Techniques' (1).

[60] For a discussion of the senses in which Machiavelli may be considered a philosophical writer, see *ME* chap. 1.

Most of Machiavelli's antitheses and deceptively normative words are drawn from a long tradition of ancient writing passed down from early Greek writers to Romans and humanists.[61] Readers familiar with the tradition—as Machiavelli's early humanist readers were—would have picked up on this method of ironic writing more quickly than readers less immersed in ancient texts. This helps to explain why it seemed clear to them that Machiavelli was dissimulating—or as Alberico Gentili put it in a nice paradox, 'making all his secrets clear' and 'revealing his secret counsels' by ironic indirection—while modern readers unversed in a wide range of ancient writings fail to see the pattern.[62]

WHY WOULD MACHIAVELLI DISSIMULATE?

If the *Prince*'s underlying judgements are decent and moral rather than subversive of traditional moral standards, some might ask, why would Machiavelli have thought he needed to dissimulate through irony? I see three main reasons.[63]

One was defensive: to protect the author of a text that hints very strongly at the hypocrisy of the new Medici authorities—whose dynastic and princely behaviour contradicted their official status as mere 'first citizens' in a free republic, recalling similar hypocrisy in the early Roman *principes*—and at gross corruption in the Church, now headed by a Medici Pope. To suggest that Florence's rulers and Church leaders fell short of generally accepted moral standards—indeed that they were two-faced, faithless, or criminal—was obviously risky and best done obliquely.[64]

A second reason was diplomatic circumspection when seeking to change readers' political judgements. Machiavelli's aim was not just to mock political and religious authorities. The *Prince* also seeks to induce rulers, and their supporters among the people, to recognize their errors and turn toward better forms of government. As ancient orators and philosophers knew well, when you want to show people uncomfortable truths it is better to sweeten the pill with ironic dissimulation than risk alienating them through uninvited lectures.

---

[61] See 'Coded words' for some general examples; more are provided in particular chapters.

[62] Gentili (1924/1594), III.9.

[63] Machiavelli perhaps also had private reasons for writing an ironic piece about princes at the time: to regain some sense of his own power—intellectual if not material—vis-à-vis the new regime, and to lighten the heaviness he and his friends felt after the Medici coup. As Worcester (1940), 142 notes, irony can offer 'an escape from mental pain, as morphine offers an escape from physical pain'.

[64] As Machiavelli observes in the *Discourses*, 'princes are spoken of with a thousand fears and a thousand hesitations.' *D* I.58.

If 'those who are discontented with a prince' are not strong enough to challenge him openly, they should, as we read in the *Discourses*,

> seek with all their industry to make themselves friends to him . . . following his pleasures and taking delight in all those things they see him delighting in. This familiarity makes you live secure . . . and affords you every occasion for satisfying your intent. . . . Thus one must play the crazy man, like [Lucius Junius] Brutus, and make oneself very much mad, praising, speaking, seeing, doing things against your intent so as to please the prince.[65]

Having gained the prince's confidence by seeming to care only about his safety and glory, his critics might then try to persuade him to give up his tyrannical ways of his own accord.[66]

A third reason is perhaps the most important, and least often recognized. Like the ancient works it refers to, the *Prince* has an educative and philosophical purpose: to train readers to discriminate between apparent and genuine political prudence. As the English philosopher and Machiavelli admirer Francis Bacon noted, dissimulation can be an excellent means of helping people to see through misleading appearances and deceptions. Prodded by subtle 'signs and arguments' to notice true qualities or judgements behind the open words, attentive readers can pick up the clues and try to decode the ironist's concealed purposes.[67] It is essential that they do this decoding for themselves, since it exercises their powers of critical observation. By mimicking the sophistries that abound in political life, the *Prince* induces readers to reflect on what's wrong with these persuasions, and thus arm themselves against their seductions.

Though formally addressed to a prince, the *Prince* speaks to ordinary citizens as well as men aspiring to political greatness. For Machiavelli as for his ancients, the ultimate source of political disorders—including tyranny of one man or empire—is not ambitious individuals *per se*, but the failure of peoples to recognize the signs of danger and causes of disorders before they grow virulent. In his own times, many Italians who had long lived in free republics eagerly embraced new self-styled princes who they hoped would help them win partisan battles or make great conquests for their cities. Having welcomed these men 'in the belief that they will fare better', they found that

---

[65] *D* III.2. Junius Brutus led a movement to expel Rome's last kings and establish a fully-fledged republic; see Conclusion.

[66] In his *Seventh Letter* 332d–333a, Plato writes that he and his friend Dion tried to teach the young Syracusan tyrant Dionysius how to be more 'in harmony with virtue'. But because he was so deficient in virtue to begin with, his resourceful philosopher-teachers did not express their ethical teaching 'openly, for it would not have been safe; but we put it in veiled terms and maintained by reasoned argument that this is how every man will save both himself and all those under his leadership, whereas if he does not adopt this course he will bring about entirely opposite results'.

[67] Francis Bacon, *Essays* (1985/1597–1625), 76–8. Compare Bacon's (2001/1605), 193–4 remark that dissimulation is a means to 'tell a lie and find a truth'.

they were deceived; in fact 'they have done worse', and were now more servile, beaten, and despoiled than before.[68] Instead of showing these misguided people the way to their hoped-for paradise, Machiavelli wrote to his friend Guicciardini, he would like to teach them 'the way to Hell in order to steer clear of it'.[69] The best way to teach human beings how to avoid evils is to show how they themselves produce them, often under self-deceptions about their own shrewdness or virtue. While seeming to advise princes to disregard moral principles, the *Prince* uses irony to show peoples how to defend themselves from their own bad judgements.[70]

In stressing the *Prince*'s educative aims, my argument differs from those of several other scholars who have recognized the work's *sotto voce* criticisms of Medici government. In an important 1986 article, for example, Mary Dietz argued that Machiavelli's purposes in the *Prince* were covertly republican, and that he wanted the Medici to give up their pre-eminent power in Florence.[71] I agree with Dietz on these points, and with her view that the *Prince*'s ironies not only mock the Medici but seek to reveal 'certain truths about princely power' that might help republicans to reconstitute a stronger government in future. But I disagree that the *Prince* is 'an act of deception' aimed at luring a gullible prince into following the book's advice, 'and thereby take actions that will jeopardize his power and bring about his demise'. My reading is closer to that of John Langton, who published a thoughtful response to Dietz's article in the same journal, arguing that the *Prince* seeks to teach princes how to convert their quasi-monarchies into republics.[72]

More than either of these arguments, however, I am interested in the *Prince*'s teachings for citizens as well as those for princes; and in its invitation to moral and philosophical reflectiveness, which goes far deeper than espousing a republican message versus princely politics. What are the qualities of a truly praiseworthy statesman? Can amoral means serve good ends? Does security depend on justice? Why bother to work hard at building and maintaining free political orders if fortune and fate control much in human affairs? What are the limits of any ruler's, state's, or empire's control over subjects? The *Prince* invites readers to consider these questions from many, often unexpected angles.

---

[68] Chap. 3.   [69] Machiavelli to Guicciardini, 17 May 1521, *MF* 336.

[70] According to Henry Neville (1681), the *Prince* shows both tyrants and 'the poor people who are forced to live under them' the danger each faces: 'by laying before the former, the hellish and precipitous courses they must use to maintain their power', and by showing peoples 'what they must suffer' if they fail to restrain over-ambitious leaders.

[71] Dietz (1986). In his 1536 polemic, Cardinal Reginald Pole (1997/1536) wrote that according to Florentines, Machiavelli's cynical advice in the *Prince* did not reflect his own view of political prudence, but aimed to mislead the Medici toward self-destruction.

[72] Langton (1987).

THE *PRINCE* AS A DISCOURSE

Machiavelli's 'little work', then, is not a treatise setting out the author's wisdom to be imbibed second-hand by uncritical readers. It is a series of highly provocative, mind-teasing conversations with the young, the impetuous, and men in power that seeks to improve their powers of political judgement. Machiavelli refers to the discussions in several of the *Prince*'s chapters as 'discourses' (*discorsi*). The word suggests that they are structured as conversations with readers, not as lectures delivered from an authorial pedestal. A discourse differs from a univocal lecture or treatise in imitating several different voices, or expressing different points of view canvassed by a participant—here the princely reader—whose own judgements are still uncertain or poorly founded. Unlike a dialogue or drama, it does not name specific discussants or announce shifts from one view to another. In the *Prince*, the impression of shifting voices or *personae* is created by a range of devices: shifting pronouns (sometimes 'he', sometimes 'you' for princes), hesitations and doubts following sweepingly assured claims, contrasts between cynical and moderate tones, or between misanthropic and philanthropic assertions in the same chapter.[73]

In content, lectures put forward carefully worked out reasons and conclusions in the voice of a single author who has thought them through. Like a dialogue, a discourse typically offers weakly reasoned but boldly asserted opinions, bringing their flaws to light as discussion progresses. The flawed opinions, however, are not necessarily renounced. The task of assessing them is left to readers, as part of the education in independent judgement that is a basic purpose of dialogical or multi-vocal writing.

What readers take from discourses depends on their own aims and dispositions. Aspiring princes in a hurry to gain power are likely to read quickly, scouring the text for nuggets of second-hand wisdom that they can apply directly to their enterprises. Since their aim is to achieve greatness and glory, they will seize on the most impressive-sounding phrases and examples, not pausing to notice subtle warnings or advice that they might be better off working through more modestly virtuous 'modes'.

As with princes, so with lay readers: those who read the *Prince* in hopes of finding a quick-fix, uncomplicated message may pick out the boldest

---

[73] As Patterson (1987), 6 says of Virgil's *Eclogues*, by throwing into question 'the location of his own voice... Virgil effectively demonstrated how a writer can protect himself by dismemberment' and a 'wickedly shifting authorial presence', effected through 'striking variations in tone and range' and 'oppositions such as serious/light, high/low, idyllic/ironic'. In view of this tradition of writing, Machiavelli's declarations in his own voice—'I say' (*dico*) or 'I judge' (*iudico*)—do not necessarily announce his own views more directly than other statements; like ancient ironists, his *dico* is often misleading, challenging readers to follow sound reasons in the text rather than the author's supposedly authoritative assertions. I thank Maurizio Viroli for alerting me to this problem.

statements and not trouble themselves too much with the caveats. If they find the amoral advice profound or intriguing, they will be disinclined to notice the subtle ways in which Machiavelli subverts it, and ignore the quietly prudent advice woven into other levels of the text. By contrast, readers who avoid falling into the snares laid by the *Prince*'s web-like writing will recognize puzzles that challenge them to think hard about what they read. If they recognize the superior logical power and practical prudence of the moderate arguments, they will be more inclined to resist the pull of the shocking ones, and work harder to decipher the underlying message. The *Prince* tests readers by moving constantly between the perspective of an impetuous, over-ambitious young man—one seeking the quickest and easiest ways to acquire power, with fortune's help—and judgements more likely to give a state firm foundations.

READING THE *PRINCE*

To understand a work that one suspects is full of ironies, of course, it is not enough to identify the 'signs' of irony—signs that the text contains meanings or messages other than those that appear on the surface. One also has to work out what those meanings or messages are, and set out reasons for interpreting them in a particular way. This is the hardest part: even if two readers may agree that a passage seems ironic, they may disagree on what deeper message it seeks to convey. The most that readers can do is to spell out the strongest reasons that led them to their interpretation. In presenting mine, I have given preference to the following kinds of evidence, in this order:

1. Other statements, terms, or examples in the *Prince* itself
2. Other texts by Machiavelli, where possible those known to have been composed before the *Prince*
3. 'External' contexts, including:
   (a) Works by other writers, giving priority to those mentioned or alluded to in the *Prince*
   (b) Historical background

A good reading clearly needs to be informed by an account of the text's origins and the particular problems its author sought to address. Nevertheless, I assume that if we want to understand a difficult text, evidence drawn from that text and others written or invoked by the same author is generally our most reliable source, and should be given primacy over purely extra-textual information—that is, information that the author did not discuss or allude to in his writings. Any reader of such a complex work as the *Prince* must overlook many nuances, and lack the background knowledge needed to understand some parts. I am all too aware of my own limitations in this regard, and hope other readers will supplement, correct, or take issue with my interpretation.

The best English translation for any reader who wants to grasp the *Prince*'s ironies is Mansfield's, which usually preserves Machiavelli's own consistent use of idiosyncratic terms instead of trying to render them more colloquial. I have used this translation as the basis for my own. I leave out page references, since my discussion proceeds chapter by chapter; most of Machiavelli's chapters are short enough that readers can easily find references without a page, while in the case of longer chapters I closely follow their order.

Needless to say, scholarship on the *Prince* is vast and exceedingly rich, although most of it deals either with general themes or particular historical, philological, or interpretative issues. Surprisingly few book-length treatments examine the work as a whole.[74] My interpretation agrees with other scholars on many specific and some general points, and disagrees on many others. I discuss our most important agreements and disagreements in the Conclusion, while keeping secondary references in the main text to a minimum. Many comparisons between the *Prince* and Machiavelli's other works are made in my *Machiavelli's Ethics* (2009). I refer to some of them in the footnotes under the abbreviation *ME*.

Whether or not others agree with my reading, I hope this book will demonstrate the need to pay much closer attention to Machiavelli's subtle uses of language. We need to take seriously the possibility that like many of the ancient writers who, as he told Vettori, inspired him to compose *De principatibus*, he used a patterned, ironic language to communicate judgements that differ from his overt declarations.

Above all, I hope to persuade readers that the *Prince* needs to be approached as a profoundly *ambiguous* piece of writing, not as a straightforward 'treatise'. Most Machiavelli scholars, and other close readers, are well aware of some of the ambiguities I discuss in this book. But the majority tend to deal with them by barely acknowledging their problematic presence, preferring to build their own interpretations on often misleading assertions about what Machiavelli 'clearly' stated or held. Others recognize the *Prince*'s ambiguities as a serious challenge. Yet they seldom consider that they might be artfully *patterned* ambiguities, which invite readers to perceive the pattern if they want to understand the *Prince*'s message. I don't expect readers to agree with every detail of my interpretation; with a writer as brilliantly elusive as Machiavelli, that would be sheer folly. I do hope that more readers might notice his book's many ambiguities, frankly acknowledge them, and then grapple with—not just seek quick and easy answers to—the hard question: why did he put them there?

---

[74] A short but valuable exception is de Alvarez (1999).

Machiavelli's ironic techniques

The *Prince* uses a range of techniques to hint at incongruities between its most apparent meanings and others that are less striking or explicit.

(1) PARADOX AND GENERAL STANDARDS

Paradoxes present two arguments or perspectives that seem inconsistent, or imply contradictory judgements or courses of action.[1] As I said in the Introduction, the *Prince* is full of paradoxes that force readers who notice them to stop and ask which of several inconsistent judgements is wiser, or which of two or more incompatible courses a prince should follow.

Machiavelli offers a surprisingly clear solution. Throughout the *Prince*, he uses the *fortuna–virtú* antithesis to signal indirect judgements of actions or maxims. Allusions to the role of fortune function like a code, suggesting that people or actions that rely on fortune are deficient in *virtú*, and unworthy of the highest praise. A secondary standard, deriving from the first, is that to secure their state, princes must avoid being hated by their peoples—or, viewed more positively, that their peoples should be satisfied. Princes who fail to satisfy their peoples may succeed for a time, but ultimately depend on unreliable fortune, thus setting their states on a dangerous path.

The same standards serve as basic touchstones for evaluating all the *Prince*'s examples and precepts. For example, Machiavelli describes Cesare Borgia as his prime case of a prince whose rise and downfall depended on fortune. This bottom-line judgement silently undermines Machiavelli's overt praise, and calls into question the quality of his *virtú*. Chapter 19 says that the Roman emperor Severus was always able to rule 'happily' because of his virtues. But in relying on soldiers and not trusting the people, he had an unstable mode of defence that fell short of the *Prince*'s basic standards. As for the claim in chapter 25 that fortune prefers impetuous young men who beat her: maybe she does, but mature and prudent readers should realize that they should not be courting fortune's favour at all, but relying on their own resources and hard work.

---

[1] See Sorensen (2005).

(2) AMBIGUITY AND NORMATIVELY 'CODED' LANGUAGE

As Plutarch writes, ambiguity 'works through the normal usage of words', so that readers must constantly ask themselves whether a writer is using a word or phrase in one sense or another. The most common form of ambiguity uses the same word in very different senses, some more complete or adequate than others. 'Happiness' (*eudaimonia*) may be understood as wealth, influence, and fame—or as secure possession of the good. 'Virtue' (*arête*) may be understood as 'reputation and influence', or as the qualities that render men and cities well-ordered, stable, and safe.[2]

Machiavelli's concept of *virtú* is notoriously slippery. It opposes fortune as half of the *Prince*'s master standard for judging precepts and examples, and is presented as the quality that princes should depend on to acquire and hold power. But what is it? Machiavelli's varied uses make it hard for even the most careful readers to pin down a clear meaning. They should, I suggest, give Machiavelli the benefit of the doubt: presume that he has a clear conception of *virtú*, and good reasons for using the word in such puzzling ways. They are puzzling because their aims are dialectical, inviting readers to work out for themselves what are merely parts or appearances of a praiseworthy quality and what its most necessary core.[3]

Machiavelli's most pervasive technique of ambiguous writing is the **normatively coded use of language**. He conveys judgements through key words and phrases that appear purely descriptive at first glance, but on close reading turn out to have systematically patterned normative connotations. Some words always express a positive sense, while others convey some kind of deficiency, often under misleadingly positive appearances. In the *Prince* such words are linked to the book's 'master' antithesis of fortune-or-*virtú*.[4] For example, statements that something makes men 'happy' (*felice*) sound positive, but often contain a veiled warning: the thing might be acquired with fortune's help, but will be hard to hold by one's own arms, and in time brings more woes than happiness. Power acquired 'suddenly' or 'quickly' (*subito, presto*) or 'easily' (*facilmente*) is infirm and unreliable, and thus too dependent on fortune. To insist on the 'greatness' (*grandezza*) or great 'height' (*altezza*) of men or actions or the high 'reputation' (*reputazione*) they confer is to warn that what appears great and confers reputation may be deceptive—or lacks secure foundations. Machiavelli's highly regular use of these and other deceptively evaluative words allows him to make indirect appraisals of actions that unsettle, and sometimes contradict, his explicit judgements.

---

[2] 'How a Young Man should Study Poetry', *PM* I.24–5.   [3] See chap. 1.
[4] See 'Coded Words'.

Other forms of ambiguity occur throughout the *Prince*. One is **complex irony**, a technique whereby a statement is true if its key terms are understood in one way, incomplete or false if understood in another.[5] Thus 'it is necessary to a prince to learn to be able not to be good' has one sense if 'good' means truly decent, but quite another if it means what corrupt men wrongly 'profess' to be good (chapter 15). On the first reading, one gets an amoral 'Machiavellian' maxim. On the second, the same statement stands in tension with or subverts the overtly amoral message.

Another form of ambiguity is **metaphor**, as when 'hunting' refers literally to the pursuit of wild game but metaphorically to chasing away tyrants or pursuing philosophical truths with friends (chapter 14). The metaphorical use of one phrase, 'one's own arms', *armi proprie*, is among Machiavelli's main devices for developing the *Prince*'s core argument that *virtú* produces firmer foundations for success than fortune. While 'one's own arms' have essential military dimensions, they also have economic, civil, juridical, and even philosophical ones (chapters 10, 12–14).

(3) PROVOCATIVE USE OF EXAMPLES

Since most of the *Prince*'s examples are not well known to modern readers, it is tempting to take Machiavelli's explicit comments on individuals or polities at face value, not asking how far these remarks might challenge contemporary views of his modern examples, or ancient and humanist views of ancient ones. This is one of the commonest but most serious errors readers make, since Machiavelli frequently uses examples to provoke further examination of actions and reputations. His choice of modern examples singled out for lavish praise would have appalled most of his contemporaries—or made them laugh. If this were not enough to indicate ironic intent, Machiavelli's other writings— most tellingly, diplomatic dispatches written before the *Prince*—cast some of these individuals in a most unflattering light.[6]

The situation is similar with his ancient examples. Some of the men or empires that the *Prince* declares imitation-worthy might seem uncontroversial to readers with only a passing knowledge of ancient appraisals. What hot-blooded prince would not want to imitate the greatness of Cyrus, Romulus, Theseus, or the Roman Empire? But readers who consult Xenophon on Cyrus, Plutarch on Romulus and Theseus, and Polybius, Livy, or Tacitus on the

---

[5] Vlastos (1991), 31–6.

[6] I often compare comments he made in his correspondence on contemporary figures—such as Cesare Borgia, Popes Alexander VI and Julius II, King Louis XII of France, Spain's King Ferdinand—to his remarks on these men in the *Prince*.

Roman Empire will encounter good reasons to pause before leaping to imitate these paragons—and suspect that Machiavelli too finds them more problematic than he openly says (chapters 3, 6). Other choices of ancient heroes are at least as eyebrow-raising as the choice of modern role models, notably the criminal Severus and Philip V of Macedon, one of the vilest characters in Polybius' and Livy's histories. On the other hand, a few more modest examples—Hiero in chapter 6, Philopoemen in chapter 14—emerge in a surprisingly positive light, and appear as more realistic models to imitate than 'higher' and 'greater' ancient men.

As a rule of thumb, then, readers should try to find out more about Machiavelli's examples before concluding that his explicit comments on them are the whole story. They should compare these comments with what he says elsewhere about the same individuals or events, and consider what he might not be saying openly, expecting readers familiar with his examples to recognize the unspoken implications.

(4) IRONIC CONTRAST

(a) Contrasting words and deeds

Another well-established technique of ironic praise is to lavish good words on a subject's actions, while describing those actions in ways that jar with the praise. In the *Prince* we often encounter statements that seem to convey Machiavelli's unequivocally positive judgements of individuals, states, or actions. Given the book's bewildering ambiguities, it is all the more tempting to seize on such statements as the basis for understanding Machiavelli's views. The temptation, however, should be resisted, since **statements** where Machiavelli seems to praise an agent or action may stand in tension with his detailed **descriptions** of the same actions. In chapter 3, for example, he seems to commend the Romans' great 'prudence and *virtù*' as they expanded their empire beyond Italy. Yet his detailed accounts of specific Roman methods, and of the long-term consequences of their expansion, raise serious doubts about their *virtuoso* quality.

This is one of the oldest techniques of ironic writing, which ancient dramatists and historians had developed into high art. Its basis is the antithesis between good words and less good deeds (Greek *logoi-ergoi*, Latin *verba-facta*). It was designed to address an age-old problem in political life: that people are easily taken in by impressive-sounding rhetoric and good appearances, and lured by good words into overlooking the dangerous errors made by men in power. Ancient writers such as Xenophon used the contrast between overt praise and accounts of problematic deeds to train readers to see through seductive rhetoric. Machiavelli, I suggest, does the same. He frequently makes actions speak more truly than words—if not so loudly that they grab our first attention.

(b) Contrasting descriptions

The *Prince* uses a further method of ironic 'blame-by-praise': instead of directly criticizing a subject, he is set alongside another person who is praised for qualities or actions that are pointedly *not* noted in the other. Whereas the method just described contrasts outspoken praise with undeclared—but richly illustrated—folly, this one offers silent or oblique criticism. Thus in chapter 7 Machiavelli warmly commends Francesco Sforza's great *virtú*, and then introduces Cesare Borgia in far more ambivalent terms.

(5) ELOQUENT SILENCES AND OMISSIONS

(a) Unstated parallels

Another form of 'silent criticism' works by implying similarities between an ostensibly decent subject and another whom the author explicitly condemns. In the *Discourses* Machiavelli comments directly on how Roman writers used this technique to imply that Julius Caesar, whom they were afraid to criticize openly, was no better than the criminal conspirator Catiline:

> Nor should anyone deceive himself because of the glory of Caesar, hearing him especially celebrated by the writers; for those who praise him are corrupted by his fortune and awed by the duration of the empire that, ruling under that name, did not permit writers to speak freely of him. But whoever wishes to know what the writers would say of him if they were free should see what they say of Catiline. Caesar is so much more detestable as he who has done an evil is more to blame than he who has wished to do one. He should also see with how much praise they celebrate Brutus, as though, unable to blame Caesar because of his power, they celebrate his enemy.[7]

Some of these unnamed writers seem to praise Caesar to the skies. But their *sotto voce*, damning judgement can be found on the one hand in comparing his actions to those of the despicable Catiline—who tried and failed to seize tyrannical power in the republic, while Caesar tried and succeeded—and on the other by comparing the greater praise they lavish on Caesar's enemy. Machiavelli's *Prince* has its own rough equivalents of the Romans' Catiline, an

---

[7] *D* I.10.

anti-hero whose deeds could be safely criticized while showing uncanny parallels with those of other men who appear more praiseworthy: Agathocles and Liverotto da Fermo in chapter 8, whose actions are similar to those of Pope Alexander VI and his son, Cesare Borgia.

(b) Misleading omissions

Machiavelli announces that he will 'leave out' discussing republics (chapter 2), the modes new princes use to gain popular favour (chapter 9), and reasoning on laws (chapter 12). In each case his omissions are misleading; he proceeds to say quite a lot about all these subjects under various paraphrases.[8] As we'll see in chapter 1, he omits the word 'tyranny'—which frequently appears in his other writings—throughout the *Prince*. Yet the actions generally associated with that word are omnipresent, and indirectly judged.

(6) IRONIC TRANSFORMATION

One of Machiavelli's favourite—and least recognized—ironic techniques starts by making claims that sound extreme or uncompromising, then adds further comments that moderate the initial claim. This may be done through **paraphrase**: subtle changes in wording when describing the same thing, action, or person; or by sudden **shifts in tone** from harsh to soft, or vice versa; or by **caveats** that harden or soften an initial statement. Machiavelli makes extensive use of ironic transformation in the *Discourses*. In the *Prince*, the most striking examples occur in chapters 16–18.

(7) HYPERBOLE AND EXAGGERATION

These are among the most widely recognized 'signs' of irony. When a text that generally has a cool, analytical tone suddenly bursts forth in extravagant superlatives, readers should be put on their guard and ask: does this hyperbole express the author's most considered views? When in chapter 14 Machiavelli insists that princes should think of *nothing* but war and military matters, can he be taken at face value? When in chapter 6 he tells princes to imitate the 'most excellent', high-soaring examples of ancient heroes, might dangerous

---

[8] The rhetorical term for this is *accisimus*, a form of irony in which a person feigns a lack of interest in something to which he actually wants to draw attention.

pitfalls lurk within this advice? In general, the more loudly Machiavelli insists on the 'greatness' or excellence of a person or action, the closer attention we should pay to elements in his descriptions that call their merits into question. His over-insistence on some qualities provokes readers to see through whatever is most effusively praised, and to recognize the less lauded conditions for stable political 'orders'.

(8) ABSURD OR OUTRAGEOUS ASSERTIONS

In an essay on reading, Plutarch notes that poets, dramatists, and historians often baffle readers by making outrageous statements or praising base deeds. Superficial readers may condemn the author for this. But they should give him the benefit of the doubt, and seek 'the means for rectifying' statements that shock them in the surrounding text—asking whether the author writes something more reasonable 'to the opposite effect' that cancels out the effect of the shocking statement.[9] Inexperienced readers tend to assume that an author must agree with all his own amoral, illogical, or unrealistic statements, when in fact he may want to test readers' abilities to see what's wrong with them. Machiavelli's *Prince* is loaded with such statements: for example, the statement that people should be 'forced to believe' in a prince's new orders (chapter 6), and many statements in chapters 15–18.

---

[9] 'Poetry', *PM* I, 24.

Coded words

The following is a non-exhaustive list of normatively 'coded' words used in the *Prince*. Some words consistently signal dependence on fortune, others reliance on *virtú*. The *virtú*-linked words convey praise, even when they sound low-key or inconspicuous. The fortune-linked words convey criticism, even when they sound enthusiastic or impressive.

	Virtú	Fortuna
Antitheses	free, freely (*libera, liberamente*)	prince (*principe*)
	people(s) (*populo, populi*)	prince
	republic (*republica*)	principality (*principato*)
	low (*basso*)	high (*alto*)
	one's own (*suo/sua proprie*)	others' (*d'altri*)
	ordinary, order (*ordinario, ordine*)	extraordinary (*estraordinario*)
	stability, stable (*stabilità, stabile*)	variation (*variazione*)
	caution/respect (*rispetto*)	impetuosity (*impetuosità*)
Near-synonyms		
	citizens (*cittadini*)	subjects (*sudditi*)
	friends (*amici*)	partisans (*partigiani*)
	prudence (*prudenza*)	astuteness (*astuzia*)
	acquire (*acquisitare*)	seize (*occupare*)
	maintain (*mantenere*)	hold, possess (*tenere, possedere*)
	order (*ordinare*)	innovate (*innovare*)
	satisfy (*satisfare*)	indulge, entertain (*intrattenere*)
	effort, pains (*fatica, affani*)	difficulty (*difficultà*)
	friendly (*amico*)	favour (*favore*)
	parsimony (*parsimonia*)	miserliness (*misero*)
Warning words		
		happy (*felice*)
		[acquiring] quickly, suddenly (*subito, presto*)
		easy, easily (*facile, facilmente*)
		great/ness (*grande, grandezza*)
		high, height (*alto, altezza*)
		rare (*raro*)
		spirited (*animoso*)
		idleness, idle (*odio, ozioso*)
		enterprise (*imprese*)
Understated praise		
	ordered (*ordinate*)	
	natural (*naturale*)	
	reasonable (*ragionevole*)	
	firm (*fermo*)	
	certain (*certe*)	
	discipline (*disciplina*)	
	knowledge, to know (*cognizione, conoscere*)	
	merit (*merito*)	

In Machiavelli's **antitheses**, both terms seem merely descriptive or of equal value. In fact the *virtú*-related term is positive and conveys praise, while the fortune-linked term is negative or ambiguous.

Near-synonyms seem almost interchangeable, although Machiavelli always links one to *virtú* and the other to fortune. They mimic the misleading resemblance between virtues and vices found in political life.

Warning words seem to express approval, enthusiasm, or high praise, but in fact signal problematic reliance on fortune behind good words or appearances.

Understated praise words seem merely descriptive or moderately positive, but in fact indicate praiseworthy *virtú* behind unassuming or neutral appearances.

While the consistent ordering of this language around the *virtú–fortuna* distinction seems to be Machiavelli's own work, a similarly patterned language can be found in many ancient writers, who also use some of the same 'coded' terms. For example, Xenophon's *Cyropaedia* begins with an opposition between democracy (*dêmokratia*) and tyranny (*tyrannia*). The work goes on to introduce a series of interrelated antitheses and near-synonyms similar to Machiavelli's. In the work's first paragraph Xenophon reflects 'how many who have aspired to tyranny have either been deposed once and for all and quickly; or if they have continued in power, no matter for how short a time, they are marvelled at [*thaumazontai*] as having proved wise [*sophoi*] and fortunate [*eutucheis*] men'.[1] This marvelling is quietly exposed as misplaced, since these men of good fortune weaken their states and enslave their people (sometimes with the latter's unconscious complicity). The opposition between what is done (*epraxan*) and what is said (*elexan*) runs through Xenophon's work, as it does through Machiavelli's: Cyrus appears and speaks as a paragon of virtue, while acting in ways that corrupt customary Persian practices.

Xenophon's ironic use of language owes much to Thucydides, who in turn drew on older traditions in Greek poetry, drama, historical writing, and philosophy. Many of Machiavelli's 'warning' words are prefigured in Thucydides' *Histories*: 'great' and 'greatness' (*megas, megalos*) are always deceptively problematic words, as are 'easy' (*rhadios*) and various words for 'quickness' when used for acquiring or changing.[2] An important contrast between problematic change or movement (*metabolas, kinêsis*) and what is stable (*bebaios*) or secure (*asphalês*) runs through his work, similar to Machiavelli's contrast between fortune's *variazione* and virtuous *stabilità* or *sicurità*.[3]

Thucydides was an important model for some of Machiavelli's favourite Roman historians, including Sallust, Tacitus, and Livy. Sallust's *Jugurthine*

---

[1] *XC* I.1.

[2] Plato's dialogues contain some particularly clear uses of these words for merely apparent goods with hidden deficiencies: for example, see *Statesman* 286d–287a, Letter VII 331a, and Conclusion n. 26 on the *Laws*.

[3] See chap. 15 and *ME* 88–97. Thucydides sets the pattern for his language in the first 19 paragraphs of his work.

War begins with a sharp opposition between virtue (*virtus*) and *fortuna*. The former is the only effective way to pursue glory, while fortune is a seductive but ultimately useless ally.[4] His *War with Catiline* employs many antitheses, near-synonyms, and words of ironic praise similar to Machiavelli's, notably the ambivalent use of 'spirit' (*animo*), 'liberality' (*liberalitas*), and 'cruelty' (*crudelitas*) (see chapters 16–17).[5]

Tacitus, whose *Histories* Machiavelli quotes in the *Prince*, writes with dark irony of the 'happy [*beatissimi*] age' inaugurated in Rome by recent emperors, who were 'increasing daily the happiness of the times [*augeatque cotidie felicitatem temporum*]'. He regularly associates 'happiness' (*felicitas*) with complacency and idleness (*otium*) that lead to decadence.[6] The theme of free speech and its suppression under the Empire runs through Tacitus' works, as does the Thucydidean theme that in corrupt times language is corrupted, so that which deserves blame is widely praised, and vice versa. His language, like Machiavelli's, frequently imitates this confusion—thereby holding up a silently damning reflection of it rather than encouraging readers to persist in their errors.[7]

---

[4] *SJW* I.Pref.

[5] Sallust's near-contemporary Cicero also admired and imitated Greek works, though his writing tends to be more direct—and thus less similar to Machiavelli's—than that of the more ambiguous Sallust, Tacitus, or Virgil. While Machiavelli quotes or mentions these other writers in his works, his rather sparse references or allusions to Cicero (or 'Tullio', as he is called in the *Discourses*) are not especially positive.

[6] *TA* 3.1, 31.4.

[7] For excellent studies of ambiguity and irony in Roman writers and their Greek sources, see McDonnell (2006) and O'Gorman (2000).

Dedication: princes and peoples

Dedicatory letter (Niccolò Machiavelli to the Magnificent Lorenzo de' Medici II)[1]

POLITICAL RESOURCES: KNOWLEDGE AND FORTUNE

'It is customary most of the time', Machiavelli begins, 'for those who desire to acquire grace [*grazia*] from a prince to come to meet him with the things of their own that they hold most dear, or with things that they see please him most.' Machiavelli might want his prince's 'grace', but he has no worldly goods to offer Lorenzo, or at least nothing like the 'horses, arms, cloth of gold, precious stones and similar ornaments worthy of [a prince's] greatness [*grandezza*]'.[2] But since he desires to offer 'your Magnificence' some 'testimony of my servitude [*servitù*]', Machiavelli presents what he cares for most among his belongings:

the knowledge [*cognizione*] of the actions of great men [*uomini grandi*], imparted to me through a long experience of modern things [*cose moderne*] and a continuous reading of ancient ones.

He has 'considered and examined' these matters 'with great diligence [*gran diligenzia*] for a long time', reduced them to a 'small volume' (*uno piccolo volume*), and now offers this 'small gift' in the hope that 'if your Magnificence considers and reads it diligently, you will know from it my extreme desire [*estremo mio desiderio*] that you arrive at the greatness [*grandezza*] that fortune and your other qualities promise'.

---

[1] Machiavelli's chapter titles and the Dedication are in Latin.
[2] Compare Isocrates' 'To Nicocles', 4: 'When men make it a habit, Nicocles, to bring to you who are rulers of kingdoms articles of dress or of bronze or of wrought gold, or other such valuables of which . . . you have plenty, it seems to me all too evident that they are not engaged in giving but in bargaining.'

Machiavelli's insistence on the contrast between the *grandezza* of his dedicatee and the smallness of his offering might seem no less aimed at pleasing the
prince than gems and gold. But perhaps there is a kind of greatness—or
something nearly as good as princely *grandezza*—in Machiavelli's little gift.
There is the 'great' diligence with which he reflected on its contents, which
include things he 'came to know and understand in so many years and with so
many hardships and dangers [*disagi e periculi*] for myself'. However small the
things of value that he possesses, he acquired them through his own industry
and discipline. He is confident that they are his for good, since while he lives
no one and no power, even fortune, can take away his knowledge. He does
not presume to identify these goods with 'one's own arms and *virtú*'. But his
description of how he acquired them resembles the second of the two modes—
fortune and *virtú*—presented in chapter 1 as those used to acquire states, and
examined throughout the *Prince*.

His prince's greatness, on the other hand, comes from fortune and 'other
qualities'. What those other qualities are, Machiavelli does not say; Lorenzo is
a new and young prince whose promise has yet to be realized. But whether
they prove to be praiseworthy qualities or not, Lorenzo and many other
princes also rise to greatness by the fortune of their birth rather than through
their own diligence, experience, and hardships. They therefore lack the secure,
hard-won knowledge that less fortunate men like Machiavelli have.

Which then is of greater value: knowledge without good fortune, or greatness
given by fortune yet unaccompanied by knowledge? Throughout the *Prince*,
Machiavelli invites readers to weigh these alternatives and choose 'in their own
mode'. Of course, most princes will desire *both* good fortune and hard-earned
knowledge. Machiavelli will try to gratify this desire by giving princely readers
'the capacity to understand in a very short time [*in brevissimo tempo intendere*]'
what he himself came to 'know and understand' (*conosciuto e inteso*) only after
many years of experience, reading, hardships, and dangers. But whatever wisdom his book may impart, it will still be second-hand, and far less firm or deep
than the knowledge one gains on one's own. At best, readers will only 'understand' what Machiavelli 'knows *and* understands'.[3] Unless Machiavelli's prince
gains experience—preferably hard experience—for himself, and supplements
what he reads in the *Prince* with a deep reading of ancient writers, he will fail to
develop the kind of first-rate brain described in chapter 22: 'one that understands
by itself [*intende da sé*]' instead of merely 'discerning what others understand'.
And the less secure his own knowledge of politics, the more a prince must rely on
fortune and 'the arms of others' to navigate its stormy waters.

---

[3] Machiavelli's words for 'knowledge' and knowing, *cognizione* and *conoscere*, occur rarely in
all his works, and always refer to highly reflective and well-founded forms of knowledge; see
chap. 14.

POPULAR AND PRINCELY KNOWLEDGE

Machiavelli identifies himself to Lorenzo not only as a man of practical experience and extensive reading, but also as 'a man of low and mean state [*uno uomo di basso e infimo stato*]'. It may, he admits, 'be reputed presumption' if such a man 'dares to discuss and give rules for [*discorrere e regolare*] the government of princes'. Most 'handbooks for princes' were the work of men whose position on the social ladder was far lower than princes. Yet they seldom apologized for presumption, assuming that superior age and political or philosophical wisdom made them eminently qualified to advise the great. In his protestations of 'servitude', his 'extreme desire' for Lorenzo's promised *grandezza*, and hopes that 'Your Magnificence will at some time turn your eyes from the summit of your height [*sua altezza*] to these low places', Machiavelli exceeds conventional expressions of deference.

Contemporaries who were aware of his recent track record in addressing Medici 'princes' are likely to have been bemused by such grandiose grovelling. This was, after all, the same Machiavelli who had been presumptuous enough to give unsolicited advice to Giovanni de' Medici (now Pope Leo X) soon after the 1512 coup, advising him to found the new Medici government on the people rather than the patrician 'great' who had backed his family's return to power.[4] It was the same Machiavelli who, having been tortured under suspicion of conspiring against that same government, had written cheekily familiar sonnets to Giuliano de' Medici bemoaning his sore shoulders and the foul stench of his prison cell. Here he was again, writing to yet another Medici prince—this one younger and less experienced than the others—in tones more appropriate for addressing a great monarch, a Roman emperor, perhaps even a tyrant.[5]

Even to readers unaware of his reputation among Florentines as a man who seldom bowed down to men of wealth or power, Machiavelli's new-found depths of deference might have smacked of irreverence. For officially, these Medici were not 'princes' or monarchs of any kind, but simply leading men in a republic. Machiavelli's humble professions of servitude ignore that fiction, insisting on a mode of address entirely out of place in a republic. The implication that the Medici expected such treatment from formally equal fellow citizens speaks louder than any direct charge of hypocrisy.

Yet the more his rhetoric dwells on the gulf between princely greatness and his own baseness, the more Machiavelli underscores the need to overcome it. Just as landscape artists go down to the plain to sketch mountains and 'high places' (*luoghi alti*), and go high [*alto*] atop mountains to consider the nature of low [*bassi*] places, so princes need to descend to Machiavelli's level if they

---

4 *Ai Palleschi* (after September 1512).
5 See chap. 1 on the absence of this word in the *Prince*.

wish to gain the knowledge needed to rule. 'To know well the nature of peoples [*conoscere bene la natura de' populi*] one needs to be prince', and 'to know well the nature of princes one needs to be of the people [*populare*]'.

Here is a classic Machiavellian transformation:[6] if at first he was a man of base and low state bowing to his 'great' superior, now he identifies himself as something quite different, one of the people. A prince looking down from sublime heights may not see the difference; to him, the base and the *populi* are the same. Once he has gained experience and read widely, however—or gained second-hand knowledge through Machiavelli's 'small gift'—he will know that the *populare* and *populi* are not at all low on the scale of *virtú*. Subjects (*sudditi*) stand beneath princes and are ruled by them, dependent on the fortunes of 'others'. But 'peoples' in Machiavelli's vocabulary are always independent and self-governing or actively striving for independence. Their 'nature' as peoples rather than subjects is defined by their active and virtuous desire for self-government. Peoples do tend to have less good fortune than princes, and lack their power, wealth, and *grandezza*.[7] Yet greater fortune, as we've seen, does not necessarily create greater worth, or even greater security in one's most treasured goods. The *Prince* will induce readers to 'examine' the *virtú* of well-ordered peoples and the benefits—and harms—they can bring princes.

Machiavelli says the knowledge he can give *qua* man of the people, as well as *qua* individual of experience and wide reading, has special value for a prince. Other princely advice books cite their author's personal qualifications as adviser. But precious few treat popular origins as one of them, or suggest that not just he but other men of the people might be able to impart equally valuable advice. In quietly putting himself on a par with princes, Machiavelli also insists on his equality with others who are 'of the people'.

Princes need a popular perspective in order to understand those whom they seek to rule. But Machiavelli's landscape metaphor suggests that they need it for another reason as well: to help them 'know well the nature of princes', that is, to know themselves. As a popular man, Machiavelli can examine their nature better than they can examine their own. His book will teach princes how to acquire and maintain power. But as a deeper foundation for this 'how to' knowledge,[8] it will also urge them to examine their own desires, strengths, and shortcomings, both personally and as princes who all—since

---

[6] See 'Ironic Techniques' (7).

[7] Unless a whole people becomes 'prince' over other peoples, as Rome did over many provinces. See chap. 3.

[8] Machiavelli generally uses the verb *sapere* for technical or purely practical knowledge of what works in particular conditions, saving *conoscere* for more reflective knowledge of the wider conditions, long-term consequences, and virtuous or un-virtuous quality of actions. See *ME* 111–12, 122–3.

they partake of the 'nature' of princes—must grapple with similar pressures and limitations.[9]

MACHIAVELLI'S FORTUNE AND THE FORTUNE OF PRINCES

Machiavelli ends by telling Lorenzo that if he should ever deign to look down from his heights, 'you will learn how undeservedly I endure a great and continuous malignity of fortune [*una grande e continua malignità di fortuna*]'.[10] Despite all his knowledge and hard work, bad fortune still cast Machiavelli down to his present low condition. But unlike *fortuna*'s less worthy victims, he doesn't simply blame it while doing nothing to improve his fate. On the contrary, his little book on principalities is an attempt to overcome his own, his city's, and Italy's bad fortune—through writing, since he is not free to act.[11]

And however harshly fortune may oppress him, Machiavelli still has one thing it cannot take: his hard-earned knowledge, which he now generously offers to share with a fortunate prince, indeed a prince whose ascendant family fortune is directly responsible for Machiavelli's malignant one. For the Medici princes may have gold and ornaments and greatness, but fortune easily gives these things and just as easily takes them away. Knowledge gained on one's own is entirely one's own, come what may; it is any person's most secure resource for future endeavours, even if he has to crawl back up from the lowest ranks, as Machiavelli will seek to do. Today he is unfortunate and base, while Lorenzo rises to great heights (*altezza*) with his family fortunes. But too high an altitude, as the *Prince* will show, can be perilous for princes. At times the book seems to urge them to reach ever higher. At others, it gives them reasons to clamber back down to earth, consult with men of the people, and stop relying on fortune to make them great.

---

[9] The *Prince* says little about what a princely perspective might contribute to popular self-knowledge. The *Discourses*, however, frequently shifts from popular to princely perspectives, thus showing peoples in republics how certain elements of their 'nature' may lead them toward principality or to tyranny if not properly checked.

[10] He will echo this pathetic line in chap. 7, where he declares that Cesare Borgia's downfall arose from 'an extraordinary and extreme malignity of fortune'.

[11] In both his practical impotence and intellectual freedom, Machiavelli had excellent company: as he later wrote in the *Discursus*, 'Aristotle, Plato, and many others' who were 'unable to form a republic in reality [*in atto*] . . . have done it in writing [*in iscritto*]'.

States

1

States and modes

How many are the kinds of principalities and in what modes they are acquired

STATES AND DOMINIONS

The *Prince*'s teachings begin by setting out some key terms: 'All states [*stati*, singular *stato*], all dominions [*dominii*]' that have held 'empire [*imperio*] over men are either republics or principalities [*o republiche o principati*].'

States and dominions are basic types of political unit. They share two main elements: territory and population. In the first few chapters, Machiavelli speaks of both as if they were essentially inanimate matter to be 'acquired' or 'held' by princes. He seems particularly indifferent to how the population of any state or dominion might feel about princes who acquire or hold them. But it will soon prove impossible to discuss these actions without considering the reactions of people at their receiving end. These reactions, it turns out, are among the most important factors that princes need to take into account if they want to maintain their *stati*.

Machiavelli's *Discourses* mention a third element in his concept of the *stato*: political organization. This may take different forms. One chapter title asks, for example, 'Whether a state could have been ordered in Rome that would have taken away the enmities between the people and the Senate'. Another asks 'In what mode a free state, if there is one, can be maintained in corrupt cities'. In these cases, 'state' refers to the internal political order, or way of ordering relations among different parts of a state's own population.[1] Other uses refer to both the internal and external aspects of a state's orders, as when

---

[1] *D* I.6, I.18. The word *stato* derives from the Latin *status*, meaning 'condition', which in turn derives from the verb *stare*, 'to stand, stay, rest, or make firm'. Machiavelli's concept of the *stato* implies that the most fully realized states are stable or firm, conditions that require well-ordered foundations.

Machiavelli writes of an 'inconvenience grown either in a state or against a state', or of 'weak states' vulnerable to both internal and outside threats.[2] For Machiavelli, the two are always connected. A strong political order is one that can defend territory and population from either sort of threat; and it needs to be firm inside if it is to withstand external dangers.

This suggests that the third element of states is in a sense the most important. One may acquire large, rich, or well-placed territories and large or robust populations, but if these raw materials lack a clear, man-made, intelligent political organization, they will be vulnerable.

While the word *stato* occurs throughout the *Prince*, *dominio* is much less frequent. At times it seems almost synonymous with *stato*. Yet there is a difference between the forms of rule typical of these two political units. In the *Discourses* and elsewhere, Machiavelli uses 'dominions' for territories and populations that are ruled by a given state but lie outside its core political orders, and are subject to less direct forms of control—as we might use 'empire' today. Since such political units are not thoroughly integrated into the ruling state's political orders, they would seem to lack the main condition for strength found in *stati*, though they may have much greater territory and populations. As chapters 3–5 will suggest, princes who dream of acquiring ever wider dominions need to realize that they are more vulnerable to internal and external threats than states based on a firmer, more unified organization.

Imperio here simply means rule 'over men'. Elsewhere Machiavelli uses the word to mean supreme authority within a state or dominion. It may be exercised in very different ways: involuntarily or based on consent, shared among several formally equal parties or held by one alone—depending on which form of political organization one finds in a state or dominion.

There are, Machiavelli tells us, only two such forms: republics and principalities, distinguished by their very different ways of organizing political authority. In republics political authority is shared among a wide cross-section of people in the state, especially the people (*populo*) and the great (*grandi*). In principalities, one man holds supreme political authority. On these criteria, dominions are far more likely to be organized as principalities than as republics, since one state unit rules by dominating other populations. States organized internally as republics can exercise *principato* over other cities or provinces, as republican Rome did over Gaul and Greece and republican Florence over Pisa, Pistoia, and Lucca.

States in the *Prince* are almost never agents. They are acquired or maintained, held or lost, but seldom act on their own. Machiavelli assumes that states are the main object of princely desires. Since he tends to speak of 'a prince's state' in the book, it might seem that *stati* are always a particular

---

[2] *D* I.33, II.15.

person's property.[3] But though states are always made by particular people for particular people, the makers and possessors are not always individuals. Republics are located in states too, and their states are by definition 'owned' by the public: *res publica* means 'the public thing'. Matters are different for principalities where, since one man holds supreme authority, the *stato* is more likely to be considered 'his' to the exclusion of others.

But while the *Prince* usually seems to take it as given that princes regard 'their' states as their personal property, it also raises the question of whether it is in a prince's best interests to see them this way. One of the book's main concerns is to get princes to think about the political and military risks of trying to monopolize state power. How far, it asks, can they do this without depriving themselves of crucial support from their populace?

REPUBLICS AND PRINCIPALITIES

Machiavelli's opening assertion that 'all' states and dominions are either republics or principalities looks like a straightforward piece of classification, in the style of numerous treatises on politics since Aristotle's. But first appearances in the *Prince* are often misleadingly bland or shocking. This first sentence sets the pattern. Behind its dry-sounding definitions lurk a deeply provocative implication, and another deeply subversive one.

The provocation lies in the stark, either–or choice between just two basic ways of organizing states or dominions. Most educated readers had learned from Aristotle that there were three main forms of government that could constitute a state's fundamental 'order': monarchy, aristocracy, and democracy. These could be 'mixed' in various ways to suit different social and political conditions. Machiavelli, too, grants that republics and principalities may include elements from these different forms. But by saying that *all* states are *either* republics *or* principalities, he implies that the three classic forms of government are not the same as what he calls 'states'. His *stato* refers to the basic organization of political power; governments are secondary, more particular ways of arranging that power. And according to Machiavelli's polar alternatives, when considered as 'states' in his sense, all the different forms of government can ultimately be classified as either republics or principalities. In every state without exception, supreme authority is either shared among a wide cross-section of the population, or exercised by one man—or one part of the populace—to the exclusion of others.

If all *stati* are either republics or principalities, how should we relate democracies, aristocracies, and monarchies to this more basic classification?

---

[3] See Mansfield (1998), 11, n.5: '*stato* is the status of a person or group while dominating someone else'. On Machiavelli's definitions, this is not true if the *stato* is a properly constituted republic.

In the *Discourses* I.2, Machiavelli begins by calling them 'states', then demotes them to 'forms of government' after declaring that all by themselves are 'pernicious' and 'pestiferous'. They are unsound because they all rest on the dominance of one part (*parte*) of a populace over the rest, and thus 'easily leap' from good to bad: 'the principality easily becomes tyrannical; the aristocrats with ease become a state of the few; the popular is without difficulty converted into the licentious'. In each case we start out with a government that assigns pre-eminent authority to one man or part of the populace—the few, the 'popular', or a prince—while conceding an inferior share of power to the other parts. But since all these governments are based on the principle that one part or person dominates the rest, as their names reflect,[4] they have a built-in flaw. Eventually, the dominant part becomes ambitious for even more power, while the parts that have less power grow discontented. In time this leads to serious conflicts, driving the dominant part of government to seek a monopoly of supreme authority. Thus, Machiavelli declares, 'if an orderer [*ordinatore*] of a republic orders one of those three states [*stati*] in a city, he orders it there for a short time, for no remedy can be applied there to prevent it from slipping into its contrary'.[5]

This suggests that the basic ordering principle of democracies and aristocracies, like that of principalities, is the dominance of one part over the others rather than shared power. Less-bad forms *try* to combine the principles of shared and monopolized power. But in practice they always tend toward the latter, since they are based on the dominance of one part and dominance easily leads toward monopoly. The more they monopolize power for the few or the 'popular', the more aristocracies and democracies resemble a kind of 'principality' of the few or the many.[6]

This means that Machiavelli's idea of 'republic' needs to be distinguished from democracy and aristocracy as well as from principality. Republics are emphatically not the same as 'democracies' in Machiavelli's vocabulary, any more than they were for ancient writers or other humanists. What Machiavelli and his contemporaries called democracy was a form of government where the 'popular' part of a city dominated the rest, and which ancient history and recent events had proved unstable. By contrast, the *Discourses* describe 'republic' as a mode of ordering laws and government that 'shares in all' the three other types, thus avoiding their deviations. Its basis is not the dominance of any one part of a populace, including the 'popular' *parte*, but the rule of laws

---

[4] The Greek *kratos* which forms the suffix of 'democracy' and 'aristocracy' means power, might, or dominion.

[5] *D* I.2.

[6] Aristotle makes a similar distinction in the *Politics*. While identifying six types of government, three sound and three corrupt deviations from the sound types, he argues that all these governments lean toward one of two more basic types of rule (*archè*): one conducted for the sake of the individual or collective ruler, and the other for the sake of the subjects. *AP* 1333a.

that stand above all citizens and require them to observe strict limits on their own power.[7] Governments in which power was genuinely shared on this basis constituted what Machiavelli would later call a 'true republic' (*una vera repubblica*).[8]

It is true that in the *Prince* and elsewhere, Machiavelli expresses particular suspicions toward the so-called 'great' (*grandi*) men and families who seek to lord it over the people at large. He prefers political orders that aim to 'satisfy' (*satisfare*) the people rather than indulge the élites. But he never defends popular *dominance* over the great, or calls for a popular monopoly of political authority. If principalities can 'easily' slide toward tyranny, democracies can just as easily 'leap' toward licentious disorder.[9]

These arguments are not merely academic. By asserting that all states are either republics or principalities, Machiavelli challenges defenders of various badly mixed governments to decide which basic 'order' they preferred. Florence, for example, had for several centuries oscillated between a more popular and a more aristocratic republic, with violent struggles often occurring between the *grandi* and the *populo*.[10] Under Medici-led governments from 1434 to 1494, and again after 1512, Florence remained a republic in name but in fact came to resemble a principality. Defenders of all these governments vigorously denied that they sought a monopoly of supreme power for the people, the 'great', or one family. All claimed to uphold the republican principle of shared power, and paid lip-service to the ideas of *libertà* and universal justice. Machiavelli's either–or division cuts through this ideological sugar-coating and demands a straight answer to the question: does your government aim to spread authority widely among the populace, or to keep supreme authority in the hands of one man or part?

As the opening line in a book dedicated to a Medici 'prince', Machiavelli's 'all states are either republics or principalities' was particularly audacious. In the tense atmosphere following the Medici return in 1512, his sharp distinction invites readers—above all the family of the prince addressed in the Dedication—to ask which kind of state Florence now resembled. By calling the Medici 'princes', Machiavelli gives his own rather undiplomatic answer. At the same time, he plays on ambiguities in the word's conventional uses. The

---

[7] See *D* I.30, I.58. Similarly, the main speaker in Plato's *Statesman* divides each of the three main kinds of government into two to make six, but argues that even the better ones are not 'correct' (*orthôs*) because all are based on faction and involve the oppression of one class. He proposes to 'separate out' the one 'correct' constitution [*politeia*, Latin *res publica*] and as a seventh, 'like a god from men'. This one alone is 'based on knowledge' (*epistêmê*) not partisan interests, and allows men to govern from a standpoint independent of faction (303b–c). Compare Plato, *Laws* 712e–713a: democracies, aristocracies, and monarchies 'are not *politeiai* but cities that rule as despots over or are slaves to parts of themselves, and each is named after the despotic power [*kratos*]'.

[8] *Discursus*, 106.   [9] For a contrasting view, see McCormick (2011).

[10] As described throughout the *Florentine Histories*.

word 'prince' (*principe*) could be used for any monarch, whether he (or she) was officially called king (or queen), duke, or emperor.[11] Or it could mean merely 'first man' or leading magistrate in a republic. The Medici claimed to be nothing more than 'first men' among fellow citizens. But anyone steeped in Roman republican traditions, as Machiavelli's well-read contemporaries were, would know that such modest claims often camouflaged far greater ambitions. Rome's first emperors called themselves *princeps* to suggest that they were merely first among equals—even as they acquired extraordinary *de facto* monarchical power. Were the Medici after 1512 'first citizens' in a republic where authority was widely shared, or were they more like Roman emperors whose principality was a monarchy in all but name?

Surely, some readers might protest, republican and princely orders can be mixed in a way that satisfies proponents of both—and in certain conditions brings more stability than one or the other by itself? This was, of course, the self-justification of Rome's first emperors, and of Medici governments both before their expulsion in 1494 and after the 1512 'restoration'. While the *Prince* does not discuss the question directly, it suggests that attempts to mix the two in practice are untenable in the long run.[12] In his 1520 *Discourse on Remodelling the Government of Florence* (henceforth *Discursus*), Machiavelli explains why those who 'order' states must make a clear choice between republic or principality. The defining principles of these two 'states' are not just different; they are fundamentally opposed. Supreme political authority cannot be both widely shared and exercised by one. Eventually, all attempts to combine these principles must fall in one direction or the other: toward evenly balanced sharing (republic) or toward the dominance, and eventual monopoly, of one (principality).[13]

Although the basic organizing principles of republics and principalities are opposed, however, they may adopt many similar institutions. Republics generally have one or more leading elected magistrates who constitute a 'quasi-regal' authority, without having the wider powers of monarchs. In the *Discourses* Machiavelli sometimes calls such leading magistrates 'princes', though being ordered under the republic's principle of shared power gives them a very different character from princes in principalities: their authority is strictly limited by the other 'parts', they are elected or chosen by lot, and they usually have fixed terms of office.[14] Principalities too may be organized

[11] Two female 'princes' are mentioned in the *Prince*: the Phoenician queen Dido (chap. 17) and the Countess of Forlì (Caterina Sforza, chap. 8).

[12] See especially chaps 9 and 19.

[13] 'States of a middle sort [*stati di mezzo*] have two ways [*vie*]: they can rise toward principality or descend toward the republic. From this comes their instability [*instabilità*]' *Discursus*, 106.

[14] Thus well-ordered republics may have 'infinite most virtuous princes' (*D* I.20), while the *Discourses'* young dedicatees 'deserve to be princes' in a republican sense (*D* Ded.). See Conclusion.

in very different ways, as the *Prince* will suggest. Machiavelli includes under this heading kingdoms containing many institutions that limit the king's power and, at the other extreme, the unchecked, violent, highly personal rule of the most hated Roman emperors. The former, more limited kind of principality may closely resemble republics that have a strong leading magistrate or 'kingly' element.

Ultimately, however, these governments are founded on one kind of supreme authority or the other, shared or not-shared. If a republic allows its leading magistrates or any other citizen to overstep established limits and acquire far more authority than the other parts of government, one can fairly say that it has crossed the line from one 'state' to the other and become a principality. This, Machiavelli would tell the Medici in his *Discursus*, was what their family's government was on the verge of doing—if it had not done it already.

SILENT TYRANNY

A further implication of the *Prince*'s innocuous-sounding first sentence was even more disconcerting for early readers. If all states are either republics or principalities, then how should one classify tyranny? In the *Discourses* and elsewhere Machiavelli calls many rulers 'tyrants', and speaks very critically of tyranny (*tirannide*). He identifies it as a 'pernicious' deviation from principality: tyranny is what you get when a prince seeks to move from dominant power toward monopoly.

In the *Prince*, the words tyrant and tyranny are conspicuous by their absence. At times, Machiavelli's silence on tyranny seems unnervingly inappropriate. When he discusses criminal 'princes' in chapter 8, or speaks of a prince's 'ascent' from 'a civil order to an absolute one' in chapter 9, or of violent and hateful Roman emperors in chapter 19, his refusal to speak of tyranny brings the word to mind more vividly than if it were used. Why does Machiavelli go out of his way to avoid using it?

Two main possibilities have been suspected over the centuries. One is that Machiavelli avoids speaking of tyranny in order to challenge the conventional, morally charged language of political analysis, thereby removing the stigma attached to some of the methods usually associated with tyranny. By discussing these methods under the more neutral-sounding heading of principality, Machiavelli implies that readers should examine their merits or deficiencies without prejudging that they are *always* bad. During the first few centuries after its appearance, the *Prince* was frequently attacked for allegedly seeking to normalize, or even whitewash, tyranny in this way. From the early nineteenth century on, however, this reading has often been associated with a more sympathetic view of the *Prince* as a pioneering treatise in the scientific, and thus amoral (though not necessarily immoral) study of politics.[15]

Other early readers suspected that Machiavelli's aims were neither pro-tyrannical nor purely scientific, but pro-republican. The basis for this reading becomes clearer when we compare the *Prince* to earlier 'handbooks' written to advise monarchs on how to rule well. Before the *Prince*, most of these works began with a robust distinction between good kings and tyrants, and told monarchs how to avoid being seen as tyrannical. By throwing this convention to the winds in its very first sentence, the *Prince* deprives princely readers of their main line of defence against those who held—as Machiavelli does in his *Discourses*—that *all* monarchies are 'pernicious' because they tend to fall towards tyranny. By using 'prince' as a broad umbrella term for legitimate and limited monarchs as well as absolute rulers, Machiavelli blurs the sharp distinction that monarchs sought to draw between themselves and bad tyrants. They belong, he implies, to the same species. Republics are a different matter: though like any man-made structure they are subject to decay, the quality of their orders places them further from the path to tyranny.

Both amoral and pro-republican readings made 'princely' rulers very nervous indeed. Among early readers, the amoral interpretation was usually advanced by monarchists and religious authorities, who loudly condemned the *Prince* and its tyrant-friendly author. The second interpretation was advanced both by monarchists who disliked the pro-republican implications and by republicans who approved of them. In Machiavelli's lifetime a Medici protégé, Agostino Nifo, published a substantially rewritten version of the *Prince* under his own name, changing Machiavelli's arguments to make them friendlier to 'good' monarchy and the Church. Nifo was clearly alert to the sweeping anti-monarchical implications of Machiavelli's republics-or-principalities antithesis, for he replaced it at the outset with the more usual distinction between legitimate kings and tyrants—and put 'princes' under the second, pejorative heading. In keeping with a Medici strategy of appeasement briefly pursued after the death of the unpopular young Lorenzo, Nifo even conceded that the earlier Lorenzo *il Magnifico* qualified as 'an amiable tyrant' under 'civil principality'—the category discussed in chapter 9 of the *Prince*—not as an altogether legitimate monarch.[16]

The great genius of Machiavelli's ambiguous writing is that it manages to sustain *both* pro-tyrannical/amoral *and* republican/moral possibilities throughout the *Prince*. Sometimes the book's arguments seem unabashedly to recommend methods that others associated with tyranny. At other times, they seem to shed a critical light on all kinds of one-man and one-party rule, and to suggest

---

[15] Nineteenth- and twentieth-century German readers were among the main proponents of a modernist 'scientific' reading of the *Prince*. It was initially cited (e.g. by Hegel, 1999/1800–1802) to justify tougher action against Germany's invaders in the Napoleonic wars, and later to argue for militaristic policies and imperial expansion; see Meinecke (1998/1925).

[16] Nifo (2008/1523) I.i, V.i, VI.xii.

that only widely shared power can save princes from ruin. Readers who notice both strands of the argument are forced either to stay in ambiguous limbo, or to decide for themselves whether one strand offers stronger arguments.

Why didn't Machiavelli simply tell them what they should think about tyranny, as other political writers did? If his implications were pro-republican, of course, it would have been impolitic—and dangerous—to say openly that the princely ways of the *Prince*'s dedicatees put them on the road to tyranny. But he may have had other reasons to want readers to examine the merits of various princely actions without prejudging them. As several chapters imply, the line between more limited forms of principality and outright tyranny is not sharp, and the 'ascent' toward 'absolute' rule often occurs gradually, even almost invisibly at first, like a sickness that is hard to detect in its beginnings. The actions and ways of thinking that put princes on the path to unlimited power often appear harmless, prudent, even great and good. Such princes seldom recognize the risks they create for themselves in seeking ever more power; many persuade themselves that they are merely doing what is necessary to defend their *stato*. This is why they and those around them need to learn how to detect the early symptoms of tyranny by studying the actions and arguments that help it along. If they merely read—yet again—that tyranny is bad, and altogether different from legitimate kingship, they may not develop these preventive-detection skills.

THE HEREDITARY, THE NEW, AND THE FREE

The chapter's title asks 'how many are the kinds of principalities'. While they may have widely diverse institutions, Machiavelli sets out just two main kinds here, in keeping with the binary structure of the analysis so far. Principalities, he declares, are either hereditary [*ereditari*] or new. New ones too come in two forms. They are 'altogether new' (*nuovi tutti*) if the prince himself was not a prince but a 'private individual' before acquiring his state, as the mercenary captain Francesco Sforza had acquired Milan and its dominions in 1447. Otherwise, new principalities are 'like members added to the hereditary state of the prince who acquires them', as the Italian kingdom of Naples was added to the hereditary kingdom of Spain in 1504.

Although the chapter approaches its subject from a princely perspective, its last sentence alludes to the experiences of populations that come under a 'new' prince's rule. Machiavelli does not yet bring them fully to life by calling them subjects, peoples, or the like. For now, he assimilates populations to political units, writing that 'dominions' newly acquired 'are either accustomed [*consueti*] to living under a prince or used to being free [*usi essere liberi*]'. The next chapter will say more about the effects of local customs and habits on a new prince's rule. If a populace is accustomed to life under some other prince, this may make it hard for new princes to establish rule over them, though far easier than when people are used to 'being free'. Machiavelli will explain what this means in chapter 5, where free 'states' are described as those that 'are accustomed to living by their own laws and in liberty'. This description covers external independence—free states live by their own laws, not those imposed by others—and internal *libertà*, a condition never directly analysed in the *Prince* but discussed at length in the *Discourses*.[17]

Many princes might think that they need not concern themselves with internal liberty, especially since Machiavelli has just implied that populations that live under princes are *not* free. The statement that dominions have *either* lived under a prince *or* are used to being free implies that freedom belongs only to the other species of state, to republics.

Princes do, however, need to concern themselves with external freedom. The *Prince* will frequently touch on the question of whether they can defend their states' independence without granting a measure of liberty to their subjects. But in striking contrast to his other works, here Machiavelli expresses no direct moral judgement about the value of freedom. Princely and free republican orders are, it seems, simply different ways of organizing states to serve different interests or suit different conditions. If he thinks one is fundamentally better than the other, Machiavelli will not presume to say so here; princes and others must form their own judgement.

FORTUNE AND *VIRTÚ*

The chapter ends with yet another binary distinction, this time concerning how new princes acquire their states or dominions: 'either with the arms of others or with one's own, either by fortune or by *virtú* [*o con l'arme d'altri o con le proprie, o per fortuna o per virtú*]'. The two distinctions are parallel, so that to acquire by the arms of others is to acquire by fortune, and to acquire by one's own arms is to do so by *virtú*.

No line in the *Prince* provides more important clues to understanding the entire book than this one. The distinction between fortune and *virtú* is the overarching standard Machiavelli applies throughout to evaluate diverse princely actions. It can, I'll suggest, be applied to every statement and example in the *Prince*, even when Machiavelli does not invoke it explicitly.

What does Machiavelli mean by *fortuna* and *virtú*? In the context of the *Prince*, fortune is above all **an amoral power that gives or takes regardless of desert**.[18] In this general sense, the upward or downward swings of fortune are

---

[17] See *ME* chap. 6.
[18] As Machiavelli wrote in his poem *Di Fortuna*, 28–9, fortune 'often keeps the good beneath her feet', while 'the wicked she raises up'.

independent of human control. Nevertheless, human beings have a choice in how they *respond* to fortune's 'variations'. They may sit back and enjoy its extraordinary gifts for a time—until they become its helpless victims at the next swing. Or they can insist on helping themselves instead of depending on fortune's alluringly generous but unreliable help.

Virtú is the quality or set of qualities that **enables people to acquire or maintain desired goods through their own independent efforts**, and therefore to merit praise. Someone who acquires by fortune deserves no praise for acquiring, since his own efforts had little to do with it. By contrast, to say that someone acquires or does anything else by *virtú* is very high praise in Machiavelli's book. What you get by *virtú* you earn, by a good use of qualities that help human beings to build 'orders' of their own that withstand the pressures of fortune and other factors beyond their control.

Fortune and *virtú* are the two possible 'modes' (*modi*) by which principalities are acquired and maintained. They are also, it will transpire, the two principal modes for conducting every action discussed in the *Prince*. In Machiavelli's vocabulary, 'modes' are not simply 'methods' used to tackle particular problems at particular moments. People tend to have a single, predominant mode or pattern of conduct that influences their actions most of the time. Although they may choose and change their habitual modes, Machiavelli stresses how hard it is to 'vary' them to suit different circumstances once they have become settled habit.[19]

Nor are Machiavelli's modes simply different 'means' (*mezzi*) to identical ends. All new princes seek to acquire states or dominions. But fortune- and *virtú*-reliant princes tend to have divergent, more basic aims that they hope to reach through acquiring. In the *Prince*, those who opt to rely on fortune are especially interested in gaining great power and reputation, and know that fortune can help them do this more quickly than their own best efforts. Those who rely on *virtú* are more interested in long-term stability than in being hailed as 'great', winning every battle, or surmounting all their difficulties overnight. A prince's choice of modes, then, tells us a good deal about his ends—and about how he can be expected to govern whatever states he acquires.

DISADVANTAGES OF RELYING ON FORTUNE

In chapter 1 Machiavelli presents his two modes in value-neutral terms. Either 'mode', it seems, may bring princes the results they want, depending on particular circumstances.

---

[19] Chap. 25.

But this first appearance of neutrality will be dispelled in chapter 6. Here Machiavelli makes it clear that *fortuna* is much the inferior mode. Though it often 'appears' that either *virtú* or fortune may relieve a prince's difficulties, 'nonetheless, he who has relied less on fortune has maintained himself more'. Since even fortune-reliant princes want to maintain their states and reputations, this means that even they would do better to rely on *virtú* and their 'own arms'. At the beginning of chapter 7, Machiavelli outlines the chief disadvantages of relying on fortune for acquiring as well as maintaining principalities:

Firstly, fortune gives princes a **deceptively quick and easy ascent to power.** Those who become princes with its help 'have no difficulty along the path because they fly there' but face many difficulties 'when they are in place'.

In concrete terms, secondly, to depend on fortune means to **depend on other, unreliable people.** Someone becomes prince by fortune 'when a state is given to someone either for money or by the grace of whoever gives it'. These princes therefore 'rest simply on the will [*volontà*] and fortune of whoever has given a state to them, which are' Machiavelli points out, 'two very inconstant and unstable things [*cose volubilissime e instabili*]'.

Finally, **states gained too quickly by another's 'grace' lack roots,** 'so that the first adverse weather eliminates them'.

Governments and institutions based on fortune, then, are inherently unstable. Fortune-reliant people often produce outcomes that look impressive for a time, but are prone to collapse at any moment. In the *Prince* and all his works, Machiavelli associates fortune with variation, instability, and weak 'orders'. By contrast, actions based on *virtú* confer firmness and security on their products. They do so chiefly by imposing good 'orders' (*ordini*). Good orders and foundations (*fondamenti*) are therefore always the product of *virtú*; foundations built on fortune are always weak. And the main question Machiavelli asks readers to weigh throughout the *Prince* is: do the general modes and particular actions described in each chapter result in strong, lasting foundations? The question of whether they bring greatness and reputation is also broached. But these things can be lost overnight if a prince lacks strong *fondamenti*.

These arguments suggest not only that it is better to rely on *virtú* than fortune; it is also better not to rely on both at once. Some princes might think that the ideal is to have as much fortune *and* virtú as possible—that the most successful individuals rise by some happy conjunction of these modes. While it is good to have and use well whatever qualities help you to earn success, they might reason, it can't hurt to get as much help from fortune as you can. Machiavelli disagrees. The more you rely on fortune, the less solidly you rely on your own *virtú*. The thinking behind this view is very ancient, and based on psychological common sense.[20] Those who succeed with fortune and others'

---

[20] The *fortune–virtue* (*tuchê–arête* in Greek, *fortuna–virtus* in Latin) antithesis has a long and rich history. Among the key texts exemplifying uses similar to Machiavelli's, by authors

arms may come to expect their continued help, and thus work less hard than they otherwise would at building their 'own arms'. And because fortune is fickle, its good effects are misleading; they can lull even virtuous people into forgetting that one should *never* count on fortune's constant friendship.[21] On the contrary, as Machiavelli put it in a poem about fortune written before the *Prince*, 'you cannot trust yourself to her as she never keeps promises'.[22] Even if you happen to *have* good fortune as well as *virtú*, then, you do better to *rely* only on *virtú*, since any hopes you bank on fortune can be overturned in a flash and upset your best-laid plans. When Machiavelli speaks of princes acquiring states by 'fortune and *virtú*', this is not his ideal, but an unstable combination of two opposed modes.

It is important to distinguish fortune from necessity (*necessità*). Both inflict unwanted pressures that cannot be entirely controlled. But necessity is not a 'mode' of action, as fortune and *virtú* are. It is a condition of extreme pressure that people may respond to in different ways. Fortune and *virtú* are the basic modes of responding to necessity, and people can always choose one mode or the other. Necessity *never* forces anyone to rely on fortune. On the contrary, the harsher the objective necessity, the more reason people have to rely on their own virtuous resources, and to work hard and intelligently to overcome their difficulties.[23]

Whereas fortune is easy and hard, good and bad in turn, necessity is always harsh. But it is also more susceptible to rational management. When harsh necessity comes down on you, you cannot change it—but you can choose to respond to it by building virtuous orders that make your life better than it was. When bad fortune strikes, on the other hand, you can do very little if you relied too much on good fortune before; your habitual modes leave you ill-equipped to deal with sudden crises. The dangerous thing about good fortune is that while people have it, they feel less pressured by necessity to work hard or to use their own intelligence to acquire and maintain political goods. In time, however, they always pay the price for their complacency.

---

mentioned directly in his *Discourses*, are Thucydides' history of the Peloponnesian War; Sallust's *War with Catiline*, 1–13; Plutarch's 'On Fortune', *PM* II.74–89, and his 'On the Fortune or the Virtue of Alexander', *PM* IV.382–487. Both Greek and Hellenophile Roman writers use the antithesis to question the wisdom of seemingly successful enterprises that rely on problematic foundations.

[21] Compare Aristotle, *AR* 1390–1391b on how goods due to fortune have bad effects on character and endanger their beneficiaries: the wealthy become insolent and arrogant (*hubristai . . . kai huperêphanoi*) and think themselves worthy to rule. Also *ANE* VII. xiii.3–5: 'because happiness requires gifts of fortune in addition, some people think that it is the same as good fortune [*eutuchia*]. But this is not so, since even good fortune itself when excessive [*huperballousa*] impedes activity, and perhaps indeed no longer deserves to be called good fortune.'

[22] Machiavelli, *Di Fortuna*, 29–30.   [23] See *D* I.1; *ME* chap. 4.

WHAT IS *VIRTÚ*?

The *Prince* associates *virtú* with a variety of qualities, including spiritedness, physical boldness, excellence, industry, foresight, caution, respect for limits, patience, discipline, good orders, and moral goodness. Some of these qualities seem to have a special connection to military organization or success in battle. Others are especially valued in civilian life, or for setting up strong political foundations. Individuals who Machiavelli describes as signally lacking in some kinds of *virtú* are nevertheless described as having other qualities of *virtú*, as when he says that the 'criminal' prince Agathocles nonetheless showed '*virtú* of spirit and body'.

Is Machiavelli just being open-minded or unsystematic—or is there some method in his various uses of the word *virtú*? When we read the whole *Prince* in the light of the opposition between fortune and *virtú*, a pattern soon emerges. Some of the qualities identified with *virtú* seem especially well suited to promote princely desires for *grandezza* and reputation. Princes whose preeminent virtues include 'spirit' (*animo*) tend to have such desires. Other virtuous qualities are most suitable for a slower, more arduous 'mode' of ascent, whose ultimate aim is lasting security rather than limitless power or impressive appearances.

Machiavelli's broad use of *virtú* acknowledges that people use the word for a wide range of qualities that deserve praise. Yet his examples and arguments suggest that they do not all deserve *equal* praise, particularly not in princes. A well-rounded prince will know how to order a military and fight battles. But military virtues are not the only virtues he needs; if he wants to maintain a state, he needs other qualities as well, those more conducive to stable political orders. Machiavelli lets readers decide which of the qualities that he calls *virtú* are most essential for princes. Along the way, he invites them to consider whether certain qualities deserve highest praise absolutely, whether they are found in military captains or rulers or ordinary people.[24] If so, does this mean that what is most virtuous in principalities is also most virtuous in republics— and vice versa?

---

[24] See McDonnell (2006) for an excellent study of how Roman writers played with the tensions between martial-Roman and more ethical Greek concepts of *virtus/arête*, provoking readers to think about the limitations of the former.

2

Maintaining states

Of hereditary principalities

ABSENT REPUBLICS

Machiavelli now announces that he will 'leave out reasoning on republics' (*lascerò indreto il ragionare delle republiche*) because he has 'reasoned on them at length another time'. This is usually taken as a reference to the *Discourses*, suggesting that he may already have done some work on this more republic-friendly book when he wrote the sentence.

Here we have another understated provocation disguised as a technical point of organization. For the *Prince*'s Medici dedicatees were not officially princes, and republican institutions and traditions still prevailed in Florence, where most citizens would have baulked at the prospect of living under a full-blown *principato*. By casually putting republics aside in a book addressed to men who ostensibly headed a republic, Machiavelli implies that they must have an active interest in learning how to run a principality. This sly implication of Machiavelli's innocent-looking omission might well have irked Medici support-ers who hoped to keep up the fiction that Florence was still a genuine republic. Nor would other Florentine readers have missed the ironic suggestion that the book's dedicatees might need advice on how to acquire and hold principalities.

In fact, Machiavelli does say rather a lot about republics in the *Prince*.[1] In the next chapter, one of his main examples concerns the foreign wars fought by a very noteworthy republic: Rome. In chapter 5 he not only discusses republics, but also argues that they contain far more 'life' and powers of resistance than any principality. Then in chapter 12 he argues that republics are better than other states at founding good military orders, permitting them to rely on 'their own arms' and *virtú*. Although the word 'republic' appears

---

[1] Machiavelli says three times that he will leave out some topic: here republics, chap. 9 the modes princes use to get popular support, chap. 12 the laws. In fact he discusses all three.

infrequently in the *Prince*, Machiavelli discusses that type of *stato* under various paraphrases, usually 'living free' or under laws (*leggi*).

Despite the book's official line of omitting or at least marginalizing republics, then, they and their distinguishing features play an extremely important role in its critical examination of princely 'modes'. Their appearances are generally low-profile, and easily missed if readers skim the *Prince*'s pages looking for its most striking remarks and examples. After all, the characteristic virtues of republics praised in the *Discourses*—steady hard work, military discipline, and respect for the laws—seem less marvellous than the greatness and lofty ambitions of princes. Except when they have to fight wars or resist oppression: in these circumstances republics display a quality of *virtú* never seen in even the strongest principalities. Machiavelli makes this memorably clear in chapter 5, one of the most powerful chapters in the book and the only one where republics openly take centre stage. His direct and indirect 'reasonings' about the *virtú* and survival strategies of republics shed essential light on the *virtú* and survival strategies of princes.

HEREDITARY PRINCES: ORDINARY AND EXTRAORDINARY

Saying nonetheless that he will 'turn' (*volterommi*) from republics 'only' to principalities,[2] Machiavelli declares that he will proceed by 'weaving the warps [*ritessendo gli orditi*] mentioned above, and disputing how these principalities may be governed and maintained [*governo e mantenare*]'. Both the image of weaving and the word *orditi* suggest an orderly, systematic process of building up an argument—and at the same time a useful work of art—from its most essential foundations to the finer details.[3]

In speaking of what princes do to states or dominions, the first chapter mentioned only 'acquiring'. This one focuses on governing and maintaining, and on the differences between hereditary and new princes. Hereditary princes, Machiavelli tells us, have far fewer difficulties maintaining their states than new ones. The reason is that those states are 'accustomed to the bloodline of their prince'. Machiavelli says that *states* are so accustomed here, not their people or subjects; he remains tight-lipped about the flesh-and-blood human element in a prince's *stato*, and how feelings among a population can affect his maintaining efforts.

---

[2] Throughout the *Prince*, Machiavelli uses the verb 'to turn' (*voltare*) to mimic fortune's destabilizing vicissitudes in principalities.

[3] The word *orditi* also foreshadows the fundamental importance of the ideas of order and ordering in the *Prince*.

Nonetheless, his next lines imply that the populaces' attitudes matter a great deal, since they can give or deprive a prince of indispensable support. For a hereditary prince, if 'extraordinary vices [*estraordinari vizi*] do not make him hated, it is reasonable that he will naturally have the good will of his own [*è ragionevole che naturalmente sia benevoluto da sua*]'. To hold his state 'it is enough only not to depart from the orders [*ordini*] of his ancestors, and then to temporize in the face of accidents [*accidenti*]'. In Machiavelli's vocabulary, accidents are events that pose temporary setbacks, but do not cause fortune's extreme highs and lows. If a hereditary prince who adopts such a 'mode' 'is of ordinary industry [*ordinaria industria*], he will always maintain himself in his state unless there is an extraordinary and excessive force [*una estraordinaria e eccessiva forza*] which deprives him of it'. And even in this extreme case, he has excellent chances of recovering what he lost; for 'if anything sinister [*sinistro*] happens to the occupier', the ejected prince 'reacquires it' with the help of his ancient lineage and his 'ordinary' industry.

Compared to new princes, then, hereditary ones who acquire principality by the mere fortune of their birth have an easy ride. Some may even conclude that they need no special skills or virtues to maintain their inherited states. The good will of their 'own', it seems, comes simply by having a princely lineage and avoiding extreme badness. The phrase 'extraordinary vices' seems to set the bar comfortably high, as if to imply that run-of-the-mill vices aren't enough to bring down a hereditary prince. And it sounds easy enough to muster 'ordinary industry', if one takes *ordinario* to mean average, common-place, or unremarkable. Machiavelli's example seems to confirm the impression that hereditary princes need not worry about cultivating personal *virtú* in order to keep their states. The 'duke of Ferrara'—in fact the episodes involved two dukes, father and son—'did not succumb' to a Venetian attack in 1484 and one by Pope Julius II in 1510 'for no other cause than that his line was ancient in that dominion'.

Yet hereditary princes would be wrong to let Machiavelli's low-key words lull them into thinking that they can rely entirely on the fortune of birth to keep them in power. First of all, if they knew their recent Italian history, they would realize that causes other than princely lineage—especially grave deficiencies in its assailants—*did* help the house of Ferrara in both cases. Later in the *Prince*, Machiavelli treats Pope Julius and Venice at the time of its attack on Ferrara as prime exemplars of agents who depended heavily on fortune, and thus had little *virtú*. The Venetians relied on hired mercenaries instead of their own soldiers to seize other Italian cities. In this mode, they made great increases for a short time—then experienced a sudden, total collapse, as fortune-dependent agents are prone to do.[4] As for Pope Julius, later chapters

---

[4] Chaps 12 and 20. Compare *D* I.1.

will comment on his reckless warmongering against Italians and foreign powers, noting the 'sad results' of his failed enterprise against Ferrara.[5] Before concluding that his fortunate blood will maintain his state for him, a hereditary prince should study these cases carefully. If his attackers are less reckless than the Venetians or Julius—and the chances are they will be—the prince who relies too much on his lineage may find resistance much harder than it was for the dukes of Ferrara.

On the other side, he should ask whether, in addition to the fortune of being born princes, these dukes also had any special *virtù* on their side. Anyone who remembered the 1484 attack, or who reads further in the *Prince*, would know that 'a union of all the other' leading Italian states defended Ferrara against maverick Venice.[6] For Machiavelli this example of military collaboration showed the possibilities for virtuous Italian self-defence. In his own, less virtuous days, a hereditary prince under attack would be most unlikely to find such robust defenders. The *Prince* says nothing further about whether his own *virtù* helped Ferrara's Duke Alfonso to withstand Julius' 1510 assault. In the *Discourses*, however, Machiavelli attributes the failure of another planned attack on Alfonso—a conspiracy to murder him—as much to the duke's own exceptional qualities as to the conspirators' incompetence.[7]

As the *Prince* will soon make clear, the personal qualities of any prince, hereditary or new, greatly influence his capacity to maintain his state. For 'ordinary industry', not departing from his ancestors' 'orders', and avoiding 'extraordinary vices' call for far more than average vigilance or quiet living. In Machiavelli's lexicon, *ordinario* does not mean 'average' or commonplace. Actions done 'ordinarily' are actions that build, reinforce, or adhere to basic 'orders' (*ordini*) in a state, or in human life generally. In this sense, ordinary industry is anything but unremarkable. It is the chief preservative quality of states.

Perhaps because of its ordinariness, *ordinario* is one of Machiavelli's most frequently overlooked, normatively coded words of high praise. Like *virtù*, to which it is closely related, it always has a strongly positive meaning. And like *virtù/fortuna* in the *Prince*, it is always part of an antithetical pair: ordinary/extraordinary. If *ordinario* modes cause order, *estraordinario* ones go against, erode, or destroy it.[8] Extraordinary actions leap out from the page, as they make a strong impression in life. They are good for shaking things up, making people marvel, and gaining a reputation for greatness. Yet they are very bad for maintaining anything one wants to hold.

By contrast, ordinary modes help a prince—or any agent—to maintain what he has. This is why not even an 'extraordinary and excessive force' that deprives a prince of his state can keep him from recovering it, so long as he has always worked 'ordinarily'—that is, in ways that tend to support good orders.

---

[5] Chap. 13.   [6] Chap. 11.   [7] *D* III.6.14.
[8] See Whitfield (1969), 141–62; *ME* chap. 10.

Force used in an extraordinary mode can acquire states suddenly and dramatically.[9] But as soon as the one who used it experiences 'anything sinister whatever', perhaps some downturn in his fortunes, he loses it again to the more *ordinario* prince from whom he seized it.

Understood in this way, the antithesis ordinary/extraordinary has a close kinship with the *virtú*/fortune antithesis. In chapter 2 *estraordinario* is associated with vices, excess, and being hated. Machiavelli uses the word in later chapters to describe excessive and arbitrary taxes on the people, which make it hard for princes to maintain their state; Roman emperors who depended on soldiers bought by money and special favours; the immediately successful but erratic and destabilizing actions of Ferdinand of Aragon; and ill-founded hopes inspired by 'extraordinary' miracles. But the book's most memorable use of *estraordinario* occurs in chapter 7, when Machiavelli blames Cesare Borgia's sudden fall from great heights on an 'extraordinary and extreme malignity of fortune'.[10]

In chapter 3, 'ordinary' is paired with the words natural (*naturale*), reasonable (*ragionevole*), and necessary (*necessario*). It refers as much to the general 'order' of human nature as to man-made political orders. The desire to acquire is 'very natural and ordinary'; it is a 'natural and ordinary necessity' that new princes must offend someone; and it is no miracle but 'ordinary and reasonable' that those who fail to act prudently always lose what they acquire. In all these instances, the word 'ordinary' does not just mean 'normal', but 'compatible with good human orders'. The next chapters point to a strong connection between what is 'ordinary' for human nature, on the one hand, and man-made 'orders', on the other. The latter, if they are to last, must be founded on a good understanding of what actions respect or violate the order of human nature. Thus acquiring is not inherently disruptive of natural order; it can be done in ways that contribute to good political orders. But extraordinary modes of acquiring violate ordinary human nature, and therefore undermine political order.

It is a very serious error to underestimate the ordinary or to overrate the extraordinary, both in political life and in reading the *Prince*. Princes who do will admire the wrong things, and shirk the more modest ordering work needed to defend their states. In particular, princes need to ask what 'extraordinary vices' violate natural and political orders, in order to avoid them. A complacent prince might think that he just needs to avoid doing anything outstandingly awful. But since 'extraordinary' means 'against orders', a prince who lacks a clear idea of what natural or good orders are won't know what

---

[9] *Forza* may be used in either an ordinary or extraordinary mode, though in Machiavelli's vocabulary it usually has a positive sense of physical power used to support orders and laws—and is thus allied with 'ordinary' modes and opposed to *violenzia*, which is almost always extraordinary.

[10] Chaps 7, 16, 19, 21, 26.

vices violate them. As later chapters show, extraordinary vices can be exceedingly hard to recognize: qualities that appear virtuous and are widely praised often turn out to be such vices, while actions that appear good turn out to do great harm.[11]

CONTINUITY AND INNOVATION

If hereditary princes never maintain their states securely without some respect for order, the chapter ends by stressing the advantages they have as compared with new princes. 'In the antiquity and continuity of the dominion,' Machiavelli writes, 'the memories and causes of innovations [*innovazioni*] are eliminated.' An 'innovation' is not simply any new method or order. It usually connotes something new and disordering, such as a conspiracy or a violent coup d'état, and is thus related to 'extraordinary' in Machiavelli's negatively coded sense.[12] This explains why innovations in a state leave memories so bitter that princes should want them to be forgotten.

While Machiavelli doesn't suggest that the ancestors of all hereditary princes used extraordinary, questionably legitimate 'innovations' to take power, he implies that some of them did. Whereas the 'antiquity and continuity' of their rule helps to erase these destabilizing memories, new princes who lack these advantages need to think about how to deal with their bad aftertaste in the shorter term. Avoiding any direct reference to the populace, Machiavelli speaks of 'memories' in the dominion without saying whose they are. Prudent new princes, however, will understand that their populaces' negative feelings about how they acquire power will be stored up in potent memories that may come to threaten their rule.

None of this is reassuring for the Medici 'princes' with their ambiguous status. On the one hand, the *Prince*'s young dedicatee Lorenzo could be considered a hereditary prince who inherited his principality through the fortune of his family line. On the other, the Medici *principato* in Florence was not 'ancient', having made its first appearance with Lorenzo's great-grandfather Cosimo only some 80 years before Machiavelli wrote the *Prince*. More importantly, it lacked continuity, since the family had been banished from Florence between 1494 and 1512. Florentine memories of the 'innovations' that made Cosimo prince, and the further controversial, extraordinary actions that made his grandson Lorenzo even more powerful, were still very much alive. If the questionable legality of those innovations had eroded popular support for Medici-led government at the time, the new post-1512

---

[11] See chaps 15–17.

[12] For examples of 'extraordinary' and harmful innovations in Florence, see *D* I.7–8.

generation of Medici princes had more recent, ignominious memories to overcome: young Lorenzo's father, Piero, had been expelled from the city after failing to resist French demands to control key military fortresses in Florentine-held territories. And while as a long-standing republic Florence had no other princely bloodline to rival the 'new' Medici, memories of its ancient and continuous republican traditions would prove hard indeed to eliminate, as Machiavelli will imply in chapter 5 and state point-blank in his *Discursus*.[13]

Whether the latest crop of Medici princes regarded themselves as hereditary or new, then, chapter 2 serves them early warning that it will not be easy to maintain their principality. It ends with a disquieting image of how each new political upheaval creates new instabilities: 'one change [*mutazione*] always leaves an indentation for the building of another [*addentellato per la edificazione dell'altra*]'. The phrase '*edificazione* of another' strikes a sinister chord. Its '*dell'altra*', the chapter's last words, recalls '*arme d'altri*'—the arms of others—and their opposition to one's own arms and *virtú*. In the light of recent events in Florence, this might be read as a reproach and a warning to the Medici: a reproach for having 'innovated' by means of a coup backed by foreign troops, and a warning that this extraordinary kind of change creates a flaw in their new building that 'another'—perhaps a foreign power—may later exploit, inserting his own building into the gap.[14]

---

[13] *Discursus*, 104–5.
[14] Foreshadowing the next chapter's argument that people should be wary of change and innovation in the hope of getting something better.

3

Empire

Of mixed principalities

Princes face their greatest difficulties, Machiavelli now tells us, in the new principality. He begins with a wide-ranging discussion of 'mixed' (*misti*) principalities: those where the prince is hereditary or of long-standing in his native state, but comes newly to power over other countries. His lessons are not reassuring for princes who hoped for an easy ride to great power.

Chapters 3, 4, and 5 form a series resembling an extended discourse within the book, in that the examples and arguments introduced in chapter 3 are examined further in chapters 4–5. Judgements that seem straightforward in this first chapter of the series are complicated in the next two. Machiavelli's text imitates reality in this respect. For the difficulties that follow from attempts to gain control over other countries do not all come at once, and those who initiate expansionist policies may not foresee their long-term consequences. Chapter 3 gives us glimpses into the future implications of policies discussed here, but withholds their full explosive force until chapter 5.

WHY NEW PRINCES FACE DIFFICULTIES

Machiavelli's first example of a mixed principality is that of France's hereditary King Louis XII adding the Italian state of Milan to his dominions. His second example of ancient Rome might seem surprising, since Rome was still a republic at the time he describes. But when considering Rome's attempts to add Greece, Spain, and other foreign territories to its empire, Machiavelli treats Rome as 'prince' in relation to these countries, noting that the Romans acted as 'all wise [*savi*] princes' do in trying to control various foreign powers.

The most salient characteristic of mixed principality, as Machiavelli observes, is its 'variation' (*variazione*)—a word he consistently associates with the random, destabilizing changes and effects of fortune. The cause of unstable *variazione* is a 'natural difficulty [*una naturale difficultà*] that exists in all new principalities', namely that 'men willingly [*volentieri*] change their lords in the belief that they will fare better'. This false belief 'makes them take up arms' to depose their old rulers, 'in which they are deceived because they see later by experience that they have done worse'.[1]

Why are new princes generally worse than old 'lords' (*signore*)? This, Machiavelli claims, 'follows from another ordinary and natural necessity [*necessità naturale e ordinaria*] which requires that one must always offend [*offendere*] those over whom he becomes a new prince'. All new princes face hostility from some people in the state they acquire. If they have to use force of arms to seize power, they presumably faced quite serious opposition at the outset. And as Machiavelli tells us later in the chapter, in the ordinary course of things new princes soon come to feel threatened even by those who helped them to power in the first place—and so begin to offend them as well. New princes therefore 'always' offend both opponents and one-time supporters 'both with men at arms and with infinite other injuries [*ingiurie*] that the new acquisition brings in its wake'.

Machiavelli says that these initial observations apply to *all* new princes, not just to cases where a prince adds foreign states or provinces to his dominions. They therefore apply to the Medici 'princes' who had returned to Florence with the help of men who 'took up arms' against their republican government in the hope of a better, more patrician or princely one. In Machiavelli's language, 'offences' are harms that may or may not have some objective justification. To send former leaders into exile offends them, but may be justified by the need to establish clear new orders. 'Injuries', however, are very serious, objective harms that cause further disorders if left uncorrected. In everyday language as in Machiavelli's, *ingiurie* was a near-synonym for injustice. And *all* new princes, Machiavelli says here, find it necessary to commit 'infinite' injuries as well as to offend. This comes close to saying that all new princes—including the *Prince*'s dedicatees—act unjustly, starting with the offensive and injurious act of using 'men at arms' to oust the previous government. Overall, chapters 3–5 make uncomfortable reading for any new prince who hopes to eliminate bad memories of his offensive beginnings as quickly as possible.

DOES NECESSITY EXCUSE INJURIES?

If there is an ordinary and natural 'necessity' that new princes offend, are their offences and injuries excused by that necessity? Not necessarily. For one thing,

---

[1] This echoes Polybius who, discussing a city in Italy that called in a foreign power, writes that pride engendered by prosperity and excessive freedom (*exousias*) naturally makes men tire of present conditions and seek a master (*despotês*); 'and having found one they soon hate him again, as the change is clearly for the worse.' *PolH* VIII.23.

people always have a choice in how they respond even to the most pressing necessity; no necessity is strong enough to eliminate all human agency. A few paragraphs on, for example, Machiavelli says that to avoid losing rebellious provinces 'it is necessary' for a prince either to go and live there himself, to send out colonies, or to hold them with direct military occupation. Although the necessity inflicted by such rebellions is extremely harsh, princes still have at least three options in how to respond—one of which, Machiavelli says, is far more useful than the others, because it causes less offence. A prince who has this choice of 'remedies' yet chooses the less effective ones, therefore, has no excuse for the injuries that flow from his bad choice.

The sources of Machiavelli's *necessità*, secondly, are not always beyond human agents' control. Some necessities arise from human or physical nature.[2] Others have a history, since they are produced by a series of choices and actions that culminate in a present, high-pressure situation where further choices are drastically limited. These kinds of *necessità* can't be avoided once they strike. But they can be avoided if people think ahead and avoid making choices that create crises over time. In many cases discussed in the *Prince*, necessity is *self-inflicted* by agents who fail to think carefully enough about the foreseeable consequences of their actions. In the present chapter, Machiavelli shows how the first offences committed in new principalities set off a cycle of reactions and counter-reactions that make a prince's offences, and hence his difficulties, worse over time. If a new prince faces the necessity to offend, then, before excusing anything he does we are still entitled to ask whether he chooses to offend in a way that was likely to establish stable new orders; and more importantly, how far his own choices brought the necessity down on him in the first place.

Thirdly, while the necessity to offend is a natural and ordinary consequence of becoming a new prince, the wish to be or to create a new prince is not itself natural, ordinary, or necessary. Many new princes and their supporters of course claim that one-man princely power is needed to deal with some critical necessity. Far from supporting this type of claim here, Machiavelli declares that it is based on a deception. In most cases, on the contrary, the people who first supported a new prince later find that they 'do worse' under him than before.

Machiavelli does not pass explicit moral judgement on the desire to become a new prince. He simply describes the inevitable pitfalls, in the tones of a cool strategist whose only concern is to help princes gain whatever they desire. If you choose to pursue a new principality, he tells them, here is what you have to look forward to. Instead of having a free hand to re-mould old orders as you wish, you will face infinite difficulties and be forced to do things you never

---

[2] See *D* I.1's discussion of sites for new cities.

contemplated at your first leap forward. These self-inflicted necessities will end up alienating your friends as well as hardening your enemies. 'You cannot keep as friends those who put you' in the principality 'because you cannot satisfy in the mode they had presupposed.' At the same time, 'you cannot use strong medicines [*medicine forti*] against them, since you are obligated [*obligato*] to them' for their initial support.

The very thought that a new prince might have to use 'strong medicines' against friends to whom he is obligated shows how far new princes are soon tempted to go against the ordinary bonds of friendship and obligation—usually seen as basic conditions for political stability. New princes start off with a deception, a false belief about the future benefits they can bring. They soon find themselves both powerless to satisfy their one-time supporters and unable to stifle their discontent, and end up unsure of whom they can rely on.

DIFFICULTIES FOR NEW PRINCES IN A FOREIGN COUNTRY

To illustrate these rather discouraging arguments, Machiavelli gives the example of Louis XII of France, who was still king at the time of writing. For the reasons just set out, Machiavelli says, Louis 'quickly occupied [*occupo subito*] Milan, and quickly lost it'. When this happened the first time, 'those people [*populi*] that had opened the gates to him, finding themselves deceived in their opinion and in that future good they had presupposed for themselves, were unable to support the vexations [*fastidi*] of the new prince'. If contemporaries were surprised that with his vast armies—the strongest in Europe—Louis could not hold a single Italian city, Machiavelli explains how this could happen: 'Even though one may be strongest in his armies', he points out, 'he always needs the favour of a province's inhabitants [*favore de' provinciali*] in order to enter it.'[3]

Here is one of the *Prince*'s first suggestions that feelings among the populace are an important factor—at least as important as military power—in successful 'acquiring'. A prince's force (*forze*) needs the complement of a population's *favore*, or the strongest armies will be unable to secure a foothold in a new province. No problem, it will transpire, is more pressing for princes than how to keep this initial favour, whether in a foreign province or a prince's native state.

---

[3] Machiavelli's *provinzia* is a more narrowly geographical term than *stato*. Provinces lack the integrated political order found in states, and often include several *stati*, as in ancient Greece or Machiavelli's Italy. He speaks of France both as a province and as a state defined by its political orders.

For now, Machiavelli takes pains not to speak of populations in a way that concedes too much independent agency to them. He speaks, somewhat awkwardly, of 'countries (*paesi*) that have rebelled' or of the favour of *provinciali*, thus assimilating peoples to territorial designations rather than highlighting their humanity. If this perspective could be sustained, it would certainly make life easier for princes. But now that he has mentioned rebellion, Machiavelli cannot avoid the word 'peoples' for much longer. In their first appearance since the Dedication, the *populi* are seen acting in a welcoming mode towards a prince rather than a hostile one, 'opening the gates' to King Louis—before finding that they cannot tolerate 'the vexations of the new prince'. This belated reaction, however, indicates that new princes' relations with peoples are likely to involve future confrontations.

There is another reason for Machiavelli's initial coyness about speaking of populations rather than territories. The words he later uses—people or peoples, subjects (*sudditi*), and citizens (*cittadini*)—indicate very different relationships between princes and populations. 'People' and 'peoples' for Machiavelli are always free agents, aware of their capacities to pursue their own collective purposes, even when they are at present under the power of a prince. Subjects are people who live under a prince, deprived of freedom. Citizens are people who share authority in a republic. Machiavelli's avoidance of all these terms in chapter 3 reflects the ambiguous status of populations who find themselves suddenly under a new prince, especially—but not only—in a 'mixed' principality. So long as the prince merely responds to their call to replace previous unloved lords, as Louis did for his Milanese supporters, those populations can still be called 'peoples'. Once he asserts control over them and they fall under his principality, they can be called his subjects. Throughout the *Prince*, Machiavelli will speak at different times of peoples, subjects, or citizens to reflect diverse or changing relationships between prince and populace.[4] His choice of terms serves dramatic as well as analytic purposes: it tells readers about the status of the relationship between prince and population at a given moment, but also dramatizes shifts toward more or less repressive princely rule that results from different policies.

Can a new prince hold on to new states or provinces when his relationship to their populations is so ill-defined? Not without growing difficulties. Having heard how easy it was for the Milanese to drive Louis out the first time, we now learn that he tried a second time to take Milan, and failed again despite overwhelming odds in his favour. To lose it a second time, Machiavelli declares, 'the whole world had to be against him, and his armies eliminated or chased from Italy'. But even without such universal opposition, Louis lost Milan again. Machiavelli will later say more about the bad political choices

---

[4] Imitating an ancient strategy used in texts that encourage tyrants to reform their tyranny into a more legitimate government; see chap. 21 on echoes of Xenophon's *Hiero* in the *Prince*.

that brought Louis' Milanese enterprise to this sorry end. Before new princes can advance to those lessons, however, they need to grasp the more elementary point pressed home in the first part of the chapter: namely, that even when people start by making a prince 'willingly', they seldom roll over and stay quiet once he is there. If they throw him out once and he tries again, he may find it easier to hold a second time, but only because the first rebellion gives him the 'opportunity' to 'secure himself by punishing offenders, exposing suspects, and providing for himself in the weakest spots'.

In other words, any prince determined to force himself on a population that has already rebelled against him must be willing to use increasingly harsh measures to 'secure himself'. The larger question, of course, is whether such measures can bring lasting security for the prince, or only lead him into greater difficulties.

So far, at any rate, Machiavelli's account of new princes—foreign or native—suggests that they all rely heavily on the 'modes' and conditions he associates with fortune. Whenever he says that gains are made 'quickly' (*subito*) or easily (*facilmente*), this is always code for unstable and easily lost, like trees that lack roots and can be blown away at the first strong gust. When a prince's support inside a state or province is positive and firm, he relies on more than fortune. When it is based only on dislike of the present ruler and the 'deception' that a new one must do better, these are 'inconstant and unstable things' that can turn against him at any moment.[5]

REMEDIES I: WHEN A PRINCE'S OLD STATE IS IN THE SAME PROVINCE AS A NEWLY ADDED ONE

Machiavelli now considers several remedies that Louis or anyone working within his 'limits' (*termini*) could have used to 'maintain himself better in his acquisition'. These remedies apply specifically to any rebellious state whose populace has shown that it rejects the new prince. Since their favour has been lost and the prince's earlier 'obligation' to them broken by their rebellion, he can now use 'strong medicine' against them.

His task is easiest, Machiavelli writes, if the states newly added to 'an ancient state of him who acquires them' are of the same province and language as the acquiring state. If they are, they 'may be held with great ease, especially if they are not used to living free [*vivere libere*]'. By observing just two other conditions, a new prince can secure his position. Firstly, he needs to eliminate the bloodline of the old prince. When this is done and there is no great disparity of customs (*disformità di costumi*) between the acquiring and acquired states,

---

[5] See chap. 7.

men will 'live quietly', as they are seen to do in 'Burgundy, Brittany, Gascony and Normandy, which have been with France for so long a time', despite certain disparities in language.[6] Thus, in a very short time, the newly acquired state 'becomes one whole body' (*tutto uno corpo*) with the old principality. If it is used to living free, however, this will be much harder even if its language and customs are similar to those of the acquiring state.[7]

Secondly, the new prince should not alter either the laws or the taxes of the 'men' in that state. Machiavelli mentions this condition almost as an after-thought, having earlier said twice that new princes must eliminate old blood-lines. While it might seem easy to implement, in fact, this condition places extensive limits on a prince or prince-state's powers. A prince who leaves peoples their laws and taxes must respect cherished local liberties, limit his or his officials' interference in local affairs, and leave intact the basic elements of self-government. Crucially, he must avoid levying special taxes on newly acquired territories, either to punish a rebellious population or to milk his new dominions for wealth that he can use closer to home. Since punitive or exploitative taxes were an extremely common means of dealing with unruly parts of a state's dominions, in ancient times and Machiavelli's, this condition is far more constraining than it might appear.

Far graver difficulties arise 'when one acquires states in a province disparate in language, customs, and orders', as when France's King Louis acquired Milan in Italy. Here 'one needs to have great fortune and great industry [*industria*] to hold them'. In this context, 'difficulties' is basically a euphemism for rebellions against a new prince's rule. Any prince who wants to establish rule over such states must be prepared to 'offend' many more people than in the first case. Consequently, each of the remedies Machiavelli outlines involves varying degrees of offence against locals. He sets out the options in clinical tones, from the perspective of a prince interested only in how he can assert firm top-down control. If the entire *Prince* considered politics only from this perspective and not also, at other times, from that of people, Machiavelli's reputation as purveyor of a cold-blooded science of princely control might seem richly deserved.

REMEDIES II: WHEN NEWLY ACQUIRED STATES ARE IN A DIFFERENT PROVINCE

One of the 'greatest and quickest remedies' for rebellions in a different province is that 'whoever acquires should go and live there in person'. This,

---

[6] In fact not very long for the first three, which came under the French crown in the second half of the previous century; Normandy had been part of that kingdom since 1204.

[7] As chap. 5 says about Pisa in relation to Florence.

Machiavelli tells readers, 'would make that possession more secure and lasting [*più sicura e più durabile*], as the Turk has done in Greece'.

These last words would probably have struck Italian readers in Machiavelli's time as shocking—or wickedly ironic. The Ottoman Turks had attacked and conquered the Greek Byzantine capital of Constantinople some 60 years earlier in 1453, making it the capital of their growing empire. By moving his capital to what had been the heart of Christian Greece, the Turkish Sultan Mohammed II asserted a direct, personal kind of control over his new 'acquisition'. These events caused great anxiety among Christian Europeans and particularly Italians, many of whom lived and had trade interests in conquered Greece. Contemporaries may have thought that by recommending the Turk's methods to other princes, Machiavelli was making light of what they saw as an ongoing threat to Italy and Christendom. Or they may have smelled pungent irony in the suggestion that if new Christian princes want to hold down foreign rebels, they might feel impelled to do exactly what they denounce as infidel despotism in others.[8]

Machiavelli's first remedy thus challenges readers to ask themselves how far they are prepared to go in order to hold on to rebellious foreign states. For as the Turk found in Greece, sometimes a foreign conqueror has no choice but to take drastic measures or lose his new 'acquisitions'. In the sultan's case, 'despite all the other orders observed by him so as to hold that state, if he had not gone there to live, it would not have been possible for him to hold it'. Machiavelli considers the effects of this policy only from the prince's stand-point: if 'you stay there', he says, switching to the direct address, 'disorders [*disordini*] may be seen as they arise, and you can remedy them'. You have better oversight over your officials, who then will be less inclined to 'despoil' (*spogliare*) the province. 'Subjects' (*sudditi*) will have the satisfaction of ready access to the prince, 'so that they have more cause to love him if they want to be good and, if they want to be otherwise, more cause to fear him.' Since outsiders (*esterni*) are more hesitant to attack if he lives there, he can lose his new state 'with the greatest difficulty'.

This would sound promising enough if, between the upbeat lines, Machiavelli didn't give princes a glimpse of the population's heavily repressed perspective. What he shows is not reassuring. Even if a prince goes to live in a rebellious country, he will not necessarily be able to establish stable orders there. On the contrary, Machiavelli takes it as given that he will be forced to deal with continuing 'disorders'. Whatever measures a new prince might take to hold down his new subjects, they will remain unquiet and cause recurring trouble. This first remedy helps princes repress them more effectively, but it

---

[8] See *FH* VI.32–3 on the Turkish capture of Constantinople. On an earlier Ottoman Turkish leader, see Machiavelli's glowing praise for Saladin's *virtú* in *FH* I.17, provocatively contrasted to incompetent Papal crusading; *ME* 144.

cannot put an end to rebellions or conspiracies, or enable the prince to live quietly in his adopted home.

Machiavelli implicitly questions the value of this first method when he goes on to offer a second, 'better' remedy for the difficulties arising from foreign conquests: to send colonies to 'one or two places' in the newly acquired province as 'fetters' (*compedes*) that help to hold the prince's state. The idea that the new state needs fetters to hold it hints at the coercive nature of the remedy, and therefore at high levels of resistance among the populace.

Colonies are the more moderately coercive alternative to a third remedy: outright military occupation. When a newly acquired state is rebellious, 'it is necessary', Machiavelli says, *either* to send colonies 'or to hold them with many men-at-arms and infantry'. While he calls direct military occupation one of two 'necessary' policies, Machiavelli also concludes that this third option is 'useless' (*inutile*). He spends as much time discussing the defects of military 'remedies' as he does the merits of colonial 'fetters'. It is far more expensive to hold a state 'with men at arms', since 'one has to consume all the income of that state in guarding it'. In this way 'the acquisition turns to loss', depriving the new prince of wealth he might have used for his benefit and giving locals endless causes for resistance. Their own resources are seized and used to pay for arms used to oppress them. And 'one offends much more because one harms [*nuoce*] the whole state as one's army moves around for lodgings'. Now Machiavelli speaks directly of feelings on the side of the populace: 'everyone feels this hardship and each becomes one's enemy: and these are enemies that can harm one since they remain, though defeated, in their homes. From every side, therefore,'—that of the prince or the conquered populace—'keeping guard in this way is as useless as keeping guard by means of colonies is useful.'

Colonies are the better solution because they are less costly and offend fewer people—'only those from whom one takes fields and houses in order to give them to the new inhabitants'. These offended and despoiled few 'can do no harm, since they are poor and dispersed'. The others 'should be quiet' because they are not offended; and if some remain unquiet, 'they are afraid to err from fear that what happened to the despoiled might happen to them'.

If Machiavelli is clear that this second remedy is far superior to the third, purely military alternative, however, its merits are comparative rather than absolute. Locals are quiet, but far from friendly to colonists. They keep quiet out of fear that their lands and houses might be seized and given away, which means that the new rulers have to control them by means of a standing threat of 'despoliation'—a term that does not lose its strongly negative sense in Machiavelli's deadpan analysis. This kind of 'holding' hardly sounds secure. It is all too easy to imagine a situation where more drastic military remedies would be called into play. If local populations are hostile to colonists, or unrest drives the prince to seize more fields and houses, military occupation will become 'necessary'. At the same time, it will be utterly useless. That is the irony of self-inflicted necessities. By insisting on courses of action that are bound to provoke natural and ordinary resistance, you end up forcing yourself into a corner where you have only unstable or useless 'remedies'.

Machiavelli is starting to speak more openly about how popular attitudes and reactions, or those of men generally, should influence princely decisions. Now he offers a general rule of thumb based on an account of how 'men' react to offences. They should, he declares:

> either be caressed or eliminated [*o vezzegiare o spegnere*], because they avenge themselves for light [*leggieri*] offences but cannot do so for heavy [*gravi*] ones. So the offence one does to a man should be such that one does not fear revenge [*vendetta*] for it.

This is the first of many similar complex, highly ambiguous statements in the *Prince*. Its key ambiguity lies in the idea that one should offend in such a way that 'one does not fear revenge for it'. This could mean: offend without scruple until you've eliminated all threats. Or it might mean: offend a few people selectively and moderately so that your actions create no new, serious threats of revenge.[9]

Given Machiavelli's remarks thus far, it seems unlikely that he sees these two responses to rebellion as equally useful. He has already warned princes about the endless difficulties that come from offending, and will tell them a few lines further on that highly offensive military solutions are 'useless'. These measures make it harder for rebels to avenge themselves, but don't stop them from doing so anyway. Instead of eliminating a prince's fear, they generate new causes for it. 'Caressing'—that is, less offensive responses—are safer for new princes than more offensive ones, because offences always elicit natural and ordinary resistance. The stark choice warns new princes about the extreme consequences they may be driven to—or drive themselves to—if they fail to choose their modes of offending with great care.

For now, Machiavelli leaves new princes a glimmer of hope that they can hold rebellious states without eliminating whole cities or putting them under permanent military occupation. The next two chapters will say more about princes whose conquering ambitions drive them to these extreme measures. Yet if a prince's policies have already deeply offended a rebellious populace, caressing may prove almost as useless a means of holding states as eliminating. The conquering prince's past choices will have driven him into a bind in which none of the remaining remedies can give him long-term security. If he responds to rebellions with light offences, the rebels will not be deterred from vengeance. If he responds heavily, they will keep avenging themselves

---

[9] Machiavelli draws here on his early, fragmentary piece, 'How to Deal with the People of the Valdechiana Who have Rebelled', where he imitates arguments attributed by Livy to Furius Camillus. Livy in turn imitated Thucydides' Diodotus in *TPW* III.36–47; see *ME* 88–97 on parallels with Machiavelli. Both Camillus and Diodotus seek to *dissuade* fellow citizens who favoured extreme military violence to adopt more measured means of dealing with rebels.

until his offences go all the way to eliminating them. Either way, a prince who insists on holding down rebellious foreign populations is in for a rough ride.

REMEDIES III: INTERNATIONAL STRATEGIES FOR HOLDING A FOREIGN STATE

Princes in a 'disparate' province need to adopt a further remedy, not as an alternative to the others but as their necessary consequence. For whoever does not conduct it well, Machiavelli declares, 'will soon lose what he has acquired, and while he holds it, will have infinite difficulties and vexations [*infinite difficultà e fastidi*] within it'. This supplementary remedy is to adopt an international strategy aimed at securing one's hold over particular states or cities in a province. The new prince should do three things to this end: firstly, 'make himself head and defender of the neighbouring lesser powers'; secondly, 'contrive to weaken the powerful [*potenti*] in that province'; and third, take care that no other foreigner (*forestiere*) as powerful as he is able to enter it.

Here we see the ever-expanding necessities of foreign conquest. If any prince thought his difficulties would be over once he eliminated rebellion in one new state, he needs to think again. Even if he manages to assert control over a particular state, as Louis XII tried and failed to do over Milan, he will need to secure it by gaining 'principality', or at least uncontested dominance, over the entire surrounding region.

Fortunately, it appears easy for a powerful foreigner to acquire such dominance, at least at the beginning. For 'it will always turn out that a foreigner will be brought in by those in the province who are malcontent [*malcontenti*], either because of too much ambition [*ambizione*] or out of fear'. Thus the Romans first entered Greece at the request of the Greek Aetolians, who were at war with other Greeks. And 'the order of things'—stemming from ordinary human nature—always leads less powerful states in a province to back a powerful foreigner, either to help them fight another local power or to defend them against other foreign states. It is easy to 'gain' some lesser powers to one's side; 'all together', Machiavelli writes, 'they quickly [*subito*] and willingly make one mass with his state'. Buoyed up by the favour of lesser powers disgruntled with the status quo, a foreign prince 'can easily [*facilmente*] put down those who are powerful' in a province, and make himself 'arbiter' (*arbitro*) of everything there.

This sounds like good news for new princes, as long as their concern is only how to acquire an initial foothold in a foreign province. At first Machiavelli plays down the less good news. The prince, he says, 'has only to think that these lesser powers may get too much force and too much authority [*autorità*]' at some later date. This 'only', however, conceals a cause for future, far from quick-or-easy wars against the lesser powers that first 'cause' you to get powerful in their province. The problem surfaces at the end of the chapter, where Machiavelli says that those who cause a new prince to become powerful are always 'suspect' to him. In time he will seek their 'ruin' so that he can dominate their province unchallenged. But if these once-helpful lesser powers become victims of their own short-sighted policy, the new prince's suspicions also spell the end of his quick and easy enterprises in a foreign province. It will be infinitely more arduous to hold it over time.

Machiavelli's coded language drops other clear warning signs. Such 'quick' and 'easy' gains are mere gifts of fortune, and thus insecure. The *favore* of lesser local powers is conditional, and not due to firm obligations or positive feelings about the foreigner. Moreover, this latest description of the pains of conquest sounds ominously similar to Machiavelli's earlier account of how 'all' new principalities must come to difficulties, only now on the larger scale of provinces rather than states. First some discontented people in a state or province 'willingly' open the gates to a new prince; then they realize their mistake; then they try to eject him, producing the familiar cycle of rebellions, new princely offences, and ever-escalating difficulties.

ROMAN FORESIGHT: THE PRINCE-STATE'S PERSPECTIVE

When they began to acquire foreign provinces, the Romans experienced exactly the same pattern of escalating difficulties as Louis XII did in Italy. But Louis lost his hold on his new acquisitions, while the Romans clung on to theirs. They managed this, Machiavelli tells us, by observing 'well' the policies just outlined. In Greece they first 'sent out colonies'; then, so that they could hold them securely, they pursued a policy of regional domination according to the rules just set out. At first they indulged (*intrattenuti*)[10] two 'lesser' Greek powers, the Achaeans and Aetolians, by making alliances to defend them against the stronger, maverick Greek power of Macedonia on the one hand and the Syrian king Antiochus on the other. After a time they brought down the kingdom of Macedonia, in accordance with the rule that larger powers in a province should be kept weak. Then they drove out the powerful foreigner Antiochus, in accordance with the rule that no foreign power in a province should be allowed to grow stronger than you.

---

[10] An ambiguous, fortune-related word used to describe the 'modes' of Philip V of Macedon in chap. 24.

The Romans were uncompromising in pursuit of these policies. Showing no regard for the merits (*meriti*) of the Achaeans and Aetolians, who wanted to increase their power in their own province, the Romans did not 'permit' them to do so. They ignored Macedonian appeals for friendship with Rome, and would not consent to let the foreigner Antiochus hold any state in Greece. In a few words, Machiavelli paints a picture of a ruthless power bent on gaining total control over a foreign province. This description is followed by more general comments on the Romans' foresight and wisdom in pursuing these policies. The Romans, Machiavelli observes:

> did in these cases what all wise [*savi*] princes should do: they not only have to have regard for all present troubles [*scandoli*] but also for future ones, and they have to avoid these with all their industry because, when one foresees from afar, one can easily find a remedy for them but when you wait until they come close to you, the medicine [*medicina*] is not in time because the disease [*malattia*] has become incurable.

In this context, the 'disease' that needs checking seems to be the threat posed by other regional powers to Roman's desire for complete domination. If these threats are not stifled early on, the prince-state will find it impossible to hold down rebellions in colonies and states it has already acquired—and then its whole empire will unravel. When it first started adding new states to its dominions, the prince-state—Rome or any other that might emulate it—had to avoid using 'strong medicines' against friends inside the new state. Now it has had to go much further than envisioned at the outset. First the prince-state used various strong 'remedies' to hold the initial, rebellious acquisition; now it uses even stronger medicine as extra insurance against losing the first conquests.

Machiavelli does not say whether the Romans foresaw the need for all these additional measures when they first started 'acquiring' states outside Italy. But by the time they reached the advanced stage we are discussing now, they did foresee future threats to their rising power in Greece, and sought 'with all their industry' to avoid them. Their foresight and industry were shown above all in wars they fought against potential rivals. Machiavelli's careful wording makes it clear that these wars were in no way forced on the Romans by others. They were offensive, not justified by any urgent need for Roman self-defence. Thus the Romans 'chose [*vollono*] to make war with Philip and Antiochus in Greece in order not to have to do so in Italy; and they could have avoided both one and the other for a long time but they did not want to [*non vollono*]'. These Roman wars of expansion, that is, were not 'necessary' in any generally accepted sense.

Writing here from the Romans' perspective, however, Machiavelli points to a non-urgent kind of necessity—if it can reasonably be called necessity—that might seem to excuse their otherwise unnecessary wars. The Romans 'knew that war may not be taken away but is postponed to the advantage of others'. While they could have avoided war for a long time, their exceptional foresight made them look far ahead of that time to the future when war must come. 'Seeing inconveniences [*inconvenienti*] from afar,' the Romans 'never allowed them to ensue so as to avoid a war.' The 'inconveniences' that they stamped out far in advance were any increases in a Greek or foreign power's ability to challenge Roman pre-eminence in Greece. For the far-seeing Romans at this stage in their expansion, even remote possibilities of future rivalries were sufficient justification for an offensive war. Nor, Machiavelli adds:

> did that saying ever please them which is every day in the mouths of the wise men of our times—to enjoy the benefit of time [*godere il benefizio del tempo*]—but rather, they enjoyed the benefit of their *virtú* and prudence. For time chases [*si caccia*] everything before it and can bring with it good as well as evil [*male*] and evil as well as good.

Does this Roman conduct epitomize *virtú* at its best? It would seem so, if we focus on the immediate context where these good words appear and don't look too closely at the actions they describe. On this narrow view, the most virtuous princes first acquire new states in foreign provinces, and when these rebel, seek to dominate the entire province by launching offensive wars. They do this not to meet urgent necessities or avoid serious troubles or difficulties, but to stamp out 'inconveniences' long before they become threatening. They do not wait for time to bring difficulties closer, but chase them down far in advance with their armies, thus getting far ahead of whatever good or bad things might come with time.

If these modes of action are the pinnacle of *virtú* for Machiavelli, his standards are stunningly different from the ideas of virtue or Roman *virtus* found in almost all ancient and humanist writings. True, the Latin word *virtus* originally stressed military valour and discipline. But those who praised these qualities did not say that they should be used to fight unnecessary wars of conquest, or that the ability to dominate others by force of arms is evidence of *virtus*. The Roman historian Livy, one of Machiavelli's main sources and favourite authors, reserves his highest praise for Roman leaders like the general Fabius Maximus who refrained from offensive wars as long as possible; he is highly critical of Fabius' more aggressive younger colleague Scipio. In the *Discourses* Machiavelli seconds these judgements.[11]

Later in the *Prince*, moreover, he offers a definition of prudence that stands in stark contrast to the one just outlined. No state, he declares, should

> believe that it can always adopt safe courses [*partiti sicuri*]; on the contrary, it should take them all as doubtful. For in the order of things [*nell'ordine delle cose*] it is found that one never seeks to avoid [*fuggire*] one inconvenience without incurring another; but prudence consists in knowing how to recognize the qualities of inconveniences, and in picking the less bad as good.[12]

---

[11] See chap. 17; *LH* XXVIII.17–21, 40–5; XXIX.14–27; *ME* 469–72.   [12] Chap. 21.

This seems to contradict the present chapter's account of Roman prudence as the ability to foresee *and* avoid inconveniences. The Romans launched offensive wars so that no future inconveniences could ensue for them, preferring even arduous wars to combat remote challenges to their power in foreign provinces. But in the passage just cited, Machiavelli tells us that inconveniences *cannot* be avoided. If prudence consists in knowing how to pick the less bad course, the prudent must also know that it is impossible—not in the natural 'order of things'—for any state to eliminate every present or future inconvenience. But this is what, in chapter 3, he says the Romans tried to do.

ROMAN FORESIGHT: THE WIDER PERSPECTIVE

The high costs of this extraordinary Roman foresight emerge only in the next two chapters, where the spiralling consequences of Rome's policies come further to light. If we glance ahead, we will learn that the Romans were still busily beating down inconveniences—and much worse—even after their offensive wars brought them to clear supremacy over Greece and other 'disparate' provinces. Machiavelli withholds this knowledge of the future in chapter 3. Here we remain with the perspective of a prince or prince-state whose foresight extends to the next obstacles to his ambitions—but not to the wider consequences of actions he takes to overcome them.

These consequences were well known to those of Machiavelli's contemporaries who had read the most famous Roman historians and philosophers: Sallust, Livy, Cicero, and Tacitus. Machiavelli's remarks on Rome in the *Prince* assume that his readers knew far more about the history of Roman conquests than he tells them. Most of the book's Roman examples relate to a critical period of history: the 50-odd years when Rome went from being a mainly Italian empire to assert control over numerous provinces outside Italy.[13] Although internally this conquering Rome still had its ancient republican 'orders', from the standpoint of its external relations it acted like a 'mixed principality': it sought supreme or princely power over foreign provinces while maintaining government based on shared power at home. With two exceptions, the *Prince*'s few Roman examples from other periods concern the 'princely' eras of Rome's internal government, before it became a republic and then after the republic was destroyed.[14]

---

[13] Culminating with the conquest of Greece and Carthage in 146 BC.

[14] The exceptions are chap. 12's reference to republican Rome's good military orders and chap. 17's reference to Scipio's 'corrupting' those orders. Romulus, mentioned in chap. 6, was one of Rome's legendary founders who founded the city as a monarchy, not a republic. By contrast, Machiavelli's *Discourses* spend more time discussing the early, more virtuous republic.

Its destruction, as Machiavelli recounts in the *Discourses*, was directly related to its modes of imperial expansion. He argues there that 'acquiring' became 'pernicious' to Rome during and after the wars with Greece and Carthage.[15] The republic's appetite for constant military expansion greatly increased the power of generals, who would later use their armies to seize power 'extraordinarily' from civilian authorities. The mass popularity of empire helped create a fashion for populist soldier-leaders—starting with Scipio Africanus, 'corrupter of the Roman military', as he is called in the *Prince*, and culminating with Julius Caesar, who dealt the final death-blow to the republic in order to make himself sole ruler. Rome's imperial overreaching thus destroyed the republic's cherished liberty. Indeed it 'eliminated all republics and all civil ways of life' up to Machiavelli's own times, so that the 'free way of life' enjoyed in Italy in earlier days was replaced by 'a servile way of life now'. Its foreign conquests also increased Romans' insecurity. The costs of maintaining a vast empire, much of it under direct military occupation, were exorbitant. And since the Romans could not trust the passive or restive 'subjects' they had created by their conquests, they were forced to rely for their defence on remote border peoples instead of on 'their own'—a 'mode' that Machiavelli says went 'against every good order'.[16]

The *Prince* tells a similar story through brief references scattered through the book. In Greece, the Romans were called in by the Aetolians to support them in regional wars. Then Rome began to assert greater control over its former protégés, and began to dictate who could and could not have power in Greece (chapter 3). These policies led to war in 146 BC after the Achaean League—a confederation of Greek states that sought to forge Hellenic unity against Rome and other foreign powers—broke into open revolt against Roman domination.[17] The Romans defeated the Achaeans in the Battle of Corinth, razed that city and dissolved the League. In the same year, they stormed and razed Carthage and conquered Spain (chapter 5). These were Rome's first full-scale conquests of non-Italian countries. Greece and the other provinces soon fell under direct Roman control, though their inhabitants frequently rebelled (chapter 4). The conquests represented a sharp departure from Rome's previous external policies, since they could no longer claim to be conquering countries outside Italy in self-defence.

Soon after Rome imposed its 'principality' over these foreign provinces, the city began to lose control over its own government. More and more, it departed from the ancient 'orders' that had preserved its republic for nearly four centuries. The provinces taken by the empire became a source of bitter rivalry

[15] Compare Sallust, *SWC* 10: after the conquest of Carthage 'fortune turned unkind and confounded all [Rome's] enterprises', leading them to 'put on the semblance of virtues that they lacked . . . When the disease had spread like a plague, Rome changed: her government, once just and admirable, became cruel and unendurable.'

[16] *D* I.18, III.24, II.2, II.30; *ME* chap. 12.

[17] Led by Philopoemen, the protagonist of chap. 14.

among leading Romans, who fought among themselves for control of the vast power they represented (chapter 4). These quarrels culminated in Caesar's audacious *coup d'état*, after which Rome became in effect a 'principality' in Machiavelli's sense: a form of government where one man, the emperor, held supreme political power. Caesar was able to topple the republic because of his vaunted 'liberality' and unprecedented conquests, which won him popular and military support against those who tried to stop him (chapter 16). Later Roman 'princes' also had to court either popular or military support. But the necessities of controlling a vast empire gave the soldiers so much power that any emperor who lacked their support soon came to grief. In a short space of time, Rome was transformed from a republic whose military leaders and soldiers were under strict civilian discipline into a *principato* whose military effectively controlled what was left of civil life (chapter 19).

When Machiavelli first mentions the Romans in the *Prince*, then, he is not showing us the earlier Romans whose great *virtù* he often praises in the *Discourses*.[18] Those Romans founded and maintained a stable, well-ordered republic. These later Romans were setting out on a course of action that would soon wreck their ancient orders. It would make Rome 'greater' than ever, in terms of size and might, but also far less secure. Readers who read ahead in the *Prince*, or who have learned about these consequences of Rome's conquests from Livy or other writers, may detect a certain irony in Machiavelli's apparent praise for Roman foresight in these matters. The Romans who began to acquire foreign provinces had too much foresight—and too little. They anticipated the remotest inconveniences posed by others, yet failed to foresee the far more serious 'difficulties and vexations' they might inflict on themselves. And in working so hard to control other states, they ended up losing control over their own. As the passage about the need to pick one's inconveniences suggests, Machiavelli often speaks of prudence—and more generally of *virtù*—as resting on knowledge of natural and ordinary human limits. To foresee inconveniences without recognizing that one can't eliminate or control them is hardly the height of prudence. It shows a naïve or arrogant belief that some 'extraordinary' human beings or states can avoid ordinary inconveniences by eliminating them far in advance.

If conquering Romans thought they could get ahead of time in this way and avoid its good and bad effects altogether, they were mistaken. The idea that their mode of expansion involved a competitive race or 'chase' (*caccia*) against time hints at the unrealistic pressures they placed on themselves. Prudence

---

[18] Though here, too, his praise is always discriminating. He shows that even in its best days, over-ambitious leaders—often cheered on by the Roman people—drove the republic beyond the limits of what was necessary for its freedom and safety. These extraordinary transgressions, Machiavelli (and Livy) suggest, would have destroyed Rome much sooner had a few virtuous individuals—notably Camillus and Fabius Maximus—not laboured to pull it back to due 'limits' (*termini*). See esp. *D* II.27–8.

and *virtú* are not qualities that can oppose time and outstrip it in the chase. They are qualities shown in human actions that always, inescapably, take place within the bounds of time. Men and states can step out of manmade orders, including the ordinary requirement that they launch wars only when they can cite some necessary cause. But they cannot step out of the natural order of things, of which time is a basic element. The best they can do is to work within the pressures of time to gain as much benefit as possible and avoid harm. The Romans, for a time, seemed to conquer time itself—until the results of their conquests sped ahead of them.

If we return to the medical metaphor discussed earlier, it now seems less clear what disease Machiavelli thinks needs to be cured before it worsens 'in the progress of time'. As the Romans saw it, the 'disease' was any threat to their quest for control over foreign provinces. From the wider perspective that unfolds over the next two chapters, however—particularly the popular perspective revealed in chapter 5—the disease that posed the greatest threat to Romans was their own limitless appetite for empire. The disease was in the prince, not the subjects.[19] As they read on, readers must decide which perspective has the deeper diagnosis:

> And it happens with this as the physicians say of consumption [*etico*], that in the beginning of the illness it is easy to cure and difficult to recognize, but in the progress of time, when it has not been recognized and treated in the beginning, it becomes easy to recognize and difficult to cure. So it happens in affairs of state, because when one recognizes from afar the evils [*mali*] that arise in a state (which is not given but to one who is prudent) they are soon healed; but when they are left to grow because they are not recognized, to the point that everyone recognizes them, there is no longer any remedy for them.

The word translated as 'consumption', *etico*, also means 'ethical'. Whether Machiavelli intended a pun or not, the etymological roots of the word *etico* as a disease or effects of a disease—*hecticus* in Latin, from the Greek *hektikós*—evoke restless, feverish motion and unquiet.[20] In a later use of the same metaphor, Machiavelli traces the sickness in modern states to the imprudent indulgence of present appetites. 'Lack of prudence in men', he remarks in chapter 13, 'begins something which, because it tastes good then, they do not perceive the poison that lies underneath, as I said above of consumptive fevers [*febre etiche*].' Perhaps the 'hectics' in chapter 3 are the foreign peoples who

---

[19] Thucydides, Plato, Sallust, Lucretius, and other ancients used medical metaphors for grave political disorders, especially those arising from imperial greed. Thucydides' famous account of the plague in Athens—a disease at once medical and ethical—describes symptoms that went unrecognized until it was too late to cure the disease, noting that at the height of their illness the sick appeared at a peak of health; *TPW* II.47–54. Sallust echoes Thucydides in *SWC* 10.

[20] The more usual words for consumption were *tisi* or *tisico*, from the Latin *phthisis*. Dante uses *etico* in *Inferno* XXX.56 in a medical and moral sense when speaking of people tormented by their own feverish greed.

challenge Rome's principality over them; perhaps they are the voracious Romans. It depends whether one adopts the perspective of acquisition-hungry princes or of peoples who seek not to be devoured.

MODERN ERRORS: THE PERSPECTIVE OF PRINCES

In the end, the quality of an agent's prudence and *virtù* has to be judged by the reasonableness of his aims as well as by his success in pursuing whatever aims he has, whether reasonable or not. Indirectly, the whole chapter poses the question: is the aim of holding principality over foreign provinces ordinary and reasonable, or bound to go against good orders? Machiavelli refrains from asking this question in so many words. In fact, he seems so determined to avoid judging princely ends that he proceeds to explain how a foreign king, Louis XII, should have gone about trying to dominate Italy. Machiavelli did not, of course, regard this aim with cool detachment, or want any foreign power to do to his native province what the Romans did to Greece. Nevertheless, he tells readers exactly how they might do this.

Whether or not the Romans' aim of controlling foreign provinces was reasonable, they were undoubtedly very good at pursuing it—unlike Louis, who 'did the contrary of the things that should be done to hold a state in a disparate province'. As the Romans were brought to Greece by the Greek Aetolians, Louis was brought into Italy 'by the ambition of the Venetians', who wanted him to help them gain half the state of Lombardy. 'I do not want to blame the course adopted by the king,' Machiavelli comments dispassionately, 'for since he wanted [*vollono*] to begin by putting a foot into Italy' and had no friends in 'this province', 'he was necessitated [*necessitato*] to take whatever friendships he could get.' Clearly, his desire to enter Italy imposed this necessity; Machiavelli does not say there was any objective necessity for Louis to enter Italy in the first place. Yet he refrains from stating his approval or disapproval of this necessity-inflicting choice. The only hints that Machiavelli might have any personal interest in the matter are his references to Louis coming to 'this province' and dealing with the powers that were great 'among us'.

Thus Louis entered Italy and 'quickly' (*subito*) gained vast numbers of 'friends' among Italian states that needed French arms either to protect them from or help them attack other Italians. This 'necessity' on the Italians' part was, in Machiavelli's view, entirely self-inflicted and avoidable. It arose because Italian states lacked good military orders of their own, so had to rely on other powers' fortune and arms. The *Prince* will later show them how to correct this fatal weakness. In the meantime, Machiavelli claims, Louis could easily have taken advantage of the Italians' desperate need for a foreign protector and asserted French dominance over the province, as the Romans did over Greece. Unfortunately for him—though not for Italians—he made numerous 'errors' in his Italian policy.

His main mistake was to violate Machiavelli's rule not to let any other external power become 'great' in a province you seek to control. Instead, the maladroit king helped Pope Alexander VI gain Romagna in Italy for his son Cesare Borgia. Then Louis agreed to divide Naples with the king of Spain, thus giving another power a firm Italian foothold. As for Italy's 'lesser powers', instead of indulging the king of Naples by making him France's willing servant, Louis expelled him—creating a cause for inconvenient war with other Italians and foreign powers. On top of all this, he made the serious error of 'putting down' the Venetians who had first let him into Italy. It would have been 'reasonable and necessary' to do this, Machiavelli remarks, if Louis had done everything else right; the Romans, after all, had moved to 'put down' their old Greek friends after expelling rival powers from the province. But since Louis had not expelled his rivals but had, on the contrary, weakened his hand by increasing the Church's power and letting Spain into Italy, he needed Venice to help keep them away from his acquisitions in Lombardy. Instead he recklessly destroyed his one potential supporter.

'Thus,' Machiavelli concludes, 'King Louis lost Lombardy for not having observed any of the limits [*termini*] observed by others who have taken provinces and wished to hold them. Nor,' he adds, 'is this any miracle, but very ordinary and reasonable [*molto ordinario e ragionevole*].' Perhaps this is a teasing reproach to Italians who saw France's ignominious departure as an act of God rather than the result of Louis' own quite human errors. Making a rare personal appearance, Machiavelli now reports that 'I spoke of this matter at Nantes with [Cardinal] Rouen' when he was serving as one of Florence's foreign emissaries at the travelling French court. When the cardinal 'said to me that Italians do not understand war, I replied to him that the French do not understand the state [*dello stato*], because if they understood they would not have let the Church come to such greatness'. The thought here seems to be that to maintain a secure external environment for any *stato*, principality, or republic, the capacity to fight wars with big armies is not enough. You also need to be good at politics, which involves knowing how to secure your foreign friends and weaken dangerous rivals.

In declaring that 'it is a truly natural and ordinary thing to desire to acquire', and that when 'men do it who can, they will be praised or not blamed', Machiavelli seems to blame Louis for not doing all he could have done to acquire Italy. But the statement that some conduct 'is' or 'will be' praised or blamed doesn't necessarily mean that it *should* be. It may mean rather that 'men' commonly make judgements in this way, though they are often wrong. Men tend to judge by asking whether someone succeeded in getting what he wanted, but do not ask whether what he wanted was good or bad for him or for others.[21] This is a fact about human nature, not an endorsement of this way of judging. When judged by the criterion of his own ambitions, Louis failed where the Romans succeeded. When judged by the quality of his aims, perhaps both 'princes' can be blamed for overstepping good orders and their own powers, since for the Romans, too, acquiring turned out to be 'pernicious'—even 'in the times when they proceeded with so much prudence and so much *virtù*'.[22]

MODERN ERRORS: THE PERSPECTIVE OF SUBJECTS

Machiavelli's personal reminiscence of his conversation with Cardinal Rouen reminds readers that from its creation in 1494 to its demise in 1512, Florence's republic had depended heavily on French military and diplomatic support. As Secretary to the republic, Machiavelli had been involved in various negotiations to secure this aid. In the republic's last years, he tried hard—and ultimately failed—to get French backing against Pope Julius II's threats to forcibly expel the republic's leading magistrate and Machiavelli's close ally, Piero Soderini, and restore the Medici to their pre-1494 eminence.

This background raises the question of what Machiavelli hoped for from Louis. It seems safe to assume that he did not want France to impose a Roman-style empire over Italy, first protecting a few 'lesser' states in the province and then using its overwhelming military force to deprive them of their independence. Machiavelli's long-term hope, as later chapters make clear, was that Italians would take his advice and build up their own military defences so that they could break their dependence on any foreign power. A key part of these defences was political: if Italians wanted to keep foreign troops off their soil, they would have to reorganize their *stato*, as well as to buy weapons and train armies. And to strengthen any single Italian state, others would have to be strengthened as well, and induced to form defensive alliances among themselves instead of allowing foreigners to take advantage of their divisions.

In the meantime, Italians had to deal with the foreign powers that had already made inroads into their province: France, Spain, the German Empire, and the Swiss. In so far as Florence had to rely on any of these powers in the past or near future, Machiavelli consistently preferred the French.[23] Some of his belated 'advice' to Louis in chapter 3 seems to suggest that if French kings could avoid his mistakes in future, they might play a valued role as a sort of 'hegemon' or leading foreign power in Italy—acting as arbiter of intra-Italian

---

[21] Compare chap. 25. [22] *D* II.19. [23] See chap. 21.

conflicts while using their military power and political skills to keep out other foreign interlopers.

From the perspective of Italians, however, the problem with this scenario is that France or any other foreign power that gained this kind of dominance might play benign protector one day, and then move toward Roman-style conquest the next. Italians or other peoples who put their security in the hands of any foreign power thus show extreme imprudence, and become helplessly dependent on the sheer luck of having a more or less competent and friendly defender. While seeming only to criticize Louis and other princes who fail to acquire when they can, Machiavelli's analysis of the king's errors is implicitly just as critical of Italians and other peoples who 'willingly' let foreign princes into their provinces. If acquiring could have been easy for Louis, this was because Italians rushed 'to become his friend' and eagerly 'jumped into his lap' (*gittati in grembo*). If their weakness put them 'under a necessity to stay with him', this weakness and necessity were of their own making, inflicted by their lacking arms of their own. Successful conquest, as the next chapter will make even clearer, doesn't just depend on the prudence or *virtú* of the conquerors; clearly Louis was deficient in both. At the crucial first step, it depends on lack of *virtú* in the conquered.

In its first steps toward foreign empire, Rome too relied more on the fortune of finding Greece weak and divided among several warring powers than on its own industry or prudence. Throughout the *Prince*, Machiavelli draws parallels between contemporary Italians and the weak and divided Greeks who first hailed the Romans as defenders and allies, then fought to drive them out, and finally fell for centuries under their yoke. Greeks then and Italians now 'willingly changed their lords' in the false belief that the new ones would make their lives better. But the chapter's closing sentence states 'a general rule that never or rarely fails: whoever is the cause of someone's becoming powerful is ruined'. While teaching princes how to conquer provinces, Machiavelli also warns *provinciali* against letting in powerful princes.

4

Absolute government

Why the kingdom of Darius that Alexander seized did not rebel from his successors after Alexander's death

Machiavelli now considers an example that seems to challenge the last chapter's argument that it is very difficult to hold 'newly acquired' states. Alexander the Great 'became lord of Asia in a few years' then died soon afterward. It 'appeared reasonable' that the 'state' of Asia, as Machiavelli calls it, would rebel soon after his death, since Alexander was a foreigner with different customs and language and had no time to put roots down in the new province. Nevertheless, his successors managed to hold his eastern conquests. Some might marvel (*maravigliarsi*) at this, imagining that they did so because of some outstanding *virtù* in Alexander or his successors. Machiavelli's analysis sets out more likely causes. Many empires endure, he tells them, not because their conquerors *possess* some marvellous quality, but because the conquered *lack* essential qualities that should 'reasonably' (*ragionevole*) lead them to rebel.

TWO MODES OF PRINCELY GOVERNMENT: DEPENDENT OFFICIALS OR INDEPENDENT LORDS

Two diverse modes of governing, Machiavelli argues, can be found among principalities 'of which memory remains'. In the first, one man has uncontested supremacy over all the other men who help him run a highly centralized system of government. These others are the prince's servants (*servi*); they help him govern 'by his grace and concession' (*per grazia e concessione sua*) as ministers and officials, but have no independent power-base that can challenge that of the prince. In 'our times' the Turkish sultan best exemplifies this form of principality. Dividing his realm into administrative units called 'sanjaks', the sultan appoints administrators to them and 'changes and varies them' as he pleases.

Princes who govern in the second mode also use other men to help them, but these men are barons (*baroni*) whose rank and power are far greater than those of the sultan's officials. They come to help the prince 'not by the grace of the lord [*signore*] but by antiquity of blood', and 'have their own states and subjects who recognize [*riconoscono*] them as lords and hold them in natural affection [*naturale affezione*]'. The prince cannot remove the barons' local privileges 'without danger to himself'. In Machiavelli's times, this decentralized type of principality was found in the kingdom of France. The king there 'is placed in the midst of a multitude of lords, recognized in their state as by their subjects and loved [*amati*] by them'. In contrast to 'the Turk', the French king's powers are limited by his barons' ancient titles and local constituencies, which can easily be rallied to challenge the king.

The distinction between more and less centralized and personalized principalities explains why Asia did not rebel after Alexander's death. Before the celebrated Macedonian defeated Persia's King Darius and annexed his empire, that empire had long been governed in the first, centralized mode. Such monarchies, Machiavelli maintains, are difficult to occupy. There are no rival lords there who can call in a foreign prince as the Aetolians called the Romans into Greece, or the Venetians called the French into Italy. And an aspiring conqueror cannot exploit local rebellions to his own advantage, for the prince's officials are 'slaves and obligated' (*stiavi e obligati*) to him, and thus too dependent to be bought off or 'corrupted' (*corrompere*) by the newcomer. But once such a principality is 'routed in the field' and conquered (*vinto*), the victor has 'great ease in holding it'. If he eliminates the bloodline of the former prince, 'there remains no one whom one would have to fear', since his ministers were wholly dependent on him and have no 'credit with the people' (*credito con e' populi*).

The answer to the chapter title's question, then, is that the mode of government in Darius' conquered state, not exceptional political skills in Alexander or his successors, allowed them to hold the empire they took from him. Once they defeated the Persian militarily, they faced no serious political resistance, either from local leaders or from the populace. All were 'slaves' whose political loyalties focused entirely on one monarch, the supreme power in the state. When he was dead, there was no one left to rebel against the foreigner, and no common cause to motivate rebellion. Used to obeying one man and depending on his 'grace' for everything, Darius' subjects presumably found it easy to switch their dependence from him to the new Macedonian prince and his successors—who in turn found it easy to rule their new subjects. No one who considers these things, Machiavelli concludes, should 'marvel at the ease with which Alexander held the state of Asia' and the difficulties of others who failed to conserve (*conservare*) their acquisitions. The difference between them comes 'not from much or little *virtú* in the victor but from the disparity in the subject [*da la disformità del subietto*]';[1] that is, from the

---

[1] Both *subietti* and *sudditi* can mean 'subjects' of a prince; here and in several other references to differences in '*subietto*' (e.g. in chap. 9), Machiavelli puns on the two meanings of 'subject'.

different qualities of various conquered states. Alexander's successors would almost certainly have lost conquests made in the second type of state, those resembling modern France.

Here the ease and difficulty are reversed. A new prince can easily enter and occupy such kingdoms by winning over some baron who 'can open the way for you' and 'facilitate victory for you', for 'malcontents and those who desire to innovate are always to be found' in decentralized states. But victory (*vittoria*) achieved by means of arms is never the end of the story for Machiavelli, since military victories need to be secured by political measures. Like Louis XII in Italy or the Romans in Greece, a prince may easily acquire such states by exploiting internal tensions, then find that 'your wish to maintain that victory for yourself brings in its wake infinite difficulties, both from those who have helped you and from those you have oppressed [*oppressi*]'. It is much harder to eliminate opposition, since many 'lords' remain even after they get rid of the old prince's bloodline, and 'put themselves at the head of new changes'. And 'since you can neither content them nor eliminate them, you lose that state whenever their opportunity [*occasione*] comes'.

TWO MODES OF ACQUIRING AND HOLDING EMPIRE

Does this mean that princes should prefer to emulate Alexander's imperial conquests rather than Rome's? At first glance, it might seem obvious that they should. While Alexander's successors eliminated Darius' ministers then ruled with 'great ease' over non-rebellious subjects, Rome had a much harder time trying to hold down independent lords and rebellious populations.

On the other hand, in devoting so much prolonged effort to subduing their conquests, the Romans seem to have relied on far more praiseworthy qualities, including the industry and foresight associated with *virtù*. By contrasting Alexander's modes of acquiring and holding empire with Rome's, Machiavelli invites readers to consider how far, and in what respects, each mode depended on *virtù* or fortune.

His analysis implies that very different qualities called *virtù* may be used to acquire and hold new states. Some of these qualities are prized because they bring military success, and thus help princes to acquire provinces even when no insiders help them. Other qualities are more political than military, and are valued because they help princes maintain what they acquire. Alexander's eastern conquests demonstrate that he had the first kind of *virtù*, but not necessarily the second. With his great military talents he was able to 'make an all-out attack' on Darius and 'drive him from the field'. But he needed no outstanding political skills to hold Darius' former state. He died soon after taking it, and his successors merely took advantage of a weakness in its internal organization, which depended so entirely on one man that it crumbled as soon as he was removed.

In terms of Machiavelli's antithesis between fortune and *virtú*, then, Alexander's successors held their empire by the good fortune of finding little political *virtú* in their subjects, not by any *virtú* of their own. That they lacked *virtú* is apparent from the squabbles that erupted among them after their leader's death. Machiavelli remarks on these disorders in typically deadpan tones, letting the deeds damn themselves without further comment. If Alexander's successors 'had been united [*uniti*]' he writes, 'they could have enjoyed' his expanded state 'at their leisure; nor did any tumults occur in that kingdom besides those they themselves incited'.

This might seem to suggest that so long as new conquerors avoid disastrous quarrels over succession, they should wish to gain an empire like Alexander's where they face no serious resistance from the locals and can enjoy their new state at leisure. But the phrase translated here as 'to enjoy at one's leisure' (*godere oziosi*) oozes negative connotations, implying that any prince who would want to rule in that way is sorely deficient in political *virtú*. *Oziosi*, 'in a leisurely manner', is associated with idleness, luxury, and dependence on fortune; the antonym of its noun *ozio* is *industria*. By choosing this loaded word, Machiavelli evokes a well-known theme of ancient writers: one that treats idleness as a consequence of too much 'ease' in holding power.[2] The 'great ease' (*facilità grande*) with which Alexander's successors held Asia evidently led to idleness, since they didn't have to do much hard political work to hold new provinces. According to ancient tradition, those who make easy gains tend to develop unhealthy appetites for power and other pleasures. If they don't meet resistance from subjects or foreigners, they will soon turn to fight against their closest colleagues or family members. This, we may infer from Machiavelli's brief description, is what happened with Alexander's successors, as it had happened to several Persian despots before them.[3] Because they had 'no difficulty in holding' their conquests but 'that which arose among themselves out of their own ambition', they inflicted difficulties on themselves.

Princes should therefore weigh the pros and cons of Alexander's model of empire before racing to emulate it. It holds a special appeal for princes who rate their own military virtues highly, and are willing to fight tough wars against formidable opponents to seize their countries, but who are less interested in working hard post-conquest to establish firm political orders. On the other side, this model has serious disadvantages that stem from the *virtú*-

---

[2] Compare Sallust, *SWC* 10: after Rome conquered Carthage, to men who had once endured all toil and adversity 'leisure [*otium*] and riches which are generally regarded as so desirable proved a burden and a curse', bringing in their train avarice, excessive pride, and deadly ambitions.

[3] See *XC* VIII and Herodotus' dramatic account of the Persian ruling family's self-destruction at the end of his history.

deficient quality of the conquered. A populace that has become used to depending on one monarch is too passive to help you hold or recover your new state should it be attacked. And since princes exercise *virtù* when they are under pressure to work hard, look ahead, and build good orders of their own, those who easily control other people tend to become complacent, relying more on the fortune of others' passivity than their own active efforts—with ultimately ruinous results.

The Roman model looks very different—at first. To acquire empire over Greece was easy for the Romans, who were fortunate in finding that province deeply divided. Though their military organization was outstanding, in making their first acquisitions outside Italy the Romans depended far less on military *virtù* than on the fortune of others' weakness. Whereas to attack a highly centralized, unified state one would need to place 'hope more in his own forces' and *virtù* 'than in the disorders of others', the opposite was true for the Romans in Greece, where people threw themselves into the conqueror's lap. A prince who wants to make quick and easy acquisitions will find this fortune-reliant mode appealing.

On the downside, decentralized states and politically divided provinces are a headache to hold. Machiavelli's remarks on Rome dash any hopes that Roman prudence and *virtù* soon nipped in the bud the difficulties he began to describe in chapter 3. On the contrary, we now learn of the 'frequent rebellions in Spain, France [Gaul], and Greece against the Romans, because of the numerous principalities that existed in those states'. Indeed the Romans 'were always uncertain [*incerta*] of their possession' as long as the memory of different principalities lasted.

Eventually, though, 'when their memory was eliminated with the power and long duration of the empire, the Romans became secure possessors [*sicuri possessori*] of them'. Surely this end result was due to the great *virtù* they showed in their long struggles against rebels? As the example of Alexander shows, however, not just any 'possession' is proof of *virtù*. Here and elsewhere, Machiavelli's language subtly distinguishes between 'possessing' a state or empire by top-down control—never a very stable condition—and 'maintaining' it in good order. *Mantenere* tends to have a special connection to order, and thus to *virtù*; to 'hold' (*tenere*) is more neutral or negative, while to 'possess' (*possedere*) is to hold in a static or oppressive manner, without stable orders.[4] When Machiavelli speaks of princes possessing or conserving a state, he usually suggests that they do so by ruling submissive, downtrodden, or 'stupefied' subjects who offer them no resistance—and no lively *virtù* of their own to strengthen the state's defences. It is much harder to possess or even

---

[4] A rare case of *mantenere* being used ironically—for Agathocles' state—occurs in chap. 8. Other examples of oppressive, badly ordered 'possession' occur in chaps 3 (the Turk), 5 (Romans in Carthage), 11 (the Church), 13 (Cesare Borgia), and 20 (Florentines in Pisa).

'hold' peoples full of life and spirit, such as those who take centre stage in chapter 5. But government over such peoples can be 'maintained'—a word that implies the need to work continuously to keep a living body in good health, whatever challenges it may face over time.

The Romans possessed their empire without maintaining it in this positive sense. They possessed it 'even though, when they later fought among themselves'—a reference to the endless, violent power struggles among ambitious leading men both in the dying republic and later under the emperors—'each took for himself a part of those provinces'. In a few disinterested-sounding words, Machiavelli conveys the terrible irony of a once virtuous, well-ordered Rome attaining secure possession over others but losing control over its own government. If we consider the long-term results of Roman conquests, it begins to look as if the *virtù* used to secure them was more military than political. It helped Romans fight successful wars and eliminate bloodlines, but did not lead to the creation of stable political orders, either abroad or at home. By the time the provinces had forgotten their former independence, making Rome more secure in its empire, its central government was disintegrating through rivalries among individuals who wanted to milk the provinces for their own private wealth—or who wanted to control the whole empire as monarchs. Once the provinces were pacified, then, the Romans showed no more *virtù* than Alexander's squabbling successors. If we look further ahead to the dire political results of empire described in chapter 19, we might wonder if all the military *virtù* the Romans used to suppress rebellions was well spent.

WHICH KIND OF STATE SHOULD A PRINCE PREFER TO HAVE?

Whether princes bent on foreign conquest imitate Alexander or Rome, then, in the long run they are likely to achieve the same problematic results. Instead of asking which kind of principality they should prefer to conquer, they might more fruitfully ask whether they should order their own states as highly centralized absolute monarchies or as decentralized kingdoms like the French.

The choice, again, might at first seem a no-brainer. Machiavelli has said that states ruled by one prince and his servants 'hold the prince in more authority [*autorità*]'. Such states, moreover, are harder for others to acquire because they are 'entirely united' (*tutto unito*). What prince would not prefer to govern obedient ministers and peoples, knowing that their undivided defences will come to his aid if he is attacked?

Perhaps one who considers what happened to Alexander's successors, the Romans, and many others after they gained 'secure possession' of their states.

Such absolute, top-down control depends on keeping subjects docile and ministers dependent on the prince's judgements. Viewed superficially, this sort of absolute personal control might seem to free the prince from depending on others' arms, since they depend wholly on him. But when Machiavelli says that princes should depend on their 'own arms', he doesn't mean that they should seek to establish one-man control over the entire state. On the contrary, he has just shown that the more a state depends on one prince or prince-state that crushes all other sources of strength in its dominions, the more readily it succumbs to the vicissitudes of fortune. Since power is not shared in it, ambitious men fight often and ruthlessly to seize supreme authority. And even if some stable process of succession can be established— as it never was in Rome under the emperors—absolute principalities still stand firm or founder on the accidents of fortune. For some princes are better at the job than others; or good at some parts of it, bad at others. Some are altogether disastrous. Any state that depends so heavily on one individual and his choice of ministers is inherently flawed.[5]

More far-seeing princes might recognize the advantages of the French model over that of 'the Turk'. It is, Machiavelli says, 'impossible to possess [*possederle*] states ordered [*ordinati*] like France with such quiet' as in the other case. But if decentralized states cannot be totally 'possessed' by their own prince, they provide far more fighting strength against outside assailants, and are better at maintaining military and political *virtù* in the prince and the state as a whole. Both kinds of *virtù* involve order and discipline, which in turn depend on setting limits to leaders' authority. The 'ancient multitude of lords' surrounding the French king keeps his powers in check, obliging him to share authority with others. The antiquity and continuity of these lords help give the state broad foundations that are lacking in the Turkish state, where the prince 'changes and varies' (*muta e varia*) administrators as 'appears' good to him. Instead of bureaucrats whom the populace obeys but does not love, the state contains several lords whose peoples 'recognize' them as legitimate and obey out of natural affection. If those lords sometimes oppose the king's wishes, this opposition is not, as Machiavelli will later suggest, a bad thing; if expressed through well-established institutions and acknowledged by the king, it can produce much better government than absolute monarchy.[6]

Machiavelli says nothing here about Italy, but his comparison of the French and Turkish 'modes' raises an intriguing question for his Italian contemporaries. At the time, Italy had no overarching political order at all; like the Greeks in Roman times, the province lacked any agreed common leadership or defence policy, while its separate states fought more bitterly against each other than against any foreign threat. If they could form some more lasting league to

---

[5] Compare *D* I.2 and I.58.   [6] See chap. 19 on France's parlements.

coordinate their security policies, they might break their suicidal dependence on foreign powers. In so far as Machiavelli contemplated a more unified political order for Italy, it resembled France's decentralized order rather than the excessively unified empire of 'the Turk'. An Italy whose defences were rooted in separate, independent states with their own laws, leaders, and local military structures, but with institutions designed to pool military resources, sometimes under a common command—this seems to have been Machiavelli's ideal.[7]

He does not presume to tell other Italians what form of government they should adopt. At the time of writing, some of the leading Italian states were aristocratic or princely republics (Venice, Florence), while others had kings or dukes at their head. But the next chapter will underscore the advantages of republics for peoples seeking to resist foreign conquest. Here in chapter 4, Machiavelli has at last alluded to the importance of 'peoples' for princes. They still appear in a passive role under 'the Turk': the prince's officials 'cannot bring their peoples with them' if they want to rebel against a foreigner, and have no 'credit with the people'. So long as they remain passive, the people give the victor nothing to 'fear' after conquest. Once activated, however, Machiavelli's *populi* are a force to be reckoned with. They are a source of great strength for princes who know how to order them well—and for those who do not, their most serious threat.

---

[7] See *ME* 478–83.

5

Free cities

How cities or principalities that lived by their own laws before they were occupied should be administered

HOW TO HOLD FREE STATES

The last chapter considered how to hold states used to living under different kinds of prince. This one asks how conquerors can hold states that are 'accustomed to living by their own laws and in liberty [*consueti a vivere con le loro leggi e in libertà*]'—that is, not under princes but under the only other type of state in Machiavelli's binary scheme, republics. But while the chapter speaks three times of peoples who 'live free', it identifies living free with republics only in the last sentence. This is the first explicit mention of republics since Machiavelli declared in chapter 2 that he would 'leave them out'. After this, we will hear nothing further of republics until chapter 8, where they are attacked and seized by 'criminal' princes.

There are, Machiavelli says, three modes for holding free states: (I) to ruin them (*ruinarle*); (II) go to live there personally; or (III) 'to let them live by their laws, taking tribute from them and creating within them a state of the few [an oligarchy] that keeps them friendly to you'. The pros and cons of Mode II were discussed in chapter 3, and are not discussed further here, presumably because they have already been judged problematic. Since the prospect of ruining free states may sound rather onerous, Machiavelli starts by appraising the advantages of the more moderate Mode III.

This mode seeks to combine two different elements. On the one hand, the conqueror leaves a free state its own laws, so that its people retain an important part of their accustomed liberty. On the other hand, that liberty is significantly curtailed in two respects. Firstly, the conqueror compels the populace to pay tribute to him, a measure widely regarded in ancient times as unjust imperial oppression. Secondly, the conqueror imposes a particular form of government on the conquered—here an oligarchical state—that makes it easier for him to control their internal and external policies. This mode has obvious attractions for anyone who hopes to squeeze wealth from once-free peoples, and to keep firm control over their governments, while upholding the fiction that they remain free in crucial respects.

Machiavelli's initial remarks on Mode III are encouraging for conquerors. 'For since such a state has been created by a prince', the men who staff it depend entirely on him and therefore 'do everything to maintain him.' Moreover, 'a city used to living free may be held more easily by means of its own citizens [*con il mezzo de' sua cittadini*] than in any other mode, if one wants to preserve [*preservare*] it'—hence the use of a few pliable natives to govern on your behalf.

Unfortunately, Machiavelli provides no examples of successful uses of Mode III—because there are none. The Spartans pioneered this 'mixed' mode before the Romans. They 'held Athens and Thebes' by creating oligarchical states there; 'yet they lost them again'. Then the Romans tried to use the same mode in Greece. They wanted (*vollono*), Machiavelli says, to hold that province 'much as the Spartans had held it, by making it free and leaving it its own laws'. But 'they did not succeed' any more than the Spartans before them, and 'were compelled to destroy many cities in that province so as to hold it'.

These examples make clear what Machiavelli does not say in so many words: namely, that Mode III is inherently unstable. On paper, it seems to strike a nice balance between certain cherished liberties of free states and the conqueror's aims of gaining economic benefits and political control. Until, that is, one considers that the balance is so obviously asymmetrical that it is no balance at all. To leave states their own laws while forcing them to pay tribute and accept a government imposed by foreigners is not freedom in any meaningful sense of that word. The Spartans and Romans wanted to have it both ways: to seem to respect certain freedoms in subject states while depriving them of others. But this supposed compromise proved unacceptable to peoples used to living free, for reasons soon to be elaborated. In the end, the Romans' desire to exert a moderate kind of principality in Greece collapsed, driving them to the extreme first mode that they had 'wanted' to avoid.[1]

Machiavelli's arguments suggest that this collapse was not due to the particular circumstances of Spartan or Roman expansion. If one pauses to think about the extreme imbalance between the freedoms left to subjects and those taken from them by Mode III, it seems clear that formerly free peoples will try to contest its terms—and that contestation may lead to violent conflict between them and their conquerors. Mode III's ultimate uselessness is therefore built in, not relative to circumstance, and foreseeable by anyone who knows how stubborn people can be who value their freedom. Machiavelli saves

---

[1] As tends to happen with Machiavelli's 'mixed' modes or 'middle ways'. See chaps 1, 9, and 23; compare *ME* chap. 12 on the Roman mode of expansion discussed in *D* II.4.

future conquerors the trouble of pointlessly trying to have their cake and eat it by setting out a tough yet inescapable bottom line: that 'in truth [*in verità*] there is no secure mode to possess [*possederle*]' free states 'other than to ruin them'. For Machiavelli can present successful examples of ruinous Mode I: in order to hold the cities of Capua in Italy and Carthage and Numantia in Africa, the Romans 'destroyed [*disfeciono*] them and did not lose them'.[2] And although they had not wanted to destroy 'many' Greek cities but were 'compelled' to do so if they wished to hold them—a self-inflicted necessity—this destruction helped them become 'secure possessors' of that province, as the last chapter said.

At the end, Machiavelli seems to soften the hardline conclusion that the *only* secure mode to hold free states is to ruin them, now saying that 'the most secure path is to eliminate them *or* live in them'. But since the latter policy's deficiencies were touched on in chapter 3, in effect we are still left with ruining/eliminating/destroying as the only safe option. For 'whoever becomes patron (*patrone*) of a city accustomed to living free and does not destroy it, should expect to be destroyed by it'.[3]

WHY CONQUERORS OF FREE CITIES MUST RUIN THEM

What is it about free states that makes them well-nigh impossible to hold unless the conqueror 'ruins' them? Machiavelli attributes their formidable powers of resistance to the memory of their old life of freedom. A state or city (*città*) accustomed to living free 'always has as a refuge in rebellion the name of liberty and its own ancient orders, which are never forgotten either through length of time or because of benefits received [*per benefizi*]'. Machiavelli doesn't say why these memories have such staying power. But he clearly implies that people used to freedom tend to value their remembered liberty more than their personal safety, more than the bloodlines of princes in principalities, more than any benefits the conqueror might claim to give them. Resistance to those who take away a city's freedom to live under its own laws, choose its own government, and determine its own external policies is, it seems, the reasonable and *ordinario* reaction of its citizens. In the *Discourses* and *Florentine Histories* Machiavelli traces this reaction to a natural human desire to live free and, therefore, to fight in defence of freedom.[4]

---

[2] Capua in 211 BC, Carthage in 146 BC, and Numantia in 133 BC.
[3] In Rome and Medici Florence, a *patrone* was a powerful benefactor who aided weaker parties who thereby became dependent and were expected to support his political ambitions.
[4] Compare *D* II.2.131–3; *FH* II.34.92–3. See *ME* chap. 6.

As we learned in the last chapter, 'power and the long duration' of an empire like the Roman can eventually eliminate memories of past freedom. But conquerors must resort to extremely harsh measures to achieve this. To wipe out dangerous memories of former princes or lords, they had simply to eliminate their bloodline. To wipe out memories of freedom is much harder. For 'whatever one does or foresees [*provegga*], unless the inhabitants are broken up or dispersed, they will not forget that name and those orders, and will immediately recur to them upon any accident', as Pisa did 'after having been kept in servitude [*in servitù*] for a hundred years by the Florentines'.

This example was bound to evoke painful memories for readers in Florence and the once proudly independent cities it now held as part of its 'dominions'. Pisa, whose republican traditions were as old as those of Florence, had special value for Machiavelli's native city as a key port. The Florentines seized it in 1405, and held it—for much of that time by direct military occupation—until 1494. In that year France's Charles VIII invaded Italy, providing Pisans with the 'accident' they needed to rebel against Florentine control. In his *Decennale*, written in 1504 to commemorate the tenth anniversary of the invasion, Machiavelli identifies Florentines' desperate desire to recover Pisa as one of the main causes of persistent Italian instability, and perhaps *the* main cause of weakness in the Florentine republic. Between 1494 and 1509, when Machiavelli's own civilian militia helped to recapture Pisa after a long and terrible siege, Florence fought many draining and fruitless wars against its neighbouring fellow-republic. Despite its eventual victory, Florence paid a high price for these campaigns, arousing the hatred of other cities in its dominions and constantly having to beg—and fork out hefty sums—for French military assistance.

Machiavelli was directly involved in these humiliating appeals for foreign military help, and deplored his compatriots' willingness to compromise their own city's independence for the sake of conquering another independent republic. The second instalment of his poem *Decennale*, composed after Pisa's re-conquest, depicts the Pisans as fierce patriots and brave fighters who were prepared to undergo the most dreadful sacrifices to defend their *libertà*.[5] As for the Florentines, in Machiavelli's view, their appetite for control harmed themselves as much as others: 'you for Pisa', he reproached his fellow citizens, 'have too strong desire'.[6] Although his militia helped bring Pisa back

[5] 'Then you moved against the Pisans . . . but because Pisa feared little or nothing, no long time you kept the field there; thus it was the beginning of very evil seed. / And if you there lost money and honour by following the universal belief, you satisfied the popular desire'—not a reasonable one. Restless with greed, 'toward Pisa you kept your eyes turned always, not being able to rest in any fashion if you did not have her', until at last 'four months you remained around her with great hardships and much toil, and with much expense you starved her. / And though she was a stubborn enemy, yet by necessity compelled and conquered, she went back weeping to her ancient chain.' *Decennale* II, 46–53, 145–65.

[6] *Decennale* I, 535–6.

into Florentine dominions, his writings before and after 1509 suggest that he was deeply unhappy with Florence's oppressive old methods of 'holding' its freedom-loving neighbour.[7] His language in the *Prince* refuses to disguise his critical judgement of his own city's conduct. Whereas other conquerors acquired or held or possessed, Pisa was 'kept in servitude' by the Florentines for a century, deprived of the freedoms that Florentines claimed to cherish for themselves. Machiavelli's close-to-home example reminds Florentine and other Italian readers that they were not just victims of greater powers' conquests; they also inflicted servitude on fellow Italians.

This self-critical perspective is developed more directly in the *Florentine Histories*, where Machiavelli shows the damage done to Florence by its wars to oppress freedom-loving cities in its dominions. The city grew safer and stronger, he suggests, when such cities managed to break free then later returned voluntarily to Florence's dominions as quasi-independent entities. Thus Machiavelli has one of the book's most prudent characters declare that if Florentines had 'received' a nearby city into its dominions 'by accord' they would have gained 'advantage and security from it'. But since they had to 'hold it by force', the occupied city would bring 'weakness and trouble' to Florence in bad times 'and in peaceful times, loss and expense'.[8] The ideal relationship between Florence and cities like Pisa was not that of prince-conqueror to subjects or servants, but one between partners who supported each other's freedom.

THE REVENGE OF FREE PEOPLES

The chapter began in the usual dispassionate tones Machiavelli employs to analyse the perspective of princes. Halfway through, he suddenly shifts to the perspective of free citizens, and the tone warms up. By the end it is dangerously hot. When Machiavelli does at last mention his previously unmentioned republics, they burst back onto the stage with a vengeance, and in formidable fighting mode. 'In republics' the final sentence tells us, 'there is greater life, greater hatred, more desire for revenge [*vendetta*]' than in principalities; 'the memory of their ancient liberty does not and cannot let them rest, so that the most secure path is to eliminate them or live in them.' This gives princes and conquering republics a strong taste of the kind of resistance they must face if they try to

---

[7] While Machiavelli was involved in military planning for the siege, he afterwards helped negotiate a moderate settlement; see Viroli (2001), 103–6.
[8] *FH* VII.30. Compare *FH* II.38 on the advantages for Florence of making its 'subject' cities into 'friends' so that 'being free' themselves, they could 'help maintain the Florentines' own freedom'; *ME* 223–4, 479–83.

'acquire' free republics. At the same time, it suggests that those who crush such fighting spirit destroy an invaluable resource that could be used to improve their own defences if, instead of ruining free republics, they make them their allies.

A further implication is that republics are better than any sort of principality at resisting conquest. Machiavelli states this conclusion rather bluntly. 'Cities or provinces used to living under a prince', he claims, are much easier to hold than republics once the old prince's bloodline has been eliminated. Since subjects are 'used to obeying' (*ubbidire*) and 'do not know how to live free', they are too slow (*tardi*) to take up arms, and 'a prince can gain them with greater ease and can secure himself against them'. Machiavelli does not say that sometimes republics, sometimes princes are better at long-term resistance. His remarks are general: republics are generally, regardless of circumstance, more suited for this task. Here he identifies their citizens' desires to protect their customary freedoms as the cause of this advantage. Later chapters will suggest that the best military orders for any state are founded most securely in republics.

Modes

6

Virtú

Of new principalities that are acquired through one's own arms and virtú

WHAT IS *VIRTÚ*? WORDS AND DEEDS

This is the first of a series of four chapters that discuss various 'modes' of acquiring and maintaining new princely states: by *virtú* (chapter 6), by fortune (chapter 7), by crimes (chapter 8), and by 'fortunate astuteness' (chapter 9).

What, according to the *Prince*, are the qualities that allow us to recognize works of *virtú*? Our answer to this question—one of the most baffling posed by Machiavelli's little book—depends on how much weight we give to two different elements in his discussions of *virtú*. On the one hand, even a superficial reading can pick out summary **statements** where the author seems to give his own judgement of certain princes or prince-cities, such as Machiavelli's remark in chapter 3 that the Romans had the benefit of their prudence and *virtú*. Yet on reading more closely, we often find that his **descriptions** of the same actions raise doubts about their *virtuoso* quality—as did Machiavelli's suggestive accounts of Rome's self-destructive compulsion to empire.

Machiavelli uses this well-established technique of ironic writing throughout the *Prince* to provoke readers to think carefully about what qualities deserve the high praise accorded by the word *virtú*. The technique is based on an ancient antithesis between good words and less good deeds. It assumes that people often lavish praise on deeds that appear praiseworthy but, on closer scrutiny, are deeply problematic. The on-paper contrast between glowing words and ambiguous deeds mimics political reality, where leaders routinely 'colour' their harmful actions with the rhetoric and appearances of virtue.[1]

Machiavelli's provocative contrasts between positive statements about certain agents and less glowing descriptions of their actions help explain what

---

[1] See chap. 15.

look like contradictory accounts of *virtú* in the *Prince*.[2] If we focus on the former, we often get the impression that a prince's *virtú* is shown above all in the boldness of his ambitions, the energy with which he pursues them, and his success in removing challenges to his will. If we focus on the descriptions, Machiavelli's account of *virtú* looks quite different: the most complete *virtú* is tied more closely to reflective forethought and other intellectual qualities than to boldness, military valour, willpower, or high spirits. The last three chapters introduced several nuances in that account that will be confirmed as we read further:

(1) Qualities that deserve to be called *virtú* may be used in ways that produce *virtú*-deficient outcomes. This happens when agents apply their *virtú* to ends that are incompatible with stable order, or when they rely too much on fortune.

(2) Success in attaining one's ends is not sufficient evidence of *virtú*. If an agent produces long-term disorder through attaining his ends, his *virtú* cannot merit highest praise.

(3) Long duration of rule is insufficient evidence of political *virtú*. Sometimes a prince or state rules for generations, even centuries, simply because the ruled lack the *virtú* to resist, irrespective of the qualities of their rulers.

(4) While some qualities associated with *virtú*—notably industry, foresight, and ordering capacities—deserve high praise in relation to any activity, other qualities deserve praise in relation to particular activities. Boldness and high spirits are especially helpful for *acquiring* new states, especially when military action is needed. They are less helpful for constructing and *maintaining* states over time, unless they are combined with intellectual and ordering capacities that go beyond military discipline.

WHY IT IS BETTER TO RELY ON *VIRTÚ* THAN ON FORTUNE

For the first time in chapter 6, Machiavelli spells out an important point about *virtú* that was merely implied before: as a general 'mode' of action, *virtú* has great advantages over reliance on fortune. It is true that fortune and *virtú* are equally efficient causes of 'acquiring'. But while fortune can help a prince make quick and easy conquests, it is far less helpful when he wants to maintain them. Indeed, 'he who has relied less on fortune' and more on *virtú* 'has maintained himself more'. If acquiring depended on either fortune or *virtú* or

---

[2] See 'Ironic Techniques' (4a).

some amalgam thereof, maintaining depends wholly on *virtú*: new princes meet with 'more or less difficulty in maintaining' their states 'according to whether the one who acquires them is more or less virtuous'.

Many individuals in the *Prince* are said to work through both *fortuna* and *virtú*. As noted in chapter 1, less reflective princes might think that some combination of *virtú* and fortune-reliant modes is the ideal recipe for success, especially since fortune makes acquiring much easier. But when Machiavelli says that 'he who has relied less on fortune has maintained himself more', he suggests that it is *never* good to rely on fortune to acquire or maintain. Since those who first acquire by fortune often find it hard to develop the *virtú* needed to maintain, the most completely virtuous princes are those who acquire *and* maintain by relying as much as possible on their own *virtú*, and as little as possible on fortune. Even when mixed with *virtú*, good fortune breeds complacency. The relative ease and impressive appearances of success it delivers pose a dangerous temptation to the virtuous, luring them to work less hard than they would without its aid—and to think less carefully about the consequences of their actions, since they expect to succeed no matter what they do. The example of Rome showed that princes or cities may possess very great *virtú*, yet be lured by success to rely less on their own foresight and ordering skills than on other people's weaknesses, divisions, and ephemeral gifts of power.

SUPERHUMAN ORDERS AND HUMAN *VIRTÚ*

The chapter begins on an upbeat tone—a welcome relief for princely readers after the previous chapter, where Machiavelli confronted them with mortal threats from peoples fighting tooth and nail for their freedom. He now entertains the prospect of princes soaring to very great heights, leaving republics and popular struggles for freedom far below. For the first time in the *Prince*, he links *virtú* to greatness (*grandezza*). In elevated tones that mimic his subject-matter, 'No one should marvel', Machiavelli declares, 'if, in speaking as I will do of principalities that are altogether new both in prince and in state, I cite the greatest examples [*grandissimi esempli*].' He then links prudence to a kind of greatness that lies beyond the reach of the ordinary run of princes. A 'prudent man' he proclaims, should set his sights high and seek to imitate the *virtú* of the most excellent (*eccellentissimi*) men of all times, 'so that if his own *virtú* does not reach that far, it at least has the odour of it [*renda qualche odore*]'.

This admits that many new princes, perhaps most, are likely to fall short of their models' qualities and achievements. Yet by imitating their *grandezza*, they can at least strive to approach the highest standards of princely greatness.

They 'should do as prudent archers do when the place they plan to hit appears too distant, and knowing how far the *virtú* of their bow carries, they set their aim much higher than the place intended'—not expecting 'to reach such height [*altezza*] with their arrow, but to be able with the aid of so high an aim to achieve their plan'.

All these accumulating superlatives—*grandissimi esempli, uomini grandi, eccellentissimi, altezza*—create the impression that Machiavelli is hugely impressed by 'greatness' in ambitions and actions, and thinks that all new princes should aspire to it. Yet something in this opening passage smells suspiciously ironic. Its grandiose language sounds out of place in a text that has so far avoided exaggerated praise of any individual or state. The elevated tone creates a feeling of remoteness from everyday political reality, at odds with all the harsh realities evoked so vividly in earlier chapters. Machiavelli seems to say that all new princes should emulate the greatest examples, even if their own capabilities are far inferior. But some readers might wonder: is this prudent? Can new princes attain reliably firm political results by aiming far above their actual capabilities? Statesmen we ordinarily consider prudent— those who know their own limitations and seek to avoid dangerous overreaching—would surely *not* aim at such targets. The word for 'height', *altezza*, is particularly worrying, since in Machiavelli's and other famous Italian writings, it is often associated with self-defeating arrogance (Latin *superbia*, Greek *hubris*), or with excessively high flight that precedes a fall.[3]

Further suspicions are aroused by Machiavelli's uncharacteristic idealization of men who 'have become princes by their own *virtú* [*per propria virtú*] and not by fortune'. The most excellent of these, he says, are Moses, Cyrus, Romulus, Theseus, 'and the like'. All but Moses were kings; the lives of all four were shrouded in legend. Since their actions cannot be known with any precision, imitators must imitate unreliable accounts rather than drawing on secure knowledge of their accomplishments. This might still lend them a whiff of borrowed greatness for a time. But would it help them to maintain their states—a task that, according to most of the *Prince,* calls for much unglamor-ous hard work to overcome great difficulties? If a prince imitates idealized accounts of heroic deeds instead of well-attested historical figures, he risks trying to do what no real-life men *can* do.

As we'll see, Machiavelli's comments on each great man's 'actions and orders' are too cursory to provide much down-to-earth guidance for imitators. In any case, before telling us anything concrete about how they manifested their *virtú*, he widens the gulf between ordinary human princes and their

---

[3] See chap. 7 and Dante, *Inferno* XXX: '*E quando la fortuna volse in basso/l'altezza de' Troian che tutto ardiva, sì che 'nsieme col regno il re fu casso . . .*' (And at the time when fortune downward hurled / The Trojan's arrogance, that all things dared, so that the king was with his kingdom crushed . . .).

heroic role models by placing one of them on a wholly different plane, beyond rational scrutiny. 'One should not reason about Moses,' Machiavelli advises, 'as he was a mere executor [*mero esecutore*] of things that had been ordered for him by God [*ordinate da Dio*].' This implies that Moses' actions and orders were not his own but God's—not the product of his *virtù*, but of divine command. Readers are entitled to ask whether taking orders from God amounts to relying on 'others' arms', or at any rate on some power other than one's own arms and *virtù*. Can it be reasonable to take as one's model a man who worked not by his own *virtù* but merely followed God's instructions? And how prudent can it be to imitate someone whose actions don't admit of rational scrutiny, about whom 'one should not reason'? Unless a new prince is confident that God has chosen him as his executor, in which case his own merely human *virtù* is essentially redundant, perhaps Moses' deeds—or rather God's deeds enacted through him—are best seen as inimitable.

Machiavelli's next remarks, however, establish some kind of equivalence between Moses and the other three men. Having questioned whether Moses' actions can be attributed to ordinary human *virtù*, and therefore explained in rational terms, Machiavelli then says that his qualities should still 'be admired [*ammirato*], if only for that grace [*grazia*] that made him worthy of speaking with God'. Machiavelli does not say whether one who deserves divine grace thereby manifests *virtù*; he normally uses that word for distinctively human qualities whose exercise in no way depends on divine blessings. The fact that Moses spoke with God sets him apart from the other paragons on Machiavelli's list, and further suggests that his example cannot be imitated at will. Yet if 'Cyrus and the others who acquired or founded kingdoms' were not helped by divine grace, nonetheless Machiavelli tells his princely readers that 'you will find them all admirable', using the same word he applied to Moses. Moreover, 'if their particular actions and orders' are examined, they 'will appear no different from those of Moses, who had so great a teacher [*grande precettore*]'.

What does Machiavelli want to suggest by first separating Moses from the pack, setting his example above even highest human *virtù*, and then identifying his divinely inspired orders with the actions and orders of the other three? The whole passage is teasingly ambiguous about the relationship between divine standards and princely *virtù*. It can be read either as inflating the *virtù* of the other three men to a Mosaic level, or as bringing Moses' merits down to earth.

From an inflationary perspective, if Cyrus and the others lacked direct guidance from God, yet their actions and orders still resemble Moses', this might mean that they performed godlike feats under their own steam. Readers might therefore conclude that Cyrus, Romulus, and Theseus possessed an extraordinary natural *virtù*, far above that of most men—and that modern princes should aspire to something like the same. All three were non-Christian leaders who were deified in their pagan traditions. Perhaps Machiavelli wants modern imitators to grant quasi-divine standing to these warlike pagans, rivalling the Christian practice of sanctifying otherworldly individuals.

From a secularizing perspective, a very different conclusion may be drawn from Moses' resemblance to the others: not that their *virtú* was superhuman, but that Moses' was essentially natural and human, even though he had God as a guide. If Moses' actions and orders owe their quality to his own *virtú*, and God made him his instrument because of that *virtú*, then the resemblance between his and the other men's actions lies in their exceptional human qualities, not in their superhuman rarity.

Machiavelli leaves it to readers to decide which kind of *virtú* can most reasonably be ascribed to Moses and the other three. For aspiring new princes, the choice depends in part on a judgement about what they can realistically hope to imitate. As men and as models for men, does it make more sense to understand these heroes' *virtú* in human terms, or to elevate it towards the superhuman? The second view is harder to square with Machiavelli's usual insistence on human-sized aims and methods, his firmly secular perspective, and the *Prince*'s earlier discussion of human beings' 'natural and ordinary' limits. But readers who imagine that they can convincingly imitate super-human *virtú* are free to consider what might happen if they try.

Either way, by subtly questioning whether Moses can after all be taken as a paragon of human, self-sufficient *virtú* before discussing the other three examples, Machiavelli signals that his treatment of these *eccelentissimi* men may not involve a straightforward call to imitate them. Readers are alerted to pay close attention to what follows, and to ask what can and cannot reasonably be taken as a target—even a remote one—for merely human princes.

OPPORTUNITY AND FORTUNE

Although Machiavelli's great four are introduced as men who became princes 'by their own *virtú* and not by fortune', he does not claim that fortune played *no* role in their ascent. Fortune did provide them with one essential condition: opportunity (*occasione*).

Speaking of Moses, Cyrus, and the others, Machiavelli declares that 'as one examines their actions and lives, one does not see that they had anything from fortune than the opportunity, which gave [*dette*] them the matter enabling them to introduce [*materia a potere introdurvi*] any form they pleased'.

This makes it sound as if fortune was actually quite generous to them, despite Machiavelli's attempt to play down its role. After all, not every prince is 'given' material so pliable that he can introduce *any* form he pleases. On the contrary, chapters 3 and 5 just discussed the far less yielding matter that the later Romans had to grapple with. They too had and seized the fortunate opportunity provided by others' divisions, but lacked the additional good fortune of malleable new subjects.

It seems, then, that fortune-given opportunities are not all equally fortunate. To take advantage of such opportunities, one has first to seize power, and then to impose one's own 'form' on new acquisitions. But some fortune-given conditions—such as those given to Alexander—make new ordering easy, while others make it very hard. Note, moreover, that Machiavelli does not say that his heroes' outstanding virtú enabled them to impose whatever form they pleased; the materia given by fortune-given opportunity enabled them to do this. They did of course need 'virtú of spirit' to recognize and seize the opportunities on offer, since without that virtú 'the opportunity would have come in vain'. Yet the expansive opportunities furnished by readily yielding matter were also needed to keep their virtú alive: 'without that opportunity, their virtú of spirit [dello animo] would have been eliminated'.

Is Machiavelli insinuating that the virtú of his four great examples owed a good deal more to fortune than their admirers might want to admit? His brief remarks on each man's deeds subtly stress the uncommonly fortunate conditions they had to work with. Of course, the opportunities each seized began as problems that cried out for a solution. Moses found 'the people of Israel in Egypt, enslaved and oppressed [stiavo e oppresso]'; Romulus was blocked from the throne of Alba to which he was rightful heir; Theseus found the Athenians dispersed; Cyrus found the Persians malcontent and oppressed by the Medes. But the Israelites were so weary of oppression that 'they would be disposed to follow' Moses 'so as to get out of their servitude [servitú]'. The people who would become 'Athenians' after Theseus unified them were too scattered to resist. Romulus had only to topple his usurping uncle to reclaim his hereditary title to rule. The Medes were so 'soft and effeminate' that Cyrus found them easy to conquer, as Alexander later found it easy to conquer the corrupt and downtrodden Persians who were produced by Cyrus' despotism.

Machiavelli's comments on his 'most excellent' four in the Discourses confirm the significant role of fortune in the actions of all but Moses, who worked more through God's agency than his own. He cites Cyrus as an example of princes who use fraud [fraude] to climb to 'sublime ranks', thereby attaining 'great fortune'. Far from praising this conduct, Machiavelli remains resoundingly silent about the virtú of Cyrus and other such princes. Another method Cyrus used to win great power was to be seen as 'humane and affable' by bribing people to become his 'partisans'—a method identified with state-destroying 'liberality' in the Prince chapter 17.[4]

Theseus appears in the Discourses as a less-than-ideally virtuous builder, since he created a new city not under hard necessity—which for Machiavelli always elicits the greatest virtú—but in order to make scattered townships

---

[4] D II.13, III.20, 23. Cyrus is described as one who rose and crashed through fortune in Machiavelli's Di Fortuna, quoted in chap. 7.

'easier to defend'.[5] While this might sound like a worthy enough motive for new founding, Machiavelli suggests that cities founded for the sake of greater advantage and easier defence tend to maintain themselves with similar aims, advantage and ease, which readily turn toward idleness and greed. For Athenians, 'it turned out happily ... because of the long idleness [*felicemente per il lungo ozio*] that the site gave them'.[6] 'Happily' here does not mean 'well': it is one of Machiavelli's strongest code words for deceptively pleasant but dangerous reliance on fortune. The irony is clear in this context, since happiness is linked to idleness, which is invariably corrupting. Athenian idleness infamously bred desires for more ease and luxury, then greed, then aggressive imperial expansion—which soon led the great city to self-inflicted ruin.[7]

In his *Discourses* Machiavelli claims that while Romulus instituted many of Rome's good orders, he did not found the city as the great and virtuous republic it later became, but as a monarchy that soon fell prey to grave disorders. Machiavelli's brief description of Romulus in the *Prince* alludes to his personal desires to rule as monarch: it was 'fitting' (*conveniva*), he writes, for Romulus 'not to be received at Alba if he wanted [*volere*] to become king of Rome and founder of that fatherland [*patria*]'. This implies that Romulus' spirited *virtú* was put to the service of his personal ambitions as much as to any wider benefit. Unlike Moses and Cyrus, who liberated oppressed peoples, Romulus aspired to be king and founder without any such necessity. According to the *Discourses*, Rome's orders remained incomplete and defective until the kings were expelled and republican orders established.[8]

Surely Romulus still deserves high praise for founding Rome, even if his foundations were flawed? Even in the republican *Discourses*, Machiavelli always speaks respectfully of Romulus and Rome's monarchical origins. Yet the first chapter gives readers a choice about who to 'take' as Rome's 'first progenitor': Romulus, who wanted to be king and killed his own brother to rule alone, or Aeneas the Trojan who fled his homeland and was forced to build a new life in Italy. Machiavelli treats Aeneas' methods, not Romulus', as a prime example of the most virtuous modes for founding new cities. Constrained by the harshest necessity to acknowledge his own limited powers as a refugee with few followers, Aeneas had to work 'by way of friends and confederates [*per via d'amici e di confederati*]' to build a new city among pre-existing populations, winning 'the consent [*per consentimento*] of neighbours where they settled'.[9] This alternative account of Rome's founding sets a

[5] The future Athenians were dispersed not in the way of a diaspora, or under compulsion, but only in the sense that they lived under many small-scale, autonomous governments, according to Thucydides, without great hardship; see *TPW* II.15–16.
[6] *D* I.1; also see *D* I.2.6 on the short life of Athenian constitutions.
[7] In the Peloponnesian War against Greek Sparta.   [8] See esp. *D* I.19–20; *ME* 418–24.
[9] *D* II.8; compare *ME* 425–32. Sallust and other writers who deplored the loss of Rome's republican virtue name Aeneas as its founder; see *SWC* 6.

moderate, diplomatic understanding of Roman *virtú* and prudence alongside the more warlike, conquest-hungry kind of *virtú* symbolized by Romulus.[10] Whether or not one prefers Romulus' modes, Machiavelli makes it clear that they were not the only—or most virtuous—way to found Rome.

THE HAPPY RESULTS OF PRINCELY *VIRTÚ*

Some readers might protest that these men deserve highest praise for what they achieved, even if fortune lent them a strong helping hand at the outset, and even if their orders were flawed in some respects. Moses and Cyrus led oppressed peoples to throw off their foreign yoke. All except Moses founded, or are said to have founded, great empires, or cities that would go on to establish great empires. All won great admiration for making their countries great and 'happy' (*felice*). Their opportunities, Machiavelli insists, 'made these men happy' personally, while their fatherlands were 'ennobled' (*nobilitata*) by 'their excellent *virtú*' and 'became very happy' (*felicissima*).

But without denying that they showed truly admirable *virtú* in some respects, Machiavelli's claims that his great men were and made their countries 'happy' signals that they were, or became, too dependent on fortune. For Machiavelli, *felice* and its cognates are always associated with the transient, unstable qualities conferred by *fortuna*. 'Happiness' is never a state of solid contentment or success, but an uncertain high that invariably precedes great difficulties.[11] The statement that something makes men *felice* contains a veiled warning: in time, that thing will bring more woes than happiness. Being happy may be compatible with personal security, for a while; Machiavelli says that princes who overcome great difficulties and are held in veneration may 'remain powerful, secure, honoured, and happy'. But how secure did their *virtú* make them—and in the longer run, their fatherlands? Unfortunately, in the *Prince* Machiavelli tells us nothing precise about how his 'most excellent' princes made themselves or their fatherlands happy and secure over time, except that they were armed rather than unarmed. Otherwise his idealizing comments are unreliably vague. As we've seen, his remarks in the *Discourses* give a more nuanced, partly critical picture of their legacies. This picture concurs with Machiavelli's main ancient sources, which were familiar to

---

[10] Petrarch vividly describes Romulus' extreme violence in his Plutarch-like 'Lives of Illustrious Men', where he emphasizes the Roman's military valour and 'spirit' but ends on an ambivalent note, inviting readers to judge freely for themselves among 'the ambiguous and multiple things' told about Romulus. Petrarch (2004b), 6–19.

[11] See esp. chaps 7 and 19.

many of his early readers. Here we find highly ambiguous appraisals of his four paragons' *virtú* and its happy results.

For Machiavelli's ancients and his well-read contemporaries, each of the four except Moses represented unbridled personal ambition that led their countries to astonishing 'greatness' in a short time—but also to self-destructive tyranny, internally and in their external relations. Romulus appears in Plutarch's 'Life' as a militaristic warlord who expanded his realm by violent means. He met a mysterious end at the hands—many suspected—of his own Senate, who feared that his tyrannical tendencies were destroying the city he had founded. Plutarch praises him for founding Rome, but implies that he also planted seeds of corruption that would plague his city throughout its long life: in particular, Romans' fatal fondness for soldier-kings and ceaseless conquests. Plutarch's Theseus, like Romulus, used violence, rape, and pillage to gain power, met a violent death, and came to epitomize Athens' self-destructive hubris in expanding its empire against other peoples' wishes.[12]

In Xenophon's *Cyropaedia*, Cyrus is depicted as an apparently ideal monarch who in fact established a legacy of corrupt despotism in Persia, at least as bad as that of the Medes whose yoke he had broken. He liberated the Persians, but could not control his desire to conquer more and more of Asia, even when the countries he seized posed no threat to his fatherland's safety. He achieved all of this while upholding appearances of good government—a façade that promptly crumbled after his death, leaving a vast, unwieldy empire torn between his squabbling heirs. Early in his career he established many good orders, notably an army of his own people to combat foreign oppression. But his insatiable appetite for conquest gradually corrupted his own good works, leading him to dismantle his own military and replace it with mercenaries. For Machiavelli and his favourite ancients, this was an unerring sign of a shift from virtuous modes toward dependence on fortune and others' arms.[13]

According to the Old Testament and later accounts, Moses struggled constantly to keep his own wayward people united and devout. Having led them to the Promised Land, he himself was prevented by God from entering it. He died alone and far from happy, leaving his Israelites free from foreign servitude, but still prone to debilitating conflicts among themselves.[14]

---

[12] See Plutarch's 'Parallel Lives' of Theseus and Romulus, *PL* I.2–201. Theseus was a highly controversial figure for Athenians, who saw him as the initiator of Athens' later, ruthless, and ultimately disastrous methods of imperial expansion; see Walker (1995). Many Athenian writers were critical of Athens' imperial ambitions and later Greek and Roman writers echoed this critical tradition.

[13] *XC* VIII; for a longer account, see *ME* 71–8. I agree with Carlier (2010), 362 that Xenophon's praise of Cyrus' monarchy is largely ironic: 'Xenophon reminds his reader, through a series of suggestive hints, that absolute monarchy is not an agreeable regime.' Compare the overtly negative views of Cyrus in Herodotus, Book I and Plato, *Laws* 694a–695b.

[14] On ambiguities in the Moses tradition see Feldman (2007). On Machiavelli's ambiguous views of Moses in the *Discourses*, see *ME* 424–32.

Machiavelli may not discuss these mixed results of his heroes' *virtú* in the *Prince*. But his remarks in the *Discourses* suggest that he did not dispute them, or seek to replace ancient writers' partly critical accounts with one-sided idealizations. The point of his ironic praise is not to cast doubt on the kind of *virtú* many people admire in men like Moses, Cyrus, Romulus, and Theseus. They all had, or had ascribed to them, genuinely admirable virtues—notably the '*virtú* of spirit' needed to recognize and take opportunities to build new empires, cities, or peoples. But throughout the *Prince*, Machiavelli uses the phrase *virtú dello animo*, *virtú* of spirit, for qualities that are highly valued for acquiring—especially in military contexts—but less valuable for building and maintaining durable orders.

One of the main themes of Machiavelli's early poems is human beings' fatal tendency to deceive themselves about how much power they can reasonably hope to sustain. He admits no exceptions, ancient or recent; uncritical admiration for any man's or state's powers is alien to Machiavelli's thinking. Like '*virtú* of spirit' or 'happy', the words 'great' and 'excellent' are almost always ambivalent in his vocabulary. To insist on the 'greatness' or excellence of actions, or the high 'repute' they confer, is to warn that what appears great and confers reputation may be deceptive—or lack secure foundations. Not even the most virtuous men can safely maintain the boundless *grandezza* sought by Cyrus 'and the like'. They can try, and many will put them on pedestals. But in the end their unchecked appetites and spirits will put an unbearable strain on virtuous orders, and make life unnecessarily dangerous for their fatherlands.

STAND BY YOURSELF AND USE FORCE

Even the most excellent princes, it seems, have great difficulties as well as great reputations. 'Men such as these', Machiavelli now informs us, 'find great difficulty in conducting themselves; all their dangers are along the path, and it is fitting that they overcome them with *virtú*.' Once they overcome them and 'begin to be held in veneration, having eliminated those who envied them for their quality, they remain powerful, secure, honoured, and happy'. But *en route* to this coveted state, they face two daunting obstacles.

These arise 'in part' from resistance to the 'new orders and modes' that these introducers (*lo introduttore*) are 'forced to' introduce. One difficulty is lukewarm (*tiepidi*) defenders. The main reason for this tepidity, Machiavelli says, is fear of adversaries with 'laws on their side'. That a new prince's adversaries may have laws on their side tells us that such princes are not always or only constructive builders of new orders; they may also violate or destroy preexisting orders and laws. Machiavelli hereby warns princes that after they acquire a new *stato*, they may have to struggle for a long time against defenders of established laws.

The second difficulty is posed by 'the incredulity of men, who do not truly believe [*non credono in verita*] in new things unless they come to have a firm experience [*ferma esperienza*] of them'. Firmness is one of the main qualities that Machiavelli associates with sound, virtuous orders. Presumably, then, it is not unreasonable for men to mistrust new rulers until they have firm experience of their rule.

Both difficulties arise, from the rather reasonable beliefs and desires of a prince's new subjects. To identify the best way of dealing with them, 'it is necessary to examine whether these innovators [*innovatori*] stand by themselves or depend on others; that is, whether to carry out their deed [*l'opera loro*] they must beg [*preghino*] or indeed can use force [*forzare*]'. In 'the first case,' Machiavelli declares, 'they always come to ill and never accomplish anything; but when they depend on their own and are able to use force, then it is that they are rarely in peril'.

The point of all this seems to be that new princes must put aside scruples about using force to impose their new orders. They are forced to assert themselves all the more vigorously because 'nothing is more difficult to handle, more doubtful of success, nor more dangerous to manage, than to make oneself head [*farsi capo*] of introducing new orders'. Force, it seems, is always virtuous when dealing with those who resist a new prince who seeks to make himself 'head' introducer, even if the resisters still have the laws 'on their side'.

Or is it? Machiavelli says that a specific kind of princely action—'*making oneself* head' of new ordering—is what makes the difficulties so formidable. Perhaps a new prince would have less trouble, and less need to use force, if his aims were more modest. And since these difficulties arise from the incredulity and tepidity of those who have 'the laws on their side', it seems likely that men who become princes without violating pre-existing laws will find it less difficult to persuade others to support their new orders, and perhaps to believe in them as well. As we'll see later, the chapter ends with a 'lesser example' of a prince who let *others* put him at the head of new ordering, and achieved great success without using force against his own people.

Those who do face resistance and disbelief, on the other hand, have to use force to 'carry out their deed'. But what is this single 'deed' (*opera*)? It sounds like a reference to a seizure of power, a *coup d'état*. By referring to these princes as 'innovators', Machiavelli reinforces the impression that their 'modes' are highly destabilizing. We tend to think of innovation as a good thing, and modern readers often assume that Machiavelli's *innovare* is connected with the creation of new and improved orders. But as chapter 2 suggested, the word has no such positive sense in Machiavelli's vocabulary. *Innovazione* subverts existing orders and makes it hard to set new ones on firm foundations.

If Machiavelli's language raises doubts about the *virtú* of new princely innovators, what about his astonishing claim that such men must be willing and able to force unbelievers to 'believe' in whatever they impose? 'For', he writes, 'the nature of peoples is variable, and it is easy to persuade them of something, but difficult to affirm [*fermargli*] them in that persuasion.' Since firmness is a desirable a quality, 'things must be ordered in such a mode that when they no longer believe, one can make them believe by force [*credere per forza*]'.

The idea that people can be forced to believe anything—that physical coercion can change innermost thoughts and convictions—is clearly paradoxical, if not absurdly unrealistic. To assert its necessity, Machiavelli must have been so dazzled by extraordinary princely power that he failed to see the absurdity. Or he is being ironic. In fact, the paradox of forcing belief was a familiar topic in ancient philosophy. In his dialogue on *Laws*, Plato presents it as a common opinion of obtuse, authoritarian men who wrongly imagine that they can control people's deepest religious convictions as well as their actions. The highly nuanced discussion concludes that force may change people's outward conduct with respect to religion, and that it is necessary for any state to enforce its own laws concerning religious practice. But force, the laws, or superstitious prophecies cannot change inner beliefs; only the hard work of persuasion can do this.[15] This position is consistent with Machiavelli's usual emphasis on the limits of power, his view that the best kind of brain is 'one that understands by itself', and the high value he places on freedom and free will in the *Prince* and elsewhere.[16] The last few chapters insisted that not even overwhelming force can stamp out people's memories and beliefs in their ancient orders, unless one physically eliminates those people or waits for time to obliterate their descendants' inconvenient beliefs.[17]

The claim that new princes should 'order' things so that non-supporters can be forced to believe in their rule seems to echo the opinions of certain impatient, impetuous princes rather than to present Machiavelli's own judgement. Like many chapters in the *Prince*, this one has a dramatic structure and movement. It starts with a naïve exaltation of ancient founders, urging new princes to imitate them without 'reasoning' too closely about their deeds. Then, somewhat belatedly, it confronts the great difficulties such princes must face, and offers force as the only solution, going so far as to recommend force to alter people's beliefs. If these are read as Machiavelli's recommendations, his initial idealizing of great princes leads him, in the space of a few pages, to endorse an unreasonable policy of forcing belief. If the same arguments are read as a dramatic imitation of how impatient new princes account for their own actions, the unrealism is theirs, not Machiavelli's. The logic of their own ambitions for one-man rule drives them to seek total control over

---

[15] Plato, *Laws* X 885c–e, 890a–d.   [16] Chaps 22 and 25.
[17] And the very act of writing the *Prince* showed that whatever force the new rulers might use against him, Machiavelli still held his old beliefs, and would work patiently through his book to try to change theirs.

their subjects' minds as well as their actions. Machiavelli merely puts up a mirror to their self-justifications by describing them honestly—as Roman poets and playwrights depicted their own corrupt society without directly judging it, or as ancient historians invented speeches to expose the flawed reasoning of leaders without directly criticizing them.

But Machiavelli's ironies do not just expose princely follies. They also have a constructive dimension, aimed at advising princes how to secure power in more modestly but reliably virtuous ways. One of his favourite ambiguity-producing techniques is a form of ironic transformation that starts with an extreme or unreasonable-sounding assertion.[18] This is followed by further claims that seem to support the first one, but in fact change key words that correct the meaning of the first claim, making it more reasonable.

Here the statement about forcing belief is followed by the claim that Moses and the others 'would not have been able to make their constitutions [*constituzioni*] observed for long if they had been unarmed [*disarmati*]'. Whereas the preceding sentence spoke of forcing belief, this one speaks only of using force to make constitutions observed. The idea that physical arms can force belief sounds unrealistic as well as draconian. The new claim that such arms are needed to make people observe constitutions is neither. Even the best, most widely supported constitutions need force to back them up, as ancient philosophers often reminded their students. And forcing people to observe laws or constitutions is a matter of setting limits on their outward actions, not of controlling their innermost thoughts or beliefs. With a quiet change of a few words, Machiavelli shows princes a more realistic way to manage 'unbelievers' than to try against the odds to force them to believe in his orders. This way still uses force, but to a far more reasonable end.

A similar transformation occurs with the claim that 'innovators stand by themselves [*stanno per loro medesimi*] or depend on others [*dependono da altri*]'. The sharp antithesis between 'themselves' and 'others' recalls the *virtú-fortuna* antithesis set out in chapter 1. It seems to suggest that virtuous new princes must be capable of radical self-sufficiency, and be willing to ignore— perhaps even run roughshod over—everyone else's beliefs and wishes. As with forced belief, this extreme mode of action sounds unlikely to succeed or bring sound orders in the long run.

But the next sentence modifies the antithesis to suggest a more reasonable prospect. If princes 'depend on their own and are able to use force [*possono forzare*]', we read, 'then it is that they are rarely in peril [*rare volte periclitano*]'. Before, 'innovators' needed to 'stand by themselves'; now they need to 'depend on their own [*dependono da loro propri*]'. The first phrase seems to suggest that new princes must depend on themselves only, controlling and ordering

---

[18] See 'Ironic Techniques' (6).

everything alone. The second implies something quite different: namely, that they should depend on others who are in some sense 'their own' people, and therefore not 'others' in the way that mercenaries, hostile foreigners, or political enemies are *altri*. The phrase 'depending on *their own*' erodes the initial distinction between self-standing and depending on others, and opens up a more realistic alternative to unilateral princely self-assertion. Before, the prospect of 'depending on others' sounded undesirable not just because it involved others, but also because it involved dependence, something control-hungry princes hate to contemplate. In the follow-up sentence, it has become both acceptable and necessary for princes to depend on someone, so long as they 'depend on *their own*' and not on *altri*.

As we'll see later, this subtle shift is extremely important for Machiavelli's understanding of political self-sufficiency. It implies that even the most virtuous princes (and prince-states) need to depend on *some* other people (and states) to achieve their goals. Their *virtú* is shown not in solitary self-assertion, but in their ability to get other people—their own subjects, soldiers, and external allies—firmly on their side, so that they help constitute their 'own arms'. On this more collaborative understanding of political *virtú*, a prince cannot impose whatever 'orders' he pleases without regard for these people's reactions. The firmest orders are founded not on the 'odour' of second-hand greatness, but on reflective knowledge of the human material all princes must work with and how it limits what they can do.

Having set up an extreme go-it-alone ideal of princely *virtú*, then, Machiavelli proceeds to undercut some parts of the ideal while transforming others into something more suited to real-life princes' limitations. His famous discussion of armed and unarmed prophets has a similar structure and purpose. Having said that princes who 'depend on their own and are able to use force are rarely in peril', Machiavelli adds: 'From this it arises that all the armed prophets conquered [*vinsono*] and the unarmed ones were ruined.' He gives a recent example—the only modern one in the chapter—of an unarmed prophet: Girolamo Savonarola, a charismatic preacher whose theocratic politics dominated the Florentine republic for several years after the Medici were expelled in 1494. Savonarola famously imitated the most exceptional of Machiavelli's four *virtuoso* men, claiming like Moses to have prophetic powers and to talk to God. But his popularity took a blow when his prophecies failed, and his devotees could not save him from being burned at the stake by order of Pope Alexander VI in 1498. Thus Savonarola 'was ruined in his new orders as soon as the multitude began not to believe in them'; and 'had no mode for holding firm [*tenere fermi*] those who had believed nor for making unbelievers believe.'

Once again, on a quick reading this passage seems to say that strong military force is the main factor needed to make people 'believe' in a new prince. But the words 'arms' and 'force' seldom are used in a narrowly military sense in the *Prince*. Although military arms are of course needed to defend political orders, chapters 10–14 will argue that good military arms cannot be constituted without good laws and political orders. Savonarola not only lacked an army, but even a legally defined political office in the republic where he exerted such a vast, disturbing influence. Without 'arms' in this wider sense of legitimate political authority, his doomsday prophecies persuaded people to believe in his authority for a time. But without earthly arms to back him up when belief flagged, his appeals to God had no clout.[19] Machiavelli's main point about Savonarola is not that he lacked military arms, but that he relied too much on the 'extraordinary' means of prophecy and appeals to God to get and keep popular support, and not enough on ordinary persuasion and political 'ordering'. His example serves as a warning to princes who think they can overcome unpopularity by claiming to be God's instruments or using religious terror like Savonarola, in pale imitation of Moses.[20]

A LESSER EXAMPLE OF GREAT *VIRTÙ*: HIERO OF SYRACUSE

If princes need examples to imitate, then, they might do better to look for some whose qualities of *virtù* are more proportionate to their human limitations. The good news is that the chapter's last paragraph offers an example of this kind of *virtù*. 'To such high [*alti*] examples' as the four already discussed, Machiavelli now adds 'a lesser [*minore*] example', that of Hiero of Syracuse. Machiavelli's references to his four *eccelentissimi* men bristled with superlatives but remained frustratingly sketchy on detail. Here, in place of all the earlier *altezza*, *grandezza*, and happiness, we get a straightforward description of Hiero's concrete deeds and results. In both modes and ends, the contrasts between greater and 'lesser' examples are striking.

In his modes of action, firstly, Hiero did not act alone, or insist on imposing whatever form he pleased. He first acquired authority 'when the Syracusans were oppressed' and they 'chose [*elessono*] him as their captain'. Afterward he did not 'put himself at the head of introducing new orders', but from successful captaincy 'proved worthy of *being made* their prince'. Since others elected him on his recognized merits as their military and then political leader, his later difficulties were perhaps less than those of men who *put themselves* at the

---

[19] This reading is consistent with the comments about Savonarola's shortcomings in *D* III.30, where Machiavelli says that he lacked legitimate political 'authority' to enforce his will.

[20] Machiavelli expressed sceptical views about Savonarola's methods in an early letter (to Ricciardo Becchi, 9 March 1498, *MF* 8–10) and in *D* I.11 and I.45.

head of new ordering—recalling that nothing is more difficult, doubtful, or dangerous than *making oneself sole* 'introducer'.[21]

Secondly, while he depended on other people to help him build new defences, Hiero knew how to make them into 'his own arms' firmly committed to his leadership. At home in Syracuse, he 'eliminated the old military and ordered a new one', actions we will hear about in more detail in chapter 13. In external affairs, Hiero 'left his old friendships and made new ones' so that 'when he had friendships and soldiers that were *his own*, he could build any edifice [*edificare ogni edifizio*] on top of such a foundation [*fondamento*]'.

Here is the *Prince*'s first use of a word for one of the most important goods that princes should seek to establish: 'foundations' that give a state firmness and security. In Machiavelli's lexicon, to say that someone could build any order on top of his carefully constructed foundations is high praise indeed— much higher than to say that he could introduce 'any form he pleased' or that he made himself or others 'happy'.

Hiero's ends also differed from those of the others in proportion to his more restrained methods. Firstly, instead of seeking to found a great empire or imperial city, he concentrated on building durable, defensive alliances for his country's safety. Polybius writes that unlike inferior rulers who try to keep their options open by frequently changing sides and breaking faith with allies, Hiero early on made a firm alliance with the Romans, and 'for a long time reigned securely in Syracuse, winning the friendly acclaim and good opinion of the Greeks'. Later in the *Prince*, Machiavelli will underline the great importance of firm alliances and the imprudence of opportunistically 'variable' foreign commitments—a precept he maintained throughout his life, and tried to make a cornerstone of Florentine and Italian policy.[22] Whereas Cyrus, Romulus, and Theseus showed insatiable appetites for territorial acquisition, Hiero focused his efforts close to home, seeking the goodwill of other Greeks instead of trying to turn Syracuse into an aggressively expansionist city. The others' empires are considered great because they were very large and dominating. Hiero's *stato* was neither. But it was stable and won great and, unlike the others, unqualified praise from his chroniclers.[23]

A second difference between Hiero's ends and those of the 'greater' others is that he did not seek to establish unrestrained one-man rule or a new dynasty. Although Polybius calls Hiero 'king' (*basileos*) and says he was declared king in Syracuse, his omission of a royal title in his eulogy suggests that Hiero deserved praise not just as ruler, but as a man whose qualities stand out

---

[21] Compare Polybius, who writes that Hiero conducted his government 'with such mildness, and in so lofty a spirit, that the Syracusans, though by no means usually acquiescing in the election of officers by the soldiers, did on this occasion unanimously approve of Hiero as their general.' *PolH* I.8.

[22] Chap. 21.   [23] See *PolH* I.16; Justin XXII.1–XXIII.4.

independently of great titles or positions. Polybius implies that those qualities and nothing else—neither inherited advantages nor other good fortune—made it reasonable that Hiero should rule. This point is spelt out in another ancient account, that of the Roman historian Justin, whom Machiavelli quotes in Latin with his own commentary. Hiero, he says, 'was of such *virtú*, even in private fortune, that he who wrote of him said "that he lacked nothing of being a king except a kingdom"'.[24] Here, then, is an example of *virtú* so great that it does not need the external trappings of greatness to be recognized. On Justin's and Machiavelli's accounts, it is unclear whether or not Hiero actually had the title of king, as Polybius says he had. But if his *virtú* so self-evidently merited kingly standing, it matters little whether he was or wasn't king in name.

Machiavelli makes the same point in his Dedication to the *Discourses*. 'Writers praise Hiero the Syracusan when he was a private individual more than Perseus the Macedonian when he was king,' he declares, 'for Hiero lacked nothing other than the principality to be a prince while the other had no part of a king other than the kingdom.' Here Machiavelli goes further than Justin in separating true princely or kingly qualities—that is, virtues—from mere names and positions. He suggests that men who are 'princely' in the sense that their virtue makes them deserve to rule need not possess kingdoms or principalities to make their *virtú* manifest. At the same time, he says that he chose to dedicate the *Discourses* to young friends who, unlike the *Prince*'s young Medici dedicatee, are not princes—but 'for their infinite good parts deserve to be'. For 'men wishing to judge rightly', he explains, 'have to esteem those who are liberal, not those who can be; and likewise those who know how, not those who can govern a kingdom without knowing how'.[25] Hiero thus forms an important link between the *Prince* and the *Discourses*, as a prime example of the truly praiseworthy *virtú* needed to support good orders in principalities or republics. This understanding of *virtú* sets reflective prudence and moral qualities far above boundless ambitions or great reputations.

The more we compare Machiavelli's greater and lesser models, the more Hiero's human-sized *virtú* looks like the more praiseworthy model for merely mortal princes. Hiero 'went through a great deal of effort [*durò assai fatica*] to acquire', Machiavelli tells us, but needed 'little to maintain'. The word *fatica*, meaning arduous effort, relates to an agent's own activity, and thus suggests *virtú*. The word used for the other princes' hardships was *difficultà*, which suggests external obstacles to such activity. The more difficulties princes face over time, the less virtuous their 'modes' must be. Cyrus, Romulus, and the others faced greater difficulties after they acquired because people opposed their 'new orders and modes'. Neither Machiavelli nor ancient historians mention comparable opposition to Hiero, who took the harder road at first

---

[24] Justin, XXIII.4.   [25] *D* Ded.

by showing that he deserved to be elected leader. The chapter's movement from the extraordinary *virtú* of Cyrus and Romulus to the ordinary *virtú* of Hiero's *fatica* draws princely readers from their initial, too-lofty ambitions toward a more mature knowledge of what it takes to build good foundations.[26]

Machiavelli says that his example of Hiero 'will have some proportion to the others'. Proportion is not identity or equality, but quality in relation to an object's size. If the extraordinary *virtú* of the first four was fitting for princes with supersized or divinely guided ambitions, Hiero's example presents *virtú* and greatness on a more modest scale, with 'ordinary' modes used to pursue more limited ends. His *virtú* and *grandezza* look less impressive than the others'. Hiero is not the most famous of heroes; he did not found a sprawling new empire, impose whatever he pleased on yielding matter, or get elevated to the rank of demigod or prophet. He merely helped rid Syracusans of a decadent tyranny, replaced useless mercenary forces with a strong civilian army, forged new alliances that made for stable peace, and improved relations with other Greeks. All these achievements fall far short of the loftiest princely ambitions. But they are easier to imitate than anything the others did, or are said to have done. And they resemble the measures that Machiavelli recommended for Florence and Italy throughout his life. His deceptively low-key praise for Hiero chimes far better with his desire to find a realistic starting-point to build up Italian strength than his apparent idealization of Cyrus, Romulus, and the rest. More than those other princes, Hiero showed a fine sense of proportion in gearing his own actions to his own limits, and to those set by the conditions he had to work with: his own people on the one hand, and foreign powers on the other.

The very concreteness of Machiavelli's description retrospectively deflates the hyperbole he lavished on the 'most excellent' others. At the same time, it ennobles the 'ordinary', unremarkable-looking qualities that create and maintain good orders. In Machiavelli's texts as in real life, the most striking words often clash with the actions being described. The actions praised most noisily are often problematic, while the most virtuous deeds are mentioned almost in passing or *sotto voce*. Machiavelli's calling Hiero 'lesser' masks a judgement that shines through in what he says about him and the greater others: namely, that when it comes to human *virtú*, firmness is worth more than *grandezza*.

---

[26] Compare Machiavelli's subtle word-shift when describing the relations between Hiero, the others, and *fortuna*: the others 'had' nothing from fortune but opportunity that 'gave' (*dette*) the others material, while Hiero 'knew [*conobbe*] nothing from fortune but opportunity'. Even in seizing opportunities he relied, it seems, more on his own knowledge of what to do—as he will again in chapter 13's remark that Hiero 'knew immediately' (*conobbe subito*) how to deal with useless mercenaries—than on fortune's gifts.

7

Fortune

Of new principalities that are acquired by others' arms and fortune

This chapter has long been considered as pivotal for understanding Machiavelli's concept of *virtú*, and indeed his whole project in the *Prince*. It is also one of the most controversial chapters in the book. In its portrait of Cesare Borgia, many readers have seen Machiavelli's ideal model of a *virtuoso* prince. Others, especially among the book's earlier readers, saw in Machiavelli's apparent praise of such an 'execrable hero' a sure sign of his ironic intentions.[1]

Cesare Borgia (1475 or 1476–1507) was the second son of the Spaniard Rodrigo Borgia (1431–1503), who became Pope Alexander VI in 1492. When still in his early twenties Cesare's father made him head of the Papal army, encouraging him to carve out a state of his own in the Romagna, a region of Italy sandwiched between Tuscany in the south and Lombardy and Venice to the north. With the help of French armies and Swiss mercenaries, Cesare attacked and deposed many local rulers. He then conceived wider ambitions to control Tuscany and Florence. In 1502, the Florentine government sent Machiavelli as an envoy to Borgia's court to dissuade him from carrying out threats to attack their city.

In trying to size up the seriousness of these threats, Machiavelli analysed Borgia's personality and behaviour in his diplomatic reports sent back home. His judgements are often ambiguous. Since there was a risk that Florence's enemies might intercept these dispatches, it would have been imprudent to pass strong judgements on a prickly young leader whom Machiavelli was meant to soften up. In the years after Borgia's fall from grace in 1503 and death in 1507, Machiavelli wrote a highly dramatic short account of one of his most infamous actions: the murder of his former allies at Sinigaglia.[2] This literary work neither praises nor criticizes Borgia—at least not unequivocally.

The *Prince*, too, sends bewilderingly mixed signals about Borgia. On the one hand, Machiavelli describes him as a prince who both acquired and lost his

---

[1] Rousseau (1964/1762), III.6.
[2] Machiavelli, 'Description of the Mode used by Duke Valentino in Killing Vitellozzo Vitelli, Oliverotto da Fermo, and others'.

state by means of fortune and 'others' arms', not by *virtú*. This alone casts doubt on the view that Machiavelli treats Borgia as an ideal model of princely *virtú*: if he did, why didn't he include him under that heading in chapter 6? On the other hand, although he memorably describes Borgia's deceptions and assassinations and admits that his rule lasted only a few years, Machiavelli seems to praise Borgia more effusively than any other individual in the *Prince*. He declares that he does not 'know how to reproach' Borgia, and says that 'he should be put forward . . . to be imitated by all those who have risen to empire through fortune and the arms of others'. Although Borgia failed to maintain his *stato*, Machiavelli suggests that if he had not backed the wrong successor to the papacy after his father died, Cesare could have prolonged his rule.

When evaluating these contradictory impressions, it helps to pay close attention to how Machiavelli applies his standard of fortune-or-*virtú* when describing Borgia's and others' actions. In fact, the chapter starts with an unusually long discussion of that standard. This general frame for Machiavelli's examples seldom gets the attention it deserves; the colourful particulars tend to arouse far livelier interest. Yet general standards supply the key needed to understand the chapter's famous paradoxes and infamous advice.

HIGH-FLYING PRINCES OF FORTUNE

Chapter 6 told us that virtuous modes make acquiring hard and maintaining easy, while fortune-reliant modes have the opposite effect. Chapter 7 begins by reiterating this view of fortune-dependence:

> Those who become princes from private individual solely by fortune become so with little trouble, but maintain themselves with much. They have no difficulty along the path because they fly [*volano*] there, but all the difficulties arise when they are in place.

The image of fortunate people 'flying' recalls the last chapter's image of princely archers with soaring arrows, aiming for an *altezza* that their own *virtú* could not reach. That high fliers like these often make huge gains, yet fail to hold them, was a recurring subject of Machiavelli's earlier poetry:

> If your eyes light on what is beyond, in one panel Caesar [Cesare] and Alexander you will see among those who were happy [*felici*] while alive . . .
>
> Yet nevertheless the coveted harbour one of the two failed to reach, and the other, covered with wounds, in his enemy's shadow was slain.
>
> After this appear countless men who, that they might fall to earth with a heavier crash, with this goddess have climbed to the highest heights [*costei altissimo*].
>
> Among these, captive, dead, and mangled, lie Cyrus and Pompey, though fortune carried both of them up to the heavens.

Their fate is summed up in a feral image of flight and fall:

> Have you ever seen anywhere how a raging eagle moves, driven by hunger and fasting?
>
> And how he carries a tortoise on high [*alto*], that the force of its fall may break it, and he can feed on the dead flesh?
>
> So Fortune not that a man may remain on high [*in alto*] carries him up, but that as he plunges down she may delight, and as he falls may weep.[3]

By likening *fortuna* to a raging eagle and high-soaring men to tortoises, Machiavelli slaps down the flattering self-images of ambitious men. They may see themselves as the more virile partner in their collaborations with fortune, pushing and shoving her to get what they want. But the truth is that she is always dominant, while they are like land-dwelling, brittle-backed reptiles, absurdly trying to imitate the king of all birds of prey.

What, in concrete terms, does it mean to acquire a state by fortune? Chapter 7's first, long paragraph makes it clear that this isn't a matter of mysterious, incalculable forces. Machiavelli analyses the notion in terms of quite specific conditions and actions. Previous chapters have already discussed some such conditions: new princes may be fortunate in finding other governments or peoples weak, disordered, or downtrodden, so that they can easily take advantage and seize power over them. Now he identifies other ways to acquire by fortune, saying that 'such princes come to be when a state is granted [*concesso*] to someone either for money or by the grace [*o per danari o per grazia*] of whoever grants it'. He gives two ancient examples. The first harks back to chapter 4's Persian king Darius, who set up client-rulers in Greek cities 'so that they might hold on to [*tenessino*] those cities for his security and glory'. In the second example, men fly to great heights not in the claws of a greater ruler, but with the help of those under their command, as in Rome 'those emperors were made who... attained the empire by corrupting the soldiers [*per corruzione de' soldati*]'. Whereas the Darius example illustrates acquiring by another's grace, the Roman one illustrates acquiring by money— using 'corruption' to buy military support for one's princely ambitions.

WHY ACQUIRING BY FORTUNE CREATES
FUTURE DIFFICULTIES

At first Machiavelli adopts the tones of neutral description, seeming not to judge these methods of acquiring as either prudent or imprudent. But appearances of neutrality are undermined by the word *corruzione*. If to say that someone acquired by money or another's 'grace' may imply no normative

---

[3] *Di Fortuna*, lines 160–83.

judgement, to say that someone corrupted others for his own ends goes beyond the purely descriptive. To corrupt something or someone is to weaken their good orders; to corrupt one's own city's soldiers is to poison the very foundations of civil order.[4] Among the 'private individuals' who became emperor by corrupting soldiers, the most famous was Julius Caesar, who Machiavelli criticizes elsewhere for dealing the death blow to his beloved Roman republic.[5] By treating corruption as among the main forms of fortune-dependence, then, Machiavelli gives his account of fortunate acquiring an unmistakably negative tinge.

Fortune-dependent modes are bad policy, since they breed future troubles for those who use them. For 'these persons', Machiavelli says of men like Darius' puppet-princes and corrupting emperors, 'rest simply on the will [*volontà*] and fortune of whoever has given a state to them, which are two very inconstant and unstable things [*cose volubilissime e instabili*]'. These unstable beginnings make it almost prohibitively hard to build anything lasting.

This is partly, Machiavelli tells us, a matter of knowledge. Most men who acquire in these ways 'do not know how' to hold what fortune handed them on a platter, 'because if one is not a man of great ingenuity [*ingegno*] and *virtú*, it is not reasonable, that having always lived in private fortune, he should know how to command'. Never having to prove their knowledge of how to govern as a condition for taking up leadership—as Hiero did, being chosen prince after proving his leadership skills beforehand—men who 'fly' to their high-ranking new job are often inexperienced and ignorant of statesmanship.

Moreover, 'they cannot hold that rank because they do not have forces that can be friendly and faithful [*amiche e fedeli*] to them'. This reminds us that, as the last chapter suggested, even the most powerful princes must depend on some other people. The question is which ones—and whether or not they are firmly 'yours', in your camp for the long haul. Virtuous men like Hiero depend on people who make commitments to them, based on common purposes and their own judgements about a prince's merit. Fortune-dependent men win wider support more quickly, since it's easier to get people on side by greasing their palms than by demonstrating that you deserve to be given power. But support gained through bribes and favours is less reliable. It tends to fall away as soon as money runs short and you lose favour, or if your enemies offer your puppet-princes a better deal, or if those princes' subjects rise up and topple them.

For Machiavelli, the difference between virtuous reliance on one's own people and un-virtuous reliance on others is epitomized by non-mercenary vs. mercenary armies. The fatal flaw in mercenary troops, we will learn in chapter 12, is that they are only motivated by pay, and care nothing for your state. When not paid whatever they demand, they abandon you. If on the other

---

[4] See chaps 17 and 19.
[5] Most fiercely, though mixed with bitterly ironic praise, in *D* I.10.

hand an army is 'your own', it will have deep-rooted incentives to fight for you, so that no pay or favours are needed. This is high-quality *virtú* that needs no admixture of fortune to maintain it, 'ordered' by a prince who knows how to build lasting friendships and fidelity.

Time and effort are needed to build new friendships and faith, as people tend not to believe in new things until they have a long experience of their benefits. The too-quick, too-easy character of fortunate acquiring is a further cause of instability, for 'states that have come to be suddenly [*subito*], like all other things in nature that are born and grow quickly [*presto*], cannot have roots and branches, so that the first adverse weather eliminates them'.

HOW TO HOLD WHAT YOU ACQUIRE BY FORTUNE: SWITCH TO RELYING ON *VIRTÚ*

The chapter's opening general remarks are almost entirely sceptical about the long-term chances for princes who acquire by fortunate modes. Such princes, it seems clear, deserve less praise than those who put in the hard work of acquiring by *virtú*. But do they deserve blame if they fail to hold what they acquire? If they had no choice in how they manage their states but were forced to depend on others after acquiring them, eventual failure would simply be inevitable, and less culpable than if they could have done differently.

But Machiavelli makes it clear that princes who acquire states by means of fortune *do* have a choice in how they try to hold them. The 'first adverse weather eliminates them' he writes, '*unless* those who have suddenly become princes have so much *virtú* that they know immediately how [*sappino subito*] to prepare to conserve what fortune has placed in their laps'. Princes of exceptional *virtú*, then, can turn things around. They may start by being 'granted' a state by another's grace or weakness, or by bribing supporters—then improve their prospects by abandoning these fortune-dependent modes and creating more self-reliant foundations for their power. In this way, 'the foundations that others have laid before becoming princes they lay afterwards'. It follows that those who do *not* opt to shift from fortunate to virtuous modes deserve some degree of blame. Those who do choose to shift modes but still fail to hold power, as was the case with Cesare Borgia, are harder to judge.

What qualities of *virtú* enable princes to keep what fortune throws in their laps? One of the most important is a kind of knowledge rarely found in princes-by-fortune. They must 'know immediately how to prepare to conserve' fortune's inconstant gifts. They must know, that is, how to move from unstable beginnings to stable foundations. This knowledge requires more than quick thinking. It also requires foresight to anticipate the very great difficulties that follow on easy acquiring, and humility to avoid the self-flattering illusion that you acquired by *virtú* what in fact came from fortune. A fortune-gifted prince needs to know, at the time when he acquires and not later, that his hold is perilously fragile. He needs to realize that whether he won his state by others' weakness, special favours, or by money, none of these methods will suffice to hold it. If he changes his 'modes', he has some chance of keeping power. If he wants to change modes but never quite understands how to do so, he will go the sad way of all fortune's favourites.

The importance of knowing 'immediately' should not be underestimated.[6] Firstly, since things born suddenly lack roots, a prince who delays the requisite hard work makes it easier for his opponents to prepare to act against him, and gives new subjects reasons to doubt the solidity of his rule. Secondly, fortune spoils its favourites. The longer they rely on it, the less they learn about how to rely on their own resources, and the more they succumb to the illusion that they owe their successes to their own *virtú*. Finally, there is a self-corroding quality in the methods Machiavelli links to fortune. Once you start courting supporters by money and favours, you create expectations that you will keep forking out more. When one day your coffers run dry, or you have no new favours to hand out, you become far less popular than if you'd never tried to buy support in the first place.[7] Like the fabled wheel of fortune, the same policy that helped you soar to greatness now casts you down, destroying whatever fantasies of control you once had.

EXAMPLES: FRANCESCO SFORZA AND CESARE BORGIA

Machiavelli now presents two examples from recent Italian history. Francesco Sforza (1401–1466) began as a mercenary captain who, taking advantage of others' weakness, seized power from the Milanese dukes who had hired him to fight their wars. Yet having become prince in this fortune-dependent way, Sforza worked 'by proper means and with a great *virtú* of his own [*per li debiti mezzi e con una grande sua virtú*]', so that the power 'he had acquired with a thousand pains [*affani*] he maintained with little effort [*con poca fatica mantenne*]'.[8]

Machiavelli tells us more about this change of modes in the *Florentine Histories*. When still a mercenary, Sforza promised Cosimo de' Medici that he would help the Florentines fight a campaign to assert control over another freedom-loving city, Lucca. But Sforza 'changed his mind with his fortune and, when he became a duke, wanted to enjoy that state in the peace that he had

---

[6] As seen again in chap. 13.   [7] See chap. 16 on liberality.

[8] Other Sforza references in the *Prince* are more ambivalent; see chaps 12 and 20. After all, Sforza remains a deeply flawed model of political *virtú*: he still acquired his state by fortune, and *virtú*-deficient modes of acquiring always make it harder to maintain well.

acquired with war. Nor,' Machiavelli continues, 'after he became duke, did he wage any wars other than those necessary to defend himself.'[9] In short, Sforza shed his dependence on fortune by limiting his ambitions to what was strictly necessary for defence, and seeking stability and peace.[10]

This suggests that fortunate princes show their *virtú* by their choice of ends as well as means. Recall the maxim set out in chapter 3 that while the desire to acquire is natural, those who desire more than they can hold are liable to be blamed. Princes should therefore consider whether the state that fortune tosses in their laps is too difficult to hold. They should be prepared to scale back their acquisitions and concentrate on what they can realistically do. Machiavelli reiterates this view in his novella *Castruccio Castracani*, whose mercenary-turned-prince hero admits on his deathbed that while he leaves his heir 'a large state,' because 'I leave it to you weak and insecure, I am very sorry'. Had he realized that 'fortune would cut off in the middle of the journey' his path 'to that glory that I promised to have through all my happy successes [*felici successi*]', Castruccio would have striven to have 'fewer enemies and less envy' by making friends of peoples he subdued and living his life 'more quietly'. His son would then have inherited 'a state, if smaller, without a doubt more secure and more solid [*più sicuro e più fermo*]'.[11]

Where Machiavelli says Sforza succeeded, however, young Borgia failed. A classic technique of ironic appraisal is to avoid criticizing a subject directly, while setting him alongside someone else who is praised for qualities that are pointedly *not* noted in the other. Machiavelli's introduction to Borgia has a rather chilling effect when set alongside the unreserved warmth of his description of Sforza. The latter consists of clear, simple, robust praise: having acquired his state, Sforza maintained it 'with a great *virtú* of his own'. Machiavelli's first remarks about Borgia are neither admiring nor clear. He omits any reference to Borgia's *virtú*; indeed, he remains reserved about his *virtú* throughout the chapter. On the contrary, Borgia first acquired then lost his state 'through the fortune of his father'. Even his fortune, in both acquiring and losing, is not his own but someone else's.

Machiavelli might seem to temper the contrast when he goes on to say that 'the duke' acquired and lost with his father's fortune 'notwithstanding that he made use of every deed [*usassi ogni opera*] and did all those things that should be done by a prudent and virtuous man'. But on closer scrutiny, this only heightens the impression that Borgia was deficient in virtuous self-mastery.

---

[9] Machiavelli cannot resist adding ironically that, 'This was cause for very great annoyance to Cosimo' *FH* VII.6.

[10] Sforza played a key role forming the Italian League, a defensive alliance of Italian states that helped to stabilize most of Italy while it lasted.

[11] In a manner typical for fortune-dependent men, however, Castruccio (*CC*, 553) persists in blaming fortune both for cutting his life short and for not 'giving' him 'so much judgement that I could early know her, nor so much time that I could overcome her'.

Machiavelli could simply have said that he *was* a prudent and virtuous man. Instead he goes to uncomfortably wordy lengths not to say this. Saying that he 'made use' of deeds implies that he merely imitated what 'should be' done by such a man rather than following his own judgement, thus achieving only a second-hand imitation of genuine prudence and *virtú*.

Another small but significant touch tells us more about the difference between Sforza's *virtú* and Borgia's reliance on fortune than any overt comparison. Machiavelli calls Sforza by his Christian name, Francesco. Borgia, however, is not Cesare but 'Duke Valentino' as he was called, Machiavelli says, 'by the vulgar' (*dal volgo*). Rather absurdly, readers are put on a first-name basis with a highly respected, *virtuoso* elder duke of Milan, now deceased—but must bear with having the very young Borgia, whose controversial rule lasted only a few years, addressed in vulgar mode throughout the chapter as 'the duke' (*il duca*). A further irony is that this title was conferred not by his own subjects or an Italian power but by 'others': a gift from a foreign power, France, not in recognition of Cesare's own merits but in exchange for favours from his father.[12]

Who are 'the vulgar' that Machiavelli mimics in this ironic naming game? When Borgia first appeared in the *Prince*, Machiavelli said that he was 'popularly called' (*chiamato popularmente*) Valentino, without the 'duke'.[13] Both vulgar and popular nicknames Italianize the foreign *Valentinois*, but the popular one drops the noble title, and thus drags Borgia down to the demotic level instead of elevating him above the people. Machiavelli's 'vulgar', then, is not a synonym for the people, or for the popular classes as distinct from social or intellectual élites. In chapter 18 we are told that the vulgar are easily taken in by impressive appearances. Thus it seems that anyone who mistakes outward appearances, titles, or self-important displays for true qualities may be called *volgo*. Together with Machiavelli's insistence on calling Sforza Francesco and not 'the duke', this recalls the last chapter's closing remarks on Hiero, who needed neither title nor kingdom to show his kingly *virtú*. The not-vulgar know that true *virtú* needs no honorifics. By calling Borgia only by his foreign title, which so impressed the vulgar, Machiavelli slyly hints that his *virtú* was less self-evident. It needed a glossy label to announce itself, whereas Francesco's and Hiero's did not.

The first really positive thing we hear about Cesare is that he 'made great foundations for future power [*grandi fondamenti alla future potenza*]'. This sounds like very high praise indeed. Yet Machiavelli has so far given us few reasons to believe it without further evidence—and good reasons to doubt it, since 'notwithstanding' all Borgia's efforts he still failed to 'put roots in those states that the arms and fortune of others had granted him'. As the last chapter noted, one of Machiavelli's favourite techniques of ironic praise is to lavish good words on a subject while describing his actions in ways that jar with the praise. When

---

[12] His official title was Duc de Valentinois, conferred by Louis XII in 1498.
[13] At the end of chap. 3.

Machiavelli declares that Borgia lay 'great foundations' for his power, readers must weigh up these good words against the ensuing account of his deeds.

If Sforza pulled off the feat of converting a state acquired by fortune into a state maintained by his own *virtù*, and Borgia did not, why does Machiavelli make Borgia his main example in the chapter and devote so many pages to his efforts— far more than any other single individual in the *Prince*? Machiavelli says that the close study of his actions can teach important lessons to new princes:

> Thus, if one considers all the steps of the duke, one will see that he had made for himself great foundations for future power, which I do not judge superfluous to discuss; for I do not know what better teaching [*precetti*] I could give to a new prince than the example of his actions. And if his orders did not bring profit to him, it was not his fault [*non fu sua colpa*], because this arose from an extraordinary and extreme malignity of fortune [*una estraordinaria ed estrema malignità di fortuna*].

A common reading of this passage is that Machiavelli made Borgia his prime example in order to illustrate fortune's utterly random power over human affairs. If even he could be hurled down by *fortuna*, this serves as a warning to all princes that brute bad luck can kill even their best efforts. On this view Borgia's ultimate failure had nothing to do with deficient *virtù*, and everything to do with forces beyond his control.

But this fatalistic view of fortune's power is hard to square with Machiavelli's analyses of how that power works through specific types of voluntary action. He has just told us that to rely on fortune is a choice, involving concrete measures: paying money, giving favours, or taking advantage of others' weaknesses. By spelling out these measures in the chapter's framing remarks, Machiavelli demystifies the metaphor *fortuna*. He sets in clear view the choices that lead people to lose control of what they gained by such means and shows that what they blame on bad fortune is often the product of their own actions or negligence. Is it plausible that having already exposed such excuses as irresponsible, Machiavelli now wants to suggest that there are notable exceptions, and that some men can reasonably blame their failures on fortune? Instead of taking Machiavelli's fatalistic judgement about Borgia's failure at face value, we should take it as a challenge to look for a more down-to-earth explanation in the details of Machiavelli's lengthy account. How well judged were the duke's actions, we should ask, if his aim was to break the apron strings of his father's fortune and secure *virtuoso* independence?

CESARE DECIDES TO GO IT ALONE

Machiavelli's narration of Borgia's deeds starts by going back to the source of his fickle fortune: Pope Alexander VI's ambitions for his son. 'Alexander had very many difficulties', Machiavelli tells us, 'both present and future, when he decided to make his son the duke great.' In particular, since 'he could not trust' those Italian arms he might otherwise have made to serve (*servire*) him, it was 'necessary to upset [*si turbassino*] those orders and to disorder [*disordinare*] the states of Italy so as to be able to make himself lord securely of part of them'.

The necessity to upset Italian orders was not absolute, but relative to Alexander's personal aims: to get others to 'serve' him and to make his son great. Machiavelli does not ask whether these were reasonable aims. But his description of the pope's modes—to upset existing orders and to 'disorder' Italian states—casts doubt on the reasonableness of the whole project. The clear implication is that the pope placed private and family aims above any wider concerns for order, to the extent of seeking to disorder Italy.[14] And this was not because he needed to create disorder before he could introduce *better* orders. Machiavelli quite pointedly omits any reference to new orders that the pope hoped to impose; his whole account of Alexander's activity exudes turbulence, instability, and distrust, with no evidence that the pope took constructive measures to find trustworthy allies in Italy. On the contrary, he greatly weakened Italians' trust in him by consenting to let France's king Charles VIII into Italy in 1494. The king's vast armies harassed and terrified locals as they streamed southward through the peninsula, while Charles demanded huge sums of money from the Florentines and others to spare them further trouble. According to Machiavelli's *Decennale*, the pope opened the door to this bullying in exchange for Charles' promise to give him a free hand in the Romagna.[15]

In short, Machiavelli shows little sympathy for the pope's policies in the *Prince* or anywhere else. His *Decennale* stresses Alexander's shortage of either practical or moral *virtú*, claiming that 'because by himself alone the pope could do nothing great, he set out to win the new [French] king's favour'. Alexander himself was thus dependent on others' arms. He was a man of fortune who used as his instrument another man, his son, who depended in turn on his father's dependent fortune. And when he died, 'slain by Heaven' for his sins:

> . . . the soul of the glorious Alexander, that it might have rest, departed to the blessed spirits;

> his sacred footsteps were followed by his three dear and intimate handmaids:

> Luxury, Simony, Cruelty.[16]

With his father's and French help, then, young Borgia 'acquired Romagna'. But he still faced two obstacles that 'prevented him from maintaining that and going further ahead'. Firstly, he did not trust the 'arms' he had relied on to take Romagna, those commanded by Rome's powerful Orsini family. Secondly,

---

[14] Pope Alexander's private aims are stressed in chap. 11.
[15] *Decennale* I, lines 169–74.   [16] *Decennale* I, lines 169–71, 463, 442–7.

although the French supplied him with additional arms and Borgia now wanted to attack Tuscany, he was impeded by the French king, who 'made him desist from that campaign'. So he decided 'to depend no longer on the arms and fortune of others'.

Machiavelli still doesn't say that Borgia thereby sought to depend on 'his own' arms or *virtú*, as Sforza did. After taking Romagna, Borgia had a choice: he could either invest time and energy in consolidating what he had already acquired—the Romagna was extremely unstable and in need of reordering—or spread his new-found wings and fly toward new acquisitions. He chose the second of these options. First, he attacked Bologna, a city whose established orders were in far better shape than those of some other cities. This audacious move, Machiavelli says, made Borgia's Orsini troops fight 'coolly'—implying that they had good reason to go cold on their commander, whose judgement they increasingly mistrusted. Next he took Urbino, another controversial move, and then attacked Tuscany, provoking the French king, hitherto his chief supporter, to put his foot down and oppose this latest ambition. Machiavelli does not say that these attempts to acquire more and more were unwise, although they came so soon after Borgia's first, already large and very tricky, acquisition. But the contrast with recent examples of stabilizing *virtú*—Hiero with his 'lesser' ambitions to establish good orders and lasting security, Sforza who scaled down his initial gains for similar virtuous ends—silently questions Borgia's prudence.

If his ends post-acquiring were not obviously oriented toward stable ordering, what means did Borgia conceive to overcome his difficulties, so that he would 'depend no longer on the arms and fortune of others'? Machiavelli describes three things he did toward this end. First, he sought to dampen partisan strife between Rome's two great families, the Orsini and Colonna, by luring the adherents of both parties to become his supporters. He did this by means of positive incentives: making the gentlemen who backed Orsini or Colonna factions into 'his gentlemen' (*gentili uomini*), giving them 'large allowances', and honouring them with 'commands and government posts', so that 'their partisan affections [*affezione delle parti*] were eliminated and all turned toward the duke'.

This policy seems to have some elements of *virtú*, particularly in trying to forge new 'arms' of Borgia's 'own' to replace untrustworthy Orsini arms. A few chapters on, however, Machiavelli warns new princes of the risks of relying on 'the great' (*grandi*), that is, the upper classes or 'gentlemen', when trying to create arms of their own; it is far more prudent, he says, to rely on the people. Neither here nor elsewhere does Machiavelli say that Borgia also had a policy for making his new subjects a component of his own arms—a very serious omission, as later chapters stress. Yet even without reading ahead, something smells fishy in the devices Borgia uses to get these gentlemen on side: buying their affections with large allowances and public posts. How is this different from what Darius or the Roman emperors did, according to the chapter's first paragraph? And if Borgia's modes resemble theirs, how could they help him to break his dependence on fortune?

His second move toward this end also focused on the *grandi*: an attempt to eliminate the 'heads' of the Orsini faction, having already 'dispersed' those of the Colonna. Borgia fought back after the Orsini incited 'rebellion in Urbino, tumults in Romagna', and created 'infinite dangers for the duke'. He 'overcame them all' Machiavelli reports, 'with the aid of the French'. While the desire to eliminate enemies sounds fair enough, the question is whether Borgia was able to do so with his own arms and *virtú*. And the answer is no: he was saved with the help of French arms, *l'armi d'altri*. Machiavelli's 1504 *Decennale* had put this in more stinging sardonic language: 'since Valentino could not escape' from his enemies' assaults, 'he had to cover himself again with the shield of France, that he might avoid the hazard'.[17] 'And when his reputation had been restored', Machiavelli writes in the *Prince*, 'he trusted neither France nor other external forces.'[18] The first clause tells us, in passing, that Borgia's fraught dealings with the Orsini and continued dependence on France damaged his reputation. The very measures he took with a view to ending dependence forced him to depend again on others' arms. If Machiavelli led us to expect a glowing report in his preface to this account, where he said that Borgia 'used better' (*usò meglio*) an opportunity that 'came well', what follows deflates these expectations.

Mistrust is emerging as a deep influence on Borgia's actions. First he mistrusted the Orsini whose arms helped him to power, now the French whose arms helped him overcome 'infinite dangers' posed by the Orsini. Readers might start to wonder whether Borgia will ever trust anyone enough to constitute arms of his own. Will his next move at last seek to build trust with other, reliable people who can help him do this? In his third attempt to go it alone, not wanting to test the fidelity of French or other 'external forces', Borgia 'turned to deceit' (*si volse alli inganni*).[19] He 'knew so well how to dissimulate his spirit [*dissimulare l'animo*]' that the Orsini were reconciled with him in 'their simplicity' (*simplicità*). By 'giving' money, garments, and horses to Signor Paolo Orsini, he lured his enemies into his hands at Sinigaglia.

Machiavelli says no more about this incident here. But it was still notorious at the time of writing, epitomizing for the general public Borgia's fabled treachery and ruthlessness. Whether or not Machiavelli admired the cunning that set this trap, notice that Borgia is still using the standard modes of

---

[17] *Decennale* I, lines 391–3.

[18] In *Decennale* I, lines 427–9 we read that after this the pope and his son sought 'again a companion who would give them other states as booty, not seeing how with the Gaul they could gain more'. Both Borgias, Machiavelli suggests, still counted on other powers to 'give' them states.

[19] Borgia's frequent 'turning' (*volse*) links his actions to the constant turns of fortune.

fortune—bribery with gifts and favours—to liberate himself from others' arms. Unlike Darius and certain Roman emperors, however, he gives gifts to and befriends those whose lives he later takes.

PACIFYING ROMAGNA: THE PIECES IN THE PIAZZA OF REMIRRO DE ORCO

Machiavelli assures us, nonetheless, that all these efforts eventually paid off. Summing up the results so far, he says that 'when these [Orsini] heads had been eliminated, and their partisans had been turned into friends, the duke had laid very good foundations for his power [*gittati assai buoni fondamenti*], since he had all Romagna with the duchy of Urbino'. Then 'it seemed to him [*parendoli*], especially, that he had acquired the friendship of Romagna, and that he had gained all those peoples to himself since they had begun to taste well-being [*bene essere*]'.

Machiavelli has given us reason to doubt that what 'seemed' to be the case to Borgia is true. It remains unclear how buying off gentlemen and getting rid of the heads of factions helped him to tackle the much larger problems of building foundations, especially the need to win over newly acquired peoples. In contrast to what he says about Borgia's own self-flattering perception, Machiavelli's diplomatic dispatches report that Borgia's subjects in Romagna were greatly disaffected by his tendency to favour his soldiers over the people—violating a maxim set out in chapter 19 that contemporary princes should favour the people more than the soldiers, and indeed make people 'their own' soldiers. Instead of using the most prudent 'mode' to build his 'own arms', Borgia's rule had created a rift between 'his' private and mercenary arms and his subjects.[20] As for how Borgia's foundations were laid, Machiavelli uses a colloquial phrase, *gittati i fondamenti*, which may be translated 'laid foundations' but also carries a sense of 'throwing' or 'tossing' them up: Machiavelli sometimes uses the word *gittare*, to throw, in conjunction with games of fortune that involve throwing dice, and in one of his favourite fortune-related phrases, *gittati in grembo*, 'thrown into one's lap'.[21]

Nevertheless, it seems that genuine improvements were made in the government of Romagna under Borgia's watch. He had, Machiavelli tells us, acquired a province 'quite full of robberies, quarrels, and every other kind of insolence' ruled by 'impotent lords who had been readier to despoil their subjects than to correct them, and had given their subjects matter for disunion,

---

[20] *Legations* 9 October 1502. As Mattingly (1958) points out, Machiavelli says nothing positive about Borgia's 'orders' in his reports.
[21] See chap. 3; *D* II.21.

not for union'. Quite reasonably, Borgia 'judged it necessary to give it good government, if he wanted to reduce it to peace and obedience to a kingly arm [*uno braccio regio*]'. In a dramatic prelude to an even more dramatic episode, Machiavelli announces: 'And because this point is deserving of notice and of being imitated by others, I do not want to leave it out.' All this sounds promising indeed. What means did Borgia employ, then, to correct and unify his new subjects?

He started, Machiavelli tells us, by installing a new governor in Romagna, Remirro de Orco, 'a cruel and ready [*crudele e espedito*] man, to whom he gave the fullest power [*potestà*]'. Then, after Remirro had successfully imposed order, Borgia seized on a pretext to accuse and then violently destroy his agent. This enabled him to rule a freshly pacified state without incurring popular blame. The incident is often thought to illustrate a classic piece of Machiavellian wisdom: use others to do your dirty work, so that necessary violence is used without making people hate you. This reading assumes that Borgia had cleverly thought the whole plan through from the outset.

But this is not what Machiavelli suggests. 'In a short time,' he writes, 'Remirro reduced [Romagna] to peace and unity, with the very greatest reputation for himself.' Only after this does Borgia recognize the risks he has incurred by giving such a successful governor fullest *potestà*, a word that implies legally limited authority rather than licence. 'Then,' not before, 'the duke judged that such excessive authority was not necessary, because he feared that it might become hateful [*odiosa*].'

Hateful for whom? Machiavelli does not say. Most readers assume that he *only* means hateful to the people of Romagna. After all, he says that Borgia 'knew that past rigours [*rigorosità*] had generated some hatred' for Remirro, and wanted 'to purge the spirits of that people and to gain them entirely to himself [*guadagnarseli in tutto*]' by showing that 'any cruelty' came not from him, but 'from the harsh [*acerba*] nature of his minister'. This is undoubtedly part of his meaning: Remirro imposed high taxes on the local rich, which made them accuse him of cruelty and contributed to his downfall.[22] But Machiavelli insinuates that Remirro also became hateful to Borgia himself, since by allowing his agent to get 'the very greatest reputation' for creating peace and unity he might have created a rival to his own kingly power. This would help explain his desire to 'gain' the people 'entirely to himself'—and away from his excessively effective governor.

The decision to then get rid of Remirro looks like another erratic 'turn' in policy rather than part of a well-considered strategy; an anxious attempt to rectify an error of judgement, not a masterstroke of *virtuoso* foresight. If this is the gist of Machiavelli's account, Borgia's conduct falls short of the standard of

---

[22] *Legations* 23 December 1502.

virtú set out in the first part of the chapter: 'immediately' knowing how to save one's fortune-given state. By this standard, if not others, Remirro might be a likelier candidate: compare his efficiency in establishing peace and unity 'in a short time'.

Then comes the dramatic climax: after having Remirro tried in a makeshift court, Borgia 'had him placed one morning in the piazza at Cesena in two pieces [*pezzi*] with a piece of wood [*pezzo*] and a bloody knife [*uno coltello sanguinoso*] beside him'. The series *piazza—pezzi—pezzo* has a wonderfully ironic lilt to it.[23] It is usually thought that Machiavelli greatly admired these ruthless actions, which showed that Borgia was superior to ordinary legal or moral constraints. 'The ferocity [*ferocità*] of this spectacle', he reports, 'left the people at once satisfied and stupefied [*stupidi*].' Some readers might wonder, however, whether people in a state of stupefaction—shock that prevents them from thinking properly—are capable of giving sustained support for a new prince's arms.[24]

Readers can surely agree, at least, that Borgia's methods of consolidating his rule are a far cry from what Machiavelli and other sources tell us about Sforza's 'proper' means and Hiero's transparent, orderly procedures. Notwithstanding all the legalistic theatrics Borgia created around Remirro's death, Machiavelli's dispatches underscore its extra-legal and arbitrary character. 'Nobody', he wrote at the time, 'feels sure of the cause of death, except that it has pleased the Prince who shows that he can make and unmake men as he likes, according to their merits.'[25] If no one knew the cause of Remirro's death, technically speaking it was not a publicly ordered execution but a murder. It is highly unusual for Machiavelli to call Borgia 'Prince' in his dispatches or anywhere else. Perhaps he was so impressed by this bold act that he decided to elevate its presumed author to an even higher rank than duke. Or perhaps the new label reeks of irony, implying that by this extraordinary act the duke took himself to a new level—not the better one *à la* Hiero or Sforza, but that of a prince who resembles a tyrant.

Either way, the key question is whether his handling of Remirro represents a more *virtuoso* shift to self-reliance and away from dependence on fortune. Once again, Borgia uses others' 'arms'—in this case whatever political skills Remirro used to impose order—to do the hard work of new ordering. Machiavelli makes it clear that the peace and unity established in the Romagna were products of Remirro's efforts, not of Borgia's. And he implies that Borgia had no far-sighted plan to scapegoat his agent, but decided to destroy him only after his efficient work gained him a 'great reputation'. Far from marking the triumph of Borgia's efforts to stand on his own virtuous feet, then, the episode

---

[23] And may bring to mind a fourth word often used in Machiavelli's poems, *pazzo* (crazy).
[24] Compare chap. 19 on the emperor Severus keeping the people 'stupefied and astonished'.
[25] *Legations* 23 December 1502.

seems to illustrate his chronic inability to escape from dependence on others' arms. His conduct typifies the fortune-dependent pattern described in chapter 3, and recurring throughout the *Prince*. Such men (or cities) 'fly' to acquire or throw up foundations with the help of others' arms. Then they lose faith in those who helped them, seeing them as rivals or obstacles to their further plans, and turn against them with deception or violence.

HOW VIRTUOUS WERE BORGIA'S FOUNDATIONS?

Having left readers breathless, Machiavelli now declares that 'the duke found himself very powerful and secure in part against present dangers—since he had armed in his own mode [*a suo modo*] and had in good part eliminated those arms which were near enough to attack him'. Once again, this sounds promising. Yet Machiavelli still shies away from speaking of Borgia's 'own' arms, or saying unequivocally that he was secure after killing Remirro. The best he can say, it seems, is that the duke 'found himself' very powerful, not that he had made himself powerful by his own well-focused actions; and that he was secure *in part* against *present* dangers 'since he had armed in his mode'.

Was this now a virtuous or a fortune-dependent mode? Whatever we make of the strained language used to describe the state of Borgia's arms, we are still missing the second part of the pair 'his own arms and *virtù*'. Through all his dramatic narrations so far, Machiavelli has not once mentioned Borgia's *virtù*. And what, after all, were his arms? They did not consist of a civilian militia in the Romagna, Machiavelli's ideal in the *Prince*.[26] Borgia's 'own mode' of being armed comprised an army of soldiers, some personally loyal to him but most paid mercenaries, drawn from all parts of Italy and including many foreigners; and a large contingent of French and Swiss auxiliary troops. Few of these men had roots or loyalties in Borgia's new state. Machiavelli's dispatches in the months before and after the Remirro incident report that Borgia's rule was under great stress, and that clashes between local people and his soldiers threatened to undermine his position. In October he wrote that although Borgia had a well-ordered artillery, 'on the other side we see his enemies armed and in order and in a position to make a sudden conflagration'; and unlike his troops, his enemies were 'all Romagna natives' who 'have not been very well treated because this lord has always shown more favour to his soldiers than to them'.[27] In November he contrasted Borgia's weak position vis-à-vis the duke of Urbino, whose state he had recently seized. Whereas Urbino's 'assembled citizens' and soldiers vowed to fight for their duke 'if the

---

[26] Set out in chaps 12–13.   [27] *Legations* 9 October 1502.

whole world were against them', Borgia could only 'spend lots of money in response'.[28]

Only a few days before Remirro's arrest, Machiavelli wrote home that the French troops were leaving Borgia's court in anger, having 'received injuries from the country people here' and fearing for their safety. In the same letter where he reports that Remirro 'has been put by this Lord in a dungeon', Machiavelli surmised that the French had left because 'the country was growing hostile' to the duke, 'being so aggravated with so many soldiers'. Borgia had thereby 'lost', Machiavelli wrote, 'more than half his forces and two-thirds of his reputation, and it is believed that he will not be able to do many things that he gave signs of earlier and that were possible'. Meanwhile he faced heavy unrest in Urbino, whose people were resisting Borgia's conquest by causing him 'great terror'.[29] Against this background, Borgia's scapegoating of Remirro looks like a desperate bid to flex his muscles and silence local dissent, at a time when his 'own mode' of arms was falling apart.

Despite Borgia's stupefying histrionics in dispatching Remirro and his enemies at Sinigaglia, the *Prince* now tells us that he *still* faced difficulties. For he now wanted to 'become lord over Tuscany'; and 'if he wanted to proceed with acquisition' he would have to 'consider the king of France', who 'he knew' would not tolerate this latest aim. Was Borgia stretching his luck in seeking 'to acquire so much empire before the pope died that he could resist a first attack on his own'? Whether he was or not, this last line tells us that at this point he was still *unable* to resist on his own. Now he was closing in fast on Machiavelli's homeland, relying on Spanish help. Machiavelli evokes the anxieties of his countrymen when he writes that had his plan succeeded, Borgia 'would have jumped on Pisa. After this, Lucca and Siena would have quickly yielded' leaving the Florentines 'no remedy'. And if Borgia

had succeeded in this (as he was succeeding the same year that Alexander died), he would have acquired such force and reputation that he would have stood by himself and would no longer have depended on the fortune and force of someone else, but on his own power and *virtú* [*potenza e virtú sua*].

At last, a reference to his own *virtú*! Yet it is a conditional reference, a 'would have': Cesare is not there yet, and at least one test of this *virtú* is whether or not he succeeds. If we review what he's achieved so far, we may feel less than confident about his prospects. After all the actions Machiavelli has described, we now learn—again—that Borgia *still* depends on 'the fortune and force of someone else' and still doesn't stand 'by himself'. Where, we may ask, have all these earlier efforts got him? We have little evidence that 'his own power and *virtú*' helped put him on the brink of success now; he has simply exchanged

[28] *Legations* 26 November 1502.
[29] *Legations* 20 and 23 December 1502; 26 November 1502.

French for Spanish backing, and could easily—in textbook 'fortunate' mode—take advantage of the divisive hatreds between Tuscan cities.

And as things transpired, 'Alexander died five years after he had begun to draw his sword' in August 1503. It is unclear whether the sword-drawing 'he' is Cesare or Alexander, and it matters little, since Machiavelli has already assimilated the son's arms and fortune to his father's. The pope 'left the duke with only the state of Romagna consolidated [*assolidato*], with all the others in the air [*in aria*], between two very powerful enemy armies, and sick to death'. In short, at the time of Alexander's death, Cesare's *stato* was in a pretty parlous state—and a hopelessly dependent one.

Machiavelli tells us that Borgia was aware of how much he still depended on his father's power, and wanted to 'secure himself' against future threats from the pope's successor. His dispatch of 8 November, written nine months before the pope died, reports that Cesare 'knows very well that the pope can die any day, and that he needs to think before his death of laying some other foundation if he intends to maintain the states he now has'.[30] A commendable realization, but one that seems to have come rather late in the day, not 'immediately' as it should to virtuous princes. Machiavelli then gives an elaborate list of 'four modes' Borgia hoped might secure him against future enemies. Further violence, despoiling, and bribery top the list. Instead of reassuring us that Borgia was a man with a plan, it heightens the impression of ill-focused hyperactivity already produced by Machiavelli's deadpan narrative, and contrasts with the straightforward modes of Sforza and Hiero.

Yet Machiavelli still tries to persuade us that without such bad luck, Borgia could have prevailed:

> And there was such ferocity and such *virtú* in the duke, and he knew so well how men have to be won over or lost, and so sound [*validi*] were the foundations that he had laid in so little time, that *if* he had not had these armies on his back or *if* he had been healthy, he would have withstood every difficulty [italics added].

Here again is *virtú*, this time in the present tense. Yet it is paired with *ferocità*, a quality that Machiavelli admires in the context of military battles, but treats as harmful unless it is disciplined by good orders.[31] He has certainly given us little hard evidence of Borgia's political ordering skills or self-discipline.

Moreover, the two 'ifs' at the end of this passage sound like a kind of special pleading that Machiavelli's fully *virtú*-reliant men don't need. Such men take the bad with the good, and face hardship as best they can, accepting full responsibility for their failures. Fortune-dependent people, by contrast, tend to

---

[30] *Legations* 8 November 1502.

[31] For example, see chap. 19 on Caracalla; *D* I.16 on the feral ferocity of peoples unused to living in *libertà*; and the *Decennale* II, lines 85–93 on Pope Julius II who, unable to check his 'ferocious spirit', vented his 'poison' on Italy by stirring up unnecessary wars.

blame everyone but themselves when things go awry, however foreseeable their fall looks to impartial observers. Men like Borgia may 'make use of every deed' that they think a prudent and virtuous man should use to put down roots. But they never quite 'own' their actions, and thus shirk responsibility for them. As 'if only' excuses pile up near the end of the chapter, readers might suspect that Machiavelli is wearing his dramatist's hat here rather than that of a dispassionate analyst, and mimicking the behaviour of fortune-dependent characters like Borgia. In a rare reference to himself, Machiavelli says that Borgia 'told me ... that he had thought about what might happen' while his father lay dying, and that he 'had found a remedy for everything, except that he never thought that at his death he himself would also be on the point of dying'. A properly *virtuoso* prince would have thought of more effective remedies before it was too late.

But here lies the problem for readers: the more blatantly Machiavelli's narration of deeds undermines his own claims about Borgia's good prospects or foundations, the more urgent his insistence that they *were* good. 'And that his foundations were good one may see', he declares, in the fact that 'Romagna waited for him more than a month; in Rome, though he was half alive, he remained secure'; his old enemies did not gain a following against him in Rome; and if he could not make whoever he wanted pope, 'at least' he still had enough influence among the cardinals to block 'someone he did not want'.

None of these arguments furnishes convincing evidence of substantial power, let alone of anything like the good foundations Machiavelli ascribes to Sforza and Hiero and discusses in more general terms later. A month is not long to wait before rebelling, especially for a region whose peoples had not been free or well-ordered for a long time, lacked coherent leadership to resist, and had recently been 'stupefied' by Borgia's violence. Machiavelli—and many of his early readers—knew that Borgia's rule in the Romagna was unpopular. Borgia's influence over the cardinals, Machiavelli has just told us, was due to bribery; his enemies' not attacking him with followers might be explained by their own internecine conflicts as well as threats from Cesare's henchmen; and his security in Rome was short-lived. The devil, so to speak, is in the details. And as Machiavelli's *sotto voce* reservations accumulate, it becomes hard to feel confident that his noisily positive claims about good foundations represent his own judgement.

WHOSE FAULT WAS BORGIA'S FAILURE?

The chapter ends with a famous contradiction. Early on, Machiavelli assured readers that if Borgia's 'orders did not bring profit to him it was not his fault, because this arose from an extraordinary and extreme malignity of fortune'.

More recently, we have been given many concrete examples of this bad fortune, and were told that if not for Alexander's death, the armies on his back, or his own bad health, Cesare would have pulled through—indeed, 'everything would have been easy [*facile*] for him'. Thus 'if I summed up all the actions of the duke,' Machiavelli declares, 'I would not know how to reproach him'. He goes on, however, to pick out one mistake that finally destroyed Cesare's hopes of holding all or part of his state after his father's death. 'One could accuse him', Machiavelli writes, in his decision to back his father's arch-rival Giuliano della Rovere to become Pope Julius II when Alexander's first successor, Cardinal Piccolomini, died after a very short papal stint. Cesare's fatal error, it seems, was self-deception in thinking that Julius could be bought off by support for his candidacy. For 'whoever believes that among great personages new benefits will make old injuries be forgotten,' Machiavelli writes, 'deceives himself. So,' the chapter concludes, 'the duke erred in this choice and it was the cause of his ultimate ruin.'

As scholars have pointed out, the claim that Borgia's failure was not his fault contradicts the claim that his own bad choice of pope caused his ultimate ruin.[32] The chapter contains so many paradoxical statements, however, and so much evidence that contradicts Machiavelli's stated judgements, that this final puzzle should not astonish. The harder Machiavelli tries to let his alleged hero off the hook, the more it appears that Borgia's main difficulties—instability in his territories, his own Orsini armies against him, his shortage of reliable friends—were the result of his own actions.

And Machiavelli's final 'reproach' merely highlights the most fundamental flaw in Borgia's foundations: when his father dies, instead of standing on his own two feet, *Cesare still depends on the Papacy to support him*. His fundamental error was not that he backed the wrong cardinal for pope, but that he failed to take measures that would have made him independent of *any* pope's support. If he decided early on to 'depend no longer on the arms and fortune of others', and tried to break away from Orsini and French military backing, Borgia made no serious attempt to separate his power-base from that of his father; so after Alexander's death, his son's survival depended on the will of his successors.[33]

As already observed, one of the un-virtuous traits that Cesare seems to have inherited from his father was an inability to trust others or to maintain their trust in him. His signature methods—intimidation, deception, violence, stupefaction—were hardly apt to make him friends. Machiavelli describes his repeated failures to build firm friendships whether in Rome, the Romagna,

---

[32] See Sasso (1987).

[33] Indeed, to say that his failure arose from an 'extraordinary and extreme malignity of fortune' can be read as a ferocious piece of irony: his failure was due to his father the pope, an 'extraordinary'—that is, order-destroying—and extreme malignity personified.

or with foreign powers, and suggests a deeper failure to appreciate their importance for his long-term security. Not long before the Remirro episode, Machiavelli tried, apparently in vain, to persuade the young duke that 'he had better make a lasting friendship than take a city he cannot hold', and that he should 'try to maintain what he has acquired rather than to acquire more'.[34]

Perversely, 'the duke' only seemed to trust others when he was wholly dependent on them—first his father, then Giuliano/Julius when he imprudently backed his papal candidacy. At the time, Machiavelli noted the rich irony that Cesare, that self-styled master of deception, was so easily tricked by the future Pope Julius' promise of money and of continued papal support for Borgia's government in the Romagna, writing home that the duke 'allows himself to be carried away by his rash confidence, believing that the word of others is more to be relied on than his own'.[35] Having secured the papacy, Julius disregarded his promises and decided to assume control of the Romagna himself. Borgia was arrested and forced to relinquish key parts of the Romagna in exchange for his freedom.[36]

Machiavelli is not particularly interested in the objective power of fortune over human beings. He is interested in how human beings react to fortune's power, and how they help to create their own good or bad fortune by their good or bad choices. Bad luck may play a large role in creating failures, but human agents always have some role as well: either their previous actions contributed to present bad luck, or they failed to rise to the occasion created by circumstances beyond their control. The power of fortune is always susceptible to human management, though not total control; even in the tightest crunch, people have some choice in how to act, and their choices show their *virtú* or lack thereof. When Machiavelli protests that Borgia bears little or no responsibility for his failure, then, he is either violating his own standards of self-responsible *virtú*, or ironically echoing fortune-dependent people who shun virtuous responsibility.

Why then does Machiavelli introduce his narration of Borgia's deeds by saying, 'I do not know what better teaching I could give to a new prince than the example of his actions', and end it with: 'it seems to me he should be put forward, as I have done, to be imitated by all those who have risen to empire through fortune and the arms of others'? Regarding the first statement, we might ask: *what kind of teaching* does Machiavelli want to give? He leaves it up to readers to decide whether the lessons are positive, or negative and cautionary. They may study Borgia's actions to learn how to avoid being fortune's plaything—or model their own actions on his, and meet a similar end.

---

[34] *Legations* 13 November 1502. [35] *Legations* 4 November 1503.
[36] Julius and Ferdinand of Aragon later feared the resurgence of a Borgia army, and in May 1504 their agents arrested Cesare and transported him to imprisonment in Spain. He escaped, but died in battle in 1507.

The second statement that Borgia should 'be put forward . . . to be imitated' is one of the most misinterpreted statements in the *Prince*. Machiavelli does not say that *every* prince should imitate Borgia, but only a particular, deficient class of princes: namely, those who have 'risen to empire' by 'fortune and the arms of others'. Princes who acquire or rise further by their own arms and *virtú* need not imitate Borgia.[37]

WHY BE IRONIC ABOUT BORGIA?

If we assume that fear of persecution must be the main motive for any author to write ironically, we might doubt that Machiavelli's praise of Borgia is ironic. He had, after all, no political reason to disguise critical views of a dead man who had few living apologists; he might even have gained Medici sympathy had he criticized the dreadful Borgia openly. But Machiavelli had other reasons to dissimulate. His descriptions of Borgia in his legations, his poems, other early literary pieces, and in the *Prince* cast him as a familiar type of character: one whose inflated self-confidence and ill-conceived ambitions make him fly high then crash. Such characters are the classic 'victims' of irony, whether comic or tragic.[38] Machiavelli's reports from Borgia's court underscore his immaturity, his arrogance, his suspicious temperament, and his imperviousness to either lessons of experience or the advice of more experienced men.[39] These qualities made him an irresistible subject for dramatic irony, which works not by announcing and denouncing such characters' self-deceptions, but by letting the readers spot them as they emerge through his actions.

---

[37] And the phrase 'rise to empire [*imperio*]' here recalls the fortune-dependent modes of 'those emperors who . . . attained the empire by corrupting the soldiers', critically examined at the beginning of the chapter.
[38] See Thomson (1927), 10–14.   [39] See chap. 17.

8

Crimes

Of those who have attained principality by crimes

Having devoted the last two chapters to his two master 'modes' for becoming
prince, Machiavelli now introduces two further modes 'that cannot be altogether attributed either to fortune or to *virtù*'. The first, which he discusses
in the present chapter, is 'when one ascends to a principality by some criminal
and nefarious path [*per via scelerata e nefaria*]'. The second, discussed in
chapter 9, is 'when a private citizen becomes prince of his fatherland by the
favour [*favore*] of his fellow citizens'.

Machiavelli's usual mask of analytical neutrality seems to slip off a bit in his
choice of the words 'criminal and nefarious' to describe the first mode. So far,
the *Prince*'s main touchstone for deciding whether princely actions were
guided more by *virtù* than fortune has been instrumental, not moral. *Virtù*
is a quality that helps princes acquire and maintain and *therefore* makes them
praiseworthy—not one that merits praise because it benefits people other than
the prince, respects their basic rights, or makes him worthy of God's grace.
Now, however, the words nefarious and criminal seem to imply that some
actions may be condemned as extremely bad, as well as unsuccessful. How,
then, are these two criteria—moral badness and practical failure—related to
each other? And how are they related to the *Prince*'s master standards of *virtù*
and *fortuna*?

DO PRINCELY CRIMES EVER PAY?

Machiavelli says that he will illustrate the first, criminal modes with two
examples, one ancient one modern, 'without entering otherwise into the
merits of this policy [*parte*], because I judge it sufficient, for whoever would
find it necessary, to imitate them'. This may seem to suggest that however
distasteful these methods, it may sometimes be necessary to use them. Yet as
we saw in the last chapter with Pope Alexander VI, when Machiavelli says that
someone might 'find' an action necessary, he implies that it may not be

objectively necessary. The necessity may arise, on the contrary, from that person's not necessarily reasonable ends. Bearing this in mind, which actions of princely criminals might be worth imitating?

As his ancient example Machiavelli chooses Agathocles, who ruled Syracuse not long before the virtuous Hiero.[1] He says that Agathocles 'became king', although in the *Discourses* he calls him a tyrant. Whatever his title, the narrative of his actions fits a classic ancient pattern of how tyrants come to power. He ascended 'not only from private fortune but from a lowly [*infima*] and abject one', being the son of a potter, and 'always held, at every rank of his career, to a criminal life'. Nevertheless 'his crimes were accompanied by such *virtú* of spirit [*animo*] and body that when he turned to the military, he rose through its ranks to become praetor of Syracuse', praetor being a leading official rank under that city's oligarchic-republican constitution.[2] Having ascended this far, Agathocles 'decided to become prince and to hold with violence and without obligation to anyone else that which had been conceded to him by agreement [*tenere con violenzia e sanza obligo di altri quello che d'accordo gli era suto concesso*]'. He first alerted Sicily's enemies, the Carthaginians, to his planned coup, thus seeking hostile foreign backing for his personal ambitions—a most unpatriotic act of treason, though Machiavelli refrains from saying so here. Then he called an assembly of the people and senate where, 'at a signal he had ordered, he had all the senators and the richest of the people killed by his soldiers'.

These violent beginnings did not, it appears, destabilize Agathocles' subsequent rule. On the contrary, he 'seized and held [*occupò e tenne*] the principality' of Syracuse 'without any civil controversy [*controversia civile*]'. And despite his initial, otherwise perfidious-looking collaboration with the enemy, he went on to fight the Carthaginians so spiritedly that 'they were compelled of necessity to come to an agreement with him, to be content with the possession of Africa, and to leave Sicily to Agathocles'. Thus, Machiavelli sums up, 'whoever might consider the actions and *virtú* of this man will see nothing or little that can be attributed to fortune'. His ascent was clearly due to his own merit and efforts, since in contrast to princes of fortune like Borgia he became prince 'not through anyone's favour but through the ranks of the military, which he had gained for himself with a thousand hardships [*disagi*] and dangers'. And having attained the principality, he afterwards 'maintained it [*mantenessi*] with a thousand spirited and very dangerous policies [*mille partiti animosi e periculosissimi*]'. The word 'maintain' here seems to suggest a more reliable kind of upkeep than Machiavelli's often insecure, too-forced

---

[1] Agathocles died 289 BC. Hiero was general from 275 and elected king in 270 BC.

[2] Machiavelli calls Syracuse's government pre-Agathocles a republic, saying that Agathocles called an assembly 'as if he had to decide things pertinent to the republic'.

'holding'.³ If we judge Agathocles' deeds by the results alone, we might be tempted to conclude that they exhibited a very considerable *virtú*.

But then in one of the *Prince*'s most surprising passages, Machiavelli bluntly rejects this conclusion. He has, to be sure, already mentioned Agathocles' *virtú* twice, and will mention it again, affirming that many of Agathocles' actions showed certain qualities of *virtú*. Yet we now learn that not all of his actions can be called virtuous. For, Machiavelli declares, 'one cannot call it *virtú* to kill one's citizens, betray one's friends, to be without faith, without mercy, without religion; these modes can enable one to acquire empire, but not glory [*gloria*]'.⁴ He acknowledges that 'if one considers the *virtú* of Agathocles in entering into and escaping from dangers, and the greatness of his spirit [*grandezza dello animo*] in enduring and overcoming adverse things', one sees no reason 'why he has to be judged inferior to any most excellent captain'. But neither these spirited sorts of *virtú* nor his success in maintaining power cancel out Agathocles' crimes. In the end, 'his savage cruelty and inhumanity [*efferata crudeltà e inumanità*], together with his infinite crimes, do not permit him to be celebrated among the most excellent men'. Nor can his acknowledged *virtú* be regarded as the cause of his achievements; 'one cannot attribute to fortune or to *virtú* what he achieved without either'.

These unusually direct moral judgements confirm a point made in previous chapters about more and less adequate kinds of *virtú*. Agathocles showed quite specific kinds of *virtú*, namely the 'spirited' kinds traditionally associated with military valour: bold determination, courage in facing dangers, ingenuity in escaping them, fortitude in overcoming adversities. But if these qualities add up to the *virtú* of a fine captain, it's not clear that they suffice to make a good statesman. Nor, Machiavelli now tells us, can men who possess '*virtú* of spirit' without other qualities of *virtú* be counted among 'the most excellent men'. Most strikingly, one of Agathocles' main aims lacked *virtú*: he wanted 'to hold with violence and without obligation to anyone else' that which had been given him 'by agreement'. This recalls chapter 3, where Machiavelli discussed Rome and other states that first acquire power in a province by the willing invitation of certain locals and later, when the same local support evaporates, proceed to hold their conquests with violence.

For the first time in the *Prince*, Machiavelli seems to suggest—indeed, to insist—that *virtú* has moral dimensions as well as instrumental ones. Not just any qualities that bring personal safety or eliminate unrest can be called *virtú*, but only those that do not transgress certain limits: in particular, limits set by obligations undertaken to other people as fellow citizens, friends, allies who

---

³ See chap. 4, n.4.
⁴ Ironically, Agathocles' name combines the Greek words for 'good' (*agathos*) and glory (*kleos*).

depend on your good faith. Machiavelli will often return to this theme of princely obligations in later chapters.

Machiavelli's next, modern example, that of Liverotto da Fermo, was less successful than Agathocles in maintaining his rule, though apparently just as successful in attaining it. Machiavelli gives us a long description of Liverotto's deceptions, betrayals, homicide committed against the uncle who had raised him, and violations of every ordinary standard of private honour or public probity. After forcing Fermo's highest magistracy to let him be made prince and killing anyone who might have harmed him, Liverotto emerged supreme. He 'strengthened himself with new civil and military orders, so that in the one year during which he held the principality, he was not only secure in the city of Fermo but had become fearsome to all his neighbours. And,' Machiavelli avers, 'to overthrow him would have been as difficult as to overthrow Agathocles, if he had not permitted himself to be deceived by Cesare Borgia' at Sinigaglia, in the episode briefly mentioned in chapter 7. Irony of ironies: just as the arch-deceiver Borgia later let himself be taken in by Pope Julius' promises of goodwill, Liverotto—who like his murderer thought he was too clever to be taken in by the cunning of others—was brought down by his own self-deceiving credulity. Thus, 'one year after the parricide he committed and together with Vitellozzo, who had been his master in his virtues [*delle virtù*] and his crimes, he was strangled'.

Again, Machiavelli has no problem acknowledging that even the vilest of men may have some kinds of *virtù*. As with Agathocles, Borgia, and many others in the *Prince*, Liverotto's specific virtues are those often associated with military prowess. He is ingenious (*ingegnoso*) and bold (*gagliardo*) in person and spirit (*animo*); qualities that helped make him 'the first man in his military'. While Machiavelli gives these kinds of *virtù* a nod, he clearly does not think they merit highest acclaim if other more important qualities are missing. In this context, his use of *virtù* oozes irony. The unusual plural 'virtues' implies that while Liverotto might have had certain qualities commonly praised by that word, Machiavelli cannot bring himself to speak in general terms of his *virtù*. The claim that he had a master of his virtues underlines their second-hand quality. And the pairing of his virtues with his crimes, followed by 'he was strangled', makes it crystal clear which of these two 'modes' mastered his sorry fate.

Agathocles' crimes deviated from *virtù*, the *Prince*'s optimal standard for acquiring and maintaining. Yet against every expectation created by earlier chapters, they still paid off. After all of his 'infinite betrayals and cruelties', this criminal prince could still 'live for a long time secure in his fatherland'. This was all the more astonishing, Machiavelli observes, since 'many others have not been able to maintain their states through cruelty even in peaceful times, not to mention uncertain times of war'. Liverotto's crimes, by contrast, did not pay off for long, though for a good year it seemed that they might. Why the difference?

Agathocles was perhaps shrewder than Liverotto and 'many others' in not letting himself be tricked by his enemies. But the more important difference, Machiavelli tells us, lies in a distinction between cruelties well or badly used (*le crudeltà male usate o bene usate*).

The key to Agathocles' success and others' failure, Machiavelli proposes, is that the former used cruelty more effectively. Cruelties are used well when they meet two criteria. Firstly, they are 'done at a stroke [*a uno tratto*], out of the necessity to secure oneself'. Secondly, they should be 'converted toward as much utility for the subjects as one can [*convertono in più utilità de' sudditi che si può*]'. Cruelties used badly, by contrast, are few at first, but multiply over time. Princes who use them well 'can have some remedy for their state with God and with men, as had Agathocles', while 'for the others it is impossible for them to maintain themselves'.

IF CRIMES SOMETIMES PAY, WHY BOTHER TO USE *VIRTÚ*?

The chapter's main message seems to be that crimes like Agathocles' are sometimes necessary and can bring a prince lifelong security. If this is right, then what, if any, are the advantages of using the virtuous modes that Machiavelli recommended in previous chapters? He has warned princes that if they use criminal modes, they must be prepared to sacrifice the glory that rewards true *virtú*. But plenty of aspiring princes will doubtless be willing to forgo *gloria* in this high-minded sense if they can attain the kind of great power and security achieved by Agathocles. Why, they might wonder, should they take the high road of *virtú*, littered as it is with hardships and toil, when well-used crimes can achieve the same results? Either Machiavelli has just admitted that even his master standard of *virtú* may sometimes be less effective than criminal modes, or he has embedded subtle doubts in the text about the utility of those modes, even as they were 'used well' by Agathocles, alongside his open criticisms of their immorality. Such doubts appear as soon as we inspect Agathocles' actions more closely.

The first criterion says that a new prince should 'review all the offences necessary for him to commit, and do them all at a stroke, so as not to have to renew them every day'. Yet Machiavelli tells us that Agathocles '*always* held, at every rank of his career, to a criminal life'. This tells us either that his initial criminal offences forced him to renew them *ad infinitum*, or that he chose to renew them. Either way, his continuous offending contradicts Machiavelli's claim that Agathocles used cruelty well.

The second criterion for 'well used' cruelty says that having got offences out of the way, a prince should convert them to utility for his subjects, for he can never 'found himself on his subjects if, because of fresh and continued injuries, they cannot be secure against him'. This criterion identifies utility for subjects with their being secure 'against' renewed injuries from the prince. The first criterion therefore defines the second; and since Agathocles violated the one, he also fell short of the other. Even if a prince serves subjects' utility by defeating foreign enemies or conferring other benefits, unless they are secure from *his* continued injuries, he will fail to found himself on them, and thus hurt his own interests. Since Agathocles 'always' held to a criminal life throughout his political career, he must have failed in this respect.

Machiavelli tells us that Agathocles maintained himself not by building firm foundations—a word conspicuously absent in this chapter—but 'with many spirited and dangerous policies'. This mode of maintaining does not sound especially secure or well founded. True, Machiavelli says that Agathocles seized and held the principality 'without civil controversy'. But he omits any suggestion that this was due to firm foundations. And there are many other possible reasons why a criminal prince might face little open controversy: fear of his ruthlessness; corruption in the leading citizens; stupefaction in the populace. So it seems that Agathocles did not use cruelty altogether well, though he undoubtedly used it better than Liverotto.

Where there is spirit and danger but no order or firmness, foundations must be weak. This seems to be the essential difference between successful criminality and virtuous modes. Machiavelli says nothing in the *Prince* or elsewhere about Agathocles' legacy, but many early readers would have been familiar with the Roman historian Justin's famous account. In his last years, Justin writes, Agathocles was greatly tormented by quarrels among his family members over who would succeed him, making him regret that his heirs had grown up in a monarchy where they expected to hold absolute power. Even before his death, the Carthaginians seized the opportunity created by Syracuse's chaotic succession struggles to launch an aggressive new bid for power in Sicily. These internal and external disorders were brought under control, according to Justin, only when Hiero came to power several years later.[5] If it first appeared that Agathocles' crimes achieved the same qualities of security and firm maintaining as virtuous modes, then this appearance was deceptive.

IS CRUELTY ALWAYS CRIMINAL?

Can 'cruelty well used' be virtuous? Machiavelli has insisted that criminal modes are sharply distinct from virtuous ones, and seems to treat cruelty

---

[5] Justin XXIII.2–4. Compare the similar disordered legacies of Machiavelli's Castruccio and Xenophon's Cyrus.

under the heading of criminal modes. This might seem to suggest that all cruelty is criminal, and therefore not virtuous. Yet Machiavelli's two criteria for well-used cruelties—do them 'all at a stroke', and in ways that make your subjects more secure—sound remarkably similar to qualities he associates elsewhere with *virtú*. The need to commit necessary offences at once recalls Hiero's prompt elimination of Syracuse's old military. Later chapters have a great deal to say about founding on one's subjects by making them feel secure. Since these criteria cut across the distinction between crimes and *virtú*, it seems that there might be forms of so-called 'cruelty' that are not criminal. Perhaps there is no real difference between 'cruelty' used really well—not how Agathocles used it, but as Hiero did—and virtuous resolution, swiftness, and toughness in establishing new orders?

We will encounter precisely this idea of virtuous cruelty in chapter 17, where Machiavelli sets out two contradictory senses of 'cruelty'. Cruelty in the proper sense of the word means excessive and unreasonable harshness. But in corrupt times, many people misuse the word. They call 'cruel' any measures that rigorously eliminate bribery or punish crimes with appropriate severity. From the perspective of such people in Syracuse, actions such as Hiero's—swiftly eliminating the useless old military, and imposing new civil and military discipline where Agathocles and his heirs had eroded it— seem cruel, though in truth they showed virtuous severity. By mimicking the corrupt use of 'cruelty', Machiavelli pokes fun at those who find any strict civil discipline cruel. At the same time, he challenges readers to notice the important difference between the names people give to actions when they want to praise or blame them—often wrongly—and the true qualities of those actions.

HOW DO CRIMINAL MODES DIFFER FROM FORTUNE-DEPENDENT ONES?

What then is the relationship between criminal and fortune-dependent modes? Are they as mutually exclusive as crimes and *virtú*? This seems unlikely, given the strong resemblance between the actions Machiavelli describes as criminal in chapter 8 and those he associates with fortune in chapter 7.

The resemblance is not complete identity. The main fortune-dependent modes discussed in the last chapter were relying on the arms, power, and connections of others; and paying money or giving favours in exchange for political support. By comparison with Agathocles' criminal—and un-virtuous— betrayals of friends, killings of fellow citizens, and breaches of faith, these fortune-reliant methods sound rather tame. On the other hand, Machiavelli's account of Borgia's career shows that the lines between these two modes are very fine indeed. In his first efforts to secure himself, Borgia relied heavily on special favours to buy off his enemies' 'gentlemen' and on his father's exchange of further special favours with the French king. But as seemingly endless difficulties kept springing up in his path, he turned to deceit, and then to multiple violent murders. When chapter 8 enumerates criminal methods that 'cannot be called *virtú*', it is hard to see why Borgia's deeds of betrayal, breaking faith, mercilessness, and homicide should not fall under the same heading, or why they should be considered any less 'criminal and nefarious' than Agathocles' actions.

Machiavelli seems to identify a clear difference in chapter 17. Though Borgia 'was held to be cruel', he writes there, nonetheless 'his cruelty restored the Romagna, united it, and reduced it to peace and to faith'. If we read this straight and take it as a sufficient statement of Machiavelli's views on Borgia, we might conclude that Borgia's cruelties deserve praise because they had beneficial results, for the people of Romagna as well as for himself. Machiavelli does not say that Agathocles' similar cruelties had such generally useful results.[6]

If we notice all the ironies in chapter 7, however, we are less likely to credit Machiavelli's later praise for Borgia. For one thing, the so-called 'cruelty' that restored order in the Romagna was not Borgia's but Remirro de Orco's. Machiavelli uses the positive word 'rigour', *rigorosità*, to describe Remirro's order-making modes. Rigour is associated with discipline and order, qualities difficult to find anywhere in Machiavelli's narrative of Borgia's actions. For another, Machiavelli gives no evidence in the *Prince*, or says anywhere in his diplomatic dispatches, that Borgia's own actions *did* 'reduce' Romagna to peace or faith.

The narrative of particulars speaks louder than any general commentary, and the similarities between Agathocles and Borgia are far more striking than any difference between them. By juxtaposing them in two consecutive chapters, Machiavelli highlights the affinities between fortune-dependent and criminal 'modes'. While not all fortune-dependent modes are criminal, they may, it seems, put those who use them on a path to crime. This happens because the modes of fortune tend to generate new obstacles rather than to remove them. Not knowing how to switch to virtuous modes, frustrated princes of fortune, like Borgia, often find themselves driven to crimes. The two modes resemble each other in being easier and quicker paths to acquiring than *virtú*, which calls for much more forethought, hard work, and respect for pre-existing orders.

Can fortune-dependent princes still be considered more virtuous than criminal ones? This seems doubtful. If we compare Borgia's background and career with Agathocles', more evidence of certain qualities of *virtú* can be seen in the latter, even if he compromised his overall *virtú* by his crimes. Agathocles

---

[6] For example, see Plamenatz (2012), 37–9.

climbed by his own efforts from base origins, and Machiavelli states that at least some of those efforts involved real merit as a military captain, not just criminal conniving. Borgia rode from start to finish on the back of his father, who secured his French title and gave him his state in Romagna. And whereas Agathocles survived to confer some benefits on his subjects, however fleeting, Borgia soon crashed.

The chapter's second example of Liverotto underscores Borgia's criminality and his defective *virtú*, and further illustrates the point that fortune-dependence tends to lead toward crimes. Their career paths look very different at first. Liverotto was 'left a fatherless child' and raised by an uncle; Borgia's entire career was utterly dominated by his father. Whereas Borgia turns to deception and crimes only after a series of frustrations, and after he has become 'prince', Liverotto hatches elaborate criminal plans to seize the principate of his native city, apparently never contemplating any other means to achieve his ends. When Borgia turns to what are self-evidently criminal modes, he does so under urgent pressure from enemies—a 'necessity' that could perhaps have been avoided by more virtuous measures taken sooner, and thus not an excuse for crime, but nonetheless one that posed a genuine threat. Liverotto's motives for embarking on his life of crime have nothing to do with personal or political safety. Machiavelli links them to pathological status-anxieties that make Liverotto obsessed with 'honour' (*onore*), in a perverse, self-serving sense of that good word. Its proper, other-respecting sense is affirmed when Machiavelli tells us that Liverotto was 'honourably received by the inhabitants of Fermo' whom, hell-bent on asserting his un-virtuous honour, he proceeds to murder in cold blood.

Despite these differences, the parallels between their actions and their downfalls suggest that if Borgia did not start off a criminal like Liverotto, he became one. Borgia perhaps had better cause to murder his enemies at Sinigaglia, including Liverotto himself, than the latter had to murder honourable, innocent fellow citizens. But murder is still murder, whatever you call it. And considered in instrumental rather than moral terms, murders—unlawful premeditated killings—have a way of creating an atmosphere of insecurity and mistrust around the perpetrator, regardless of his motives. In Borgia's case they also reveal deep anxieties in the murderer, showing that he does not trust his own legal orders enough to let them punish conspirators. He evidently failed to commit necessary offences 'at a stroke', and thus found himself 'always under necessity to hold a knife [*coltello*] in his hand'. Although this reference to a *coltello* occurs in chapter 8, it echoes the memorable line in chapter 7 about Borgia's murder of Remirro: that he was found in two pieces in the piazza with a knife '*coltello*' beside him—Borgia's knife, undoubtedly.

There are other ironic echoes of Borgia's deeds in Machiavelli's Liverotto narrative. Liverotto murders the honourable people of Fermo at a 'most solemn banquet' after softening them up with 'certain reasonings about weighty things [*ragionamenti di cosi gravi*]' relating to 'the greatness of Pope

Alexander and of Cesare Borgia, his son, and their enterprises [*imprese*]'.[7] Then, of course, Liverotto allows himself to be deceived by Borgia just as Borgia—as we already know from chapter 7—will later be deceived by Pope Julius II. Whatever their different starting-points and motives, then, in the end the two men share the common fate of criminals, many of whom fall victim to the next criminal waiting in the wings.

By hinting at these differences and similarities between Liverotto and Borgia, Machiavelli invites readers to reflect carefully on responsibility for crimes. Liverotto seems more blameworthy than Borgia because he was the fuller 'owner' of his actions: they were not initiated by another's ambitions, and they were not a response to any threat. Borgia might look more like a victim of circumstances. His fortune was really his father's, and later his enemies' (including Liverotto's) plots forced him toward crime. But the contrast with more *virtú*-reliant men and actions presses the question: if Borgia *did* not fully own his actions for these reasons, he could and *should* have done. He could have done a better job of making himself independent of his father, but failed; and if he hadn't failed, enemy plots would have threatened him less, since he would have had other arms of his own to defend him. To excuse these shortcomings by invoking fortune is hardly virtuous.

DOES MORAL *VIRTÚ* MATTER?

Let us conclude by returning to a question posed at the start of this chapter: what do Machiavelli's examples say about the relation between *virtú* in the moral sense that Agathocles lacks, and the kind of *virtú* that enables people to achieve lasting order and security? Does moral badness tend to produce practical failure and moral *virtú* success?

Close attention to his subjects' deeds and their effects suggests that there is a strong connection between practical failure and the kinds of immoral behaviour Machiavelli mentions: violating obligations, not keeping faith, killing friends and citizens. It seems that if a prince wants to build well-ordered foundations that last beyond his own lifetime, he *must* be concerned with his obligations to others, and with their welfare and feelings of security. At the very least, then, high quality *virtú* must involve a reflective kind of prudence that takes other people's concerns very seriously. It thus has an important moral dimension.

---

[7] *Imprese* is often ironically linked to fortune; see chap. 21 on the not-so-great *grande imprese* of King Ferdinand (and Pope Julius II), and *FH* I.17 on the *generosa impresa*—a pointless and failed Crusade—of Pope Urban II.

Machiavelli has repeatedly implied that there are more and less reasonable ends for princes. The highest quality *virtú* is shown in actions and qualities that help secure the most reasonable ends for princes, especially safety for themselves and their state. Safety depends, in turn, on firm, well-ordered foundations. What makes foundations firm and 'ordered' in Machiavelli's understanding of order is not extraordinary force, but knowledge of the natural, inescapable *limits* that constrain any prince's actions, no matter how powerful he is. These limits reside, on the one hand, in princes' own capacities and in the natural and reasonable desires, drives, and resistance of the people princes seek to control. The main defining quality of what Machiavelli calls good 'orders' is respect for such limits.

When princely ends are based on a good understanding of order in this sense, they embody both instrumental and moral *virtú*: they serve a prince's best interests and respect other people's most important interests. Princely ends are un-virtuous when they ignore these natural and *ordinario* limits— when they overstretch the capacities of merely human princes, and underestimate the constraints imposed by other people's capacities and desires. For Machiavelli, it makes little difference whether one describes this lack of *virtú* as morally wrong or merely imprudent, since violating natural order is *both* immoral—because it injures other people—*and* dangerous for the violator. But when addressing princes whose first concern is their own greatness and safety, it makes more sense to describe it as imprudent and self-defeating, since many would rather succeed as Agathocles did than win prizes for moral *virtú*.

9

Fortunate astuteness

Of the civil principality

Machiavelli now considers how 'a private citizen becomes prince of his fatherland' without using 'crime or other intolerable violence' in the manner of Agathocles and Liverotto, but rather 'with the favour [*favore*] of his fellow citizens'. This mode of becoming prince 'could be called', Machiavelli says, a civil principality, *uno principato civile*.

CIVIL PRINCIPALITY: MIXED MODE OF GOVERNMENT OR OXYMORON?

After making frequent appearances in the last chapter, where criminal princes seized power in republics, the word 'republic' is conspicuously absent from chapter 9. But by stressing that both the aspiring 'civil prince' and his supporters are 'citizens' (*cittadini*), the opening lines identify the initial context of this 'mode' as a republic. Civil princes, that is, are men who are handed princely power within a republic, with the help of fellow citizens who elevate one of their own to the superior status of first man or *princeps*.

Machiavelli does not specifically say that such princes are 'made' by means of unofficial or questionably legitimate means rather than by established, transparent laws and procedures. But the whole chapter implies this. A civil prince is not a man who holds the official post of leading man in a republic, such as the Florentine republic's post of Gonfalonier (Standard-bearer) for life, one of the 'orders' dissolved by the new Medici government after 1512. Holders of such elective posts were magistrates, whose authority was subject to strict legal limits. But at the end of the chapter, Machiavelli opposes the 'civil' prince to the magistrates who try to stop him from seizing 'absolute authority' (*autorità assoluta*). His power is thus 'extraordinary' from the outset, since it is neither acquired nor regulated by formal institutional orders.

By introducing an extraordinary princely element into a republican constitution, the creation of a civil prince effects a fundamental change from one form of *stato*, republic, towards its sole alternative, principality. Since those who seek this 'innovation' avoid criminal or 'intolerably' violent methods, the mode of civil principality may appear painless, and the changes it introduces seem less radical than those brought by violent coups or revolutions. Indeed, they may be so subtle that they are scarcely noticed—until the prince seeks to 'ascend from a civil order to an absolute one'. The very name 'civil principality' has a respectable ring to it, and might seem to weld Machiavelli's two basic forms of government into a happily balanced union: the republican rule of laws and the principality's rule of one man combined. But happy marriages of opposites have no place in Machiavelli's book. Republics have 'princes' in the sense of leading magistrates, but these magistrates are still subordinate to civil laws and held in check by others who share supreme power. Principalities may have magistrates, but they are ultimately subject to the prince's will. Instead of deceiving themselves that the 'civil' part of the *principato civile* secures them against princely desires for more absolute power, readers should ask: since 'civil' and 'principality' identify mutually competitive sources of supreme authority, aren't civil principalities doomed to fall toward one or the other?

THE SHADOW OF THE MEDICI

Machiavelli would pose this last question directly in his 1520 *Discursus*. Here he points out that all the Medici governments so far—including the one headed by the *Prince's* recently deceased dedicatee Lorenzo II—were neither republics nor principalities, but an unstable mix of these forms. For no government, he argues, can be stable (*stabile*) unless it is a true principality or a true republic (*vero principato, vera repubblica*). All hybrid governments inevitably 'rise' toward *principato* or descend to *repubblica*. Florence's 'princes' would thus make life far easier for themselves, and win the highest praise of their compatriots, if they reformed their state in the direction of one and away from the other.[1] If they failed to do this, their cities' fragile orders would soon rise to tyranny or collapse into licentious violence.[2]

Chapter 9 of the *Prince* expresses a similar analysis of civil principality, though indirectly. Florence's princely family is not named here, but its shadow looms over the whole chapter. Among the four 'modes' of becoming prince discussed in chapters 6–9, this one most obviously resembles that family's

---

[1] In fact Machiavelli completely ignores the option of reforming toward principality and recommends establishing a true republic, offering detailed advice about its magistracies and councils.

[2] Machiavelli could now be blunter in his criticisms of this hybrid 'mode' because of the very different political environments in 1520 and 1513.

signature political methods. The Medici were 'private citizens' in a republic whose vast wealth and connections enabled them to acquire great influence, far beyond any formal offices they held. Recounting their extraordinary 'ascent' in his *Florentine Histories*, Machiavelli suggests that in the midst of exhausting conflicts between the city's élite citizens or *grandi* and the non-élite *popolo*, Cosimo de' Medici was able to present himself as an impartial mediator standing above the fray. Without holding formal princely office, he and his offspring managed to acquire ever greater control over the state by exploiting an impressive range of non-violent yet quasi-legal means: 'liberally' handing out monetary favours, manipulating the selection of magistrates, and punishing opponents through a variety of questionably legal expedients.[3]

NOT FORTUNE OR *VIRTÚ*, BUT A FORTUNATE ASTUTENESS

Machiavelli alludes to the profound instability of civil principality when he stresses its ambiguous relation to his master standards: 'neither all *virtú* nor all fortune is necessary to attain' civil principality, he declares, 'but rather a fortunate astuteness [*una astuzia fortunata*]'. This phrase might seem to place the modes of civil princes worlds away from the nefarious cruelty of criminal princes. Like the term civil principality, 'fortunate astuteness' sounds rather respectable. Since astuteness is an ability to size up people and situations in order to gain one's advantage, it might even seem akin to virtuous prudence. Becoming prince through the favour of fellow citizens sounds good too: *favore* is support given voluntarily rather than forced, and no 'intolerable' violence is involved in the initial rise to princedom. In name and at first appearances, at least, this mode seems remote indeed from those used by criminal princes.

But good names and appearances can seldom be taken at face value in the *Prince*. The key question is whether civil principality is better at producing and maintaining stable orders than criminal or purely fortunate modes. The label 'fortunate astuteness' gives rise to doubts that it is. Any quality linked to fortune must be that much further from *virtú*, and is thus deficient as a mode for maintaining. In the *Discourses* Machiavelli observes that Venice, his prime example of a fortune-dependent city, failed to hold its empire because it was acquired 'not with war but with money and astuteness'—so that 'when it had to put its forces to the proof, Venice lost everything in one day'.[4] Like the fortune-reliant, the astute are good at acquiring power but less skilled at building durable foundations.

---

[3] See *FH* VII.1–6.   [4] *D* I.6; compare II.5.

As this passage suggests, the word *astuzia* is extremely ambiguous in Machiavelli's normatively coded vocabulary. In the *Prince* it almost always involves cunning, dishonesty, faithlessness, or transgressions of established orders and customs, under cover of decent causes. In chapters 15 and 18 *astuzia* is opposed to *integrità*, meaning integrity or honesty. Machiavelli treats *integrità* as a positive quality, while *astuzia* is the opposite, noting 'how praiseworthy it is for a prince to keep his faith, and to live with integrity and not by astuteness'.[5] Other passages associate *astuzia* with unscrupulous opportunism: the knack for exploiting divisions, such as those between the people and the great, to advance one's own ambitions even if this harms one's city.[6]

In the present chapter Machiavelli declares that 'there is more foresight and more astuteness in the great' than in the people—which might sound virtuous until it turns out that the *grandi* aim only to 'save themselves', while seeking to oppress the people through their astuteness. The *Histories* note 'with what deceits, with what astuteness, with what arts the princes, soldiers, and heads of republics conducted themselves so as to maintain the reputation they have not deserved'.[7] In the *Discourses*, *astuzia* sometimes appears as a valuable quality in military combat, enabling soldiers and generals to take advantage of their enemies. Otherwise, especially in civilian life and politics, it tends to do harm under a shadow of decency.[8] Their relatively inoffensive appearance compounds the harm astute methods eventually cause, since they prevent people from recognizing the disease until it is too advanced to cure.[9]

In its deceptively attractive features and affinities with fortune-reliance, *astuzia* could almost be shorthand for what Machiavelli says elsewhere about the Medici family's hallmark 'modes'. As he writes in the *Histories*, the most celebrated founders of the Medici dynasty, Cosimo (1389–1464) and his grandson Lorenzo 'the Magnificent' (1449–1492), were famously adept at using 'decent' (*onesto*) words to cover 'indecent' (*disonesto*) deeds. If they lacked certain qualities of *virtú* needed to make their city strong, they were past masters at generating appearances of strength and legitimacy, even while their actions—bribery, political favours, and shrewd manipulation of opponents—undercut civil order.[10]

---

[5] In chap. 19 Machiavelli calls the emperor Severus, an extremely ambivalent character in the *Prince*, a 'very astute fox'.

[6] Thus 'many judge', we read in chap. 20, 'that a wise prince, when he has the opportunity for it, should astutely nourish some enmity so that when he has crushed it, his greatness emerges the more from it'.

[7] *FH* V.1.186.   [8] For example, see *D* II.12, III.17.

[9] Both *D* and *FH* link astuteness to tyrannical ambitions, which are openly condemned throughout both works. *FH* IV.30 has one of the work's most prudent characters warn Florentines, on the brink of Medici coup, 'that courses of action, whether astute or bold, appear good in the beginning but then turn out to be difficult to deal with and harmful to finish'.

[10] See *FH* VII.1–6 and VIII.36; *ME* 17–28. Machiavelli often describes Medici actions as fortunate and extraordinary, but never as straightforwardly virtuous.

In the *Prince*, however, Machiavelli avoids identifying this or any mode too obviously with Florence's 'first family'. Here he plays the role of an adviser whose brief is not to question the wisdom of princely ends, but simply to suggest the best way to rise toward principality within a republic.

WHY PRINCES SHOULD FOUND THEMSELVES ON THE PEOPLE

A private citizen rises to civil principality in his native city, Machiavelli tells us, through the support of one of two sets of fellow citizens: either the people (*populo, popolo*) or the great (*grandi*). Machiavelli asserts that these 'diverse' parts of the citizen-body are always at odds with each other, unless their conflicts are somehow held in check. Each part may try to deal with opponents by making a private citizen 'prince'. The people do this when they want a strong individual to protect them from the predations of the great, who seek to 'oppress' (*opprimere*) them. The great make one of their fellow citizens prince, so that they can 'vent their appetites' (*sfogare il loro appetito*) against the people, 'under his shadow' (*sotto la sua ombra*).[11]

Machiavelli defines *populo* and *grandi* by their general opposition to each other more than to particular political or socio-economic characteristics.[12] This opposition is rooted in conflicting 'humours', *umori*, a word that Machiavelli uses to denote basic dispositions, drives, or desires. Thus he says that 'diverse humours' are found in every city because 'the people desire neither to be commanded nor oppressed by the great, and the great desire to command and oppress the people'. The desires or 'appetites' (*appetiti*) of the great and the people are fundamentally incompatible, since the one wants what the other seeks to avoid.

Which of the appetites described is more dangerous to an aspiring prince? This question will decide which 'part' of the republic's citizens he should look

---

[11] 'Under the shadow' was a well-known topos of Roman and humanist writings referring to imperial rule, with ambiguous allusions to an emperor's benign protection and/or sinister and 'shady' lack of transparency. Machiavelli plays on this ambiguity in *A W* I.12–17, where he writes that instead of doing things 'in the sun' like the Romans in their best days, matters of public import are now decided 'in the shade' (*sotto l'ombra*) in the manner of 'false and corrupt' examples from antiquity.

[12] In contemporary Florentine usage, the word for 'great', *grandi*, was applied to various upper-class élites: it might mean landed nobility, the wealthiest families, or some mixture of these elements. The term for 'the people', *il popolo*, was used in a range of different ways. In a political sense, it could refer to all those who were eligible to participate in political life; this sense of 'people' was coextensive with 'citizen', or with families whose heads of household were citizens. In a socio-economic sense, the word *popolo* could refer to non-élite citizens, sometimes including the 'labouring classes of artisans and salaried workers', but especially 'the non-élite middle classes' of tradesmen, professionals, and small landowners. Najemy (2006), 36–7.

to for support in his rise to power. Machiavelli has no doubts. He offers three arguments in favour of relying on the people as against the great.

The first argument is that the *grandi* with their desires to command and oppress are far less reliable supporters, and far more threatening to a new prince's own ambitions.[13] 'He who comes to principality with the aid of the great' finds it harder to maintain himself than one who relies on the people, for the former finds himself 'first man' among top-ranking citizens 'who appear to be his equals, and because of this he can neither command them nor manage [*maneggiare*] them in his own mode'.

This argument indirectly conveys key information about the desires or appetites of so-called civil princes. Equality, Machiavelli implies, is intolerable to such princes, since it threatens their first-man status. After a civil prince has risen to principality, in order to remain there he needs to establish a clear superiority over everyone else in the state. He must be able to command and manage in his 'own mode' even the wealthiest, noblest, and most powerful fellow-citizens who brought him to the principality in the first place. Whatever mode a prince uses to acquire power at first, the defining feature of principality—the supreme authority of one—propels him to seek to ever-greater, unopposed control. Machiavelli does not ask whether this end is reasonable, or good for a prince's or his city's health. For now, he merely shows that it cannot easily be gratified by the *favore* of the great, since desires of the great for power inevitably clash with the desires of princes for ever-greater control.

The second argument is that while the people's desires not to be commanded or oppressed by the great can be satisfied without actually harming the *grandi*, a prince who collaborates with them to oppress the people 'injures' the latter. Machiavelli casts this argument in unusually direct moral language. 'One cannot', he declares, 'satisfy [*satisfare*] the great with decency [*onesta*] and without injury to others, but one can satisfy the people; for the end [*fine*] of the people', he explains, 'is more decent [*più onesto*] than that of the great, since the great want to oppress and the people want not to be oppressed.' Whereas the desires of the great are aggressive and shady, those of the people are defensive and transparent. The former want to 'vent their appetite' under a prince's 'shadow', while the people openly seek protection through a prince's 'authority'. This argument suggests that prudence coincides with respect for 'decent' ends. Since the desire not to be oppressed is natural, reasonable, and decent, its satisfaction tends to produce stability and security for whoever satisfies it. Thus even a prince who cares little about whether his actions are just or harm the basic interests of others—and so seeks to avoid 'injuries'—can

---

[13] Soon after the Medici 'restoration' in 1512, Machiavelli wrote to Giovanni de' Medici (in *Ai Palleschi*) advising him to found his new state on popular support rather than that of the great—a move that may have angered powerful Medici partisans and exacerbated Machiavelli's already precarious position.

recognize the advantages of a policy that keeps injuries and oppression to a minimum.

Machiavelli's third argument has a different quality from the first two. So far, he has advised the prince to seek popular support because the people's desires are less competitive with his and more decent than those of the great. Both arguments hold out better prospects of top-down princely control over his fellow citizens. If anyone imagined that the people are easier to manage than the great, however, they were wrong. Princes need the people on side not because the *onesto* people are less threatening than the oppressive *grandi*, but because they are far *more* threatening when they stand against him. 'A prince can never secure himself against a hostile [*inimico*] people', Machiavelli tells us, 'as they are too many; against the great, he can secure himself, as they are few.'

It is true that while 'the worst that a prince can expect from a hostile people is to be abandoned by it', the hostile *grandi* may both abandon and attack him. But if Machiavelli takes pains here to present the people as non-aggressive, he implies that even their defensive hostility makes a prince less secure than the more aggressive enmity of the great. After all, the prince can afford to lose the friendship of any particular group of *grandi*, since these are just a handful of families who can be stripped of their titles or wealth, or sent into exile. By contrast, 'the prince always lives of necessity with the same people'; he cannot 'make and unmake them every day' as he does with the great. Different élites come and go, made and unmade by the whims of princes and fortune. The people, however, are always there, in every city—setting very substantial, inconvenient, yet inescapable limits on what princes can do. Since a prince cannot unmake them, he had better learn how to live with them.

All this suggests that aspiring princes not only do better with the people than with the great. They also, it seems, *need* the people as much as they need him. 'Therefore', Machiavelli says, summing up his arguments, 'one who becomes prince through the favour of the people should maintain them as friendly [*amico*] to him.' This should, he adds, 'be easy for him because they ask of him only that they not be oppressed'.

This tells us that the people desire not to be oppressed *in general*—not simply by the great, but also by the prince. It also introduces a warmer word than the previous 'favour' for what the prince needs from the people: 'friend-liness'. Machiavelli's low-key verbal modulations suggest that, on reflection, a prince might need considerably more from the people than their *favore* if he wants to enlist their help in maintaining his principality. And the costs of failing to win firm friendship increase a few lines later, when Machiavelli repeats the same refrain with important variations: 'I conclude only that for a prince it is necessary to have the people friendly; *otherwise he has no remedy in adversity*.' We have moved from arguments about the relative disadvantages of going with the great to a more absolute set of claims where popular friendship is a necessity—and where survival, not mere advantage, is at stake.

If it's clear that aspiring princes should cultivate the people, how should they manage those irksome *grandi*? Perhaps the people would be best satisfied if their protector dealt harshly with their erstwhile oppressors? 'To better clarify this issue', Machiavelli explains, the civil prince should avoid tarring all the great with the same brush. Those among the great who 'are obligated in everything to your fortune' and 'not rapacious' should be 'honoured and loved' (*onorare e amare*). Those who are 'not obligated' should not be lumped together either, but 'examined' to identify the reasons for their tepidity. Those who naturally lack 'spirit' (*animo*) need not be feared, and some may be useful counsellors. Only those who oppose the prince 'by art and for an ambitious cause' (*per arte e per cagione ambiziosa*) deserve to be seen as serious threats. Still, Machiavelli does not recommend attacking these dangerous *grandi* or letting the people avenge themselves on them. The prince should simply 'be on guard against them, and fear them as if they were open enemies'.[14]

MODES OF FOUNDING ON THE PEOPLE

'The prince can gain the people to himself', Machiavelli tells us, 'in many modes; and since they vary according to the subject [*variano secondo el subietto*], one cannot give certain rules [*dare certa regula*] for them, and so they will be left out.' There is a distinct whiff of irony in this omission. If there are no certain rules for gaining popular *favore* or friendship, this is not only because the modes commonly used by civil princes are various, but also because some are 'extraordinary' and therefore break rather than follow established rules: giving private favours and bribes, masking indecent deeds behind decent appearances, or taking advantage of civil strife to increase one's own power.[15]

Instead of spelling out specific modes of gaining the people, Machiavelli presents a single, apparently positive example: Nabis, 'prince of the Spartans, withstood a siege by all Greece and by one of Rome's most victorious armies', defending 'his fatherland and his state against them'. And when 'danger supervened', Machiavelli writes, 'it was enough for him to secure himself only against a few, which would not have been enough if he had had a hostile people'.

Knowing no more about Nabis, readers might think that Machiavelli means to hold up as an example to Italians a plucky prince of a beleaguered state who, against heavy odds, still defended his fatherland by securing popular goodwill. But there is often more to Machiavelli's ancient examples than meets the eye.

---

[14] Compare chap. 19.

[15] To 'vary' is to follow fortune, as Machiavelli hints these princes do.

Many early readers would have been familiar with Polybius', Livy's, and Plutarch's extremely critical accounts of Nabis' rule.[16] They portray him as a murderous tyrant who exploited popular rage against Spartan élites to maintain his power, sending many wealthy citizens into exile and parcelling up their estates. Such measures are far too extraordinary and destabilizing for Machiavelli's taste. In a chapter in the *Discourses* entitled 'Much as the founders of a republic and of a kingdom are praiseworthy, so much those of a tyranny are worthy of reproach', Machiavelli classifies Nabis as a tyrant whose methods should be strenuously avoided as both un-virtuous and unsafe.[17] For ancient writers and perhaps for Machiavelli, Nabis' most serious shortcoming was his implacable hostility to other Greek cities. Despite winning some impressive battles, Sparta eventually lost its independence under his watch—and an assassin sent from another part of Greece murdered Nabis.[18]

Though in the *Prince* Machiavelli 'leaves out' any critical comment on these long-term results of Nabis' methods, he surely expected readers to investigate them for themselves. The lesson they might draw is that while attacks on the great might persuade an angry populace to back you, even they cannot save you—or themselves—if you lead them down unreasonably confrontational paths at home or abroad. This is implied in Machiavelli's next remarks. Firstly, he reaffirms the value of founding on the people: 'let no one resist my opinion on this with that trite proverb, that whoever founds on the people founds on mud'. This saying is true only 'if a prince allows himself to think that the people will liberate him if he is oppressed by enemies or by the magistrates'— an error made by 'the Gracchi in Rome and Messer Giorgio Scali in Florence'. These men were what might today be called 'populist' leaders who, playing on popular anger against the *grandi*, stirred up civil unrest in order to increase their own power. Both the Gracchi and Scali failed to maintain princely authority for long. Yet their actions so intensified suspicions between the great and the people that their respective cities never managed to restore good internal orders.[19] Nabis' modes and legacy were not so different.

In terms of Machiavelli's most general modes, these particular methods of 'founding' on the people—especially winning support by negative attacks on the great or in external wars—have far closer ties to fortune than to *virtú*, and are thus unlikely to achieve firm foundations at all. As we saw in chapter 7, this kind of favour can evaporate or turn against you as quickly as it gets whipped

---

[16] *PolH* IV.81, XIII.6-8; *LH* XXXII.38-9, XXXIV.41; *PL* 'Philopoemen'. Sometimes with, sometimes against Philip V of Macedon (chap. 24), he fought against the Greek Achaeans led by Philopoemen (chap. 14), who appear in a favourable light throughout the *Prince*.

[17] *D* I.10.

[18] Sparta was defeated by and absorbed into the Achaean League. Machiavelli mentions the plot against Nabis in *D* I.40.6 and III.6.7.

[19] The Gracchi name was a byword for buying favour and wreaking havoc in republics. Scali was a tyrannical head of the plebs, discussed in *FH* III and IV.

up. Solidly virtuous foundations need more than *favore*: they depend on *satisfying* people's reasonable, decent desires, such as the desire not to be oppressed. This, perhaps, is the most promising way to win popular friendship. But the characteristic methods of those who seek to become princes in republics do not aim to satisfy reasonable desires; they merely indulge unreasonable popular appetites for revenge against the great.[20]

Then Machiavelli mentions a very different way to 'found' on the people. Things go better for a prince, he argues, who 'can command and is a man full of heart [*uomo di cuore*], does not get terrified, does not fail to make other preparations and with his spirit and his orders keeps the generality of people inspired [*tenga con lo animo e ordini suoi animato l'universale*]'. Such a prince 'will never find himself deceived' by the people, 'and it will appear that he has laid his foundations well.'

This passage could be read as a parody of the belief that all a prince has to do is make indeterminate 'preparations', fire up the masses with his great heart and spirit, and that will suffice to win over the people regardless of his concrete policies. Keep the people animated and put on a good show; so long as it appears you have laid good foundations, no one will worry about their true quality. Or it may point princes toward essential elements of a well-founded state: good command, which Machiavelli will say more about in the chapter's closing paragraph; further preparations, which later chapters will discuss; and 'orders' as well as spirit since, as often seen before, *animo* without good *ordini* can harm cities. The ambiguity lets princes choose between more spirited and order-driven 'modes'.

THE PERILS OF ABSOLUTE POWER

This encouraging passage about how a prince can lay—or appear to lay— foundations well is followed by more ominous reflections. Civil principalities 'customarily run into peril when they are about to ascend from a civil order to an absolute one [*salire da lo ordine civile allo assoluto*]'. The peril arises from the extraordinary character of this 'ascent'. Princes who move toward absolute power violate customary and ordinary limits, and thus quite reasonably come to danger. This view is echoed in the remark that in emergencies the prince 'does not have time to seize absolute authority because the citizens and subjects, who are accustomed to receive commands from the magistrates, are not ready, in these emergencies [*frangenti*], to obey his'. Civil orders accustom citizens to obey the magistrates, not a prince. It is consistent with that custom for them to oppose or withhold support from a prince who usurps the magistrates' authority.

---

[20] See *ME* 299–306.

By saying that princes who seek to make their authority absolute lose the support of 'citizens and subjects', Machiavelli hints at the ambiguous civil status of those governed under a civil principality. At the beginning of a prince's 'ascent', the *populo* are citizens of a republic. But once they have granted one man more than ordinary authority, the distinction between citizen and subject becomes blurred. Almost imperceptibly, citizens are converted into subjects, just as the free cities discussed in chapters 3–5 became subjects of foreign powers after willingly handing the latter power to act as their 'arbiter'.

Machiavelli says that civil principalities come to peril *when* they move toward absolute principality, not *if* they do. This implies that the passage 'from civil order to an absolute one' *must* eventually transpire. The necessity seems to arise from uncertainty about how civil princes should exercise command. 'For these princes', Machiavelli explains, 'either command by themselves or by means of magistrates.' The first method is personal or 'private', the second civil or public. At first, civil princes who rise in a republic may follow the second method, according to established custom. But such princes are seldom satisfied with commanding through magistrates for long, since 'their state is weaker and more dangerous because they remain altogether at the will [*stanno al tutto con la volontà*] of those citizens who have been put in the magistracies'.

It seems inevitable that once the people or the *grandi* make a prince in a republic, conflicts will arise between these two sources of ultimate authority in the state, civil and princely. Instead of being content with constraints on his personal power, the prince soon realizes that the magistrates 'can take away his state with great ease either by turning against him or by not obeying him'. Growing wary of these 'ordinary' restraints on his authority, he is apt to turn towards the other, personal method of command and seek more 'absolute' authority.[21] A prince who does this effectively abandons the 'civil' part of his principality and plumps for straight *principato*—if not for tyranny.

Far from giving the green light to princes tempted to pursue this course, the entire chapter has quietly underlined the dangers that confront those who seek unbounded personal power in republics. It is always dangerous to try to 'seize absolute power', since in a clash between prince and magistrates 'the citizens and subjects' will hesitate between these rival authorities, or choose to obey the 'customary' magistrates' commands. Machiavelli's analysis suggests that the people have reasonable grounds for their reluctance to back a prince's aspirations for absolute authority. There is, in fact, a basic tension between the desire of the people not to be oppressed and the desire of princes for 'absolute' command. Herein lies the greatest danger for civil princes. They need to keep the people friendly; yet the people want not to be oppressed. If—or rather when—a civil prince moves toward absolute power, many among the people

---

[21] As *D* I.2 says eventually happens in all principalities; see chap. 1.

will understandably see him as an oppressor. Chapter 5 stressed how implacably hostile the people are to whoever oppresses them; the present chapter has reminded us that 'a prince can never secure himself against a hostile people'.

A 'wise prince' who recognizes these perils must think about how to make his citizens need him and his state, 'always and in every quality of time', for then 'they will always be faithful to him'. This seems to advise the prince to establish a clear hierarchy of dominance and dependence, making sure that his subjects 'need' him and are loyal out of need. In a similar vein, earlier in the chapter, Machiavelli stated that 'men who receive good from someone from whom they believed they would receive evil [*male*] are more obligated [*obligano*] to their benefactor', and 'the people immediately [*subito*] wish him well more than if he had been brought to the principality with their favour'. Wearing the mask of solicitous adviser, Machiavelli flatters the prince's hopes of gaining and holding power without worrying about popular desires to avoid oppression. No need to put yourself out trying to satisfy those desires, he seems to say, so long as you keep the people on edge, fearing that you might do 'evil'. If you then surprise them with good, their relief will suffice to make them obligated.

But the flattering adviser's voice—a voice that frequently pipes up in the *Prince*—is not in total command of the chapter. It expresses only one set of opinions among more thoughtful reflections, including the view that a dangerous contradiction exists between a prince's desire for absolute command and the people's inconvenient desire not to be oppressed. So the truly 'wise' prince might have to consider other ways to make citizens need 'the state and himself' than to take absolute power in a republic. He might, for a start, have to think harder about what *he* needs from the people. In the course of the chapter, what princes need moved from 'favour' to the warmer 'friendliness'. Now at the end—indeed, this is the chapter's last word—he should aspire to keep them always 'faithful' (*fedeli*). Faith is even harder to get and keep than friendship, especially unwavering faith. Yet this is not the first time in the *Prince* that Machiavelli has hinted at the importance of lasting faith for a strong state, nor will it be the last. The next chapter will suggest some concrete measures that might help to give peoples faith in princes.

If these undertones warn princes about the risks of seeking absolute authority in republics, they also serve warning to the citizens who help to create such monsters. Beneath its detached analysis, the chapter tells a perennial human story, as sadly familiar in our own times as in those of Machiavelli and his ancients. In a republic fraught with economic or political inequalities, the people hand extraordinary power to one man, hoping that he will protect their interests from grasping, power-hungry élites. But it soon transpires that they deceived themselves: they did not foresee that their protector-prince would transgress his limited remit, and come to oppress the entire city. The same story, told in a thousand different ways throughout human history, was the stuff of Greece's greatest tragedies and histories, and of Roman histories and satires. Machiavelli retells it in his own way in the *Prince* and other works. The *Discourses* nicely sum up its main message: 'one should be mindful of the works of citizens because many times underneath a merciful work a beginning of Tyranny is concealed'.[22]

---

[22] The title of *D* III.28.

Foundations

Foundations

10

Abundance and necessity

In what mode the forces of all principalities should be measured

When assessing the quality of a prince's foundations, Machiavelli now tells us, a key consideration is 'whether a prince has enough of a state that he can rule [*reggersi*] by himself when he needs to, or whether he always has the necessity of being defended by others'. Military defences are the main condition for self-sufficiency. 'I judge those capable of ruling by themselves', Machiavelli declares, 'who can by abundance of either men or money, put together an adequate army [*uno esercito iusto*] and fight a battle against whoever comes to attack him'. By contrast, 'those always have necessity of others who cannot appear in the field against an enemy, but are necessitated to take refuge behind walls and to guard them'.

If princely readers hope to hear more about how they can acquire enough men or money to assemble an effective army, they'll be disappointed. Instead, Machiavelli assumes that his readers are poor and short of fighting men—and thus find it necessary to fortify their towns and depend on others. How, he asks, can princes reduce their chances of failure in these far-from-ideal conditions?

HAVE A STRONG TOWN AND AVOID POPULAR HATRED

When princes have a scarcity of men or money, Machiavelli begins, 'one can say nothing but to exhort' them 'to fortify and supply their own towns [*terra*], and to take no account of the countryside [*paese*]'. With his 'one can say nothing but', Machiavelli seems to give cold comfort to princes who have only moderate wealth and middling or small populations at their disposal. But what follows suggests that these modest defensive measures, fortifying and supplying 'well', can go a long way toward deterring attackers. For 'whoever has fortified his town well', Machiavelli tells readers, 'and, concerning other governing, has managed relations with his subjects as was said above and will be said below, will always be attacked with great hesitation [*con gran respetto assaltato*]'. Though ideally, princes should have armies that can meet attackers on the battlefield, those who lack an army can ward off assaults by constructing solid defences inside their towns. 'For', Machiavelli points out, 'men are always hostile to undertakings where difficulties may be seen, and one can see it is not easy to attack one who has his town strong [*gagliarda*] and is not hated by the people.'

Machiavelli stresses, however, that military fortifications and munitions are insufficient defences. How a prince 'manages' other matters of government with his subjects is no less important for his security against outside attacks. So what measures does a prince need to take to build a strong town and avoid being hated by the people?

WHY FREE CITIES HAVE GOOD DEFENCES

Machiavelli touches on these questions in his example of German cities, *la città della Magna*. These cities, he says, 'are very free [*liberissime*]', and 'have very small rural areas [*contado*]'. This last circumstance presumably makes it easier for these cities to take his earlier advice: concentrate on defending the town while taking 'little account of the countryside'. The chapter discusses freedom chiefly in terms of individual cities' relations with other powers, omitting any explicit discussion of internal freedoms.[1]

Machiavelli states that German cities are 'very free' since they 'obey the emperor when they want to; they do not fear either him or any other power [*potente*] around, because they are fortified [*affortificate*] in such a mode that everyone thinks their capture would be toilsome and difficult'. This makes a clear connection between the defensive capabilities of individual cities and their freedom. Good defences help make them free, in the sense that they can freely choose when to obey others and do not fear them. The cities' formidable defences rendered them free, on the one hand, in relation to foreign powers; on the other, in relation to the German emperor, who held leading or princely rank in the wider German *stato* that embraced the individual cities. While formally associated with the empire, the cities—some governed by their own 'princes', others as republics—were able to choose when to obey his commands,

---

[1] Though indirect implications are raised below. Compare what Machiavelli says about German cities in *D* I.55, where their free way of life is linked to lack of corruption and observance of laws, 'so that no one *from outside or inside* dares to seize them'. This suggests that their fierce resistance to external oppression arises from internal freedoms, while loss of freedom corrupts citizens and weakens cities' external defences.

and have strong enough defences of their own not to fear repercussions if they choose not to obey.

Machiavelli doesn't say whether this kind of freedom in its constituent cities produces better defences for the German Empire as a whole. He judges strong defences here from the standpoint of the individual cities rather than that of the empire or emperor. In this respect, he echoes his earlier essay on 'German Affairs'. Here he acknowledges the value of a weak imperial power that could act as arbiter in conflicts among German cities, helping them to avoid fratricidal wars of the sort that were driving Italians to self-destruction. But whenever an emperor became too strong, he threatened to ruin this good order by undercutting the individual cities' freedoms: he would 'dominate and belittle' the separate German cities and princes, using them to serve his wishes and not when it suited them. Emperors who turned the empire into an instrument of their private enterprises instead of treating it as a means to common ends might increase their own reputation and 'greatness'.[2] But an empire made up of cities whose cherished freedoms have been stripped away by a prince might face the kinds of rebellions Machiavelli alluded to in the *Prince*, chapter 5.

Instead of risking the endless troubles that result from such attempts to dominate free peoples and cities, a prudent 'prince' of an empire—whether a vast one like the German or a smaller one like the Florentine dominions—should perhaps try to preserve the *defensive* powers found in individual free cities, drawing on them as a source of common defences. In both early and later writings, Machiavelli frequently suggests that the best defences for any state consist of the pooled resources of independent cities, especially those governed as free republics. And in so far as his German example presents an ideal of good orders that might fruitfully be adapted by contemporary Italians, it seems clear that in the *Prince* Machiavelli's preferred Germans are those who desire to live in their own cities without oppression, not those who want to dominate others imperial-style. To contemporaries, his German model held up the possibility of a defensive Italian union with a weak central authority, with the participating city-states maintaining primary responsibility for their own defences.[3]

FORTIFICATIONS I: MILITARY AND ECONOMIC

Having said that fortifications in free German cities deter 'everyone' from attacking them, Machiavelli explains what constitutes these impressive defences.

---

[2] *GA* 22–3.   [3] Compare *D* II.19.

All of these cities, Machiavelli writes, 'have suitable [*convenienti*] ditches and walls, and sufficient artillery'. The words 'sufficient' and 'suitable' remind us that these defences are still supposedly a poor alternative to having an 'abundance' of men or money. But as we read further about the very considerable advantages they bring, we might start to wonder whether sufficiency without abundance isn't, after all, a perfectly good basis for defensive strength.

The next lines suggest that fortifications and the 'forces' (*vires*) measured in the chapter's title are not just walls and artillery. They also include well-stocked public stores of food and drink. And Machiavelli points to other conditions for successful defences that are not military in a narrow sense. In particular, the plebs [*plebe*] should be kept well fed 'without loss to the public', because they are given work 'in employments [*esercizi*] that are the nerve and life of that city'. *Esercito* is Machiavelli's usual word for 'army', although *esercizi* may have the wider sense of exercises or employments. Here it means both. The *plebe* were the lower classes of city-dwellers. In Machiavelli's Florence they did not hold full political rights as citizens. Machiavelli suggests here that they should be employed in *esercizi* as the city's key military defenders. The plebs' *esercizii* include regular military exercises performed by all able-bodied male citizens, as the next sentence says: 'They should hold military exercises [*esercizii militari*] in repute, and . . . have many orders [*ordini*] to maintain them'. Machiavelli implies that these supportive orders are not exclusively military. The plebs are not to be employed only as soldiers, but given work in various *esercizii*—in the broader sense of employments—that help to fuel 'the industries [*industrie*] from which the plebs are fed'.

A basic condition for good fortifications, then, is material security for the people who provide the core of their city's defences: a secure employment and livelihood, and freedom from fear of hunger. To express this in terms of princely interests, a well-ordered political economy that ensures a decent living for all a city's people is among the necessary foundations of a prince's military power. Civil orders should enable the plebs to feed themselves without depending on a prince's largesse or the charity of the great.

At first, Machiavelli's exhortation to keep the plebs fed might have sounded like advice to treat them like cannon fodder, giving them a barely sufficient livelihood in exchange for them putting their lives on the line. A closer reading transforms this first impression. Far from simply keeping their martial herds alive, princes have to meet more than their basic, bestial survival needs. They should also start viewing them as men on whom a prince's own security depends—and who deserve respect, since their employments, military and industrial, are the very 'nerve and life' of their city.

Machiavelli's discussion of what it means 'to fortify' (*fortificare*) a city thus expands the term from its narrowly military sense to include the ordering of a city's political economy. The economic advantages of Machiavelli's German model are connected to their motivational benefits. Even lowly plebs need to be motivated to defend their city. If they are able to feed themselves through highly valued work, they will also be more content with their princes, and more willing and able to perform their military duties. And princes whose people are 'very free', secure in their livelihood, respected, and self-respecting will be harder to attack than those who lack such robust 'arms'.

FORTIFICATIONS II: GOOD ORDERS AND JUSTICE

This provides some initial answers to the question posed at the end of chapter 9 about how princes can ensure that their people are 'always' faithful, bridging the dangerous gulf between prince and people that constantly imperils the former's *stato*. Chapter 10's last, long paragraph picks up this recurring theme, affirming that 'a prince who has a city ordered thus and does not make himself hated cannot be attacked'; and if someone did hazard an assault on him, he would soon 'have to retreat in shame', since a city armed with well-fed, respectfully employed plebs can withstand siege 'for a year' within its walls. If this optimistic assessment is right, one might wonder again whether such defensive forces aren't sufficient for a prince to 'rule by himself when he needs to'.

Of course, if he does reorder his city's lower classes to serve as its premier defenders, he will not be wholly self-sufficient, but dependent on the plebs and other city-dwellers to fight in case of a siege. Some princes might baulk at this point, preferring to wait for fortune to endow them with abundant men or money rather than to make the most of their current scant resources, if this means depending on lowly *plebe*.

But it is starting to sound as if a really adequate army might be better assembled *without* an abundance of men or money. Machiavelli's discourse on German cities suggests that excellent defences depend more on the quality than on the quantity of men and resources. And your own self-imposed orders—that is, orders built by *virtù*—can produce a better quality of defensive fighting than sheer masses of men or weapons purchased by money.[4]

As to men, Machiavelli would make this point quite directly in his *Art of War*. The best ancient armies of the Romans and Greeks, he declares there, 'made war with few, fortified by order and by art'; less admirable armies fought with 'a multitude' (*moltitudine*), a word Machiavelli generally uses for disordered, ill-disciplined collections of people.[5] A few fought more effectively in

[4] Compare *D* II.8.4.
[5] In contrast to well-ordered 'peoples'. See *D* I.58 where Machiavelli distinguishes between disordered multitudes 'unshackled by laws' and those that become ordered 'peoples' once they are constrained by good laws. The distinction has ancient roots in the Greek contrast between *ochlos* (mob) or *plēthos* (crowd, many), and the well-constituted *dēmos* (people). Compare Hobbes (1998/1642), VI.1–2.75–7.

these cases because virtuous order and discipline had to make up for other deficiencies.[6] As to money, Machiavelli underscores the *advantages* of relative scarcity over abundance in his 'German Affairs'. He presents the Germans as paragons of thrift and self-restrained appetites, qualities that allowed them to live far more healthily on sparse supplies than their self-indulgent Italian counterparts. This frugality extends to military defences, where 'they spend nothing on soldiers, as they keep their own men armed and drilled'.[7] Virtuous measures, it seems, can more than compensate for lack of abundance.

At the beginning of the chapter Machiavelli wrote that those capable of 'ruling by themselves' need an *iusto* army. The word *iusto* has connotations of strength, but can also simply mean 'just'. Are the good orders Machiavelli describes in his German example also 'just' in a moral sense?

He does posit a very strong connection between good orders, military strength, and justice in both early and later writings.[8] In a series of proposals for reforming Florence's military written in 1505–6, Machiavelli regrets that his city lacks the two essential pillars of any political order, justice (*iustizia*) and arms, and argues that 'the only way to recover the one and the other is to order arms through public deliberation, and maintain them with good orders [*ordinarsi all'armi per deliberazione pubblica, et con buono ordine et mantenerlo*]'.[9] His main argument in another early proposal offers specific reasons why well-ordered military defences cannot be maintained without general political and legal justice. The plebs or citizens who are expected to serve as their city's *armi* are less likely to avoid service, and more likely to observe good discipline, if they are confident that no exceptions to general conscription are made in exchange for political or monetary favours.[10]

In these earlier writings the impartiality of the laws, or basic legal justice, is treated as a necessary condition for well-ordered civil defences. Machiavelli omits these legal arguments in the *Prince*, maintaining the conceit that princely readers of his book care too little about laws or justice to take them seriously. But he will suggest that good laws are needed to constitute strong civil 'arms' in chapters 12–14. For now, he touches on the relation between socio-economic justice and effective civil defences, proposing that the latter depend on giving the lower classes a decent share of public goods, especially work that serves the public interest, and is recognized as 'the nerve and life' of

---

[6] Compare *AW* 131–2.

[7] *GA* 20–1. Tacitus' *Germania* held up a similar German ideal to corrupt Romans. In his poem *The Ass* (Asino), 5.64–8 Machiavelli says that Florence was content with controlling a smaller territory around her, and her people stood firm when threatened by great kings and emperors. But 'Now that she has extended her power to the lands around about and become great and vast, she dreads everything, not merely huge armies.'

[8] In particular, the *Art of War* argues strongly that general justice is needed to order and maintain strong military forces; see *AW* 130–1; see *ME* 293–4.

[9] *Cagione*, 26–7.   [10] *Provisione*, 41–2.

that city. It seems reasonable to infer from this that some sort of distributive justice is a condition for creating strong civil defences.[11]

Machiavelli makes the case for this kind of justice in purely instrumental, self-regarding terms, suggesting that princes should adopt these measures not out of a concern to respect others' reasonable claims, but because they can help him defend his private interests. But readers who reflect on why it pays to treat other people justly—here, by giving the plebs employment and a livelihood that allow them to merit their share of public recognition—may come to recognize a moral reason to do so as well. If decent work and public respect motivate people to fight for your state, this is because people are not chattel. They are human beings who want good reasons to act at others' command, and who have the capacity to reject or rebel against such commands. Anyone who recognizes basic human capacities to demand reasons and choose to obey commands or not—capacities of reasoning and free agency—will have good moral as well as self-interested reasons to treat people justly. Machiavelli will say more about the coincidence of princely self-interest and justice in later chapters, especially when discussing the justice of keeping faith with allies in chapter 21.

MAKING *VIRTÙ* OUT OF NECESSITY

At the beginning of chapter 10 Machiavelli misleadingly told readers to expect that he could do no more than show princes who lacked abundant men or money how to scrape by in a bad situation. Instead, he embarks on a far more ambitious enterprise, telling them how to turn these supposed shortcomings to their advantage. A cash-strapped prince who does not control huge populations can, if he adopts the measures recommended here, do much *better* than princes who have an abundance of money and men. He will have taken the first steps toward forming an army of citizens capable of defending his state even more effectively than any larger, expensive army of mercenaries or foreign auxiliary troops. Machiavelli's German example shows that princes can construct more virtuous defensive orders without abundance than with it, because they have to work harder to get the best from the little they have. Instead of imagining that they can solve all problems of defence with large quantities of money and men, scarcity forces them to think about redesigning political

---

[11] In the *Discourses* Machiavelli describes social equality as such a condition: 'those republics in which a political and uncorrupt way of life is maintained do not endure that any citizen . . . either be or live in the usage of a gentleman; indeed, they maintain among themselves a full equality [*tanta equalità*]' D I.55. He makes the same point in 'German Affairs', speaking of the Swiss Germans who 'enjoy a true freedom [*libera libertà*] without any differentiation between men, apart from that which results from holding public office.' GA 22.

'orders' to improve their military defences, and to contemplate making fundamental improvements in their economic, social, and legal institutions.

An apparent downside of these reforms is that princes who implement them end up depending on some others—their own plebs and other subjects—to deter attackers and fight back in case of attack. On the bright side, these good orders can bind these people to a prince, so that 'so long as he does not make himself hated' they can be trusted to defend his state. And as chapters 12–13 elaborate, 'arms' made up of one's own well-disciplined, highly motivated subjects or citizens are more formidable and reliable than multitudes of troops recruited from elsewhere, paid for with an abundance of money. It turns out that some ways of depending on others are perfectly compatible with *virtú*, and necessary for good defences.

These arguments had, of course, a pressing practical import for Machiavelli. He wanted to persuade any Florentine government, whether republican or princely, that a civilian militia would make the city less dependent on mercenary and foreign troops for their defences. He had to reassure his more conservative compatriots that a militia would be neither very expensive nor dangerous for the élites, who feared that the lower orders might use their arms and discipline to seize more power for the populace. But like other chapters, this one grounds arguments for practical reforms on a bedrock of philosophical positions developed in the *Discourses* and *Art of War* as well as the *Prince*.

One of Machiavelli's basic precepts is that some of the best things, indeed the qualities and works of highest *virtú*, can be coaxed out of scarcity, poor sites, and a few men—that is, out of necessity.[12] But not all princes recognize the advantages of ordering their defences under necessity, and the disadvantages of depending on abundance. Necessity looks different to the fortune-dependent and to the virtuous. The former regard all the unavoidable constraints Machiavelli calls *necessità* as a threat to their ambitions. The virtuous see the same constraints as stimuli to more effective ordering. People who rely too much on fortune tend to expect an easy ride to success. Thinking that they should be able to 'fly' unimpeded to whatever goal they might have, they fail to understand that they might sometimes have to bow to necessity and work within its limits.

By contrast, people who exhibit *virtú* in Machiavelli's optimal sense realize that they *always* have to work within certain constraints that they neither choose nor completely control. They know that no human being, however powerful, can escape the limits imposed by necessity—least of all the limits set by the existence of other people with whom they must share the world, who have needs and desires that often collide with their own. The *virtú*-reliant don't try to escape all such constraints on their actions. Instead they learn to

---

[12] See *D* I.1, *ME* chap. 4.

distinguish those that are inescapable, or rooted in quite 'ordinary and rea-sonable' human desires, from obstacles that can be ignored or forcibly removed.

HOW PRINCES AND PEOPLES CAN UNITE THROUGH SIEGE

In the chapter's dramatic conclusion, Machiavelli describes how powerful bonds between prince and people may be forged out of harshest necessity: here, through the common experience of being under attack. He imagines a sceptical respondent to his discourse who doubts that the people can ever be relied upon to stand by the prince in a long siege. 'Someone might reply', he writes, that 'if the people have their possessions outside, and see them burning' they will soon lose patience, 'and the long siege and their care for their own [*carita propria*] will make them forget the love [*amore*] of the prince'. Machia-velli responds that the people will not abandon 'a prudent [or powerful]¹³ and spirited [*animoso*] prince' in a crisis; he 'will always overcome all these difficul-ties' by inspiring his subjects with hope or with fear of the enemy's cruelty.

The first impression created by the passage is that 'spirited' princes who know how to inflame their subjects' spirits against the enemy can prevent them from giving up when their own homes and belongings are attacked. A closer reading suggests that high spirits are only one source of the bond that may form between prince and people through a siege. By enduring a long attack on their city and *contado*, the people 'come to unite [*unire*] with their prince so much the more, since it appears he has an obligation with them [*abbia con loro obligo*], their houses having been burned and their possessions ruined in his defence'. This quietly subverts the conventional princely wisdom that princes should defend the people, who are then obligated to him. Here Machiavelli urges princes to recognize, on the contrary, that their subjects are in fact *their* best protectors. If a prince asks them to let their houses burn and their possessions get ruined 'in his defence', he must acknowledge obligations of gratitude and respect toward them at least as strong as any they have to him.

The words 'unite' and 'obligation' evoke a firmer, more lasting kind of bond than the transient cooperation that results from spirited resistance in a crisis. Machiavelli makes it clear that the most binding obligations between princes and subjects—or indeed any people—are formed reciprocally, on an equal basis: for 'the nature of men is to be obligated [*obligarsi*] as much by benefits [*benefizi*] they give as by benefits they receive'. A prince who wants to unite his

---

¹³ Some versions of the original text have *prudente*, others *potente*.

people to him and make them 'always faithful' can do so, then, by means of reciprocal obligations, not asymmetrical dependence. Obligations are more reliable than feelings of love for the prince, which can flare up and subside or turn to hatred overnight. The people are more likely to stand by him over time, and not just when an enemy attacks, if he gives them the respect and security in their livelihood that they earn through their sacrifices in defending his *stato*.

At the end of chapter 9, Machiavelli advised princes to think of ways to make the people be 'always' faithful to them. Now he depicts a movement from subjects toward prince as 'they come to unite with their prince so much the more'—a voluntary movement motivated by virtuous princely policies. To be sure, such two-way obligations impose very considerable limits on a prince's ability to do whatever he wants. They will appear inconvenient if he aspires to absolute independence. But the more virtuous a prince is, the more he will realize that such ambitions are unrealistic. Even the strongest princes have to depend on some others, and it is safer to depend on people you can trust to act as your 'own arms' than on temporary or purchased *favore*. So the right question for princes is not: how can I avoid depending on anyone other than myself, but rather: how can I choose the best possible 'others' to rely on, then order their actions and relations with me so that our dependence is reciprocal—and willing?

A single word choice in its last sentence enhances the chapter's movement from the top-down perspective of princes toward a more popular standpoint. So far, Machiavelli has spoken of those under princely government as subjects (*sudditi*). Now, having said how prince and subjects might 'unite' through two-way obligations, he declares: 'it should not be difficult for a prudent prince to keep the spirits of his citizens [*cittadini*] firm in the siege'. The quiet change in name marks an important transformation in the relationship between a prince and his people—one brought about by the modest, *ordinario* measures proposed in the chapter.

11

Popes

Of ecclesiastical principalities

OTHERWORLDLY STATES

The last chapter spoke of the earth-bound human needs that generate or thwart virtuous defences: of *terra* and countryside, food and drink, the loss of worldly possessions, and the raw fighting spirit that endures such losses. States that adopt his measures—Machiavelli did not refer to them as either principalities or republics—face undoubted hardships in setting up their own defences. But the hard work pays off once potential attackers see how hard it is to defeat them.

Turning from earth to higher places, chapter 11 examines a species of principality that has little need of ordinary human *virtú*. Ecclesiastical principalities, Machiavelli tells us, have difficulties only before they are possessed (*posseghino*). They are acquired 'either by *virtú* or by fortune', but 'maintained without one or the other'. Surprising as this sounds, Machiavelli has an explanation. Such principalities do not need to concern themselves with the usual modes of maintaining because they are 'sustained [*sustenati*] by orders that have grown antiquated with religion [*antiquati nell religione*]'. These antique *ordini* do the supportive work that either fortune or *virtú* must do in secular states. Indeed, they do much more, for they 'have been so powerful and of such a quality [*tanto potenti e qualità*] that they hold [*tengono*] their princes in the state in whatever mode they proceed and live'.

Princes in these states are thus wonderfully blessed. They can, it seems, live and act however they like without worrying about the consequences of their actions. The sustenance they derive from antiquated religious orders furnishes so much power that they need not think about the difficulties, inconveniences, and risks that Machiavelli urges every other kind of prince to appraise before acting. The prop of religious orders gives them, in effect, a political and military *carte blanche*. These princes 'alone have states and do not defend them; they have subjects, and do not govern them'. Extraordinarily, their states, 'though undefended, are not taken from them', and their subjects neither care that they are not governed nor 'think of becoming alienated [*alienarsi*] from such princes, nor can they'.

To have states and subjects held without question no matter what you do, without any need for the arduous tasks of governing and defending, and yet without having to fall back on fickle fortune—what a pleasant way to rule! Exalted above ordinary people, indeed above the ordinary run of princes, the princes of the Church do nothing, or do the worst, and get away with it. Since they derive power from an otherworldly source, they are 'held' without ordinary human efforts, and seem eternally immune from difficulties and enmities. 'Thus,' Machiavelli observes, 'only these principalities are secure and happy [*sicuri e felici*].'[1]

HOW THE CHURCH GREW GREAT

Having described all these marvellous advantages, he now checks himself. Perhaps such states are too unique, and the sources of their power too mysterious, to bear Machiavelli's usual exact analysis of the actions that support or undermine any political order. Since 'they are upheld by superior causes [*retti da cagione superiori*], which the human mind does not reach', he declares, 'I will omit speaking of them. For,' he explains, 'since they are exalted and maintained by God, it would be the office of a presumptuous and rash [*presuntuoso e temerario*] man to discourse on them.'

These scruples dissolve the moment after Machiavelli expresses them. 'Nevertheless'—his recurring *nondimanco*—'if someone were to ask me how the Church came to such greatness [*tanta grandezza*] in temporal matters', then Machiavelli could hardly restrain himself from hazarding an examination of the purely human causes of this phenomenon. He now launches into precisely the kind of reasoned, down-to-earth discussion he just said he would omit, for fear of appearing presumptuous and rash.

Until King Charles VIII of France marched into Italy in 1494, the province 'was under the empire' (*imperio*) of several leading Italian powers, including the pope.[2] The other powers managed to check the popes' ambitions, and each others', for a long time. But in the traumatic aftermath of the French invasions, Pope Alexander VI launched an aggressive campaign to

---

[1] That is, 'both' secure and happy: since happiness in Machiavelli's ambivalent sense is fortune-dependent and thus at odds with genuine security, 'only' states sustained by some otherworldly cause can hope to have both.

[2] The Pope, Venice, Naples, Milan, and Florence.

increase the Papacy's—and through it, his family's—power in Italy. 'Of all the pontiffs there have ever been', Machiavelli declares, Alexander 'showed how far a pope could prevail with money and forces', using his son Duke Valentino 'as his instrument' (*lo instrumento*). Although that duke was eliminated (*spento*) soon after his father's death, nevertheless 'what he did turned to the greatness of the Church', which inherited the fruits of his labours.

This unprecedented worldly *grandezza* was further increased under Alexander's arch-enemy Pope Julius II, who 'found the path still open to a mode of accumulating money, never used before Alexander'. Machiavelli refrains from saying what this mode was, but it was presumably the sale of ecclesiastical offices to men who agreed to support an individual pope's ambitions. Julius also continued Alexander's and Cesare's policy of restraining the great Orsini and Colonna factions in Rome. Machiavelli ends his historical excursus, and the chapter, with a reverent bow to the effective head of the Medici clan at the time of writing, Pope Leo X. This first Florentine pope, he writes, 'has found this pontificate most powerful [*potentissimo*]; one may hope', he continues, 'that if the others made it great with arms, he, with his goodness and infinite other virtues [*con la bontà e infinite altre sua virtú*], can make it very great and venerable'.[3]

CAN ANY HUMAN PRINCE DO WITHOUT EARTHLY FOUNDATIONS?

A reader unaware of Machiavelli's reputation as a secular-minded critic of the Church, and unfamiliar with his ironic vocabulary, might read this as an exemplary political success story with Pope Alexander VI as its hero. Before Alexander, other Italians—not only the so-called great powers but 'every baron and lord'—held the Church 'in low esteem in temporal affairs'. Because of Alexander's shrewd use of 'money and forces', the Church rose in a few years to astonishing greatness, becoming involved in territorial wars and vying with other 'powers' for dominance over Italy. If we assume that, for Machiavelli, the ends of *grandezza* and reputation excuse whatever means attain these ends, we might think that he sees nothing wrong with Alexander's methods: extending the use of bribery among Church dignitaries on the one hand, and using his son, backed by foreign troops, to pursue a programme of military expansion in Italy, on the other. True, Alexander's 'intentions were not to make the Church great, but only the duke', whereas his rival Pope Julius

---

[3] This praise is somewhat dampened by Machiavelli's reference to Leo's 'virtues' in the plural—echoing the same atypical formula used for Liverotto in chap. 8—leaving open the question of how well integrated his *virtú* will turn out to be.

deserves 'all the more praise inasmuch as he acted for the increase of the Church and not of some private individual'. But regardless of his motivations, Alexander's actions brought unheard-of greatness to the Church. If Machiavelli's basic criterion is how individual states or princes can gain as much power and *grandezza* for themselves as possible, all the actions he ascribes to Alexander and Julius are commendable. They allowed the Church to 'surge' forth, breaking free from the various checks that had long 'held it down' (*tenere bassi*).

If we apply the *Prince*'s general standards to judge the same actions, however, a less flattering account emerges. More than previous popes, Machiavelli claims, Alexander and Julius relied heavily on money—both given and taken in exchange for ecclesiastical offices and other favours—to pursue their political and military ambitions through the Church. It may be that 'superior causes' helped them out, and God exalted their enterprises. *Nondimanco*, when viewed from an ordinary human perspective their methods look uncannily similar to those presented at the start of chapter 7 as typical modes of agents who rely on fortune. The devil, again, lurks in un-virtuous details that undermine what might otherwise look like high praise. In keeping with his attitude of mock veneration for 'princes' whom divine protection shields from ordinary criticism, Machiavelli refrains from calling the popes' actions 'corrupt'. But the actions he describes in such amoral language undeniably merit that label, in the sense in which he uses it elsewhere in the *Prince* and other works.[4]

Even before we reach the discussion of specific popes, the first part of the chapter suggests that ecclesiastical principalities are inherently so paradoxical that there is no good reason—assuming that some readers judge such matters by reason more than faith—to trust them to do the basic work expected of any political order. Ecclesiastical princes have states 'yet do not defend them', although earlier chapters made it clear that no human state can last without *its own* defences. Later chapters will reiterate that only those defences that 'depend on you yourself and on your *virtù*' are good, certain, and lasting, and one should not depend on God 'to do everything'—precepts that ecclesiastical principalities, being sustained by causes superior to fortune and *virtù*, seem to violate.[5] Their princes' subjects 'though ungoverned, do not care, and they neither think of becoming alienated from such princes nor can they'. But

---

[4] Recall the *Decennale*'s bitterly satirical encomium to Alexander and his 'dear and intimate handmaids: Luxury, Simony, Cruelty' cited in chap. 7. In his several appearances in the *Prince*, Julius II is the epitome of a fortune-reliant, *virtù*-deficient 'prince'; see esp. chaps 13 and 25. The *Decennale* says of him that 'Julius the Second was made gatekeeper of Paradise, to heal the world of its afflictions' (I, lines 460–1), and refers to his 'ferocious spirit he could not check', making him vent his 'poison' on Italians (II, lines 85–93). Machiavelli's letters describe Julius as 'irascible and demonic' and capricious, violent, impetuous, and stingy; Machiavelli to Vettori, 29 April 1513, *MF* 232 and 236. Compare *D* I.12, II.22.

[5] Chaps 24 and 26.

the last chapter and the next insist that virtuous states have forces comprised of faithful subjects (or citizens), who *do* care about how they are governed.

The conclusion that only these principalities are 'secure and happy' sums up these paradoxes, which arise from ecclesiastical principalities' attempts to have their cake and eat it. They want to hold earthly dominion over lands and peoples, fighting wars to control territory and topple secular governments, without thinking about how to govern, defend, or maintain a state. Machiavelli's down-to-earth analysis gives readers little reason to expect much good to come of this approach. Such princes are 'happy' in the way that fortune-dependent people often are in Machiavelli's writings: they make huge gains in a short time without much hard work, and for the moment seem sure to fly ever higher above other mortals. But 'if the times and affairs change', as they always do, they come crashing down, bringing ruin to many others. Alexander had become pope little more than 20 years before Machiavelli wrote the *Prince*. That is a very short time in which the Church appeared great and exalted by God in its temporal enterprises. Its religious orders might be antique and venerated by many, but its ambitions for temporal power might still lead Italy to ruin.

12

Arms and laws

In what mode the forces of all principalities should be measured

In chapters 12–14 Machiavelli turns from wider political questions to focus on the military. At the most obvious level, he makes a case here for the main political reform he sought for Florence: a militia of citizens to end dependence on mercenary armies. Machiavelli remained committed to this project throughout his life. He began campaigning for a Florentine militia in his early days as second chancellor of the republic and Secretary to the Ten, the republic's military magistracy. The militia was established in 1506 under his supervision, and helped recover Pisa for Florentine dominions in 1509. When the Medici returned in 1512, they stripped Machiavelli of all his posts and dissolved the militia. When he composed the *Prince*, he was still convinced that the only way to save his city from falling under foreign control was to build up its 'own arms'.

He had, of course, originally wanted a citizen militia to help defend a specific form of government: a broad-based republic where power was widely shared among different parts of the citizenry, and where courts and magistrates were subject to strict scrutiny. But however remote this ideal seemed in 1513, Machiavelli still wanted Florence to have the best possible military defences. And he hoped to persuade the new rulers that his civilian militia fitted that bill.

The *Prince*'s Medici addressees might, however, wonder whether such a quintessentially republican institution could serve their military needs. Although the Medici scrupulously upheld the fiction that their government was still a republic, by addressing them as princes throughout the *Prince* Machiavelli confronts the 'effectual truth' that they govern as princes. This raises the question: what special challenges might a prince face in trying to establish a militia comprising his own subjects or citizens? If he starts by narrowing the discussion to military matters, Machiavelli soon widens it as he examines the political and other conditions needed to build a strong military suitable for principalities.

WHY GOOD ARMS NEED GOOD LAWS

Whereas he previously 'discoursed in particular' on various qualities of principalities, Machiavelli says that he will now 'discourse generally [*discorrere generalmente*] on the offence and defence befitting each of those named'. The discussion that unfolds over the next three chapters is indeed 'general' in an important way that contrasts with preceding discussions. In previous chapters we learned that different kinds of prince—natural, new, criminal, spiritual— have diverse modes of governing. All of them, moreover, are different from those of republics. By contrast, he insists that *any* prudent prince or republic must follow the generic modes of military ordering outlined in chapters 12–14, though they may vary in certain details. The same kinds of military organization are needed for principalities and republics, or indeed for any government that seeks to build lasting foundations.

Machiavelli starts by setting out one of his book's most general criteria for appraising any prince's efforts to consolidate his rule: 'it is necessary for a prince to have good foundations for himself; otherwise he must of necessity be ruined.' But what are good foundations? Earlier chapters offered a few specific examples. The first, in chapter 6, concerned military foundations: Hiero the Syracusan 'eliminated the old military and organized a new one . . . and when he had friendships and soldiers that were his own, he could build any building on top of such a foundation'. This foreshadows the present chapter's central argument: that arms are only useful if they are 'one's own arms'. The most recent mention of *fondamenti* occurred in chapter 9, where it concerned the social and political basis of a prince's power. Machiavelli argued that a prince who founds himself on strong popular support, 'and with his spirit and his orders keeps the generality [*universalità*] of citizens inspired', always finds that 'he has laid his foundations well'. A prince has good political foundations, then, if his primary supporters are the generality of citizens, not the 'great' or any other particular part of society.

Now in chapter 12 we get a much broader analysis of good foundations: 'The principal foundations that all states have, new ones as well as old or mixed, are good laws and good arms.' This standard applies to *all* states, whatever their form of government: it is a general—one might say theoretical—proposition about the basic preconditions for stable government in 'any city whatever'.[1] We shall indeed hear more about these in the next chapter. But we shall not, Machiavelli tells us, hear about good laws, 'because there cannot be good laws where there are not good arms, and where there are good arms there must be good laws'; so 'I shall leave out the reasoning on laws and shall speak of arms'.

---

[1] This phrase appears in the title of the first chapter of the *Discourses*, signalling that work's theoretical purposes.

A common interpretation of these remarks is that military arms are a *more important* foundation of states than civil laws. We will consider below whether Machiavelli's discussion supports this implication. For now, at least one thing is clear: princes need to found themselves on laws as well as on arms, and not just on any laws that suit their whims, but on 'good' laws.

The *Prince* does not tell us what makes laws good. But it does give us Machiavelli's most important criterion for good arms, framed in terms of an antithesis: the arms used by a prince to defend his *stato either* are his own *or* mercenary, auxiliary, or mixed—all types of arms that are not one's own. It is worth stressing that Machiavelli's antitheses are mutually exclusive choices: good arms cannot be *both* one's own and others'. As soon as you mix some of your own arms with those of others, you undermine your capacity to order and discipline them for your own purposes, and they lose the strong sense of commitment to you. The sharpness of this choice makes it clear that Machiavelli's most basic criterion for good arms is not pragmatic. When discussing arms and just about everything else, he has clear *general* standards that rule out many of the policies that might seem effective or expedient in the short term or in particular circumstances. The standards provide a more reflective standpoint for judging what to do than just deliberating on the basis of particular, empirical facts-on-the-ground.

This theoretical level of the *Prince* was introduced at the end of chapter 1 in the antithesis that frames the entire work: dominions are acquired 'either with the arms of others or with one's own, either by fortune or by *virtú*'. In chapter 12 Machiavelli brings the *one's own vs. others' arms* part of this standard into sharper focus, while reminding readers that these two kinds of arms are not simply different, appropriate for different circumstances or forms of government. To rely on one's own arms is to rely on *virtú* not fortune, and therefore always good for maintaining oneself, as prince or republic, individual or state. To rely on others' arms is to rely on fortune, which is changeable and not subject to intelligent ordering, and therefore not good for building firm foundations.

WHY MERCENARIES ARE USELESS

Having set out his general standards, Machiavelli applies the antithesis *one's own arms* = *virtú*/*others' arms* = *fortune* to a concrete assessment of various kinds of military. Both mercenaries and auxiliaries, he declares bluntly, are 'useless and dangerous' since both fall under the negative heading 'the arms of others'. Chapter 12 focuses on mercenaries, who, Machiavelli says, can never constitute 'firm or secure' foundations because they have no motivation to fight except 'other than a small stipend, which is not sufficient to make them want to die for you'. Mercenaries want to be in your pay while you are not at war; but as soon as war and its attendant hardships come, 'they either flee or leave'. Machiavelli then offers a sweeping diagnosis: 'the present ruin of Italy', he asserts, 'is caused by nothing other than its having relied for a period of many years on mercenary arms'. Their utter uselessness has been revealed whenever foreign troops threatened Italy, notably in 1494 when France's Charles VIII brought 25,000 troops into Italy to pursue his claim to the throne of Naples. Lacking any means of self-defence, one Italian city after another had to accede to whatever he demanded. This example was guaranteed to strike a special chord for Medici princes, since Charles' pressures on Florence led to the banishment of the Medici from Florence in 1494.

A further problem with mercenary arms concerns their captains. They are 'either excellent men of arms or not' and, either way, dangerous for whoever hires them. Non-excellent captains ruin you by avoiding risks and hard work. Excellent ones cannot be trusted because their ambitions drive them to turn their arms against you or against others, 'contrary to your intention'. Machiavelli gives one of the sorriest examples in recent Florentine and Italian memory—that of the mercenary captain Paolo Vitelli. Hired to fight their war against Pisa, the Florentines suspected him of having been corrupted by the enemy when he failed to attack at a crucial moment. He was summarily tried and beheaded. Machiavelli perceived that such rough justice would not be necessary for a city whose captains were drawn from its own citizen body and subject to strict legal controls. A reluctant or unworthy captain could be legally dismissed, obliged to fulfil his command, and checked if he 'stepped out of bounds' (*passi el segno*). An effective mercenary captain is always a potential threat, since nothing but death could guarantee that he would not go over to your enemies, as Francesco Sforza did against Milan, or seize your liberty, as Philip of Macedon did to the Thebans.

Machiavelli anticipates the usual response, which he doubtless heard many times when trying to sell his militia to the republic: surely any armed captain poses such risks, mercenary or not? He answers that the risks posed by over-ambitious, non-mercenary captains are more easily contained than those posed by mercenaries. Princes can avoid the threat of usurping captains by performing the office of captain themselves. Republics do the same through laws designed to eject or constrain military men whose ambitions take them 'out of bounds'. 'A republic', Machiavelli writes, 'has to send its own citizens, and when it sends one who does not turn out to be a worthy [*valente*] man, it must change him' by procedures that establish civilian control over military appointments. And if he is worthy, the republic must 'hold him back with laws so that he does not step out of bounds', since even the best captain may become too ambitious and seek more than his authorized share of power. 'And by experience', Machiavelli concludes, 'one sees that only princes and armed republics make very great progress', while 'nothing but harm ever comes from mercenary arms'. And 'a republic armed with its own arms is brought to obey one of its citizens'—that is, a military leader who tries to seize political power—'with more difficulty than is a republic armed with external arms'. Such well-ordered, transparent controls are lacking in the case of mercenaries, who can only be punished by 'extraordinary' means, i.e. means not regulated by public laws that apply to citizens.

GOOD ARMS AND REPUBLICS

Machiavelli has strayed a little too far from princes toward republics here, despite his assertion in chapter 2 that he will leave out republics. He has even stumbled into talking about laws, though he declared that he would leave these out of the present *discorso*. In fact, this apparently narrow military chapter mentions both republics and laws more than ever in the *Prince*: each word appears five times in chapter 12, far more than in any other.[2] Indeed— recalling the question whether good military arms are a more important foundation of states than good laws—it now appears that the former are at least partly constituted by the latter, at least in republics, since part of what makes one's own arms good is that they are subject to regulation by civil laws. Machiavelli will make this point explicitly in the first book of his *Art of War* (1521). 'Arms given by the laws and by order', we read there, 'on the backs of one's own citizens or subjects, never do harm', a maxim that holds true both for monarchs and republics.[3]

The *Prince* does not say whether good laws are also necessary for good princely arms. Perhaps no laws are needed to regulate captains, if the prince himself is captain? Machiavelli mentions the difference between methods suitable for princes and republics in passing, but does not directly discuss the obvious next question: do princely and republican methods produce equally sound foundations for good arms, as judged by the general standard *one's own arms = virtú/others' arms = fortune*?

If one ponders the text's unstated implications, it is hard not to see that the task of turning subjects or citizens into 'one's own' soldiers might pose particular challenges for princes. In republics, good military orders have built-in procedures for changing incompetent or over-ambitious captains. But what if a prince who makes himself captain proves incompetent, over-ambitious, or otherwise unworthy? If the office of captain is unregulated by

---

[2] The word laws (*legge*) occurs only nine other times in the book, including three times in chap. 5; republic or republics only seven other times.
[3] *AW* 24.

laws that can replace an unworthy captain, even if he is the prince himself, this exposes the state's defences to various flukes of fortune. Security will depend on the good luck of having a prince who is a highly competent captain; of his remaining good over time; and of his being able to adapt to the needs of peace as well as war. If by rare chance one man meets these criteria throughout his own life, the chances that his successors will do so are minuscule.

Republics, by contrast, can select the best men for the job out of a wide pool of able citizens, and replace them if they step out of bounds, or if changed circumstances call for a man of different humours and talents. In the *Discourses* Machiavelli explicitly praises these aspects of the Roman republic's military orders. More generally, whereas principalities rely on fortune to give them a succession of good princes who can maintain their foundations, republics 'through the mode of election' can choose 'infinite most virtuous princes' to lead their government in succession.[4]

This discussion of captains is followed by a string of examples that insinuate—rather less subtly—that free republics have the best arms: 'Rome and Sparta stood for many centuries armed and free. The Swiss are very well armed and very free.'[5] The chapter offers no examples, however, of princes who served successfully as their own captains. Their absence reinforces the impression that Machiavelli wants to drive home the special military merits of republics. His examples suggest that good arms and political freedom go hand in hand; you are unlikely to maintain one for long without the other.

Machiavelli's statement of his objection to mercenaries further implies that when it comes to good arms, republics have a distinct edge over principalities. Mercenaries 'have no love nor cause to keep them in the field', he asserts, other than their small stipend, which is not enough 'to make them want to die for you'. This gives us an important clue as to what kind of motivation makes soldiers constitute arms that are properly one's own, and therefore *good* arms: they should have enough love for a prince or their country to *want* to die for you. For arms to be your own it may not be enough that they are native instead of foreign, and under a prince's formal command; 'your' troops should also be actively willing to fight and die on your behalf. This is quite a tall order for 'new' princes who, as previous chapters made clear, face special difficulties in trying to win over subjects' hearts and minds. It is easier in republics, where citizens—not subjects but active participants in self-government—identify with the *stato* as a public patrimony.

So beyond the chapter's most obvious message—that mercenaries are pernicious—Machiavelli also makes it clear that militias formed by a prince's

---

[4] *D* III.9, III.36; I.19–20.

[5] The words *libere/liberissimi* here refer to internal forms of government as well as to freedom from foreign domination.

own people make the best arms, because they are subject to political and legal controls; and he drops fairly broad, *sotto voce* hints that the most effective controls are found in republics. Republics have better arms partly because of the primacy they give to laws over the special claims of individual men, including princes, and partly because citizen soldiers are more willing to die for their leaders. Not wanting to offend princely readers, Machiavelli does not spell out these implications; those who draw the consequences of what they read can work them out for themselves.

VIRTÚ BADLY USED

The chapter concludes by sketching a brief history of the 'origin and progress' of mercenary arms in Italy so that 'one can correct them better'. Machiavelli describes how rivalry between the Holy Roman Empire and the papacy led to the fragmentation of Italy into many *stati*, and to civil conflicts between the nobles and citizens—*cittadini* here used for those who wanted more popular forms of republic, *nobili* for the titled aristocracy or 'great' who sought to dampen those civic aspirations. Since the Church and 'a few republics' that now governed Italy were run by priests and citizens who did not understand arms, they 'began to hire foreigners'. The closing paragraph exemplifies Machiavelli's talent for using irony to dull the pain of confronting Italy's current, tragic situation. Within a relatively short time, mercenary captains had made themselves 'arbiters of Italy'. 'And the result of their *virtú*', Machiavelli declares dramatically, 'has been that Italy has been overrun by Charles [VIII], taken as booty by Louis [XII], violated by Ferdinand [of Spain], and insulted by the Swiss.' The Italians' mercenary warriors 'used all their industry to rid themselves and the soldiers of trouble and fear' by avoiding actual battles, *not* going against towns at night, *not* building defences around their camps, and *not* campaigning in winter. The irony of anyone using all their industry and *virtuoso* ordering powers to *avoid* hard work would be laughable if the results were not so devastating. Devising all these 'military orders' solely 'to escape trouble and dangers', they 'have led [*condotta*, a sly play on *condottiere*] Italy into slavery and disgrace'.

The paragraph's rich ironies are produced by tensions between the good words used to describe actions and the awfulness of what they describe. If qualities normally associated with *virtú* are used in ways that result in their opposite, do they deserve in these instances to be called true *industria*, *disciplina*, *ordine*? And if the 'result of . . . *virtú*' is to expose those on whose behalf it was exercised to the worst possible *fortuna*—that is, to insecurity and constant upheaval and dependence on unreliable others—can it be called *virtú* at all, even if some kind of effort and organization was mixed in it? A prince who wants to develop true *virtú*—or the fuller *virtú* of a statesman, rather than simply that of a soldier—must learn to discriminate between surface appearances of order and the real thing, and find properly *virtuoso* modes of industry and discipline that are likely to be genuinely good *fondamenti*. This philosophical theme will be further developed in the next two chapters.

13

Arms and *virtú*

Of auxiliary, mixed, and one's own soldiers

HOW USING OTHERS' VIRTUOUS ARMS
CAN HARM YOU

The title signals that we can expect to learn more about the positive value of 'one's own arms' here than we did from chapter 12. Auxiliary arms are 'those of a [foreign] power that is called to come with its arms to help and defend you'. Like mercenaries they are useless, but for different reasons. Whereas mercenaries harm you with their laziness (*ignavia*), auxiliaries may hurt you with their *virtú*—that word being used here in connection with the qualities just discussed, especially good discipline and order. Mercenaries are bad 'in themselves' because they lack these qualities, as well as the motivation to die willingly for whatever cause they fight for. Auxiliaries may be well ordered and disciplined, and thus 'useful and good in themselves'. But for the party that calls them in 'they are almost always harmful, because when they lose you are undone; when they win, you are left their prisoner'.

Some readers might ask: wouldn't you be 'undone' in the same way if your own troops lost? Machiavelli answers this question in the negative. 'A wise prince', he says, always prefers 'to lose with his own [arms] than to win with others, since he judges it no true victory [*non vera vittoria*] that is acquired with alien arms.' This is partly a matter of the self-esteem and confidence that come from knowing that you have achieved something under your own steam, and thus can feel that you 'own' the success. But it also has to do with the political conditions for securing any military victory. If you win with your own arms, you can determine the political outcome. If troops belonging to a foreign power win for you, they become masters of the outcome, and may make you their 'prisoner' in various ways—in the worst case by 'refusing to leave' your territories after they have won for you, as the Turks did in the Greek Eastern

Empire; or by trying to control your internal affairs and future foreign policies, or threatening to do so unless you pay them many ducats. As Secretary in the now-defunct republic, Machiavelli had constantly to deal with such humiliating threats and blackmail from foreign powers called in to help Florence's efforts to recover Pisa.

The example of Pope Julius II allows Machiavelli to answer anyone who might object that auxiliaries don't *always* seek to dominate you. He concedes that the pope's 'course of thrusting himself entirely into the hands of a foreigner' by getting military help from Spain's King Ferdinand did not end in disaster for Julius, who 'came out a prisoner neither of his enemies . . . nor of his auxiliaries'. But he insists that this result was a mere fluke, due to nothing but Julius' saving 'good fortune' in this instance. Although his Spanish auxiliaries were defeated, Swiss mercenaries unexpectedly rose up against the other side and forced the victors to flee, so that the pope won by default, 'beyond all expectation', and despite his own 'bad choice' (*sua mala elezione*).

In short, Machiavelli warns readers not to take isolated examples of non-disaster as evidence that auxiliary arms can be useful. The essential criterion should not be whether these arms sometimes have happy outcomes, but whether the outcomes are founded on unstable fortune and the arms of others—in this case, those of the Swiss who were not Julius' auxiliaries—or on *virtù* and one's own arms. For, quoting (but not naming) Tacitus, 'it has always been the opinion and judgement of wise men that "nothing is so infirm and unstable as fame for power not sustained by one's own force".' For both Tacitus and Machiavelli, the force in question is intellectual as well as physical, involving qualities of judgement as much as material power. Julius' astonishing rescue from defeat had nothing to do with his own choices, which were bad, or with prudent foresight or discipline. On the contrary, his policy 'could not have been less well considered'. And those who win by means of fortune may be happy for a time, but they store up trouble for the future. To underline this point, Machiavelli recycles a medical metaphor he used in chapter 3 when discussing the importance of foresight. 'Lack of prudence in men', he remarks, 'begins something which, because it tastes good then, they do not perceive the poison that lies underneath, as I said above of consumptive fevers [*febre etiche*].'[1]

Note a further implication of Julius' case, and of the medical metaphor used in both chapters. It warns readers not to judge by short-term results and appearances when deciding what arms are useful, since, as at the beginning of a fatal illness, the long-term poisonous consequences of relying on others' arms and fortune are 'difficult to recognize'. If your end is true victory, it matters less whether you win or lose specific battles than that you fight with your own arms and virtuous means—including thinking things through and

---

[1] As noted in chap. 3, Machiavelli uses the term *etico* for consumption there and *febre etiche* here for consumptive fevers, though the more usual term for consumption was *tisico*.

choosing wisely—because no other means can *ever* produce true victory. One should, it seems, judge as much or more by the means than by the results.

FOUR EXAMPLES

Having issued these warnings against auxiliaries, Machiavelli sets out four apparently positive examples of men who improved their situation after ex-changing others' arms for their own. The first, Cesare Borgia, began to conquer Romagna with French auxiliaries. When these 'no longer appeared safe' he turned to mercenaries. When these in turn proved 'doubtful, unfaithful, and dangerous' he eliminated them, and finally turned to his own arms. This, Machiavelli tells us, greatly increased Borgia's reputation, since 'everyone saw that he was the total owner [*intero possessore*] of his own arms'. Then he gives three examples from outside Italy: Hiero of Syracuse, David confronting the Philistines, and in modern times Charles VII of France, all of whom increased their countries' safety by rejecting foreign arms in favour of their own. The chapter concludes with an apparently simple solution to all the military problems Machiavelli has mentioned: for anyone who discourses on the orders of these four and on Philip II of Macedon, father of Alexander, 'the mode of ordering one's arms will be easy to find'.

Or is it so easy? The examples make it easy enough to see the need to get rid of auxiliaries and mercenaries—Machiavelli's *critical* point. But we have still been told very little about the *constructive* work of building and ordering one's own arms. Are the four examples all equally good models for new princes to imitate?

On closer inspection, Machiavelli's remarks reveal fundamental differences among these men who turned to their own arms. At first glance he seems to treat the example of Cesare Borgia as particularly commendable, declaring that 'I shall never hesitate to cite' him and his actions. But this favourable impression fades when Machiavelli's lengthy description of the errors Borgia made before he finally 'turned to his own arms' is compared with the second example of Hiero.

Machiavelli prefaces his discussion of both men with a general statement: 'A wise prince . . . has always [*sempre*] avoided' mercenary and auxiliary arms. As ever in the *Prince*, such general statements should be taken seriously and applied to evaluate particular cases, even those that Machiavelli seems to praise. Hiero 'knew immediately' (*conobbe subito*) that the mercenaries hired by Syracuse were useless, and promptly 'had them all cut to pieces [*tagliare a pezzi*]' by sending them to fight a battle he knew they could not win.[2] If we

---

[2] See Polybius: Hiero sent the mercenaries among his troops into battle, and 'allowed them to be all cut up by the Campanians', then 'retired safely to Syracuse with the citizens' among his soldiers. *PolH* I.9.

compare Hiero's resolute clarity to Machiavelli's plodding, convoluted narration of Borgia's stab-in-the-dark trials and failures—his use of auxiliaries, then mercenaries, and only after much trouble and danger resorting to his own arms—Cesare begins to sound like a slow learner. He realized late what Hiero knew 'immediately' and David, in the next example, worked out 'as soon as' he tried on borrowed arms, and before he went out to fight with his own 'sling and his knife [*coltello*]'. The words *pezzi* (pieces) and *coltello* (knife) ironically echo chapter 7's account of Borgia's killing of Remirro de Orco, presenting more virtuous ways to cut men into pieces and use a knife than his. Hiero had mercenaries cut into *pezzi* on the open battlefield, not in a shady extra-legal killing. David openly owned and wielded his own *coltello*, whereas the owner of the knife left beside Remirro's corpse did not declare himself.

If Hiero's far-sighted modes were better than Borgia's lack of clear military vision, his foundations were better too. This was suggested in the earlier Hiero–Borgia juxtaposition in chapters 6 and 7, where Machiavelli presented Hiero as the prime example of a *virtuoso* prince who built solid foundations without relying on fortune, while Borgia was the prince of fortune par excellence. Hiero relied on his and his citizens' *virtú* alone, and therefore built a well-founded *stato*.[3] Borgia, one might infer from these remarks, recognized the need for firm foundations too late, if he ever did. Unsurprisingly, his state crumbled to dust almost immediately after his father's death—notwithstanding Machiavelli's wry observation in chapter 7 that it managed to hold for a whole month afterward in Romagna, as if a month without serious revolt could count as evidence of firm foundations. Borgia's 'reputation' may have increased once 'everyone saw that he was a total possessor of his arms', but that reputation was not enough to prop him up without his father the pope. And it is hard not to smell the irony in calling Cesare the 'total possessor' (*intero possessore*) of arms that depended so utterly on another's fortune, and that he lost almost overnight.[4]

The example of King Charles VII provides food for thought for monarchs contemplating Machiavelli's advice. Having 'liberated France from the English with his fortune and *virtú*', Charles saw the need to arm his kingdom with 'his own arms', and laid down an ordinance to this effect. Had this order been 'expanded or preserved', Machiavelli opines, 'the kingdom of France would be unconquerable'. But Charles' son Louis XI repealed part of that *virtuoso* ordinance and hired Swiss troops, thus increasing French reliance on fortune and weakening their military *virtú*. Spoiled by relying on Swiss help, French

---

[3] In the *Discourses* David is a more ambivalent case. His *virtú* was sufficient for him to leave a strong kingdom to his son, but by the third generation his foundations were undermined by civil strife—a pattern typical for monarchies discussed in that work. See *D* I.19 and I.2 on the short life cycles of monarchies.

[4] The word *intero* here contains a further irony, since it also means 'honest'—not a word that springs to mind on reading chap. 7's account of Borgia's deeds.

troops stopped believing they could win without it, and France became less secure than before. The example shows that while monarchs can make 'good arms' out of their own subjects, civilian militias are less well founded in hereditary kingdoms or principalities than in republics. In the former they are subject to the whims of individual monarchs who may decide to dissolve them. In republics they are founded on independent laws and orders that underwrite their longevity, and protect them from corruption.

The chapter ends with a final puzzle: why does Machiavelli tack Philip II of Macedon onto his list of examples to be 'discoursed on', without a word about what his 'mode of ordering arms' was? The only other mention of this Philip in the *Prince* occurs in chapter 12, where he was presented not as an example of military self-reliance, but as a foreign captain who took the liberty from the Thebans who enlisted his aid.[5] Though this might seem a characteristically 'Machiavellian' manoeuvre on Philip's part—while pretending to defend others, cleverly take advantage of their dependence on you to seize control over them—Machiavelli does not commend any auxiliary or mercenary captain in these chapters.

The *Discourses* provide more promising clues as to why he adds Philip. In a series of references scattered through that work, Philip emerges as a new prince who worked by deception, force, and 'very cruel' and inhuman modes to gain mastery 'of the world'. By the end of his prematurely shortened life he only went out flanked by a private armed guard of 1,000 men—a hallmark of a prince-turned-tyrant who cannot trust his own people. As the *Prince* repeatedly reminds us, a prince who lacks popular support lacks an essential component of 'good arms' and strong foundations. Despite his fear-inspiring retinue, Philip was killed outdoors by a mere youth. If the great king's personal fortunes collapsed suddenly, so did his empire, after the even shorter lifetime of his son Alexander.[6] On Machiavelli's criteria, states that last so briefly and crumble so fast seldom qualify as good orders, however impressive their initial gains. They lack firm foundations because the industry and discipline that produces them is used to strengthen one man alone. This makes their survival depend on his personal qualities, which may be corrupted by growing power, and not enough on the *virtú* of many citizens who might have supported him and maintained good orders after his death.

Once again, it seems that not all men and actions that appear *virtuoso* meet Machiavelli's demanding standards for *virtú* in the most reflective sense of the word: as a quality or set of qualities that confer lasting (though never eternal) stability on human works.[7] The examples of Philip and Cesare Borgia

---

[5] To be distinguished from the later Macedonian Philip V discussed in chap. 24.

[6] *D* I.20, I.26, I.59, II.13, II.28, III.6.

[7] *AW* 117: 'For you know that everything desires rest [*riposo*], as well as security, for to rest and not to rest securely is not perfect rest.'

underline the need for princes to discriminate carefully before they rush to imitate what looks impressive on first appearances.

A puzzling sentence in the final paragraph reinforces this point: one's own arms, Machiavelli declares, 'are composed of either subjects or citizens or your creatures [*creati' tua*]'. Earlier chapters have already touched on the sensitive question: do subjects and citizens make equally good foundations for one's own arms? Are arms ever fully one's own when they consist of subjects rather than free and willing citizens? In the light of these arguments about military foundations, princes will need to ponder these questions as they read on.

14

Knowledge and discipline

What a prince should do regarding the military

The chapter's title again seems to confine the discussion to military matters. At first glance, so does the content. Princes, Machiavelli asserts, should concentrate entirely on war 'and its orders and discipline' as 'the only art which is of concern to one who commands'. Whenever princes have 'thought more of amenities than of arms, they have lost their states'. Being unarmed 'makes you contemptible' so that soldiers do not esteem you and you cannot trust them. Therefore 'a prince should never lift his thoughts from the exercise of war, and in peace he should exercise it more than in war'.

He should do this, Machiavelli says, 'in two modes, one with deeds [*opere*], the other with the mind [*mente*]'.[1] As to deeds, he 'should always be out hunting' as the best way to inure his body to hardships, and to learn the nature of sites as a basic component of military knowledge. A prime exemplar is Philopoemen, 'prince of the Achaeans', who 'in times of peace ... never thought of anything but modes of war', often discussing military strategy with friends while on campaign. As for exercising the mind: princes 'should read histories and consider in them the actions of excellent men' in wars. They should pick out and imitate some excellent man in the past who himself imitated another who had been 'praised and glorified before him'. A prince who does these things will be able to resist adversities when his fortune changes.

MILITARY AND CIVIL ORDERS

All this seems to suggest that princes should give primacy to military over civil orders, laws, and other considerations discussed in preceding chapters. Perhaps the best princes are first and foremost military leaders? This might appear to be the basic message—if one is unperturbed by the chapter's many oddities.

---

[1] Compare Sallust, *SWC* 1–2 on mental and physical virtue in war.

It opens with a series of egregious overstatements: princes should have *no other* object, nor *any other* thought than war, should *never* lift their thoughts from the exercise of war, which is the *only* art that concerns them. Such exaggerated emphasis on military priorities makes one wonder why Machiavelli bothers to discuss any of the wider political themes broached in the *Prince*. Then there are the platitudes, which fly at the reader thick and fast: being unarmed makes you contemptible; unarmed princes get no respect from armed soldiers; hunting is good training for war; princes should imitate excellent men found in histories. Finally, in the discussion of hunting we get a strangely insistent repetition of the word *cognizione* (knowledge), a word used very sparingly in all of Machiavelli's writings: in the *Prince* it occurs only in this chapter, four times in one paragraph, and once in the Dedication.

Such oddities should not be passed over in haste, but taken as an invitation to pause and consider possible reasons why Machiavelli put them there. Important clues to all of them are found in 'the writers' Machiavelli mentions in the chapter—the unnamed *scrittore* who praise Philopoemen and Xenophon, the first of only two writers named in the *Prince* (the other is Virgil in chapter 17). When Machiavelli says 'as to the exercise of the mind, a prince should read histories', this is more than the bland advice it might appear to be. Readers can already start this kind of exercise by reading the works Machiavelli alludes to here, following the traces and clues given in this very chapter.

THE BENEFITS OF HUNTING

To begin with hunting, Machiavelli's rather banal-sounding description of its uses contains some puzzling details. A prince should always be out hunting: really, always?[2] His remarks about the advantages of gaining detailed knowledge (*cognizione*) of sites are even odder. That through hunting one 'learns to know one's own country, and . . . better understand its defence' sounds reasonable enough, if glaringly obvious. But it is far less obvious why 'through the knowledge of and experience with those sites, once can comprehend with ease every other site that it may be necessary to explore [*speculare*, lit. speculate on] as new'. Machiavelli explains: 'For the hills, the valleys, the plains, the rivers, and the marshes that are in Tuscany, for example, have a certain similarity to those of other provinces', he writes, 'so that from the knowledge of a site in one

---

[2] The *Art of War*, Machiavelli's main work on military orders and training, nowhere discusses hunting. Indeed, Machiavelli implies throughout that work that the art of war should *not* be the master art of those who are responsible for government: the dialogue's chief interlocutor Fabrizio Colonna, a famous mercenary, says that unlike less scrupulous mercenaries 'I have never used war as an art, because my art is to govern my subjects and to defend them, and, so as to be able to defend them, to love peace and know how to make war' *AW* 19.

province one can easily come to the knowledge of others'. But surely the sites and landscapes that a commander needs to know tend to be quite individual, so that to presume their similarity might prove dangerous in war? Taken literally, the statement that the topography of one country is much the same as another's is so clearly false that sharp-nosed readers must smell some less banal message beneath the paradoxical surface.[3]

A first key to a solution might be found in ancient texts that treat hunting and knowledge of sites as complex metaphors, linking them to military and other forms of knowledge. A passage similar to the one just cited occurs in Plato's *Laws*, where the dialogue's main speaker says that 'everyone who means to play his part in keeping his country safe must throw himself heart and soul' into hunting 'and other kinds of chase'. They should 'examine the entire country, summer and winter, in arms, to protect and get to know every district in succession'. Each hunter should take turns serving as master and servant, never working 'for their own private needs, but only for public tasks'; and 'everyone should come to know with precision all of his own country [*akribeias epistasthai pantas tên hautôn chôran*]; probably no study is more valuable'.[4] Here the initial military purpose of hunting is subtly expanded to include exercises in serving the public good and careful self-examination.

Did Machiavelli expect at least some readers to recall this passage when they read his similar remarks—which reappear, with an even stronger resemblance to Plato's passage, in the *Discourses*' remarks on hunting? If so, he may have wanted to signal that his advice in this chapter treats good military defences as inseparable from good civil orders and the kind of deep, critical self-knowledge that the ancients called philosophical.

Like Plato a student of Socrates, Xenophon also treats hunting as an extended metaphor in his deceptively practical essay *On Hunting*. He urges readers 'not to despise hunting or any other education, for these are the means by which men become good in war and in all things out of which must come excellence [*kalôs*] in thought and deed'. Hunting is part of an education in virtue. It teaches prudent moderation, discourages rashness, and 'teaches a man to observe laws'. Huntsmen who absorb this education are the best defenders of their countries, since they gain both military skills and a love of justice. Well-armed with these mutually supportive kinds of knowledge, they protect fellow citizens against any wild human animals who refuse to stay within the bounds of law and justice—the tyrannical individuals who threaten cities from inside as well as without. The best huntsmen are able to check tyrants before they grow too strong to control, because through constant reasoning with others they have learned not to trust appearances when judging whether men and actions

---

[3] The *Discourses* make a nearly identical, paradoxical claim about the general military value of knowing one's site in III.39.
[4] Plato, *Laws* 763a–c.

are virtuous. Of such philosophically disciplined citizens, Xenophon insists, 'are good soldiers and good generals made'.[5]

Is it possible that Machiavelli's 'hunting' has a similar, extended set of meanings—including military training, of course, but implying that good military commanders and 'orderers' also need these other intellectual and moral virtues? If so, this might account for the otherwise unusual repetition of *cognizione*, a word Machiavelli always uses for highly reflective forms of general knowledge, not for know-how skills or the understanding of particulars (for which he tends to use *notizia* and the verb *intendere*, to understand, rather than *conoscere*, to know). His example of a leader who practised hunting to good military effect, Philopoemen, strengthens the suspicion that he wants to draw attention to the intellectual and ethical benefits of hunting. Machiavelli tells us that when the Achaean leader 'was on campaign with friends . . . [he] often stopped and reasoned with them about questions of military strategy . . . listened to their opinions, gave his own, supported it with reasons'. And 'because of these continued cogitations there could never arise . . . any accident for which he did not have the remedy'. Whatever the specifically military benefits of such reasoning and cogitations, Machiavelli also stresses the general benefits of self-questioning through dialogue with others, echoing the Socratic themes in Xenophon's many-sided hunting.

COMPLETE MILITARY *VIRTÙ*

If we consult some of the writers who Machiavelli says praised Philopoemen, we soon discover more such echoes. Plutarch's Philopoemen is a philosophical soldier-prince par excellence, foreshadowing Machiavelli's next paragraph about the need for martial princes to exercise their minds. Plutarch refers to the Achaean leader's love of philosophy and his philosophical uses of hunting, which were interwoven in military exercises. He studied the writings of philosophers with a view to ethical self-improvement, focusing on teaching he found beneficial for virtue, and saw war as 'affording a most manifold basis for the practice of virtue'.[6] Polybius, the main source for Plutarch and Livy— and together with Justin, a possible source for Machiavelli's earlier, glowing remarks about Hiero—presents Philopoemen as a moderate leader who strove to observe the highest standards of personal virtue, and refused to overstep the bounds of legality and justice in matters of war and peace.[7] Had Machiavelli wanted to highlight only military aspects of hunting, as his title and blunter assertions seem to insist, his choice of Philopoemen as an example is puzzling;

---

[5] The essay ends by saying that huntsmen should include huntswomen; Xenophon, 'On Hunting', *Scripta Minora*, pp. 443–57.
[6] *PL* 'Philopoemen' I.4, IV.4–6.   [7] *PolH* XXIV.11–13; also X.21–4, XI.8–10.

he could have picked many less philosophical and ethical 'princes' who used hunting for military training in a narrower sense.[8]

On reading these writers' remarks about Philopoemen, further implications emerge that may shed further light on Machiavelli's idea of the kind of leadership Italy needed in his own times. Some are military in the narrower sense. Finding the Achaean military badly disciplined by its aristocratic commanders, the stubbornly egalitarian Philopoemen ignored their protests and 'went around to the different cities' on his own to train the young men to fight better.[9] Other implications are political. Philopoemen was 'prince' not in the sense of a monarch who held an inherited or permanent rulership, but a military and political leader (*strategos*) of the Achaean League, appointed to his post many times because of his proven merits. The League (280–146 BC) was a confederation of Greek cities and kingdoms formed to defend the independence of each against encroachments by aggressively expanding empires, notably the Macedonian and the Roman.

In both their wars with these stronger powers and their struggles to build defensive unity among the Greeks, the Achaeans resemble the Italians of Machiavelli's day.[10] Polybius praises Philopoemen as the last Greek statesman to stand up to Roman bullying. In referring readers to this praise, perhaps Machiavelli also reminds them that if ultimately the Greeks proved too divided to resist, Philopoemen's intelligent efforts to unify them are still exemplary for Italians who seek to defend their freedom.[11]

GOOD AND LESS GOOD IMITATIONS OF GREAT MEN

The point that the great military princes worth imitating were also exemplary in intellectual and moral virtue is confirmed by the chapter's final paragraph. Again, the overt emphasis is narrowly military: princes are advised to exercise their minds on warfare by reading histories, where they may find some 'excellent man' to imitate, enabling them to be as 'praised and glorified' as their models. Thus 'Alexander imitated Achilles: Caesar, Alexander; Scipio, Cyrus'. Machiavelli seems to accept unquestioningly that all these men deserved their reputations for greatness. In particular, 'whoever reads the life of Cyrus written by Xenophon will then recognize in the life of Scipio how much glory that imitation brought him, how much in chastity, affability, humanity, and liberality Scipio conformed to what had been written of Cyrus by Xenophon'.

---

[8] Including Cyrus; see below.

[9] *PL* 'Philopoemen' VII.2–5; as Machiavelli had done a few years earlier.

[10] In *D* II.4 Machiavelli associates the Achaean League with the earlier Tuscan League in Italy.

[11] The Achaeans are mentioned three times in the *Prince*. Including these, ten of the book's examples come from the period of the Greeks' last resistance to Roman conquest, which ended with the Battle of Corinth in 146 BC. No other ancient period figures as prominently in the book.

But if we take his 'whoever reads...' as a challenge to read Xenophon's *Cyropaedia* for ourselves to get a more precise idea of what Machiavelli might have in mind, we soon discover far more nuanced and critical accounts of these men. Xenophon treats hunting as part of the old Persians' excellent moral and political education, as well as military training. In all these fields, the highest virtue consists in self-control; the well-educated hunter learns when to stop pursuing his game as well as how to capture it. The young prince Cyrus' attitudes to the sport, however, soon prove symptomatic of his personal flaws: unrestrained competitiveness and *pleonexia*, the insatiable desire for more than one's share. As an adult ruler, he continues to show an obsession with chasing game, only now the human kind—expanding his empire far and wide, and neglecting matters close to home.

In his own lifetime Cyrus was so skilled in the arts of persuasion that his subjects seem secure and happy. But he turns once-virtuous Persia into a despotism founded on one man's power. With such thin foundations, the empire falls into chaos and tyranny on his death. Masked by his charming manners and relentlessly reasonable-sounding words, Cyrus' greed for power makes him destroy even his own good works. In his youth he created a Persian civil militia, arming and training subjects. By the end of Xenophon's book he has disbanded it, disarmed the people who once supported him, and entrusted the military to a small group of close friends whom he sets as superiors above the rest.[12]

If they read carefully instead of skimming the surface—which like Machiavelli's *Prince* seems to praise Cyrus—'whoever reads the life of Cyrus written by Xenophon' might suspect that Machiavelli is giving them an example of the kind of 'exercise of the mind' that princes need to become good military leaders. This exercise, it now turns out, involves much more than finding some big-name model to imitate. It involves learning how to spot potentially corrupting flaws behind virtuous appearances, in great men themselves and in what is written about them. Recall Machiavelli's list of men who themselves imitated an earlier model of excellence—Achilles, Alexander, and Caesar as well as Cyrus and Scipio: all were famously flawed, and failed to leave a lasting legacy of good internal and external orders for their countries.

And this raises the question: did the men who imitated an earlier model of excellence do so uncritically, failing to see their heroes' weaknesses, or mistaking their flaws for strengths? Perhaps Scipio was so dazzled by Cyrus' short-term achievements that he ignored his contribution to Persia's corruption, insecurity, and eventual ruin. In chapter 17, Machiavelli will suggest that this was the case. Like Xenophon's Cyrus, the celebrated Roman conqueror of Carthage had a flair for projecting appearances of virtue even when his deeds showed an ambition

---

[12] *XC* I.ii.6–10, iv.5–9, VII.v; see *ME* 71–8, 116–24. Like Machiavelli, Xenophon conveys these criticisms with the subtlest hints; the *Cyropaedia* is a masterwork of dissimulation, seeming to praise its subject while subtly exposing Cyrus' well-concealed flaws as a statesman.

unbecoming in a republic. Always courting his soldiers' favour with a view to securing support for his political ambitions, he showed 'excessive mercy' in failing to discipline unruly troops. For Machiavelli lax discipline is one of the worst failings in a military leader, especially the failure to punish soldiers who violate standards of order in dealing with the enemy.[13] The only thing that prevented this 'damaging quality' from destroying Scipio's reputation, Machiavelli says, was that he lived in a republic 'under the government of the Senate' which opposed some of his reckless impulses, allowing him to keep up the good appearances that 'made for his glory'.[14]

Behind the narrowly military mask he wears in this chapter, then, Machiavelli suggests a fuller and more interesting answer to the title's question 'what a prince should do regarding the military' than first appears. A prince who wants to build solid defences must learn to be a discriminating judge not just of strategy and soldiers, but also of what it takes to construct political foundations, and of what superficially attractive qualities tend to destroy them. Cyrus' and Scipio's chastity, affability, humanity, and liberality gained them many supporters at first, but they used these qualities to increase their private power at the expense of the public good. Princely readers who imitate an idealized Cyrus or Scipio may win personal popularity. But their foundations, however impressive looking, will prove ephemeral and subject to fortune's vicissitudes; and they may precipitate the decline of whatever good their countries had before, as Machiavelli thought Scipio did.[15]

Like Xenophon, Machiavelli gives subtle lessons to princely and non-princely readers: don't trust first appearances or reputations, exercise your own judgement about what you read, and remember that what is truly excellent and imitation-worthy is seldom the most loudly praised. Hiero and Philopoemen are not as celebrated as Cyrus, Caesar, or Alexander, and made far less grandiose conquests. But they might, for all that, be better models for contemporary Italians.

---

[13] This is the point of the Locrian example in chap. 17. Compare *D* II.27–8 on the Romans' failure to punish the Fabii who violated the law of nations.

[14] Chap. 17. Machiavelli's critical views on Scipio in the *D* and the *Prince* echo Livy's: see Livy, XXVIII.17–21, 40–5, XXIX.14–27, XXX.26, 32.

[15] *D* I.46, II.4, III.34; *ME* 468–72. Following Livy, Machiavelli implies that Scipio (like Caesar later) violated one of the most fundamental maxims in his *Art of War*: that art should be used only on behalf of the public, not for a captain's private ends. *AW* 16–17.

Virtues and vices

15

Praise and blame

Of those things for which men and especially princes are praised or blamed

Having advised princes on how to acquire and hold their states, 'it now remains', Machiavelli says, 'to see what the modes and government of a prince should be with subjects [*sudditi*] and with friends [*amici*]'. A prince's relationships with subjects are governed by very different 'modes' than those with friends.

This and the next three chapters contain some of the most ingenious double-writing in the *Prince*, and indeed in all Western literature. While seeming to tell princes how to acquire, hold down, and deceive subjects when necessary, Machiavelli teaches those who recognize his ironies how to govern in a mode that instead makes friends.

MACHIAVELLI'S SUBVERSIVE NEW TEACHING

Knowing that many have written on the matter of relations with subjects and friends, Machiavelli says that he fears he will be held presumptuous for doing so again, all the more since 'in disputing this matter I depart from the orders of others'. It appears, then, that we are about to get some radically new advice on a tired old subject. His next words insinuate a specific criticism of what 'others' have written. 'My intention is to write something useful [*utile*] to whoever understands it', he states—implying that other writings have not been particularly useful.

The reason for this, he suggests, is that others have considered princes' 'modes and government' with subjects and friends from a misleading standpoint of 'imagination' (*immaginazione*). To avoid their errors, Machiavelli declares, 'it has appeared to me more fitting to go directly to the effectual truth [*alla verità effettuale*] of the thing than to the imagination of it'. He seems to set himself against the tradition of moral and political philosophy associated with Plato and others who 'have imagined republics and principalities that have never been seen or known to exist in truth [*mai visti né conosciuti in vero essere*]'. Machiavelli, by contrast, will 'leave out' what is 'imagined about a prince'—presumably also leaving out imagined republics—and discuss only 'what is true'.

What is true but not admitted by others is that, try as they might, princes cannot always display all the qualities that are highly praised, or avoid those that incur blame. 'All men', Machiavelli begins, 'and especially princes, since they are placed higher [*più alti*], are noted for some of the qualities that bring them either blame or praise [*o biasimo o laude*].' He then lists some of the qualities that incur blame or praise. Thus 'someone is held [*tenuto*] liberal, someone mean; someone is held a giver, another rapacious'; others are called cruel, merciful, breakers of faith or faithful, effeminate and pusillanimous or ferocious and spirited, honest or astute, hard or agreeable, heavy or light, and so on. Everyone, Machiavelli asserts, 'will confess that it would be a very praiseworthy [*laudabilissima*] thing to find in a prince all of the above-mentioned qualities that are held good.' But:

> because he cannot have them, nor entirely [*interamente*, also 'honestly'] observe them, since human conditions do not consent to it [*non lo consentono*], it is necessary for him to be so prudent as to know how to avoid the infamy [*infamia*] of those vices [*vizi*] that would take his state from him and to guard against those that do not, if possible. But if one cannot, one can let them go with less hesitation [*respetto*, also 'respect'].

This passage is positively riddled with ambiguities, including the ambiguous meanings noted in brackets.[1] Its main point, of course, is that human limitations make it impossible for any prince always to avoid the 'infamy' of certain vices if he wants to keep his state. But the most perplexing ambiguity here is whether princes should avoid the *infamy* of certain vices—or the *vices* themselves. Throughout the chapter, Machiavelli speaks far more of how people are 'held' (*tenuto*) than of how they really are, of what 'appears' to him and others about what should be praised or blamed, and about the 'infamy' or 'fame' of vices and virtues rather than of the qualities that deserve those labels. He worries about being 'held' presumptuous, remarks that people are 'noted' for certain qualities, and says that princes 'are placed' higher than others— perhaps in truth, perhaps in some people's misguided minds.

Exactly what, then, does Machiavelli think princes should avoid? Does he want to teach princes how to *be* 'in truth' if they want to maintain their state, or only how they should seek to *be held* by others?

MISLEADING APPEARANCES AND NECESSARY VICES

Machiavelli makes it very hard to answer this question by running together two quite distinct arguments. Argument (1) says that since men in general are

---

[1] And of what should a prince 'let go' (*lasciare andare*)—his *scruples* about exhibiting vices, or 'the *vices* that would take his state from him'?

not always good, princes sometimes need to lower their moral standards in order to preserve their state. It starts with a set of claims about the essential 'human conditions' that limit moral possibilities. 'It is so far from how one lives to how one should live', Machiavelli tells us, 'that he who lets go of what is done for what should be done learns his ruin more quickly than his preservation.' How one 'should live' according to conventional moral standards may be dangerously misleading in a world where many people fall short of them. In view of the yawning gap between 'is' and 'should', 'a man who wants to make a profession of good [*professione di buono*] in all regards must come to ruin among so many who are not good'. From these claims about *what is* and how people *are*, Machiavelli draws the practical conclusion that a prince who wants to maintain himself needs '*to learn to be able not to be good*, and to use this and not use it according to necessity'.

Here Machiavelli underlines the potential for conflict between moral notions of what should be done, and what is useful or necessary for self-preservation. When conflicts occur, he states clearly, princes should give priority to the latter, presumably non-moral considerations. The argument seems to identify two sets of standards—one moral, one concerned solely with self-preservation— that coexist side by side, each having its proper place in a prince's repertoire of 'modes'. But they have unequal weight. Ultimately, the most important standards are those that help princes maintain themselves. And the actions that best serve this aim are not always 'good' (*buono*).

Argument (2) says that appearances of moral virtue and vice may be dangerously misleading. 'If one considers everything well', Machiavelli declares in the chapter's closing sentence, 'one will find something appears [*parrà*] *virtú*, which if pursued would be one's ruin, and something else appears vice, which if pursued gives rise to one's security and well-being [*bene essere*].' Because of this, 'one should not care about incurring the *infamy* of those vices without which it is difficult to save [*salvare*] the state'. A prince, that is, **shouldn't mind being 'held' vicious**, so long as his actions result in his state's security and well-being.

The two arguments seem to concur on the most essential point: since self-preservation is a prince's basic aim, it is sometimes necessary for him to maintain himself and his state by means that are not good—or that are not held or do not appear good. But which is it? The difference between means that *are* not good and those that are not *held* or do not *appear* good is hugely important, though Machiavelli teases readers by fudging it. Argument (1) says that since what *is* good may cause harm, princes should learn not to *be* good. Argument (2) says only that since what *appears* virtuous may cause ruin, princes shouldn't care about the *infamy* of vice, that is, of being 'held' vicious. It doesn't say that princes should *be* or not care about *being* vicious. It merely implies that because people sometimes—wrongly—condemn beneficial qualities as vicious and praise harmful qualities as virtuous, princes should ignore these wrong-headed views, and act according to what they judge beneficial.

On closer inspection, it turns out that the differences between the two arguments run very deep. For one thing, they rest on competing explanations of why standards of virtue and vice may be dangerously misleading. According to Argument (1), the problem lies in unrealistically high standards of moral virtue. According to Argument (2), the problem lies not in those standards, but in the muddled thinking of people who misunderstand their proper content.

This suggests a further, still more fundamental, difference: the two arguments rest on sharply contrasting accounts of the relation between moral virtue and 'real' human conditions. Argument (1) suggests that there is an *inescapable* conflict between lofty moral ideas of virtue and down-to-earth human realities, since it understands virtue as a kind of standard that sets the bar above what human beings are capable of achieving. Argument (2) allows that conflicts between moral virtue and the precepts of self-preservation dictated by 'human conditions' might be merely apparent. If they are rooted in a misunderstanding of the appropriate content of moral virtue, then perhaps a correct understanding of that content can *dissolve* the conflicts.

Finally, these diverse accounts point in very different practical directions. If a prince thinks Argument (1) is right, he will sometimes opt not to be good— according to moral standards of goodness—in hopes of saving his state. If he agrees with Argument (2), he will simply ignore people who criticize him for his *apparent* vices, and do what promotes security and well-being. These deeds, in turn, may call for qualities praised as good by those who have a *correct* understanding of moral virtues and vices.

If the two arguments have such different implications, which one does Machiavelli want readers to accept? Is he telling princes to *be* bad when necessary, or only not to mind *appearing* bad to some people, while in fact doing good? This question cannot be answered on the basis of what we read in this chapter alone. Here Machiavelli simply introduces the central ambiguity that will unfold over chapters 16–18, where he continues to speak in two voices that offer princes quite different kinds of advice. He signals these different registers by frequent shifts between the language of being—what is done, what princes should be—and the language of being 'held', 'appearing', 'professing', 'infamy', or 'fame'.[2] At one moment we read that princes should be able to *be* 'not good', at another only that they should not want to 'make a profession of good in all regards'. But is it the profession of good or being good that may cause harm? Machiavelli plays with readers' sense of reality, even as he claims neatly to separate the true from the imaginary.

---

[2] Aristotle shifts between the language of appearing and being in discussing how tyrants can strengthen their rule in *AP* V.ix–xx.

EFFECTUAL TRUTHS

Machiavelli's equivocation between being and appearing highlights a related ambiguity in one of the *Prince*'s most worked-over phrases: the 'effectual truth of a thing', which Machiavelli contrasts to 'the imagination of it'. What constitutes the effectual truth (*verità effettuale*) princes should care about, and how can they recognize it among all the misleading appearances that many follow to their ruin? The usual reading says that what 'is done' by actual human beings constitutes the effectual truth, as opposed to idealistic notions of what 'should be' done. The truth about the quality of actions can presumably be identified by observing what people 'do' in one's own times, or in other periods of history.

But what if that which is most conspicuously 'done' is unwise or corrupt, a possibility Machiavelli considers in the next two chapters? Should such conduct nonetheless be taken as the effectual truth about humanity that ought to guide prudent princes? This *seems* to be the point: in corrupt times when most men—in particular, most political leaders—are not good, anyone who seeks to act more nobly than them will soon be torn apart. But what if in corrupt times people are especially prone to precisely the kind of order-destroying error identified in Argument (2): namely, that things appear virtuous that would bring ruin if pursued, and other things appear vicious that would produce security and well-being?

The idea that, in corrupt times, people tend to invert qualities of good and bad, regarding harmful deeds as praiseworthy and blaming salutary ones as harmful, was a favourite theme of ancient writers. Thucydides, one of its earliest exponents, wrote brilliantly about how hard it is for citizens and leaders to judge political matters rightly when their moral standards have been turned upside down. This confusion arises because, in pursuit of private ambitions, people change 'the accepted sense of words' in order to cover the injustice of their deeds. Bent on gratifying their bloated appetites, they ruin themselves and their cities under the self-serving illusion that they are exalting both.[3] Later writers used this theme to criticize their own corrupt times. The habit of investing vices with the names of virtues, Plutarch argued, is both symptomatic of grave civil disorder and tends to aggravate it. The man on the street grows accustomed 'to treat vices as virtues, so that he feels not disgusted with them but delighted, which also takes away all shame for his errors'.[4]

Machiavelli invoked this ancient theme to frame his own tragic history of his native city. In the dedication of his *Florentine Histories*, Machiavelli announces that 'in all my narrations I have never wished to conceal an indecent deed with a decent cause [*una disonesta opera con una onesta cagione*

---

[3] *TPW* III.82–3.   [4] 'How to tell a flatterer from a friend', *PM* I, 300–5.

ricoprire], or to obscure a praiseworthy deed as if it were done for a contrary end'.[5] In a speech he gives to a group of decent citizens, 'moved by love of their fatherland', Machiavelli highlights the difficulties of recognizing true qualities behind the spin given to good appearances. In Florence, the main speaker declares ruefully:

> an oath and faith given last only as long as they are useful; so men make use of them not to observe them but to serve as a means of being able to deceive more easily. And the more easily and surely the deception succeeds, the more glory and praise is acquired from it; by this, harmful men are praised as industrious and good men are blamed as fools.[6]

If this is the message of the second, less strident voice in the *Prince*, it suggests that we need a more reflective account of how to identify the 'effectual truth' than one that derives truth from 'what is done'. The next three chapters make readers work hard toward this end.

---

[5] *FH* Ded.   [6] *FH* III.5.

16

Giving and spending

Of liberality and parsimony

THE DANGERS OF BEING HELD LIBERAL

Machiavelli begins with the first item on the last chapter's list of qualities that are praised or blamed, liberality (*liberalità*): the quality of appropriate giving or spending. Aristotle, Cicero, Sallust, and other ancient writers said a good deal about this virtue. The properly liberal man, according to Aristotle, gives the right amount to the right people for the right purpose. Liberality (*eleutheriotês*) is the virtuous mean between two vices relating to giving: the excess of prodigality or extravagance (*asôtia*), or giving too much to the wrong people for the wrong purposes, and the deficiency of meanness (*aneleutheria*).[1] Roman and humanist writers echoed these distinctions in the tripartite distinction between *liberalitas* (virtue), *luxuria* (excess), and *avaritia* (deficiency).[2]

At first Machiavelli seems to question these traditional distinctions. It would, he concedes, 'be good to be held liberal'. Nonetheless, when liberality 'is used so that you may be held liberal'—that is, 'virtuously and as it should be used'—it offends you and brings you the infamy of being thought illiberal. So 'if one wants to maintain a name [*nome*] for liberality among men', he must behave like a spendthrift who does not 'leave out any quality of sumptuousness [*suntuosità*]'.

But this is a sorely inadequate solution. Princes who rely on 'sumptuous' spending and giving to gain a reputation for liberality may win over many supporters in a short time. But this soon leads them to ruin, since such princes squander all their resources. Desperately seeking other means to maintain a good 'name' for liberality, the big-spending prince then 'burdens the people extraordinarily' with heavy taxes and other unpopular measures. The upshot, inevitably, is that his subjects grow to hate him for taking their property, and despise him for his poverty. Then, 'having offended the many and rewarded

---

[1] *ANE* IV.i.1–22, II.ix.2.   [2] See Tacitus, *TH* I.30.1 and examples below.

the few with this liberality of his, he feels every first hardship and danger' that comes along. Nor can he safely reverse his initial bad policy, for when he recognizes his error and tries to retreat from his former excesses, 'he immediately incurs the infamy of miserliness [*misero*]'.

If these are the results of so-called liberality, Machiavelli reasons, princes should shun the conduct that currently goes under that name. Whether a prince is *reputed* to have particular vices or virtues is less important than the *true* qualities and effects of his actions. So to safeguard the state instead of ruining it, he should do the exact opposite of what those praised as 'liberal' do. Instead of pandering to unreasonable expectations, a prudent prince should prefer to be 'held' miserly rather than liberal.

At first he will face bitter complaints. To people who expect political leaders to be extravagant givers—bribing them with gifts, huge tax breaks, or expensive public spectacles—those who run a prudent economy *appear* stingy. They will blame a prince who exercises fiscal prudence, avoids wasting public money on self-promoting displays, and does not try to buy supporters. Fearing such criticism, some princes may be tempted to throw moderation to the winds, and do whatever it takes to make people 'hold' him liberal.

Machiavelli says: don't do it. For 'there is more wisdom in maintaining a name for miserliness, which begets infamy without hatred', than in following ruinous policies that are 'held' liberal. In the long run, a moderately bad reputation is less harmful to a prince than a terrible reputation that also turns people violently against him. A prudent prince knows that sound policies don't always win love. But if he does what saves the state and avoids outright hatred, he can weather subjects' scepticism and win them over in the end. 'For with time he will always be held more and more liberal' when people realize that by refraining from the extravagance others use to buy supporters, he has built a strong, self-reliant state. They will come around 'when it is seen that with his parsimony [*parsimonia*] his income is enough for him, that he can defend himself from whoever makes war upon him, and that he can undertake campaigns without burdening the people'. Thus increasing his subjects' actual security and well-being, he builds much firmer foundations for his own state than princes who court favour by big spending. 'Therefore', Machiavelli concludes, 'so as not to have to rob [*rubare*] his subjects, to be able to defend himself, not to become poor and contemptible, nor to be forced to become rapacious [*rapace*], a prince should esteem it little to incur a name for miserliness.'

WHAT'S IN A NAME: TRUE AND APPARENT VICES

Here, then, is the first so-called 'vice' that Machiavelli recommends as necessary to 'save' the state: the appalling vice of fiscal responsibility. How, then, do the actions and qualities he associates with this necessary 'vice' differ from those that are traditionally called virtuous?

Not much at all. The policies Machiavelli recommends conform to what ancient writers called the virtue of *parsimonia*, or wise economic restraint.[3] Good parsimonious practice also leads to properly restrained liberality, the virtue relating more specifically to appropriate giving and spending.

And indeed, when spelling out the advantages of restraint in these areas, Machiavelli shifts from speaking of being 'held' miserly to saying that 'with his *parsimonia*'—now the real thing—a prince can build strong foundations. Here is one of those subtle word shifts found throughout the *Prince*, which takes us from an initial, defective view—here that economic restraint deserves the bad name of 'miserly'—to a more reasonable understanding that renames such restraint virtuous 'parsimony'. The chapter moves from *seeming* to recommend the vice of miserliness to *actually* recommending the old-fashioned virtue of *parsimonia*. Perhaps for this reason, its title is 'Liberality and parsimony', not 'Liberality and miserliness'. Whereas the next chapter's title has a traditional (Christian) virtue–vice antithesis, cruelty and mercy, this one consists of two traditional (Greco-Roman) virtues.

Machiavelli's preference for virtuous *parsimonia* doesn't mean that he treats liberality as a vice. He distinguishes quite clearly between the appropriately moderate virtue of *liberalità* and the immoderate spending or *suntuosità* that many people *wrongly* praise as liberality. While certain qualities that are mistakenly 'held' liberal are vicious, other virtuous qualities do deserve their good name. Thus Machiavelli writes that if liberality 'is used virtuously and *as it should be used*, it may not be recognized', so that 'you will not escape the infamy of its contrary'; and advises the prince to accept this infamy only because he 'cannot, without damage to himself, use the virtue of liberality in such a mode that it is recognized [*conosciuta*]'. It is the misrecognition of true virtue that causes problems, not the unrealistic demands of the virtue rightly understood. The behaviour 'held' virtuously liberal isn't virtuous at all, but extravagance or profligacy; the conduct held miserly by the same defective standard isn't vicious, but moderate and virtuous. If properly liberal actions aren't recognized as such, this is because observers lack a proper measure of what virtuous liberality is and how it should be used.

So far, then, Machiavelli is telling princes to set aside what is 'held' virtuous not by the standards of 'traditional' ethics upheld by ancient writers, but only

---

[3] In English, 'parsimony' means excessive penny-pinching and thus appears synonymous with Machiavelli's 'Tuscan' vice, *misero*, or the Latin vice *avaritia*. But for Roman writers, *parsimonia* meant virtuous thrift: see Cicero, *De Officiis* I.92, Seneca, *De Beneficiis* 2.34 ('*Parsimonia* is knowing how to avoid unnecessary expenditure, or the art of thrift'), Livy, *LH* Pref.11 (poverty and *parsimonia* were honoured in ancient, virtuous Rome), and Tacitus, *TH* I.37. Machiavelli plays with the superficially similar meanings of *misero* and *parsimonia*, speaking as if both were vices when one is properly a virtue.

by the inverted standards that some people apply in everyday political life. This was not a radical new argument, although Machiavelli gives it a misleadingly shocking appearance. In his *Nicomachean Ethics* Aristotle stresses that virtues are often held to be vices that closely resemble them. In times where excessive spending is rife, people mistake extravagance for the praiseworthy 'mean' and misidentify moderate liberality as stinginess. Some extremes bear a certain likeness to the 'mean' virtue, as big-spending extravagance may look like appropriately generous liberality. This makes it easy for 'opposite characters to claim the same quality, for instance the extravagant [*asôtos*] man claims to be the same as the liberal [*eleutheriô*]'.[4] People rightly called extravagant do just the sorts of things that Machiavelli's mistakenly-called liberal people do: they take from the wrong sources, and become rapacious (*lêptikoi*) because 'they want to spend, but cannot do so freely because they come to an end of their resources, and so are compelled to obtain supplies from others'.[5]

Other writers also elaborate on this theme. Warning that we should be 'on our guard against extravagance being called liberality', Plutarch, following Thucydides' famous passage on the subject, points to the disastrous political consequences that ensue when leaders and ordinary citizens confuse actual vices with apparent virtues.[6] One of Machiavelli's favourite Roman historians, Tacitus, describes how ambitious politicians exploit the potential for confusion in moral language for their own illicit ends. His *Histories* show the would-be tyrant Otho courting the mob by accusing prudently parsimonious opponents of shameful avarice (*avaritia*). Otho does what a long tradition of Greek and Roman writers show aspiring tyrants doing: seeking to win mass support so that they can seize power from legitimate authorities, they use the 'names' of vices to defame moderate opponents, criticizing virtuous restraint and fiscal discipline as unduly harsh and punitive. Tacitus has one of Otho's virtuous adversaries urge Romans to see through these rhetorical sleights-of-hand, warning of deceptions that 'luxury imposes by its false show of liberality [*luxuria specie liberalitatis*]'.[7]

In the first part of chapter 16, at least, Machiavelli's position is wholly in accord with these ancient writers and their high standards of virtue. Like Aristotle and Tacitus, he treats liberality as the virtue in between two vices, extravagance and miserliness. Parsimony is not opposed to liberality; it is a more general virtue related to economy. The problem with these standards, Machiavelli suggests, is not that they are too high, but that people often misunderstand or misapply them, inverting what should be blamed and praised. He doesn't advise princes to ignore true virtues, but only what people wrongly consider virtues, since these 'if pursued would be one's ruin', as we read at the end of chapter 15.

---

[4] *ANE* II.vii.2–3; *Eudemian Ethics* III.v.2.

[5] They also give to the wrong people: 'they make men rich who ought to be poor, and will not give anything to the worthy, while heaping gifts on flatterers and others who minister to their pleasures.' *ANE* IV.i.34–5.

[6] 'Flatterer', *PM* I, 300–5.   [7] *TH* I.37, I.30.

By setting out good policies under a bad name, Machiavelli reverses his usual ironic procedure in the *Prince*, which involves describing bad actions under good names. Readers who fail to notice the difference between *misero* and *parsimonia* will fall into the trap of Otho-like rhetoric—and think that Machiavelli is telling princes to practise a traditional vice when in fact he tells them to practise a traditional virtue, without minding if it is 'held' vicious by the morally confused.

What then should we make of his declaration that 'in our times we have not seen great things [*gran cose*] done except by those who have been held miserly', while 'the others have been eliminated'? This is a typical Machiavellian test. While 'great' men did all these 'great things', it does not follow that they deserve equal praise. Machiavelli's three examples challenge readers to distinguish between more and less prudent actions that go under the 'name' of vicious *misero*.

The first and third examples portray bad modes of penny-pinching. The miserliness of both Pope Julius II and Spain's king Ferdinand consisted in their imposing excessive taxes to fight unnecessary wars. Julius, in typical fortune-dependent mode, oscillated uncontrollably from excessive and inappropriate spending to excessive and inappropriate taxing. He 'made use of a name for liberality to attain the papacy', but didn't bother to maintain it later since 'to be able to make war', he could not afford to spend on other things. The reference to Julius' initial liberality is a sly dig at his notorious use of bribes and favours to win favour among those who chose the pope. He ceased to care about liberality—that is, he became less lavish in his favours and burdened people with taxes—not for the sake of good order, but in order to make endless violent and unnecessary wars. This is hardly the kind of 'great' action that Machiavelli recommends. Nor does it involve the kind of so-called 'miserliness'—truly parsimony—that he deems necessary to save states.

The third example says only that 'If the present king of Spain [Ferdinand] had been held liberal, he would not have been able to make or win so many campaigns [*imprese*].' Machiavelli's word for campaigns or enterprises, *imprese*, often has ironic connotations; if some wars are necessary and required to maintain good orders, what he calls military and religious *imprese* are almost always unnecessary, extraordinary, and harmful.[8] Chapter 19 will tell us that Ferdinand 'was able to sustain armies with money from the Church and the people', implying that he relied on others' fortune by drawing from the former and on 'extraordinary' taxes imposed on the latter. Ferdinand erred in the direction of excessive *misero* in the sense Machiavelli gives that word in chapter 15: he refrained too much from using what was properly his, instead using what belonged to others to conduct his badly ordered *imprese*.

Machiavelli's second example presents a more reasonable kind of state-saving 'miserliness', or rather parsimony, as Machiavelli calls it here. 'The

---

[8] See chap. 8, n.7.

present king of France [Louis XII] has carried on many wars without imposing an extraordinary tax on his subjects', Machiavelli claims, because 'the extra expenses were administered with his long-practised *parsimonia*', a quality that allows princes to fight wars without overburdening their subjects.

ARE MORAL AND INSTRUMENTAL *VIRTÚ* DIFFERENT?

How does Machiavelli relate the traditionally *moral* virtues of (true) liberality and parsimony to the standards of prudent self-preservation set out in the *Prince* so far, under the 'name' of *virtú*? Are moral virtue and Machiavelli's *virtú* two distinct standards that sometimes overlap, sometimes conflict in practice? Or are the ancient moral virtues of liberality and parsimony essentially identical to the qualities needed to preserve the state?

So far, again, it is hard to see any 'effectual' difference between them. Machiavelli's vocabulary, of course, doesn't distinguish between moral and purely instrumental senses of *virtú*. He uses the same word for qualities that are valued for moral reasons—concern for other people's well-being, or respect for their desires and reasonable claims—and those valued because they help to secure or advance one's own well-being or satisfy one's desires. The fact that the same word can be used in different ways is hardly evidence of a unified conception of instrumental and moral *virtú* in the *Prince*. Nevertheless, Machiavelli's reflections on the qualities that contribute most to stable orders, security, and good foundations do point toward such a conception. The same virtuous qualities that help promote a prince's reasonable aims also induce him to be concerned about other people's well-being—as parsimony induces him to avoid wasting public resources (extravagance/*suntuosità*) on the one hand, and oppressive taxes (miserliness/*misero*) on the other, and as careful military ordering induced him to take an active interest in the welfare of his 'plebs' in chapter 10. In the next chapter, the same qualities of self-restraint and temperance that help princes avoid hatred also induce them to show respect for other people's desires for security and non-arbitrary punishments. As we saw at the end of chapter 8, a prince who reflects carefully on the qualities that help him maintain his state will begin to see that a concern for others' well-being and respect for their reasonable desires is necessary for his own safety.

CAVEAT I: BE LIBERAL TO ACQUIRE, BUT
NOT TO MAINTAIN

In the second half of the chapter, however, Machiavelli introduces caveats that seem once again to separate his position from traditional virtue ethics. Having set out reasons to avoid seeking a 'name' for liberality, he now considers two possible objections to this argument. Both suggest that there are some conditions in which excessive 'liberality'—that is, extravagant spending—is necessary for princes.

Machiavelli's first imagined challenger insists that 'Caesar attained the empire with liberality, and many others, because they have been and have *been held* to be liberal'. Machiavelli responds: if you are already a prince 'this liberality' is damaging. 'Caesar', he notes, 'was one of those who wanted to attain the principate of Rome; but if after he had arrived there, had he remained alive and not been temperate [*temperato*] with his expenses, he would have destroyed the empire.' But if you are still *en route* to acquiring princely rank, 'it is indeed necessary to be held liberal'.

This seems to relativize virtues and vices to an individual's particular aims. It may still be true that economic restraint is necessary for a prince to *preserve* his state. But if a man's aim is to acquire rather than to maintain, he needs to operate with an entirely different set of virtues; indeed, he needs the opposite of those qualities that help princes maintain what they've acquired. He needs to spend wildly, using pay-offs and bribes, to buy his way up to princedom as Caesar did—then stop once there and clean up his act.

If this is Machiavelli's advice, however, it sits uncomfortably beside his earlier observations about how princes who gain supporters through their excessive 'liberality' risk losing their support if they try to switch toward a more restrained mode. If someone who is already prince becomes hated and despised by those who once loved him for his extravagance, why shouldn't the same happen to someone who tries to 'draw back' from his excesses once he becomes prince? If support can be withdrawn from one who has been prince for some time, it can be withdrawn at least as easily from one who has recently risen to princely rank.

By claiming that princes need to be spendthrifts to acquire power in a republic, but parsimonious to maintain it, Machiavelli challenges readers to ask whether it's *possible* for any prince to maintain his state by the opposite 'modes' from those he used to acquire it. If new princes had no need of other people's support once they reached the peak of power, then of course they could rule as they please. But all princes need someone, and have to keep supporters satisfied. If even the immensely popular Caesar's fans would have turned against him if he'd survived and adopted frugal policies, why should his modern imitators think that they can switch from extravagance to parsimony without turning their partisans into enemies? Moreover: if excessive spending is *both* necessary to acquire princely power in a republic *and* ultimately harmful, then perhaps the very aim of seizing princely power is unreasonable?

CAVEAT II: BE LIBERAL WITH OTHERS' PROPERTY, BUT NOT WITH YOUR OWN

Machiavelli next considers a further objection to his argument that princes should not want to be held liberal. If another imagined interlocutor protests that many princes have done great things 'with their armies who have been held very liberal', Machiavelli replies that 'either the prince spends from what is his own and his subjects', or from what belongs to someone else'. He should be sparing with the former, but 'not leave out any part of liberality' in giving away the property of others.

Here again, we seem to have a blatantly self-serving distinction that subordinates virtue to a prince's own advantage. Machiavelli has already emphasized the advantages of avoiding rapacity, both in truth and in reputation, when dealing with his own subjects: rapacity, the chapter's last sentence says, 'begets infamy with hatred', a potentially lethal combination for any prince. Now he seems to suggest that no similar advantages can come from being 'sparing' with the property of non-subjects. On the contrary, princes should have no scruples whatever in taking and using that property to gain a 'name' for virtuous 'liberality'. Machiavelli's examples mention two different instances of 'others' property' that princes may use to be held liberal. For a prince 'who goes out with his armies and who feeds on booty, pillage, and ransom, this liberality is necessary', since without it 'he would not be followed by his soldiers'. And 'one can be a bigger giver [*piú largo donatore*]' of 'what is not yours or your subjects', as can be seen with Cyrus, Caesar, and Alexander; because spending that which belongs to others increases your reputation, while 'spending your own' brings you harm.

Both cases involve princes who woo support by taking and spending what belongs to others who are not their subjects. But there are important differences between them. The first speaks of princes in the specific context of war where the plundered party is a declared enemy, plundered within limits. According to generally accepted practices of war in ancient times and Machiavelli's, victorious soldiers were permitted to take booty from the defeated party until terms of capitulation were agreed. So long as soldiers and princes 'fed on' booty and pillage within customary limits, and did not try to take more, this way of being 'liberal' with others' property could be considered an 'ordinary' part of warfare.

It is one thing to spend what one takes from a declared enemy in war to feed and reward one's soldiers. It is quite another to do what Cyrus, Caesar, and Alexander famously did. To get a name for liberality among supporters, they took and gave not just booty but control of country after country, without concern for customary limits or prudence. Machiavelli subtly contrasts the two cases by saying that liberality is 'necessary' in the first, while in the second he speaks not of necessity but of the luxury born of excess: one has the luxury of being a 'bigger giver' of that which is not one's own when one takes as much as these three insatiable conquerors.

A further consideration might lead readers to doubt whether Machiavelli thinks prudent princes should imitate Cyrus and the others. The peoples they conquered thereby became subjects. But it is dangerous to spend what you take from your own subjects, since this makes them hate you. So long as you gain supporters by giving them what you take from others, you need to keep taking from others, and find new countries to plunder. But as soon as you conquer and make them subjects so as to plunder them more easily, you also make ever more enemies from among 'your own'. This vicious spiral might lead thoughtful readers to the next chapter's quite different argument that a prince should 'above all' keep his hands off the property of others, except where such 'rapacity' is authorized by customary practice in war.

Far from setting out reasonable exceptions to the advice that princes should avoid using excessive 'liberality', then, Machiavelli's distinctions between acquiring/maintaining and one's own subjects'/others' property look like superficially plausible but, ultimately, ineffectual attempts to save big-spending princes from the consequences of their actions.

Machiavelli is fond of using specious distinctions and other rhetorical fallacies to exercise readers' skills at seeing through corrupting persuasions. Those encountered so far are child's play, however, compared with some of the tricks he pulls out of his hat in the next two chapters.

LIBERALITY AND CORRUPTION

If one of Machiavelli's reasons for writing ironically about virtues is to arm readers—whether aspiring princes or ordinary citizens—against specious excuses for lowering moral standards, ancient writings on liberality cast light on another reason for his stylistic strategy. Machiavelli was not the first to deplore the loss of stable moral bearings while eschewing overtly moral language in his own critical writings. Many ancient writers argued that in corrupt times when people invert the qualities of virtues and vices, to insist on the traditional meanings of words will not help the fight against corruption. People will simply ridicule your naïvety, or suspect that you're trying to manipulate them. The best strategy for correcting widespread errors about virtue is to feign indifference to moral standards and to other people's interests, discussing only what is expedient for the people you want to correct.[9]

---

[9] See *ME* 95–6.

This strategy is used by Cato, the foremost defender of Rome's ancient republican virtues on the eve of the republic's destruction, in Sallust's *War with Catiline*. Sallust has Cato declare that the state of Rome is so rotten that there is no point in discussing 'whether our morals [*moribus*] are good or bad'; he will only concern himself with the question of Rome's self-preservation. Corrupt Romans, he claims, habitually praise to the skies qualities that threaten the republic's survival. 'For a long time now', he tells his countrymen, 'we have ceased to call things by their proper names. To give away other people's property is called *liberalitas*, while criminal daring (*audacia*) goes by the name of courage (*fortitude*). That', he claims, 'is why our republic is in such extreme straits.'

Cato refuses to lecture Romans on the proper senses of words. 'If such is our standard of morality', says Cato, 'let Romans be liberal if they want to.' But this false and harmful liberality is exposed by ironic indirection at the end of the work, where Sallust compares two of Rome's great men, Cato and Julius Caesar. While seeming to praise the virtues of each even-handedly, Sallust's normatively coded language conveys harsh criticisms and high praise. 'Caesar', he states, 'was esteemed for the many kind services he rendered and for his lavish generosity [*munificentia magnus*]'; Cato for consistent uprightness (*integritate*), and for 'never offering presents'. Cato's taste was for restraint, propriety, and above all, austerity (*modestiae, decoris, severitatis*). And—presumably unlike Caesar, though Sallust does not say so directly—Cato 'was more concerned to be a good man than to be thought one'.[10] Machiavelli was a close reader of Sallust's work; in the *Discourses* he comments on the Roman author's ironic techniques for condemning Caesar's corrupt qualities while seeming to praise them.[11] His own examination of so-called liberality and virtuous *parsimonia* has similar aims: to rescue the virtues of moderate restraint while pretending to care only about a prince's self-preservation.

Machiavelli was too cautious to imply that the Medici had used similar corrupting methods to attain princely power in a republic. But it was well known that conspicuously lavish spending and building, generous gifts, and other forms of 'liberality' had enabled the super-wealthy banking family to rise to extraordinary heights. In the *Florentine Histories*, Machiavelli uses the ancient ironic code to praise Medici *liberalità* while implying that the deeds widely applauded under this 'name' corrupted good republican orders. Along with 'astuteness', liberality repeatedly appears as a hallmark virtue of the men who founded the Medici dynasty. Cosimo de' Medici 'took care to benefit everyone and with his liberality to make many citizens into his partisans'— noting that 'partisanship' for Machiavelli is always divisive and hence corrupt.[12]

---

[10] *SWC* 52. Compare Cicero, *De Officiis* I.xiv.44.   [11] See 'Ironic Techniques'.
[12] Compare *XC* VIII on Cyrus' similarly lavish giving.

These arts of appearing decent made it hard to reproach Cosimo, especially since so many benefited from his liberality: he helped many powerful people with his money, handing out or writing off loans to his prospective supporters, and secured public positions for friends. Machiavelli has Cosimo's chief opponent Niccolò da Uzzano, described as one of the most prudent and law-abiding characters in the *Histories*, speak of Cosimo much as Sallust's Cato speaks of Caesar. Uzzano 'perfectly understood' that these 'extraordinary' money-giving modes of gaining support undermine republican liberties, and 'send men flying [*volando*] to a principality'. But most Florentines, he says sorrowfully, are taken in by Cosimo's 'liberality', as they call his efforts to help 'everyone with his money . . . and not only the Florentines but the condottieri [mercenaries]', in order to pull 'this or that friend to higher ranks of honour'.[13] In both his *Histories* and the *Prince*, Machiavelli exposes the disastrous consequences that flow from inverted standards of virtue and vice. Like earlier writers, he inverts these standards not to repudiate or mock traditional morality, but to find a different way back to it.

---

[13] *FH* IV.27; compare VII.5, VII.10.

17

Fear and punishment

Of cruelty and mercy; and whether it is better to be loved than feared, or the contrary

TOO MUCH MERCY CAN BE CRUEL

The next chapter presents a similar inversion of the values ascribed to the 'vice' of cruelty and the 'virtue' of mercy. Machiavelli starts by declaring that princes should 'desire to be held merciful [*piatoso*] and not cruel [*crudele*]'. Nevertheless, they 'should take care not to use this mercy badly'.

What is mercy used badly or well? Machiavelli illustrates each case with recent examples. Hoping to 'escape a name for cruelty', the Florentine republic used mercy badly towards the city of Pistoia, thus allowing that city to be destroyed. Pistoia was a city under Florentine dominion, famous for its violent internal factions. In the *Discourses* Machiavelli writes that the Florentines should have clamped down on Pistoian factions by dealing harshly with the leaders of 'tumults', and by forcing both sides to put down their arms. Instead of taking firm action, however, the too-merciful Florentines tried to reconcile the warring factions. This policy failed dismally, and allowed the factions to tear their city apart.

By contrast, Cesare Borgia used mercy well. Though he 'was held to be cruel', nonetheless 'his cruelty [*crudeltà*] restored the Romagna, united it, and reduced it to peace and to faith'. When this case is 'considered well', 'one will see that he was much more merciful than the Florentine people' in their dealings with Pistoia.

Notice the usual ambiguity in this account: was it Borgia's so-called but wrongly held cruelty that had such good effects or his 'cruelty' in the correct sense of that word? Either way, Machiavelli uses these contrasting examples to propose that it is 'more merciful' to be held cruel, or perhaps to be cruel, in order to bring unity and peace to one's subjects than to let violent disorders rage among them. When cruelty or so-called cruelty has such results, it is far better than policies that 'for the sake of too much mercy allow disorders to continue, from which come killings or robberies; for these', Machiavelli points out, 'customarily hurt the generality of people [*una universalità*], but the executions [*esecuzioni*] that come from a prince hurt one particular person'.

Just as the last chapter said that if a prince does what is 'held' miserly (vice) he will soon be judged 'liberal' (virtue) in a truer sense, this one says that if he does what is held cruel (vice) he will be more truly merciful (virtue). But there seems to be a difference in the two chapters regarding who mistakenly 'holds' certain actions vicious. The actions Machiavelli described as miserliness in chapter 16—more correctly called parsimony—were not at all vicious by the high standards of traditional ethics; they were only 'held' vicious by people whose judgement was confused or corrupted. It's not immediately clear that the same is true here. If Borgia's actions exemplify conduct that is held cruel but is truly merciful, then those who 'hold' them viciously cruel would include most ancient and modern philosophers. If Machiavelli is seriously proposing Borgia's policies in the Romagna as a model of 'virtuous cruelty', this would indeed constitute an audacious challenge even to the tough-minded standards of virtue upheld by ancient Roman and Greek moral writers, as well as to more mercy-oriented Christian understandings of virtue.

It would appear even more shocking had Machiavelli not added a moral-sounding condition: namely, that to count as *merciful* 'cruelty', a policy should bring unity and peace to one's subjects, or at least end the disorders that 'hurt the generality of people'. Nothing quite like this criterion has yet been stated in the *Prince*. Now it sounds as if Machiavelli is setting out a condition for princely *virtù* that requires princes to take the good of a wider body of people as one of their chief ends. This may be a 'good' only in the narrow sense that it helps other people to avoid serious harm. But it still suggests that in redefining mercy as cruelty, thus assimilating a virtue to a vice, we need not abandon all moral standards. We merely have to trade in standards that judge virtue and vice by considering a person's 'modes' of action—here mildness and extreme harshness—for standards that judge by results, where the results that excuse so-called cruelty are those that help or avoid harm to a wider cross-section of people and not just the prince.

Machiavelli's next remarks further soften his initial tough-talking remarks. A prince, he says, should not 'make himself feared' but should 'proceed in a mode tempered with prudence and humanity [*procedere in modo, temperato con prudenza e umanità*]'. In this way he ensures that 'too much confidence does not make him incautious [*incauto*] and too much diffidence does not render him intolerable [*intollerabile*]'. This seems to suggest that getting one's modes right is necessary, or at least helpful, for achieving the right results. Do temperance, prudence, and humanity produce a better quality of actions than intemperance, imprudence, and inhumanity? That the right modes produce better results certainly seems to be Machiavelli's view throughout the *Prince*;

over and over, we have seen various intemperate modes produce impressive-looking but trouble-engendering outcomes.

But having advised princes to use humanity for their own good, he again turns around abruptly and declares that men in general are hardly worth it: they are 'ungrateful, fickle, pretenders and dissemblers, evaders of danger, eager for gain', and worse. Readers' sense of unease about the status of humanity is heightened at the end of the chapter where Machiavelli praises the Carthaginian general Hannibal, declaring that the remarkable unity in his armies 'could not have arisen from anything other than his inhuman cruelty [*inumana crudeltà*]'.

SEVERITY AND MILDNESS

From one moment to the next, the chapter strikes jarringly different tones. Its dominant position—that princes should not mind being held, or perhaps being, cruel—is expressed in harsh overtones, as if imitating the harsh 'mode' being recommended. But this is only part of the story, since statements in this tone are followed by gentler caveats that soften the initial hard line. What is Machiavelli doing with all these modulations?

One possibility is that the tempering caveats don't substantially modify the harsh precepts, but simply tell princes how to 'use' them so that they avoid becoming 'intolerable' to subjects. Another is that princes who take the caveats seriously won't be able to be 'cruel' in any ordinary sense of that word, since the caveats call for modes of action that preclude genuine cruelty. In this case the 'soft' caveats *do* modify the hard-line precepts, which then have to be either abandoned or understood in a more moderate sense than the one they first appeared to have. Perhaps if a prince is 'held' cruel rather than merciful in the heavily qualified way Machiavelli recommends, he ends up exhibiting some other virtue that many people *misidentify* as cruelty—as they misidentified virtuous parsimony as stinginess in chapter 16?

If so, Machiavelli would be renovating rather than subverting an ancient ethical tradition: one that discusses common mistakes in thinking about the relation between *clementia* (clemency or mercy) and *crudelitas* (cruelty). Ancient writers discussed both qualities under the heading of virtues or vices in punishing offences. The Roman philosopher Seneca expressed the traditional view, writing that clemency, or 'mildness in inflicting punishment', should generally be considered a virtue; while cruelty, understood as 'harshness of spirit [*atrocitas animi*] in exacting punishments', is a vice of excess. If this were all Seneca said, Machiavelli would obviously disagree with him. But the Roman goes on to warn about a common, extremely damaging error made by those who consider clemency the primary virtue in matters of punishment. The more essential virtue governing punishments is *severitas,* meaning reasonable severity or strictness. When people forget that *clementia* needs to be governed by *severitas,* they go soft and fail to impose sufficiently strict punishments on offenders. Excessive clemency, Seneca argues, can become one of the most insidious causes of corruption in a state, since both subjects and rulers think they can get off lightly when they commit serious crimes. These people come to think that the opposite of *clementia* is not cruelty but severity, and loudly blame any strict, deserved punishment of wrongs as merciless, vicious, and 'cruel'.

Applying the same excessively 'softened' moral standards, people often confuse virtuous clemency with a quality that resembles it, but is really a vice: pity (*misericordia*). Although 'many commend it as a virtue', Seneca argues that this is 'a mental defect' which ought to be avoided: 'for under the guise of clemency' we may fall into excessive *misericordia.* Thus, Seneca concludes, we should be wary 'lest the plausible word *clementia* should sometimes deceive us and lead us to the opposite extreme' of vice and corruption. Clemency that goes hand in hand with severity is virtuous. But when it breaks away from its sterner partner and hooks up with pity, it fatally weakens standards of strict discipline needed to uphold good order.[1]

Machiavelli does not speak directly of severity in chapter 17. But he describes actions that vividly recall ancient arguments about the need to value *severitas* as highly as *clementia.* It is significant that he contrasts cruelty not with the virtue of clemency, but with *pietà,* translated here as 'mercy'. The Italian word *pietà* differs from the Latin *clementia* in several respects. For one thing, it has the senses of mercy, pity, or mildness not specifically in matters of punishment, but more generally. For another, it is a virtue valued more conspicuously in the Christian than in the Roman tradition: *pietà* also means religious 'piety', and would have carried that primary meaning for many of the *Prince's* early readers. Finally, in some of its senses—in particular pity, and Christian 'piety' understood as devotion to otherworldly concerns—*pietà* comes closer to the Roman vice of *misericordia* than to virtuous *clementia.*

In the chapter's title, *crudelitas* and *pietas* look like a vice and its opposing virtue. But the Romans traditionally contrasted cruelty not to *pietas* (pity, piety to the gods, or dutiful conduct generally) but to *clementia.* Recall that chapter 16 had two qualities in its Latin title, *liberalitas* and *parsimonia,* that at first seem to be opposed as virtue and vice—because that is how people wrongly 'hold' them—but turn out to be two mutually compatible virtues. Chapter 17's title, '*De crudelitate et pietate*', hints at the inverse kind of mistake made about qualities relating to punishment. Here, too, the first appearance that cruelty is opposed to *pietas* proves deceptive, since *pietas* is not a suitable antidote to cruelty at all; *severitas* is.

Both chapter titles, then, misleadingly present non-opposed qualities as if they were opposed virtue and vice, imitating very common yet dangerous errors of judgement. If the titular qualities of chapter 16 were both virtues, those of chapter 17 are both traditional Greco-Roman (though not Christian) vices, so long as *crudelitas* is not tempered by humanity and *pietas* ungoverned by due severity. Is Machiavelli subverting ancient ethics here—or challenging readers to spot the errors in order to correct them? If the latter, his judgements have more in common with Seneca's than first appears when he criticizes excessive mercy/*pietà*, and contrasts it to duly moderated cruelty/*crudeltà*.

Chapters 16 and 17 invert each other in another way. Both contain dominant overtones modified by caveats. But in chapter 16, the caveats were harsher than the overtones. Having set out the moderate-sounding precept (to paraphrase): 'be parsimonious rather than excessive in giving, and in time you'll be held moderately liberal', Machiavelli then said (Caveat I) that Caesar-style excess is necessary when trying to acquire principality, and (Caveat II) that excess in giving what belongs to others increases your reputation. Here in chapter 17, on the contrary, the overtones take a hard line and excuse cruelty, while the caveats temper them.

A reason for the difference is suggested by ancient thinking about how to avoid errors in matters of vice and virtue. Aristotle says that in order to hit the virtuous mean, one should lean sometimes to the side of excess and sometimes to that of deficiency.[2] In matters of spending, Machiavelli implies, excess causes more harm than deficiency; thus it is safer to err in the direction of little spending than to give too much to the wrong people. When it comes to punishing serious crimes, the situation is reversed: too light a punishment corrupts people more than too severe. If serious violations go unpunished, lax attitudes creep in, and soon cause general ruin. So whereas the dominant statements in chapter 16 lean toward the 'deficient' vice of miserliness, trying to pull princes back from excessive and corrupt spending, those in chapter 17 lean toward the 'excessive' vice of cruelty, pushing readers to get tougher against crimes and disorders.

When reading chapter 17, then, we need be wary of one-sided interpretations that focus on the harsh, amoral-sounding major statements while ignoring the tempering development that follows them. Machiavelli's reasons for discussing cruelty and mercy in predominantly harsh tones become clearer when we encounter similar ancient treatments of the subject. The same writers who criticize misuses of the good word 'liberality' also discuss how ambitious men seek to be 'held' merciful by being excessively lenient toward criminals.[3]

---

[2] *ANE* II.ix.9.
[3] 'To get a name as merciful, humane, and compassionate [*eleēmones kai philanthrōpoi kai sumpatheis*]', Plutarch observes, 'many release wrongdoers from the punishments they deserve.' 'On Compliancy', *PM* VII 84–5.

To discredit opponents who seek due punishment for crimes, they denounce such virtuous severity as 'cruelty'. Sallust dramatizes the problem in his *War with Catiline*. In contrasting speeches, he first has Caesar urge senators to be lenient toward a group of men who conspired to overthrow the Roman republic. Then he has Cato warn the Senate to 'mind what you are doing with your mildness and pity (*mansuetudo et misericordia*)'; if the conspirators take up arms again, 'you may regret your leniency'. In Sallust's concluding contrast between Caesar and Cato—described as two men of 'diverse morals' (*diversis moribus*)—we read that Caesar was renowned for his mildness and pity, while Cato had earned respect by his severity (*severitas*). Caesar won fame by his readiness to give, to relieve, to pardon, and was thus praised for his good nature; Cato, who never offered gifts or indulged criminals, 'was a scourge for the wicked, admired for his firmness [*constantia*]'.[4]

CAVEAT I: PROCEED IN A TEMPERATE MODE WITH PRUDENCE AND HUMANITY

If we take the chapter as a whole, considering the caveats as well as the overtones, does Machiavelli advise princes to be more like the severe Cato or the cruel Cesare Borgia? Machiavelli certainly seems to make Borgia his model of necessary 'cruelty', though his description of what qualities merit praise is teasingly ambiguous: Borgia '*was held* to be cruel', Machiavelli writes, 'nonetheless *his cruelty* restored the Romagna, united it, and reduced it to peace and to faith'. It's unclear what did the work of restoring, uniting, and reducing here: Borgia's so-called cruelty—which may have been appropriate strictness and discipline rather than excessive harshness—or his cruelty according to a correct meaning of that word. Machiavelli says here that princes 'should not care about' incurring '*the infamy* of cruelty', not that they should not mind *being* cruel. And then come the incongruously moderate caveats. 'Nonetheless', he declares, a prince:

> should be slow [*grave*, also meaning serious, weighty, rigorous] in believing and moving, nor should he make himself feared, and he should proceed in a mode tempered by prudence and humanity, so that too much confidence does not make him incautious [*incauto*] and too much diffidence does not render him intolerable.

Here Machiavelli speaks clearly of how a prince should *be* and behave, not how he should appear or be held. But can these qualities be combined with cruelty in such a way that one's actions are still recognizably cruel? If cruelty is by definition excessive or unreasonable harshness, then it's hard to see how it

---

[4] *SWC* 52, 54.

can be tempered by prudence and humanity without becoming something other than cruelty. Harsh methods of punishment tempered by prudence and humanity are no longer unreasonable or excessive. They are therefore not cruel, but virtuously severe.

The last part of the sentence strikes a distinctly moderate chord: the 'mode' princes adopt should make them neither incautious from overconfidence nor intolerable out of diffidence (*diffidenzia*). The former is too harsh a mode, the latter too soft and weak. Machiavelli's caveats steer princes away from both extremes toward a more moderate mode, one governed by caution and gravity rather than excessive speed or sluggishness, overconfident credulity or timorous inaction. Recall too that gravity, temperance, and reasonable caution all contrast with the qualities attributed to fortune-dependent princes in chapter 7. Those princes fly hard and fast to greatness, high on self-confidence born not of wisdom or personal achievements but of what others have thrown into their laps.

Did Cesare Borgia's methods of dealing with the Romagna respect the limits set out in these caveats? The answer is a pretty resounding No. His 'modes' as described in chapter 7 were assuredly not tempered by humanity. On the contrary, he seems to have plumped for violent methods at every turn. Nor did they display the kinds of prudence mentioned here. Far from showing gravity and circumspection in evaluating his options, he seized on policies that later failed to hold, or threatened his authority—as when he used Remirro de Orco to impose order, then concluded afterwards that his agent's 'cruelty'—or was it really virtuous severity?—brought trouble on himself.

And while Machiavelli says little about it in the *Prince*, Borgia's overconfidence in his own abilities was legendary, and frequently noted in Machiavelli's diplomatic correspondence. Indeed, Machiavelli wrote home that he tried to instil caution in the arrogant young man by warning him that 'times change, and bad fortune and good fortune do not always find a lodging in just one place'. After his father's death, Borgia remained unrealistically confident about his prospects for holding on to the Romagna. 'The duke', Machiavelli wrote at the time, 'allows himself to be carried away [*lascia traportare*] by his spirited confidence [*sua animosa confidentia*], believing that the word of others is more to be relied on than his own'. In the manner typical for fortune-dependent people, however, at the first inkling of failure he began to oscillate desperately between overconfidence and diffidence. Borgia now appeared 'inconstant, irresolute, and timid, not standing firm in any decision [*vario, inresoluto et sospettoso et non stare fermo in alcuna conclusion*]', perhaps 'by nature', perhaps 'because these blows from fortune have stunned him [*stupefacto*], and, since he is unaccustomed to receive them, his mind is confused'.[5]

---

[5] *Legations* 20 and 22 November 1502, 4 and 14 November 1503. Recall that Borgia's murder of Remirro 'stupefied' the people of Romagna; later, fortune's blows stupefied him.

In chapter 17 Machiavelli seems to excuse Borgia's undeniable excesses because their result was the restoration of unity, peace, and faith in the Romagna. But as chapter 7 suggested, Machiavelli's ironies there and 'straight' remarks in his correspondence raise doubts about whether he seriously attributed these benefits to Borgia. On the one hand, he implies that whatever order was imposed on the Romagna resulted from Remirro de Orco's actions, not Borgia's. On the other, no shred of unity, peace, or faith appears in Machiavelli's letters when he discusses the situation in Romagna just before and after Remirro's murder. On the contrary, he depicts a new 'state' beleaguered by angry subjects, abandoned by the foreign troops that were supposed to form its main defences, and surrounded by hostile neighbours. Machiavelli may be serious when he says that princes should avoid excessive 'mercy' that hurts 'the generality of people'. But it isn't clear that he thought Borgia's cruel methods brought the Romagnoles any lasting benefits, or even short-term benefits that could be attributed to him.

Whatever Borgia's shortcomings, though, surely Machiavelli's point is that his harsh modes are comparatively better than the alternative, exemplified by Florence's too-merciful policies in Pistoia? Perhaps. But if we take his caveats seriously, *both* alternatives look equally deficient. If Borgia's modes look too harsh by the standards set out in the caveats, the Florentines' policies toward Pistoia look too soft, diffident, and thus 'intolerable'. The general thrust of Machiavelli's arguments in the chapter is that when dealing with civil crimes and disorders in corrupt times, excessive softness is *more* insidious than excessive harshness. This position agrees with that of Sallust's Cato and other ancient moralists. But if a first question is: which vice is worse in matters of punishment, excess (cruelty) or deficiency (mercy), the deeper question behind Machiavelli's and ancient discussions is: what is the non-vicious 'mode' for punishment? Are cruelty and mercy the only alternatives?

Not in the case of Pistoia, according to Machiavelli's remarks in the *Discourses*. Here he sets out *three* options for dealing with Pistoia's self-mutilating factions. The Florentines could, firstly, kill the leaders; secondly, get rid of them by sending them to prison or exile; or thirdly, try to force the factions to make peace with each other 'under obligations not to offend one another'. This third, comparatively 'soft' method, Machiavelli declares, is the most harmful, uncertain, and useless, 'for it is impossible where very much blood has run, or other similar injuries that a peace made by force can last'. Yet this was the method used by the Florentines in Pistoia, with disastrous results. 'So, worn out, they came to the second, tougher mode of removing the heads of the parties', putting some in prison and keeping others in exile 'so that the accord they made would remain'. The results were good, for 'it has remained until the present day'.

Machiavelli adds that the first method of killing leaders 'would have been most secure'.[6] It's not clear, however, that even this—the harshest of the three methods—necessarily involves 'cruelty' in the proper sense, overstepping the bounds of reasonable harshness set by Machiavelli's caveats and Roman standards of virtuous *severitas*. As we'll see shortly, a second set of caveats in the present chapter says that if a prince has to 'proceed against someone's life, he must do it when there is suitable justification and manifest cause for it'. If Pistoia's leaders were executed without such justification, this would be cruel rather than merely severe. If they were executed in a manner consistent with both the second and first caveats—after taking time to weigh their guilt and the penalty, in a way that does not make the prince feared, and 'in a mode tempered by prudence and humanity'—then this punishment should not be 'held' cruel.

All this suggests that there are several workable alternatives to Borgia's extreme cruelty on the one hand, and excessive Florentine mercy on the other. In fact, Machiavelli's initial Borgia-cruel/Pistoia-merciful opposition is so extreme that it looks like a trap set for readers to test their political judgement— and their skills at seeing through easy excuses for policies that err toward both excessive harshness and leniency. The opposition claimed that since excessive mercy may be harmful, this excuses the opposite extreme of cruelty. This is a well-known rhetorical fallacy of the 'false alternative': it offers only two polar options when in reality others are available. Readers who fail to spot the fallacy may try to imitate Borgia's cruelty, and end up with similar happy-then-unhappy results. Those who recognize it will pause before seizing on either of the flawed initial options, and read further in search of intermediate ones.

Machiavelli's example of the Carthaginian queen Dido conveys a similar temperate message under deceptively harsh appearances. When Machiavelli asserts that 'it is impossible for the new prince to escape a name for cruelty because new states are full of dangers', this seems to say that new princes are forced to lower high moral standards and not to mind being 'held'—perhaps even to be—cruel. Dido was a Phoenician queen who, having fled from a violent tyrant at home, set up shop as the new ruler of Carthage.[7] Machiavelli quotes Dido's welcoming speech to the Trojan refugees who washed up on her country's shores, as imagined in Virgil's *Aeneid*: '"the harshness of things [*res dura*] and the newness of the kingdom compel me to contrive such things, and to keep a broad watch over the borders"'.[8] If we turn to Virgil's poem, we find that while Dido has taken reasonable precautions to secure her new state, her

---

[6] *D* III.27. Here Machiavelli points out that Florentine 'mercy' was not the basic cause that harmed Pistoia; Florentines helped create their own problem by thinking they could hold Pistoia more easily if they kept the city divided into factions. By punishing Pistoian 'leaders of tumults', they merely scratched the surface of a self-inflicted problem.

[7] The chapter mentions two Carthaginians, including Hannibal later; both come out rather well.

[8] Virgil, *Aeneid* I, lines 563–4.

vigilance is tempered by hospitality and humane concern for the Trojans' plight. Machiavelli's *Discourses* treat her—with Aeneas—as an example of the most virtuous kind of founder of cities: a 'free' builder who, not being native to the place where he or she builds, must maintain herself 'by way of friends and confederates' through 'the consent of neighbours where they settled' instead of by brute force.[9] This shows that tempered severity may be an alternative to cruelty even under the harsh necessities that constrain new princes.

THE BADNESS OF HUMAN NATURE

The caveats just discussed include the straightforward assertion that a prince should *not* 'make himself feared'. But this view is complicated, if not set aside altogether, as Machiavelli goes on to discuss 'a dispute' about 'whether it is better to be loved than feared [*amato che temuto*], or the reverse'. The proper response, he says, 'is that one would want to be both one and the other; but because it is difficult to put them together, it is much safer to be feared than loved, if one has to lack one of the two'.

His tone then changes without warning. From cautiously weighing different possibilities and urging temperance and humanity, Machiavelli launches into a foul-tempered tirade against humankind:

> For one can say this generally of men: that they are ungrateful, fickle, pretenders and dissemblers, evaders of danger, eager for gain. While you do them good they are yours, offering you their blood, property, lives, and children, as I said above [in chapter 9], when the need for them is far away; but, when it is close to you, they revolt. And that prince who has founded himself entirely on their words, stripped of other preparation, is ruined . . . And men have less hesitation to offend one who makes himself loved than one who makes himself feared, for love is held by a chain of obligation [*uno vinculo di obbligo*] which, because men are wicked [*tristi*], is broken at every opportunity for their own utility; but fear is held by a dread of punishment [*timore è tenuto da una paura di pena*] that never abandons you.

This intemperate passage is often plucked out of context and treated as an unambiguous expression of Machiavelli's bleak view of human nature. Relocated among all the chapter's shifting tones, however, it sounds more like one of several very different voices imitated by Machiavelli the dramatist than like his own univocal judgement. Readers who notice the competing voices are invited to weigh more and less moderate arguments.

One glaring fallacy in the passage is its implication that the human characteristics it describes make men 'wicked' rather than simply human. Of course,

---

[9] *D* II.8.

princes who seek total control over others may complain bitterly of human tendencies that make it difficult to assert such control. But Machiavelli's general view—as distinct from that of this nameless, violent disputant—is that these tendencies are simply part of the human animal. This view of human nature is neither a new nor a shockingly amoral one. Long before Machiavelli, others declared that:

> most men are rather bad than good and the slaves of gain and cowardly in times of danger ... And those who are able to ill-treat others are to be feared by those who can be so treated; for as a rule men do wrong whenever they can.[10]

This passage, with its striking similarities to Machiavelli's, comes from Aristotle's *Rhetoric*—a book that, like parts of the *Prince*, mingles straightforward analyses of rhetorical practice with subtler teachings about how to avoid being tripped up by various rhetorical fallacies. Like Machiavelli, Aristotle implies that these unappealing features of human nature are what they are. But the prudent response to them is not bitter exasperation, but an effort to contain the damage they can cause.

Another fallacy in Machiavelli's—or his misanthropic prince's—tirade is its assumption that human ingratitude, fickleness, hypocrisy, greed, and the like can only be restrained by means of love or fear. In Machiavelli's terms, this is another false alternative. He agrees that fear of punishment is necessary to deter offenders from harming good orders, and that 'love' is an unreliable basis for support. But the passage mentions a third, better alternative: obligations or commitments based on people's own choice and judgement. As earlier chapters stressed, firm political foundations are built on two-way obligations assumed voluntarily, *as well as* on fear of punishment. Moreover, in the examples just discussed, various kinds of human 'badness' are best dealt with by transparent 'modes of proceeding' backed by fear of punishment, not by fear alone. Neither fear nor love can suffice to rein in others' badness and render them trustworthy.

The *Discourses* state more clearly that, in order to build a well-ordered polity, it is best to 'presuppose that men are bad [*rei*]' and 'more prone to evil than good'. These presuppositions do not excuse those who found states primarily on fear of punishment. They merely remind political builders that since they can't expect angelic goodness from subjects or citizens, they need to design orders and laws that encourage their better qualities while discouraging the worse. Well-designed laws both oblige and force people to behave better than they would by nature alone; people are not altogether good or bad by nature, but 'the laws make them good'.[11] The natural badness of others is therefore no excuse for giving one's own similar badness free rein, since there are far better ways to deal with it. Machiavelli avoids spelling out these arguments in the

---

[10] *AR* 1382b 7–9.   [11] *D* I.3, I.9.

Prince, since principalities in his scheme tend to be founded more on force than on law. The view of human nature voiced to justify such foundations, however, looks too one-sidedly pessimistic to sustain lasting orders.[12]

CAVEAT II: HOW TO BE FEARED WITHOUT BEING HATED

The misanthropic passage is followed by a series of incongruously humane caveats, switching the mood once more from bitter exasperation to respect for basic human needs and desires. First we read that a prince should not make himself feared—then that it is safer to be feared than loved. Machiavelli's second set of caveats begins by qualifying this tough-sounding statement. 'The prince', he declares, 'should nonetheless make himself feared in such a mode that if he does not acquire love, he escapes hatred', since 'being feared and not being hated can go together very well'. He will 'always' do this, Machiavelli declares,

> (1) if he abstains from the property [*roba*] of his citizens and his subjects, and from their women;[13] (2) and if he also needs to proceed against someone's life [*sangue*, literally blood], he must do it when there is suitable justification and manifest cause [*iustificazione conveniente e causa manifesta*]. (3) But above all, he must abstain from the property of others, because men forget the death of a father more quickly than the loss of a patrimony.

These caveats warn princes against using specific, excessively harsh measures associated with arbitrary rule—or tyranny, a word omitted from the *Prince* but unmistakably evoked by these lines. Chapter 16 has already advised princes to abstain from the property of their own subjects and citizens (1). Now Machiavelli extends the prohibition on seizing property to 'others' more generally (3)—contradicting the last chapter's assertion that princes should be liberal in giving away the property of others. Now this expedient is said to be dangerous 'above all' for a prince. For whereas men always find 'causes for taking away property' that lead them down a dangerous path of rapine, 'causes for taking life are rarer and disappear more quickly'—assuming that we are speaking of *reasonable* causes here, those found to have 'suitable justification and manifest cause'.

When these caveats are seen as an essential part of Machiavelli's preferred modes of dealing with criminal offences, it becomes clear that he does not judge these modes solely by their results. Results are important, of course, but his arguments throughout the *Prince* imply that you can't get good results—for

---

[12] The *Discourses* also says that men don't know how to be altogether bad or good (I.26–7) and that the world has as much good as wicked in it (II.Pref.). See *ME* 190–7, 201–6.

[13] Machiavelli paraphrases Aristotle here; compare *D* III.26.

yourself or for the *universalità* in your state—unless you use the right modes. Modes and the 'means' they govern can't be neatly separated from and subordinated to ends, because modes and means affect ends in fundamental ways. They either help or hinder your pursuit of desired ends (acquiring) and, if you attain them, make them easier or harder to hold (maintaining).[14] And excessively harsh modes knock you off the path of *virtù* as much as excessively soft ones. If princes use cruelty 'well' when it benefits the generality of people, as we read earlier, perhaps they need to realize that such benefits seldom come through intemperate or unjust means.

CRUELTY WELL USED

The chapter concludes by discussing a case when it is 'above all' (*al tutto*) necessary for a prince 'not to care about a name for cruelty'. Indeed, it is better to have such a name when a prince is 'with his armies and has a multitude of soldiers under his government', since without it, 'he never holds his army united, or disposed to any action [*fazione*, also negative "faction"]'. As in the last chapter when he allowed princes to be liberal with booty in war, Machiavelli suggests that certain uses of what appear vices for civilians are permissible, and even virtuous, in the specific contexts of war and military life. Many people wrongly condemn the virtuous 'use' of cruelty by commanders, Machiavelli observes, because patriotic bias led certain ancient writers—mostly Romans—to misjudge the qualities needed to maintain strict military discipline. They applaud the 'mercy' or 'humanity' of Roman generals who failed to punish their soldiers' misconduct, while condemning enemy generals who upheld strict discipline.

Machiavelli challenges these double standards by contrasting the modes of two ancient generals, the Carthaginian Hannibal and his Roman rival, Scipio Africanus. Among Hannibal's 'admirable actions' was that 'when he had a very large army, mixed with infinite kinds of men, and had led it to fight in alien lands, no dissension ever arose in it, neither among themselves' nor against Hannibal, 'in bad as well as in good fortune'. Astonished that their country's mortal enemy was able to maintain such remarkable unity, Roman writers assert—and Machiavelli seems to affirm—that Hannibal could not have achieved such good results by 'anything other than his inhuman cruelty [*inumana crudeltà*]'.

But it's far from clear that Machiavelli agrees with this opinion. Whenever he says that someone showed the ability to order for steady self-reliance in

---

[14] See *ME* chap. 9.

'any fortune', this is praise of the highest order, indicating the presence of exceptional *virtú*. This raises a suspicion that the qualities writers 'hold' cruel and inhumane in Rome's arch-enemy are more correctly identified with virtuous severity. Machiavelli slyly intimates this by pointing out that Hannibal's Roman detractors contradict themselves. They admire the Carthaginian's well-ordered army, but 'condemn the principal cause of it', his use of strict discipline or *severitas*.

These Romans mistake Hannibal's severity for cruelty not just because he was the enemy, but also because standards of discipline in the Roman military were corrupted. Machiavelli notes that during and after the wars with Carthage, Hannibal's adversary Scipio gained a reputation for 'mercy' among his fellow Romans. Following Livy—like Sallust and Tacitus, a Roman writer who does *not* idealize his own country's virtues or brand all its enemies as vicious— Machiavelli is unusually forthright in stating his own critical judgement of Scipio's methods. Towards his own soldiers he showed too much mercy [*troppa pietà*], allowing his soldiers 'more licence than is fitting for military discipline'. The senior statesman and general Fabius Maximus publicly reproved Scipio's so-called mercy, Machiavelli notes, calling him 'the corrupter of the Roman military'. Machiavelli evidently agrees with Fabius' reproach that under the good name of merciful leniency, Scipio let his soldiers get away with unnecessary violence when he should have corrected them—'all of which', Machiavelli comments ironically, 'arose from his easy [*facile*] nature'.

Even if Scipio's armies ultimately defeated Hannibal's, Machiavelli—like Livy—refuses to follow those who judge the Roman general's 'modes' by this particular success. Here, and in the *Discourses*, he implies that Scipio's excessive mercy undermined the strict standards of military and political order that sustained the Roman republic. When later generations of military men such as Julius Caesar imitated what they took to be Scipio's virtues—courting support among their troops by means of 'liberality' and light punishments—good republican orders were finally destroyed. Machiavelli's remark that Scipio was 'very rare [*rarissimo*] not only in his times but also in the entire memory of things known' thus reeks of irony, especially since he immediately adds that 'his armies in Spain rebelled against him'. Whatever praise some writers might heap on Scipio, a simple description of his actions suggests that he was no different from other ambitious military men on the make, in the all-too-familiar, fortune-seeking mode of other aspiring princes before and since.[15]

Machiavelli's so-called cruelty turns out to be much the same, then, as Seneca's and Sallust's virtuous *severitas*, or reasonably tempered strictness. Like these earlier writers, Machiavelli holds that in corrupt times people become self-indulgent, and consider it cruel when they or their friends are

---

[15] Recall the remark in chap. 14 that Scipio imitated Cyrus—a monarch, not a leader in a republic.

duly punished. Machiavelli says: If what corrupt men call cruelty is the quality of actions that correct serious offences and bring order to disorder, then princes shouldn't shun a 'name' for cruelty.[16]

The stakes were as high in his native Florence as they were for ancient Romans. In the *Florentine Histories* Machiavelli has Cosimo de' Medici's chief opponent remark that his impeccably decent appearances make it hard to pin any crime on him, despite his corrupting ways of seeking excessive power; to the general public he appears simply 'merciful [*piatoso*], helpful, liberal, and loved by everyone'.[17] The *Prince* chapter 17 contains the same warning as the *Histories* and *Discourses*, where we read that 'many times works that appear merciful, which cannot reasonably be condemned, become cruel and are very dangerous for a republic if they are not corrected in good time'.[18]

---

[16] Compare another paragon of Roman *virtú* in the *Discourses*, Camillus, who was unreasonably 'hated' because he was 'more severe [*severo*] in punishing' his soldiers 'than liberal in rewarding them.' *D* III.23.

[17] *FH* IV.27.   [18] *D* III.28.

18

Deception and good faith

In what mode princes should keep faith

Chapter 18 presents an all too familiar political drama: one dominated by the voice of a prince who sets off down the path of infidelity, thinking this will help him fly to greatness, then looks for ever more plausible-sounding excuses for his conduct. As Machiavelli does so often in the *Prince*, he imitates his subject—here the deceptive appearances spun by 'astute' princes 'in our times'—and exercises readers' skills at seeing through these appearances. A masterpiece of dissimulation, the chapter piles one optical illusion on top of another. It challenges us to spot various rhetorical fallacies that princes use to ensnare others—and deceive themselves.

WHY BREAK FAITH?

'How praiseworthy it is', Machiavelli begins, 'for a prince to maintain faith [*fede*], and to live by honesty [*integrità*] and not astuteness, everyone understands'. This is the end of the chapter's praise for good faith. Whatever faith's well-understood moral and practical merits, princes have a reason to disregard it and cultivate *astuzia*, cunning opportunism, instead of integrity. The reason is that, as 'one sees in our times', princes 'who have done great things [*gran cose*] are those who have taken little account of faith'. A prince who hopes to do great deeds must, it seems, value greatness above praiseworthiness—and then find ways to gain praise without worrying too much about genuine worth. What 'everyone' understands does not, perhaps cannot, extend to his high-soaring ambitions. With astuteness such a prince can 'get around men's brains' and take advantage of 'those who have founded themselves on loyalty'.

At first, a prince's wish to perform 'great' actions is the main reason to prefer cunning to good faith. As the discussion proceeds, we encounter a different and perhaps better reason: *necessità*. It 'has to be understood' that a prince 'is often under a necessity, to maintain his state, of acting against faith, against charity, against humanity, against religion'. The excuse of necessity only appears toward the end of the chapter. In the middle, we read that violations of faith are excused because men 'are wicked [*tristi*] and do not observe faith with you', so 'you also do not have to observe it with them'. This grim view of human nature helps to explain why princes are often necessitated to break faith, and the necessity to break faith is linked to the further necessity to deceive. Both necessities arise, then, from other people's untrustworthiness.

It isn't clear how the initial reasons to break faith—desires for greatness—are related to these later reasons of *necessità*. Is it that 'great deeds' are necessary to preserve a prince's state? This isn't what Machiavelli has suggested so far. On the contrary, he has repeatedly shown that ordinary, self-restrained actions are often the most effective means to lasting power. In view of these more thoughtful judgements, the claim that bad faith triumphs over 'those who have founded themselves on loyalty [*fondati in su la realtà*]' sounds particularly ironic in the original. The word translated 'loyalty' here is *realtà*, which also means 'reality'.[1] Since Machiavelli seldom misses a chance for mischievous wordplay, it would be surprising if the ambiguity were unintended. The joke is on whoever claims that faithlessness and deception can overcome those who found themselves on loyalty/reality. If such people deceive their honest victims, they also deceive themselves, seduced by the siren-call of *grandezza*.

LAWS AND FORCE, BEASTS AND MEN

Then comes another infamous teaching:

> You must know that there are two kinds of combat: one with laws [*leggi*], the other with force [*forza*]. The first is proper [*proprio*] to man, the second to beasts; but because the first is often not enough, one must have recourse to the second. Therefore it is necessary for a prince to know well how to use the beast and the man.

This is usually taken as advice to rely less on law and more on force than conventional morality dictates. Prudent princes, it seems to say, need to know when to thrust legal constraints aside and use force to pursue their advantage.

But on a closer look, nothing in the passage suggests the need to subordinate law to force. On the contrary, it says that a prince must know how to use *both* the beast *and* the man. While the chapter will soon say more about good uses of specific beasts, foxes and lions, it also declares that 'a prince needs to know how to use both natures', for 'the one without the other is not lasting [*non è durabile*]'.

Since laws are the expression of 'properly' human nature and the mode of combat suited to it, what would be a 'good use' of the laws, and the proper

---

[1] Mansfield's translation takes it as an unusual spelling of *lealtà*, loyalty. See the editor's note on its ambiguity in Machiavelli, *Opere* I, 872.

relationship between laws and force? If *leggi* and *forza* were antithetical modes, then Machiavelli's advice to use both would imply a trade-off whereby princes who use force rely less on law. But this kind of opposition between laws and force is fallacious. For Machiavelli as for ancient philosophers, force is a necessary element of law.[2] Human laws need to be backed by force, of course, or they become ineffectual in a world where men are not perfectly good. But by the same token, force needs to be regulated by law, or human life becomes merely bestial. Machiavelli never says that princes should dispense with laws or subordinate them to force, but only that fighting with laws is not *sufficient* without force. Moreover, he describes law as a 'mode of combat', not as a mode of regulating human beings that renders all forms of fighting unnecessary. Laws are needed to do constant battle with human appetites and 'humours' that would debase human life if left unregulated.[3]

If he sees laws and force as complementary, why doesn't Machiavelli balance his discussion by saying that force needs to be guided by laws as much as laws need to be backed by force? By seeming to oppose these two 'modes' and giving force primacy, Machiavelli exercises readers' skills in recognizing a common rhetorical sleight-of-hand used by ambitious political leaders. Asserting a false antithesis between law and force, such leaders try to win support with the following specious argument: 'In an ideal world, men would only use laws to combat bad behaviour. But since in the real world laws are not enough, it is often necessary to use force. It is therefore necessary that I, the prince, sometimes use force without recourse to laws, thus acting above the law'.

It is easy enough to agree with the proposition that laws without force are not enough, and that it's often necessary to use force. But the necessity to use force in no way reduces the necessity to use laws to regulate it. If people accept the false conclusion that legal restraints should be relaxed merely because force is often necessary, they allow themselves to be ensnared by one of the oldest tricks in the princely tyrannical book.

The necessity to use *both* force and laws arises because of human beings' 'mixed' nature. As the last chapter suggested, we are neither all bad nor all good in Machiavelli's book. Though often driven like other animals by appetites and impulses, we also possess natural capacities to regulate them with our

---

[2] Aristotle writes that since the many are persuaded more by punishment (*zêmiais*) than by appeals to what is fine (*tô kalô*), laws must be given compulsory force and impose punishments that chastise the disobedient. *ANE* X.xi.12.

[3] See *D* I.1, I.18, I.58. Compare Aristotle *ANE* V.v.4: 'law exists among those between whom there is a possibility of injustice'. The idea that both law and force, and modes of men and beasts, are needed to sustain human orders can be found in Plato, *Republic* 589b–590b. Here Socrates says that those who want to preserve justice in cities should make the lion's nature their ally; so long as they do not subordinate their human reason to it, this alliance involves no debasement of human character.

reasoning powers and to build orders and laws that raise human life above the bestial—so long as the orders hold firm.[4]

Read in this light, Machiavelli's next, enigmatic comments about the centaur Chiron take on a different colouring than if we assume that he had a thoroughly pessimistic view of human nature. The way to use the beast and the man, he says, was 'taught covertly [*copertamente*] to princes by ancient writers, who wrote that Achilles, and many other ancient princes, were given to Chiron the centaur to be raised, so that he would look after them with his discipline [*disciplina*]'. Machiavelli then explains the significance of this for modern princes. 'To have as teacher a half-beast, half-man', he says, 'means nothing other than that a prince needs to use both natures; and the one without the other is not lasting'. This is often read as implying the necessity to lower excessively high moral and legal standards to deal with human bestiality. But nothing in the passage unambiguously supports such a reading. It says that princes need *both* natures, and that *neither* is 'lasting' without the other. And significantly, Machiavelli's Chiron does not teach princes to be more ruthless, or to break faith and laws and other man-made constraints on their actions. On the contrary, the centaur looks after princes with his 'discipline'—a word that Machiavelli always associates with well-ordered restraints.

Chiron is an apt symbol for the theme of misleading appearances. Like Machiavelli's text, he looked more bestial than he was. His body was half-beast half-man, but by birth he was more than half divine, the offspring of Cronos and half-brother of Zeus. Despite his monstrous outward form, Chiron's distinctive talents lay in the arts of medicinal healing, civilization, and moderation as well as in the arts of war; he sought to tame aggressive heroes as well as helping them to fight better.[5] By surrounding his reference to Chiron with remarks that seem to treat the good centaur as teacher of the bestial 'modes' of force, Machiavelli leaves room—as usual—for different interpretations of the *Prince's* aims.

FOXES AND LIONS

Turning from the human to the bestial, what precise parts of 'the beast' should princes learn to use? 'Since', Machiavelli declares:

a prince is necessitated to know well how to use the beast [*usare la bestia*], he should pick the fox and the lion [*la golpa e il lione*], because the lion does not

---

[4] *ME* 186–97.
[5] See Plato, *Lesser Hippias* 371d, *Republic* 391c, *Statesman* 291b, 291e, 303c. Xenophon's *Cyropaedia* also has interesting philosophical things to say about combining the human and animal natures of centaurs; see *XC* IV.317.

defend itself from snares and the fox does not defend itself from wolves. So one needs to be a fox to recognize snares [*conoscere e' lacci*] and a lion to frighten the wolves. Those who stay simply with the lion do not understand this.

The usual reading is that princes should combine lion-like ferocity with fox-like cunning. Note, however, that the passage identifies not the strengths of foxes and lions that princes should imitate, but their distinctive shortcomings. Lions do not defend themselves against snares; foxes are vulnerable to wolves. Human beings often display the same weaknesses.

The first thing to learn from these beasts, then, is their means of *self-defence*. Thus one must be a fox to 'recognize snares' and a lion to 'frighten off' wolves—both defensive, not aggressive, aims.

The skills needed to do these things, moreover, are not what they've often been taken to be. Most importantly, the fox's distinctive skills are not cunning and fraud. Machiavelli's foxes are quite unlike Cicero's. Whereas the Roman treats foxes as creatures of deception [*fraude*], Machiavelli presents deceit as a quintessentially human skill, not practised by other animals.[6] His imitation-worthy foxes are not cunning fraudsters; they are simply good at recognizing snares. In the next chapter he will invoke a more Ciceronian view of foxes, describing the emperor Severus as 'a very astute fox [*una astutissima golpe*]'. But cunning astuteness and the ability to spot snares are altogether different qualities. And as chapter 9 suggested, it is doubtful that Machiavelli thinks princes should imitate fox-like *astuzia*, while he clearly advises them to learn from foxes how to recognize snares.

If we assume that Machiavelli identifies foxes unambiguously with deceit, we risk overlooking the important difference between skills needed to *generate* appearances and those needed to *see through* them. Foxes can do the second but not the first. By contrast, human beings do have many ingenious ways to create traps by covering decent deeds with less decent words and appearances. Men hardly need to learn arts of appearance-making from foxes, since those arts are altogether human. But they are deplorably bad at recognizing snares created by their fellow human beings. They fail to see through seductive appearances because they rely too much on one misleading sense, sight; and spin-adept leaders know how to colour their deeds in appealing shades. To recognize these traps, human beings need, like foxes, to use all their senses, 'touching' what others 'are' as well as seeing their surface. Foxes know how to do this by instinct; humans, however, have to work hard to develop an ability to 'recognize snares'. In corrupt times they fail to do this work, and thus become bad at defending themselves.

Machiavelli's philosophical zoology is therefore rather generous to foxes, and critical of the human beings who project their own damaging traits on to other animals. His discussion of foxes questions the Christian and Ciceronian

---

[6] Cicero, *De Officiis* I.xiii.44–7, widely viewed as a reference for Machiavelli's chapter.

assumption that human beings who 'use' the beast thereby *lower* standards of human conduct. Ignoring the usual negative descriptions of 'bestial' behaviour, he ascribes positive traits to foxes and lions, and implies that the lowest standards of conduct found in the animal kingdom are not 'subhuman' at all—they are, in fact, set by human beings.[7]

Princes also need to 'use' the lion's ability to 'frighten wolves', since men, too, must combat predators. Machiavelli tells princes to imitate the lion's defensive, not aggressive, abilities, and stresses the disadvantages of acting *only* like lions. Ferocity without vigilance, he suggests, shows deficient understanding. Since no similar warning is issued to those who imitate foxes but not lions, we might conclude that princes should give priority to those 'bestial' behaviours that have a large cognitive element—stressed in the word *conoscere* for what foxes do—not to those rooted in simple instincts of self-preservation. Princes remain vulnerable who use lion-like ferocity to defend themselves when attacked, but lack the ability to defend themselves pre-emptively by means of prudence.

WHEN FAITH MAY BE BROKEN

Returning to the question of when to keep or break faith, the next lines seem to urge princes to shed moral scruples:

> A prudent lord, therefore, cannot observe faith, nor should he, when such observance turns against him, and the causes that made him promise have been eliminated.

But is this advice really subversive of traditional ethics concerning promises, oaths, contracts, and treaties? In fact, it sounds more or less amoral depending on how one interprets certain ambiguous phrases. 'When such observance turns against him' is such a phrase. By itself, it seems to say that a prince may break faith 'when keeping faith is no longer to his present advantage', regardless of what caused the change that made him promise in the first place. This does sound immoral.

But if observance 'turns against' a prince because the other parties violated their side of an agreement, and reciprocal good faith was one of 'the causes that made him promise', the statement looks quite different. In the first case, observing turns against a prince because he could get more out of non-observance, taking advantage of other parties' naïve fidelity to seize what they too might have seized if not under an agreement. In the second, continued fidelity is unreasonable because other parties' non-observance defeats the whole point of the agreement, which is based on the condition of reciprocity. Understood thus, the statement is not shockingly amoral but expresses a generally agreed view on when contracts, oaths, and treaties may be broken.

---

[7] For a similar argument, see Plutarch's satire 'Beasts are rational', *PM* XII 492–533.

The next lines undoubtedly evoke the first, more cynical position: 'And if all men were good, this teaching would not be good', but 'because they are wicked [*tristi*] and do not observe faith with you, you also do not have to observe it with them'. But this statement clashes loudly with Machiavelli's more general arguments about how to create strong foundations. If he really believed that all men are *thoroughly* bad and *generally* fail to observe faith, it is odd that he places so much emphasis on reciprocal trust and obligations in his proposals for stronger defences. His recurring insistence on the need for firm obligations between princes and people presupposes that *some*, perhaps most, men aren't *all* bad and generally do observe faith when both sides uphold it. If a prince embraces the maxim that he should break faith whenever he likes, he deprives himself of the main resources set out in the *Prince* for maintaining stable states—the support and commitments to mutual safety undertaken by subjects, citizens, or allies. If he violates agreements with them whenever he thinks he can gain more in this way, his gains are unlikely to last long or bring him genuine security.[8]

The sloppiness of the statement's reasoning is another reason to suspect irony. Whereas Machiavelli's general arguments and writing style are rigorous, consistent, and logical, the claim that 'because men are wicked and do not observe faith with you, you also do not have to observe it with them' contains not one but two textbook rhetorical fallacies.

The first is a fallacy of exclusion: it presents one possible response to other people's badness—to lower standards to their level—as the only option, although others are available. A more effective response to human badness is to hold it in check with good orders and punish transgressors.

The second fallacy assumes that since *some* men are wicked and break faith with you, this is a good reason to break faith pre-emptively with *anyone* under any conditions. The argument that a prince should violate his agreements whenever it suits him because some men are sometimes faithless, whether or not the particular men he contracts with have demonstrated infidelity, is both terrible reasoning and a recipe for the most violent disorders. If everyone followed it, or even just every political leader, it would be impossible to establish any decent civil life or sustain basic security.

If Machiavelli is presenting the licence to infidelity not as his own maxim, but as one followed in the practice of over-ambitious princes, this makes more sense of the following, pungently ironic passages. When he declares: 'Nor does a prince ever lack legitimate causes to colour his non-observance [*cagione*

---

[8] A few years before he wrote the *Prince*, Machiavelli underlined this point in his diplomatic correspondence, reporting to his superiors that he had lectured a two-faced ally on 'the value and importance of good faith'. Since 'everyone knew' that this man had undertaken an engagement to Florence, if he violated it they would 'charge him with ingratitude and bad faith, and would regard him as a stumbling horse which nobody would ride for fear of getting his neck broken'. *Legation* to Baglioni, 11 April 1505.

legittime di colore la inosservanzia]' the word *colore* slyly implies that such causes are meretricious appearances or pretexts, not genuinely legitimate reasons. There is an even stronger whiff of irony in the next lines: 'One could give infinite modern examples of this' legitimate 'colouring', 'and show how many peace treaties and promises have been rendered invalid or vain through the infidelity of princes'. Is Machiavelli saying this to warn his prince against the infidelity of other princes—or to warn all his readers against the faithlessness of princes generally, including those who rule them? The ambiguity extends to his declaration that 'the one who has known best how to use the fox has come out best'. This could mean that since all princes are potentially cunning tricksters, they must all try to outdo each other in faithlessness. Or, recalling Machiavelli's ambiguous play on the different characteristics of foxes, it could mean that those who know how to see through appearances and snares come out best.

DISSIMULATING ABOUT DECEPTION

The discussion of infidelity now turns, almost imperceptibly, into a discussion of when princely deception is excused. Different ways to take advantage of others by dishonest means are proposed—so far not in the name of reasonable necessity, but first for the sake of greatness and then because 'men' are bad and faithless. Some princes will buy these bad arguments, finding them wise or useful. But readers who are more receptive to Machiavelli's subtle lessons in seeing through appearances might detect irony in the next, audacious lines:

> But it is necessary to know well how to colour this [fox-like] nature, and to be a great pretender and dissembler [*gran simulatore e dissimulatore*]; and men are so simple [*semplici*] and obedient to present necessities that he who deceives will always find someone who will let himself be deceived.

Here, princes are told to be what 'men generally' were said to be in the previous chapter: pretenders and dissimulators, *simulatori e dissimulatori*. In trying to surpass other men and seeking to rule them by their greatness, princes need to become as bad as all the others whose badness they claim as justification for their actions. This is either deep-thinking 'realism' or an absurdly vicious circle. It all depends on whether you think that there are other, more effective responses to human badness than out-badding everyone else.

And where at one moment this voice describes men generally as cunning pretenders, in the next they are gullible, and the prince alone is so clever that he never gets taken in. This kind of dangerously self-deceiving arrogance recalls the examples of Liverotto da Fermo, who successfully deceived everyone else but was finally destroyed by the deceptions of Cesare Borgia; and the nearly identical experience of 'Duke Valentino', who was taken in by Pope Julius despite his own impressive record of deceptions, imprudently 'believing that the word of others is more to be relied on than his own', as Machiavelli wrote at the time.[9] Is it the generality of men who are most easily hoodwinked by their inability to see beyond 'present necessities'? The really simple ones, these examples suggest, are princes who think only about what short-term gains infidelity might bring them, not realizing that they thereby inflict far more pressing *future* necessities on themselves.

In what should be a fairly easy test of readers' skills in seeing through dissimulation, Machiavelli lavishes praise on Borgia's extraordinary father, Pope Alexander VI. 'I do not want to be silent', he proclaims grandly, 'about one of the most recent [*freschi*] examples' of modern deceivers:

> Alexander never did anything, nor ever thought of anything, but how to deceive men, and he always found a subject to whom he could do it. And there was never a man with greater efficacy in asserting a thing, and affirming it with greater oaths [*iuramenti*], who observed it less; nonetheless, his deceits succeeded at his will [*ad votum*], because he knew this aspect of the world.

An example of highest princely prudence, or a passage loaded with ironic praise? Whichever one decides, one ironically coded implication is worth noting. The claim that Alexander's 'deceits succeeded *ad votum*' is wickedly provocative. In ancient Rome, a *votum* was a promise made to a deity; the word comes from the Latin verb *vovere*, meaning solemnly to vow or to promise.[10] To say that Alexander's deceits (*inganni*) succeeded *ad votum* suggests that they succeeded by his solemn promise—to God, or perhaps the Devil? Either way, a deceit underwritten by a promise is both logical nonsense and self-defeating practice.

APPEAR MORE VIRTUOUS THAN YOU ARE, AND VARY WITH FORTUNE

One self-inflicted necessity leads to another. The supposed necessity to be faithless made it necessary to deceive; now the necessity to deceive makes it necessary to *appear* to have good qualities that one lacks. For Machiavelli now makes a disturbing new claim. When it's impossible to 'observe' all the qualities that are—or are held—virtuous, he tells us, it's all the more necessary to *appear* to have them. 'It is not necessary', he argues,

---

[9] *Legations* 4 November 1503.
[10] The *votum* is connected with the contractual nature of Roman religion, a bargaining expressed by *do ut des*, 'I give that you might give'.

for a prince to have all the above-mentioned qualities in fact [*in fatto*], but it is indeed necessary to appear to have them [*parere di averle*]. Nay, I dare say this, that by having them and always observing them, they are harmful [*dannose*]; and by appearing to have them, they are useful, as it is to appear merciful, faithful, humane, honest, and religious, and to be so; but to remain with a spirit built [*stare in modo edificato con lo animo*] so that, if you need not to be those things, you are able and know how to change to the contrary.

This appears merely to elaborate on the last three chapters' advice. In fact, it is a stunning turnaround. In chapters 15–17, Machiavelli said that false appearances of *virtú* were harmful. He told princes that it is necessary to *ignore* what is 'held' or 'appears' praiseworthy, and instead to do what actually secures their state. Though at first people would criticize them, over time, they would see that what they wrongly praised was bad, and shed their misperceptions.

Now princes are told to place appearances above reality when their actions go against what is 'held' virtuous. Instead of showing critics why their initial judgements were wrong, thereby restoring a correct understanding of *virtú* among subjects or citizens, princes should leave them their illusions—even cultivate them by trying to appear as people want them to be. Instead of treating such errors of judgement as harmful to the prince or his state, Machiavelli now says that princes can go further by pandering to confused beliefs about what deserves praise or blame than by trying to correct them. Either he has changed his mind on this fundamental issue, or he is dissimulating.

The new *necessità* to appear virtuous leads to another, even more surprising, new requirement—one that brings the chapter's dominant voice into head-on collision with the *Prince*'s most reflective understanding of *virtú*. For in order to appear virtuous at every turn, a prince

> needs to have a spirit disposed to change as the winds of fortune and variations of things command him [*volgersi secondo che e' venti della fortuna e la variazione della cose gli comandano*], and as I said above, not depart from good, when possible, but know how to enter into evil [*male*], when necessitated.

The qualities needed for flexible appearance-making are antithetical to the qualities Machiavelli has so far credited with producing security and well-being. Chapters 15–17 urged princes to stand firm, move slowly, stay their unpopular course if need be, and use their own judgement instead of following the mistaken or corrupt opinions of others. Now they are advised to conform to others' opinions, whether reasonable or not, at every turn. Many readers have seen these flexible modes as the height of Machiavelli's *virtú*. But he never says that it is; the word *virtú* makes no appearance in the chapter. By the end, on the contrary, fortune is firmly in command, and princes are told to obey it.

The precept that princes should change with the 'winds of fortune' contradicts the most fundamental teachings of Machiavelli's book. If a prince changes at every turn to keep up virtuous appearances while being something quite other than virtuous, he may win over many supporters, at the price of becoming fortune's plaything. A prince's main concern, Machiavelli avers, is to get results, for if he can 'win and maintain' his state, 'the means [*mezzi*] will always be judged honourable, and will be praised by everyone'. But what kind of results matter most: winning popularity by appearing good, or securing good order in your state, even if this sometimes makes you unpopular?

Machiavelli links the necessity to change as fortune commands to the necessity, at times, to enter into evil. This was perhaps the solemn pact of deception made by Pope Alexander—if not a devil's pact *per se*, still a pact that leads to evil, and harms the prince as well as the victims of his deceits. But necessity doesn't come out of nowhere. What might cause a necessity to do evil?

If we retrace the chain of necessities that runs through the chapter, we find that it has one of two sources: the badness of men or the desire to do great things. There are, however, different ways to respond to the badness of human nature, and responding with evil is not the *Prince*'s most frequent or well-reasoned advice. In the order of the chapter, the unchecked desire to do great things came before intemperate assertions about bad human nature. And while following the chapter's descent from the necessity to break faith to deception to evil, one has the impression that if 'princes' like Pope Alexander did not insist on doing what they consider great things, none of the rest would have to ensue.

JUDGING BY RESULTS

In the context of a discussion of political appearance-making, to 'change with the winds of fortune' can be a metaphor for pandering promiscuously to whoever can help you to win at the moment. This is what the chapter's amoral speaker now advises. 'A prince should thus take great care', he declares,

> that nothing escape his mouth that is not full of the above-mentioned five qualities and that, to see him and hear him, he should appear all mercy, all faith, all honesty, all humanity, all religion. And nothing is more necessary to appear to have than this last quality.

Prudent princes might worry that if they go this way, they will be founding themselves—if one can speak of founding at all—on little more than hot air and spin. Pope Alexander VI, on the other hand, was blessedly free from such worries. So was 'a certain prince of present times, whom it is not well to name'. This anonymous prince is named quite openly in chapter 21, where Machiavelli says of Spain's Most Catholic King Ferdinand that 'in order to undertake greater enterprises' he was 'always making use of religion'. Ferdinand 'never preaches [*predica*] anything but peace and faith, and is very hostile to both'. This hypocrisy was evidently necessary to him, since 'if he had observed both, he would have had either his reputation or his state taken from him many times'.

Machiavelli's scathing judgements of Ferdinand are set out in letters written in 1513, when he was almost certainly drafting the *Prince*. In his recent enterprises, he opined, 'the king of Spain unnecessarily endangered all his territories—always a reckless [*temerario*] course of action for any man'. If one examines his actions, he concludes in what would become the *Prince*'s critical code, 'you will realize that the king of Spain is a man of astuteness [*astuzia*] and good fortune *rather than of wisdom and prudence*'.[11] His hypocrisy might make some observers suspect that some brilliant strategy lay behind all his hyperactive, 'spirited' manoeuvres. But Machiavelli had no doubt that the king's astuteness would not get him far.

Not all observers will recognize the true quality of such princes because 'men in general [*i universali*] judge more by their eyes than by their hands, because seeing is given [*tocca a vedere*, literally "seeing touches"] to everyone, sensing [*sentire*] to few'. Deceitful princes can therefore feel safe in their hypocrisy, since only a few are sensitive enough to detect the truth about them; while 'everyone sees how you appear, few sense [*sentono*] what you are'. Perhaps these few are those who master the skills of better-quality Machiavellian foxes, who know how to recognize snares. Princes need not fear this minority, according to our speaker, for 'these few dare not oppose the opinion of many, who have the majesty of the state to defend them', and whom the prince hopes will back him. Moreover:

> in the actions of all men, and especially of princes, where there is no court to appeal to [*iudizio a chi reclamare*] one looks to the end [*fine*]. So let a prince win and maintain his state: the means will always be judged honourable, and will be praised by everyone. For the vulgar [*volgo*] are always taken in by the appearance and the outcome [*evento*] of a thing, and in the world there is nothing but the vulgar; the few have no place there when the many have somewhere to lean on.

So long as a prince is or appears to be successful, whatever means he uses will be thought honourable. But can a prince found stable power on such poorly founded opinions? The passage makes it clear that judging by outcomes is a default mode of judgement, and by no means a reliable one; people resort to it only when 'there is no court' to help them separate appearances from the truth. This view is confirmed in the passage's final sentence, where judging by outcomes is treated as a dubious recourse of the 'vulgar' who are taken in by impressive appearances. The greatest, most vulgar victim of deception, however, is the overreaching prince himself. The whole chapter speaks in the voice of such a prince, ensnaring himself in his own deceptively self-serving arguments.

---

[11] Machiavelli to Vettori, 29 April 1513; italics added.

19

What princes should fear

Avoiding hatred and contempt

Harking back to chapter 15, Machiavelli says that he has now discussed the 'most important' of the qualities mentioned there that bring men praise or blame. He will now 'discourse on the others briefly' under the general heading (*generalità*) 'that the prince, as was said above in part, should think how to avoid those things that make him hated or contemptible [*odioso o contennendo*]'. If we take him at his word, we should expect a 'brief' discussion. Instead, this chapter turns out to be by far the longest in the *Prince*.[1] And its main subject is a matter of life and death: how princes can escape conspiracies.

The argument that other people's hatred and contempt pose the greatest threats to rulers, especially tyrannical ones, was famously set out in Aristotle's *Politics*:

> There are two causes that chiefly lead men to attack tyranny, hatred and con-
> tempt [*misous kai kataphronêseôs*]. The former, hatred, always attaches to
> tyrants, but it is being despised that causes their downfall in many cases.[2]

More than ever in the *Prince*, the word 'tyranny' constantly springs to mind in this chapter as Machiavelli sets out the actions of the cruellest, most detested Roman emperors. He calls some of these emperors 'tyrants' in the *Discourses*, and speaks freely—and always very critically—of tyranny there and in the *Florentine Histories*. Here, however, he upholds the *Prince*'s strict policy of omitting the word. In a chapter whose examples practically scream out the presence of the phenomenon, Machiavelli's tight-lipped refusal to speak of tyranny feels oppressive, as if he were imitating a tyrant determined to muffle attempts to call things by their proper names.

---

[1] The longest chapter in the *Discourses* (III.6) also concerns conspiracies.
[2] *AP* V.viii.20.

GETTING AWAY WITH INFAMIES

Chapter 19 purports, as usual, to teach princes how to take advantage of their subjects without incurring hatred and violent revenge. When a prince avoids things that bring hatred and contempt, Machiavelli writes, 'he will have fulfilled his part, and will find no danger in his other infamies [*infamie*]'. Some princes will take this to mean that they can get away with committing whatever offences they like, so long as they avoid hatred and contempt. But as earlier discussions made quite clear, actions experienced as offensive or injurious naturally and 'ordinarily' arouse feelings of strong aversion. Machiavelli drives this point home again, by repeating earlier arguments on the theme of avoiding hatred. The generality (*universalità*) of men live content, he says, so long as 'one does not take away either honour or property [*né onore né roba*]' from them. For what makes a prince 'hated above all, as I said, is to be rapacious and a usurper of the property and the women of his subjects'.

Chapter 17 said that the prince 'will always' escape hatred if 'he abstains from the property of his citizens and his subjects, and from their women'. The two chapters' statements are almost identical, except that citizens have now vanished. Now, it seems, our prince has only subjects. For readers who've followed the frequent comings and goings of *cittadini* in the *Prince*, and of the elusive republics that are ordinarily their home, the omission of one word evokes a different quality of prince: one who still wants to rule subjects, not citizens who are more nearly his equals. Previous chapters suggested that princes greatly strengthen their foundations when they exercise self-restraint, treat subjects with respect and meet their basic needs, and entrust them with the all-important duties of defence. Here, however, Machiavelli seems to be addressing princes who are too power-hungry or suspicious to see that a stronger populace is their own best source of strength.

Machiavelli has already said a good deal about avoiding hatred. His remarks about how to avoid contempt open up a new theme, and raise hard questions for princes who hope to conquer difficulties by going with fortune's flow. What makes a prince contemptible, he declares, is 'to be held variable, light, effeminate, pusillanimous, irresolute [*vario, leggieri, effeminate, pusillanime, irresoluto*], from which a prince should guard himself as from a shoal [*scoglio*]'. Several of these qualities were mentioned in chapter 15, but not discussed further. Until now, the vices of variability, lightness, and irresolution may have seemed less damaging to princes than cruelty or rapacity, which make them hated. But this impression turns out to be wrong, for these qualities incur contempt, and thus bring special hardships to princes who underestimate the risks of using the 'modes' associated with them.

Variability, lightness, irresolution, and the like are typical qualities of actions that depend more on fortune than on *virtú*. But the last chapter ended by saying that princes should 'know how to change to the contrary' of how they appear or are, 'as the winds of fortune command'. Princes who think they need to practise this kind of 'variability' to keep their power may want to hold on to this first-named quality, considering it part of *virtú*, while gladly spurning the other four. Others might wonder whether one can be variable and follow fortune's commands without also being (or appearing) light, irresolute, pusillanimous, and effeminate. If Machiavelli thinks one can, it seems odd that he places variability at the head of the list of qualities to be guarded against 'as from a shoal'—a metaphor that evokes an image of a prince sailing confidently into the shallows and crashing against unseen underwater rocks. Can a prince who changes with every gust of wind ensure that 'his judgements in the private concerns of his subjects' are irrevocable, as Machiavelli says they should be? And isn't such firmness in judgements needed for a prince to 'maintain such an opinion of himself that no one thinks either of deceiving him or of getting around him [*aggirarlo*]'?[3] Of course not, fortune-addicted princes might reply: the best protection against deceivers is to be changeable and deceptive oneself. But the *Prince*'s examples suggest otherwise; its arch-deceivers Liverotto and Cesare Borgia were themselves victims of others' equally 'astute' hypocrisy.

HOW TO AVOID CONSPIRACIES

Reputation seems to be more important in the next paragraph than true qualities. 'The prince who gives [an] opinion of himself' as difficult to deceive 'is highly reputed, and against whoever is reputed it is difficult to conspire' or 'to mount an attack'. This light, upbeat tone then turns grave as Machiavelli moves from the shallows of repute and opinion to a topic that some princely readers might prefer not to face: their own fears. 'For a prince', he states baldly, 'should have two fears [*paure*]: one within, on account of his subjects; the other outside, on account of external powers [*potentati esterni*]'. As we read on, it becomes clear that the greater fear relates to subjects.

How difficult is it to defend oneself against them? This depends on how far princely readers have grasped the *Prince*'s earlier advice. Machiavelli sums up his previous teachings by saying that from subjects 'one is defended with good arms and good friends; and if one has good arms, one will always have good friends'. This might sound like the blandest of platitudes, unless we recall that Machiavelli set out many demanding conditions for ordering good arms. Princes who see the wisdom of his arguments for a civil militia will understand

---

[3] The same word for 'getting around him' was used in chap. 18 with reference to the prince 'getting around' people's brains by deceit. Now he is the potential victim.

that this 'order' calls for much more than military reforms. If they establish it according to Machiavelli's advice, their subjects will be reconstituted as good arms and good friends, so that princes will have no need to fear them. Lightweight, higher-flying princes tend to underestimate the hard work needed to get good arms and friends, thinking that they can buy both with money and favours. Since they don't trust their subjects with defences or understand how to build military orders, in time they find themselves in fresh danger.

By comparison with subjects, relations with external powers are less important to a prince's safety. On the one hand, the absence of external threats does not guarantee internal security; though 'things inside will always remain firm [*ferme*] if things outside are firm', a prince's position still depends on whether it is 'disturbed by a conspiracy'. On the other hand, the presence of external threats need not arouse great fear if internal 'things' are in order. For 'even if things outside are in motion [*movessino*]', if the prince 'has ordered and lived *as I said*, as long as he does not abandon himself he will always withstand every thrust [*impeto*], as I said Nabis the Spartan did'.

But what exactly did Machiavelli say about these matters? About how princes should order and live, he has said quite contrary things: sometimes that they should adopt firm modes, move slowly and with gravity, and trust subjects or citizens as their own arms—then that they should vary with fortune, fly high to greatness, and put no faith in the generality of men. As for Nabis, he was described in chapter 9 as a prince who rose to power in a republic. Essential information was omitted there, and again here: namely, that Nabis did *not* in fact withstand every external thrust, but was killed in a conspiracy. Machiavelli reveals this in the *Discourses'* very long chapter on conspiracies, where he also calls Nabis a tyrant. Once again, readers must choose their own way to interpret and apply Machiavelli's message. They may read histories to find out the truth about Nabis, and try to avoid his errors. Or they may imitate Nabis' crowd-pleasing methods and end up wildly popular— until someone offended by their aggressive policies murders them.

Different responses to *motion* tell us a lot about a prince's true qualities and the likelihood that he will avoid hatred and contempt. In the passage just cited, motion outside or inside appears as potentially harmful, whether it is produced by involuntary natural processes or by human agency. Whatever its cause, its harmful effects can be partially counteracted by deliberate actions aimed at 'ordering and living' as Machiavelli said. This idea is well captured in chapter 25's image of firmly built dykes and dams able to resist fortune's violent floods. But while some people meet disordering movement with their own firm orders, others respond to it by trying to move just as fast and in the same direction. Alternatively, they deliberately foment disturbing movements in which they appear great and spirited and forceful, thus avoiding their subjects' contempt and hatred for a time.

The next lines mimic this view, presenting external motion as a useful distraction from internal threats: 'when things outside are not moving, one has to fear' that one's own subjects 'may be conspiring secretly'. This is a classic princely anxiety—that unless subjects' minds are occupied by constant external threats, they might turn their frustrations against the prince. Of course, a prince who has ordered virtuously will lack deeply frustrated subjects, and not have this worry. It is more likely to torment a prince who doesn't trust his subjects to defend him, and who instead depends on foreigners, or on a professional military separate from the general populace and potentially inimical to it. As chapters 12–13 said, professional soldiers thrive on war and cause disturbances in peacetime. A prince who mistrusts his own people thus depends for his defence on a constituency that is deeply invested in constant motion, disturbance, and war. If this helps him ward off conspiracies, it makes him unsafe in innumerable other ways.

On the upbeat side, Machiavelli focuses on the prohibitive difficulties of pulling off a successful conspiracy. 'One sees from experience', he observes, 'that there have been many conspiracies, but few have had a good end.' A conspiracy (*congiure*) is not a general uprising, but a secret plot by a handful of people to overthrow or kill a prince. Machiavelli discusses two main conditions for success, both very hard to meet. Firstly, conspirators should have good reason to think that 'they will satisfy the people with the death of the prince'. If a prince is popular, or if for other reasons his death would 'displease the *universale*', the conspirators will end up having 'the people as enemies' and consequently face 'infinite difficulties'—as the killers of Caesar famously discovered. Secondly, they need trustworthy co-conspirators, who are very hard to find; the plotters risk betrayal by malcontents who might benefit from exposing them.

If less prince-friendly readers hope that Machiavelli might covertly encourage conspiracies, they'll be hard-pressed to find signs that he does so.[4] The language he uses to describe conspiracies is unambiguously negative. Conspirators 'ordinarily'—that is, reasonably—'have to fear' (here *temere*, a word Machiavelli often uses for rational fear or awe) 'before the execution of evil [*male*]'. He 'must fear afterwards too, when the excess [*eccesso*]'—another negative word—'has occurred, nor can he hope for any refuge'. His example of a recent plot in Bologna against the Bentivoglio family bluntly calls the killing of a criminal 'homicide' (*omicidio*), and provides the cautionary information that 'immediately after that homicide the people rose up and killed' the whole family of the leading conspirators.

At the time of writing, of course, Machiavelli had recently been accused of participating in a conspiracy against the Medici. He may have been keen to show that whatever his views on Florence's new princely government, he saw conspiracies as an inefficient or counterproductive way to effect political

---

[4] For example, Mansfield (1979), 318–43. See *ME* 373–9.

change. Here and in other works, his analysis of their shortcomings is devastating, and so consistent with his other warnings against taking unnecessary risks in politics that it seems designed to discourage conspirators rather than to egg them on.[5] There were other, far more prudent ways to get rid of unwanted rulers. One was the well-ordered, genuinely popular uprising, a method Machiavelli discusses favourably in the *Florentine Histories*.[6] Another was to persuade princes to scale down their own powers, or—if a commoner dared to ask this much—to give them up in favour of a more broadly based form of government. Machiavelli tried a direct version of this method in his 1520 *Discursus*, addressed to Giulio and Giovanni de' Medici. There are more than a few signs that the *Prince* contains less direct persuasions to this end.

Summing up his position in 'brief terms' (*brevi termini*),[7] Machiavelli declares 'that on the part of the conspirator there is nothing but fear, suspicion, and the anticipation of terrifying punishment', while

> on the part of the prince there is the majesty [*maestà*] of the principality, the laws, the protection of friends and of the state which defend him, so that when popular benevolence [*benivolenzia populare*] is added to these things, it is impossible that anyone should be so reckless [*temerario*] as to conspire.

Does this mean that princes should forget their fears of subjects and rest easy after all? The lighter, shallow-thinking breed of princes might think so. Others will realize that while conspiracies often destroy the conspirators and destabilize states, princes still get killed along the way. Or if they survive, they live in constant 'fear and suspicion' of further attempts on their lives, as much as conspirators live in fear and anticipation of 'terrifying punishment'.[8] Machiavelli's discouraging description of a conspirator's terrors applies just as well to those of princes whose subjects hate or despise them. If a prince doesn't relish living in a constant state of anxiety, he had better avoid the causes that drive subjects to conspire. This he will do if he does what's necessary to secure the above-mentioned conditions: the majesty of his office, supplied partly by his properly restrained bearing and partly by good orders and laws; and the protection of the right kind of friends and popular benevolence, both founded again on good orders and laws.

HOW TO SATISFY THE PEOPLE

When the *Prince* discussed fear (*paura*) before, the question was whether and how far subjects should fear princes. Now the tables have turned, and princely

---

[5] See *ME* 373–80.   [6] *FH* II.39.
[7] The idea of limits or checks (*termini, frenare*) makes frequent appearances in the chapter.
[8] See *FH* VIII.2–10 on the Pazzi conspiracy and Lorenzo de' Medici's response.

anxieties about subjects take centre stage. 'A prince should take little account of conspiracies', Machiavelli reassures his readers, 'if the people show benevolence to him. But if they are hostile and bear hatred for him', he warns, 'he should fear [*temere*] everything and everyone.'

This is some very serious fear. The solution should be obvious by now: 'one of the most powerful remedies against conspiracies', Machiavelli tells us, 'is not to be hated by the people generally'. While refraining from rapine certainly helps, an even better insurance against hatred is to keep the people 'satisfied' by means of more positive benefits; indeed, 'this is necessary to achieve, as was said above at length'. Since 'this is one of the most important matters that concern a prince', Machiavelli declares, all 'well-ordered states and wise princes' have thought diligently about 'how not to make the great desperate and how to satisfy the people and keep them content'. Note that wise princes and well-ordered states don't play off the great against the people, or pander to popular hostility against the great. They take care not to offend the *grandi* unnecessarily, but otherwise concern themselves more with the reasonable desires of the people, which need to be satisfied if princes want to feel safe.

What concrete 'orders' provide the popular satisfaction needed to guarantee secure princely rule? Machiavelli has already discussed civilian militias, and touched briefly on the social, legal, and economic measures needed to support them. Now he gives an example of a legal and political institution that can help princes to guard against conspiracies. It comes from a modern monarchy where the king's powers were strictly limited. France has one of the 'well-ordered and governed kingdoms in our times'; it has 'infinite good institutions [*constituzioni*] on which the liberty [*libertà*] and security of the king depend'. This is the first time Machiavelli has spoken of the 'liberty' of a monarch—whether prince or king—in a chapter where, also for the first time, he speaks of a prince's fears. These fears, it seems, are best addressed by orders that provide liberty as well as security. And it turns out that the French king's liberty and security depend on institutions that limit his authority rather than expanding it, by transferring an important office to an independent authority.

Among good French institutions, Machiavelli singles out 'the parlement and its authority [*il parlemento e la sua autorità*]'. In his time, the parlement of Paris was not a law-making body but an assembly with ancient rights of consultation and deliberation. Judicial functions had been added in the thirteenth century, so that the parlement served as a court of law; several provincial parlements were created in the half-century or so before Machiavelli wrote the *Prince*. His discussion focuses on the parlement's judicial functions, recalling the end of chapter 18: 'where there is no court to appeal to, one looks to the end'.[9] Now he makes clear that the absence of courts and judging

---

[9] See *D* III.1.212: the kingdom of France 'lives under laws and under orders more than any other kingdom. Parlements are those who maintain these laws and orders, especially that of

by the end are not natural necessities, but deficient conditions that can be rectified by 'ordering' courts that judge by sounder standards.

Machiavelli describes the parlement as a 'third judge' set above the rival 'humours' of the great and the general populace, with the authority to set limits on both. This court is not identified with the personal judgement of the king, but passes judgements on its own independent authority. The unnamed orderer[10] of France's parlement wanted to put 'a bit in their mouths to correct' (*uno freno in bocca che gli correggessi*) the great, but

> did not want this to be the particular concern of the king, so as to take from him the blame he would have from the great when he favoured the popular side, and from the popular side when he favoured the great; and so he constituted a third judge [*uno iudice terzo*] to be the one who should beat down [*battesi*] the great and favour the lesser side without blame for the king. This order could not be better, or more prudent, or a greater cause of the security of the king and the kingdom.

The aim of 'beating down the great' and favouring the lesser, popular side hardly sounds like impartial justice. Is Machiavelli advising princes to 'order' ostensibly independent courts that are charged with promoting a particular, partisan end: to crush the great while favouring the people?

This seems unlikely. Though his mischievous glee is palpable whenever Machiavelli writes about reining in or beating down the *grandi*, his basic position is the classic republican one: leaders who play extreme partisan politics destroy their countries' liberty and security, while good orders restrain the harmful effects caused by *both* great *and* popular 'humours'. A well-ordered 'third judge' would satisfy the people not by attacking the great arbitrarily, but by keeping them down and favouring the people when—to borrow an expression used in chapter 17—'there is suitable justification and manifest cause for it'.[11]

There is, of course, generally more cause to 'beat down'—or, in Machiavelli's more moderate phrase, 'correct'—the great. They constantly seek more than their fair share of political offices and other goods, and have an unfair advantage of power and wealth over the 'lesser', though far more numerous, people. Nevertheless, in a typical Machiavellian twist, the paragraph's initial prejudice against the great is counterbalanced by its last sentence. 'Again I conclude', Machiavelli declares, 'that a prince should esteem [*stimare*] the great, but not make himself hated by the people'. The appropriate way to deal with the great is not to 'offend' them, but to esteem them for

---

Paris. They are renewed by it whenever it makes an execution against a prince of that kingdom and when it condemns the king in its verdicts.'

[10] Machiavelli refers to 'The one who ordered that kingdom'.

[11] Compare *D* I.16 where a great merit of French 'orders' is that they include the 'universal security' of subjects, as well as submitting the king to good 'orders and laws': that kingdom 'lives secure because of nothing other than that the kings are obligated by infinite laws in which the security of *all* its peoples is included' (italics added).

their services to their prince and country without letting them get away with more than their due.[12]

Machiavelli's closing remarks on the French parlements strike a more cynical-sounding note. From this example, he declares, 'one can infer another notable thing: that princes should have anything blameable administered by others, favours [*quelle di grazia*, literally "things of grace"] by themselves'. At first, this might recall Cesare Borgia's use of Remirro de Orco as a frontman for his 'cruel' reordering of Romagna. On second thoughts, however, the differences become obvious. Parlements are well-ordered institutions designed to last beyond the reign of any particular king, while Remirro was installed as a temporary expedient. And whereas kings cannot 'ordinarily' eliminate parlements, since their authority is independent of his, Borgia could eliminate Remirro at his will and by the most 'extraordinary' means.

Keen readers of Machiavelli's ancients would be aware of more ancient references for his claim that 'princes should have anything blameable administered by others, favours by themselves'. In an earlier work well known to Machiavelli, Xenophon's dialogue *Hiero*,[13] the poet Simonides persuades the eponymous unhappy tyrant (not to be confused with the later, virtuous Hiero in chapter 6) that he will be less hated and feel safer if he takes several radical measures. The first is that the tyrant should assign unpleasant tasks to others, reserving the pleasant ones for himself. One of the least pleasant tasks is that of inflicting penalties on wrongdoers, since those who punish tend to be unpopular. The job of meting out punishments should therefore go to an independent judicial authority, while the tyrant may keep for himself the privilege of awarding prizes for merit—an office that makes him more loved than hated.[14] Like Machiavelli, in advising these reforms Simonides appeals only to his addressee's desires to avoid personal harm; he never invokes justice or the common good. But almost imperceptibly, while appearing only to teach Hiero how to strengthen his tyranny, Simonides advises measures that, in effect, undermine its tyrannical qualities.[15] Might Machiavelli have a similar programme in mind for his prince?

WHO TO SATISFY: THE PEOPLE OR THE SOLDIERS

Many readers, Machiavelli acknowledges, might cite examples contrary to his 'opinion' that the most secure princes are those who satisfy the people in the

---

[12] See chap. 9, *ME* 299–309.
[13] Machiavelli refers to it directly in *D* II.2; see chap. 21.   [14] *XH* 30–57.
[15] Similarly, Aristotle sets out two opposed modes by which tyrants may preserve themselves; one involving extremely harsh measures, the other moderate ones that tend to eliminate the government's tyrannical features. One device of the moderate mode is for tyrants to distribute rewards themselves, while getting others to inflict punishments by the agency of other magistrates and law courts. *AP* V.ix.1–20.

ways he has said. For on examining the lives and deaths of Roman emperors, 'one may find someone who lived outstandingly [*egregiamente*] and showed great *virtú* of spirit, and nevertheless lost empire or was killed by his own [*da sua*] who conspired against him'.

Several clues identify this sceptical questioner as one of Machiavelli's less attentive learners. He still persists in thinking that the way to avoid hatred is to live outstandingly and show great *virtú* of spirit, although the *Prince* has repeatedly shown that *virtú* of *animo* is insufficient for good ordering, and often works against it. *Egregiamente* is an unusual word in the *Prince*, but the Latin *egregio* is widely used by Roman authors in an ironically ambiguous way, similar to Machiavelli's *estraordinario*: while it can mean 'outstanding' in a positive sense, it carries sinister undertones of outstandingly bad, excessive, or unjust.

That Machiavelli's questioner would take his examples from the Roman emperors raises further doubts about whether he's learned a key lesson of earlier chapters, and indeed of the last few pages: namely, that princes had better build good orders early on in their reign, not start worrying about this when their principality is already well down the road toward 'absolute' power. For educated readers in Machiavelli's time, the centuries of rule by emperors that followed the destruction of Rome's good republican orders were synonymous with the heaviest tyranny. Whatever the widely different merits of various emperors, the structure of imperial rule was almost universally acknowledged to be corrupt, oppressive, and insecure for emperors and subjects alike. If some seemingly bad emperors thrived while other good ones were killed, this shouldn't surprise anyone who realizes how deep corruption ran in imperial Rome. Machiavelli's imagined interlocutor, it seems, is unaware of this.

Nevertheless, Machiavelli will respond to his questioner's 'objections' (*obiezioni*) by discussing 'the qualities of certain emperors, showing the causes of their ruin to be not unlike that which I have advanced', offering for special consideration 'things that are notable for whoever reads about the actions of those times'. As with his reference to Xenophon's *Cyropaedia* in chapter 14, this invites readers to compare what Machiavelli says about the emperors with what others say. They can either take him as a sufficient guide, or supplement or question his observations in view of what they read elsewhere.

So far, Machiavelli has insisted *ad nauseam* on the need for princes to satisfy and avoid being hated by the people. But the people did not kill Roman emperors, however badly the latter oppressed them. In every case Machiavelli discusses, the emperors who were killed in office died at the hands of Roman soldiers, members of their own bodyguard, or someone else close to them. This happened because, as Machiavelli notes, 'whereas in other principalities one has to contend only with the ambition of the great and the insolence of the people', Roman emperors 'had a third difficulty, of having to bear with the cruelty and avarice of their soldiers'. Notice the shifting perspectives on the people. Before, the great were held insolent; now the people are too, although a few lines on we read that the Roman people 'loved quiet [*amavano la quiete*]'. All these shifts seem to reflect the 'variable', unsteady perspectives of princes: at one moment they see the people as much-needed supporters, at another as threatening or ungrateful.

Some readers might think that having the additional 'difficulty' of the soldiers excused the harshness shown by several of the emperors Machiavelli discusses. Others might wonder if there is *any* good excuse for a mode of rule that allows the soldiers to hold so much power. Imperial Rome's corruption is especially glaring to those who read Livy and other writers who, as Machiavelli notes in the *Discourses*, praised republican Rome's many good orders and laws for maintaining strict civilian control over the military. Machiavelli himself has mentioned some of these laws in chapter 12, and recently seconded Livy's (and Fabius Maximus') criticisms of Scipio Africanus for 'corrupting the soldiers'—the first of a long line of popular military leaders who pandered to their troops' desires in order to win support for their own unseemly ambitions. This kind of corruption, in Livy's view and Machiavelli's, ultimately destroyed the Roman republic.[16] If the emperors had to grapple with the disruptive 'humours' of soldiers, then, this was not at all a feature of Rome's good ancient orders but a gross corruption of them.

The question, then, is what is the most *virtuoso* way to deal with such disordered circumstances? Should a prince who inherits such a powerful army, used to making and breaking Roman rulers, try to curtail the soldiers' power? Or is it more prudent to increase that power even more and use it to check the great and the people, so long as it can be harnessed to his own ends? In the examples Machiavelli discusses, one set of emperors tried to limit the soldiers' power, while the other did not. The main problem all of them faced, however, was not simply that the soldiers were too demanding, but that 'it was difficult to satisfy the soldiers and the people'. In place of the conflict between the great and the people that had dominated politics in the Roman republic, under the emperors, we have an irreconcilable conflict between the people and the soldiers. At its root, Machiavelli suggests, lay very different conceptions of leadership:

> For the people loved quiet, and therefore loved modest [*modesti*] princes, and the soldiers loved a prince with a military spirit [*animo militare*] who was insolent, cruel, and rapacious. They wanted him to practice [*esercitassi*] these things on the people so that they could double their pay and give vent to their avarice and cruelty. These things always brought the ruin of those emperors who by nature or by art did not have a great reputation such that they could hold the one and the other in check [*in freno*].

Here, then, is the ideal standard: an emperor who could hold both people and soldiers 'in check'. Machiavelli will suggest that the two who did this, Marcus

---

[16] See chap. 3.

Aurelius and Severus, avoided conspiracy for this reason, while those who failed to check both people and soldiers did not.

They had, however, extremely different modes for this dual restraining. The philosopher-emperor Marcus' modes exhibited the qualities 'loved' by the people, modesty and quiet. The military man Severus' modes showed the spirit, insolence, cruelty, and rapacity admired by the soldiers. If judged from outside the one-sided perspectives of the soldiers or the people, it's unclear whether any of these qualities should be regarded as virtuous. If qualities such as industry and ordering skills are among Machiavelli's most praiseworthy virtues, then perhaps modest princes who simply guarantee quiet are too low-key to win highest acclaim. On the other hand, 'high spirits' are always a mixed blessing in Machiavelli's princes, while insolence, rapacity, and outright cruelty—as distinct from due severity—cause disorder and incur hatred. If one had to choose which qualities are more supportive of order-producing *virtú*, those loved by the people are the clear winner. Modest princes encourage quiet, and quiet, if well ordered, brings firmness. Insolent and rapacious princes relish constant motion, upheaval, and disorder.

Most of the emperors, Machiavelli tells us, on recognizing 'the difficulty of these two diverse humours, turned to satisfying the soldiers, caring little about injuring the people'. He then advances the view that:

> This policy [*partito*] was necessary; for since princes cannot fail to be hated [*odiato*] by someone, they are at first forced not to be hated by the generality of people [*università*]; and when they cannot continue this, they have to contrive with all industry to avoid the hatred of those communities [*università*] which are most powerful.

Having recently heard so much about the necessity for princes to avoid being hated by the people, what are we to make of this new claim that it is necessary for them not to care about injuring the people—a policy that *must* make them hated? This supposed necessity arises, one suspects, from the failure of these emperors to consider ways of dealing with the people/soldiers divide other than to play one side off against the other. If they can't be held responsible for creating the division—that was done over generations by over-ambitious men in the republic—those emperors can be blamed for playing into the conflict and making it worse. The un-virtuous quality of the argument shines through in its claims that princes are 'forced' to do contradictory things: first 'not to be hated' by the general populace, then to do what makes them hated. A prince who is forced into such conflicting and perilous positions has lost control over his actions, if he ever had it. He lets fortune and necessity push him around instead of regulating both with his *virtú*.

'And so', the *virtú*-deficient voice continues, 'those emperors who because they were new had need of extraordinary favour adhered to the soldiers rather than to the people.' For Machiavelli, there is never an objective need for extraordinary favour or modes of any kind; people who rely on them do so by choice, because they are too impatient or ambitious to use ordinary modes. In the context of the people/soldiers opposition, his identification of soldiers with extraordinary (disordering, questionably legitimate) modes links the people with ordinary (order-producing, legitimate) ones. The former are associated with fortune, the latter with *virtú*. Those emperors who chose to rely on the soldiers' favour therefore placed themselves under fortune's command.

The excuse of 'being forced' is wheeled out again in the claim that

> A prince who wants to maintain his state is often forced [*sforzato*] not to be good. For when that community of which you judge you have need to maintain yourself is corrupt, whether they are the people or the soldiers or the great, you must follow their humour to satisfy them, and then good deeds are your enemy.

We have already noted the fallacies in this type of argument. Chapters 15–17 insist that no really prudent prince is forced to follow his supporters' corrupt humours; he always has the option of ignoring them in favour of what he judges necessary for stable orders. It is true that in the empire's deeply corrupt conditions, as Machiavelli's ensuing discussion suggests, there was precious little room for *virtú*. But there were still some signs of it—and he will try to track them down.

PATHOLOGY OF TYRANNY: THE ROMAN EMPERORS

A number of the *Prince*'s Roman examples have pointed the way toward the reign of the emperors. Chapters 3–5 discussed the first wars of conquest outside Italy, mentioned the rebellions that followed these conquests, and spoke of the Romans being forced to destroy cities whose people refused to give up their freedom. Chapter 13 fast-forwards several centuries to the later Roman Empire that, Machiavelli tells us, was ruined by hiring foreign mercenaries for its defence. Chapter 16 mentions Julius Caesar as an imitator of Scipio; chapter 17 says that this same Scipio was publicly accused of being the 'corrupter of the Roman military'. And now we have the emperors. Machiavelli will not call their rule a 'tyranny' in the *Prince*. But nor can he bring himself to call it a 'government', 'order', or a 'state', since all those things presuppose functions and qualities that were destroyed by the empire.

These scattered examples outline a sad story of corruption. Machiavelli's *Discourses* tell the story in greater detail. There he identifies the root of these corruptions in Rome's boundless military conquests, whose very successes fed an unhealthy appetite for more. Men always err, Machiavelli declares, 'who do not know how to put limits [*termini*] to their hopes, and by founding themselves on these without otherwise measuring themselves, they are ruined'.[17] In more virtuous times, he notes ruefully, the city of Rome 'had a defence'. But 'after it had conquered Carthage and Antiochus' and 'no longer feared wars, it appeared to it that it could commit armies to whomever it wished, with regard not so much to *virtù* as to other qualities that gave them favour among the people'. Rome's conquest of Carthage seemed to make Italy safer from foreign wars. Instead it created more licence for civil wars between over-ambitious rivals for princely power: 'first between Marius and Sulla, then between Caesar and Pompey, and later between the killers of Caesar and those who wanted to avenge his death'.[18]

Caesar was killed in a conspiracy by the 'great': patricians who opposed his attempts to make himself tyrant with the support of soldiers and the people. Their failure to defeat Caesar's avengers spelled the end of Rome's ancient order of leadership: one that had two elected consuls at the head of government instead of one monarch, and changed office-holders annually to prevent them from growing too attached to supreme authority. Under Rome's new system of rule, there was no well-ordered method for selecting emperors, who now ruled alone and for life. As Machiavelli's discussion indicates, some inherited supreme authority by mandate from their predecessor, who was often their biological or adoptive father; others were chosen by powerful members of the Senate; still others—more and more as time went on—were chosen by the most powerful military legions. Unwilling to dispense with the fiction that Rome was still a republic, for a long time the emperors called themselves by the modest title of *princeps*, which originally meant 'first man' among equal citizens, not a hereditary or royal office. Machiavelli cuts through the whitewash and calls the first men 'emperors' (*imperadori*)—except when he describes some of their actions as typical for 'new princes'. The unstated implication that new princes are typically on a path to tyranny could hardly be more audible.

The *Prince* has presented many 'modes' of action that at first seem necessary or even praiseworthy, but turn out to have consequences that drag unwary princes into deeper and graver difficulties. Rome's great fortune-seeking men, backed by people and soldiers who longed for great conquests, pushed back the limits needed to uphold Rome's good orders and led her to this pass. Now Machiavelli's description of the emperors shows how hard—perhaps impossible—it is to stop the rot once one has crossed the thin line that separates corrupt republics from tyrannies. Although Machiavelli first names the emperors he discusses in their chronological order, his discussion reshuffles them to serve his own purposes.[19]

---

[17] *D* II.27.   [18] *D* III.16; *FH* II.2.

[19] Chronological order: Marcus, Commodus, Pertinax, Julianus, Severus, Caracalla, Macrinus, Heliogabalus, Alexander, Maximinus. Machiavelli's order of discussion: Marcus, Pertinax, Alexander, Severus, Caracalla, Commodus, Maximinus, Heliogabalus, Macrinus, Julianus. Compare *D* I.10.

His order presents three distinct sets of emperors. The first set consists of those who showed the qualities loved by the people: modesty, quiet, and respect for ordinary limits. The second set comprises emperors who had qualities loved by the soldiers: insolence, cruelty, rapacity, and extraordinary disregard for limits. The third set consists of emperors whose qualities were loved by no one. Thus:

Popular *virtú*	Soldierly *virtú*	No *virtú*
Marcus Aurelius	Severus	Heliogabalus
Pertinax	Caracalla	Macrinus
Alexander	Commodus	Julianus
	Maximinus	

Machiavelli's order depicts a single, steep line of descent that starts with the most virtuous emperors and declines toward the worst. According to this order, the qualities the people value in princes are closer to the virtues that are most necessary to found and maintain well-ordered states. Those valued by soldiers rank lower. While qualities of spiritedness and ruthlessness are necessary in military enterprises, they are less valuable in *political* leaders, unless other qualities of ordered restraint contain them. Since insolence, cruelty, and rapacity defy restraint and cause disorder, emperors who display them fall short of optimal political *virtú*, and pave the way for the others who show little sign of *virtú* at all.

On this reading, Machiavelli's account of the emperors looks like a devastating pathology of the disease of tyranny passing through its various stages, from the decent Marcus Aurelius 'the philosopher'—still able to impose some semblance of order in deeply corrupt conditions—to Pertinax and Alexander trying but failing to do the same. They are followed by the spirited, insolent Severus' success in oppressing the people without falling victim to a conspiracy—and then by Caracalla, Commodus, and Maximinus, all soldiers' emperors who were killed by their own centurions, armies, or others close to them.

Machiavelli's remarks on individual emperors confirm the impression of a rapid descent into a moral and political black hole. 'From the causes mentioned above', he tells us, 'Marcus, Pertinax, and Alexander, all living a modest life, lovers of justice, enemies of cruelty, humane, kind [*benigni*], all, except for Marcus, came to a bad end [*tristo fine*].'[20] The causes Machiavelli mentioned were the corrupt division between people and soldiers, fostered by the corrupt habit among Roman leaders of pandering to these different constituencies; he never suggests that these emperors' modesty or humanity caused their bad ends. If Marcus came out better, this was partly due to good fortune, partly to

---

[20] Here is the book's first use of the word 'justice'.

his 'many virtues that made him venerable' and helped him to keep the 'orders' of both soldiers and people 'within its limits' (*termini suoi*). By virtuously setting limits on *both* sides of the people/soldiers divide, Marcus managed to escape hatred and contempt from either; indeed, he gained their respect.[21]

Alas, he was the last Roman ruler to pull off such a feat of even-handed ordering. The next two emperors had qualities that might have endeared them to the people, but made them hated or despised by the soldiers, who were used to licentious living and unable to 'tolerate the decent [*onesta*] life to which Pertinax wanted to return them'. The latter was struck down by a soldier of the Praetorian Guard after only three months in office, after trying to impose discipline on the pampered soldier-élites. Alexander comes next in Machiavelli's order, though chronologically he came much later. In the 14 years of Alexander's reign, Machiavelli tells us, no one was ever put to death without a trial. But the soldiers despised his respect for legal propriety as 'effeminate', so 'the army conspired against him and killed him'. Regarding these two emperors, Machiavelli notes that 'hatred is acquired through good deeds as well as bad ones', since corrupt men hate those who try to make them better. Where there are no good orders left to correct men's bad dispositions, good leaders can only do so much.

The destruction of the good and the just brings Machiavelli to his second group of emperors, the soldier-friendly Severus, Antoninus Caracalla, Commodus, and Maximinus. In 'discoursing on' their qualities, Machiavelli says, 'you will find them very cruel and very rapacious'. Among these four, only Severus avoided a bad end. He did so by having 'so much virtue' that

> by keeping the soldiers his friends, although the people were overburdened by him, he was always able to rule happily [*felicemente*] because his virtues made him so admirable in the sight of the soldiers and the people that the latter remained somehow stupefied and astonished [*stupidi e attoniti*], while the former were reverent and satisfied.

The Roman people's 'stupefied' reaction to Severus echoes the Romagnole people's stupefaction after Cesare Borgia's murder of Remirro de Orco. Cesare, too, relied on his soldiers more than on the people, though with more ephemeral success than Severus. As foundations go, stupefaction and astonishment are not as firm as reverence or satisfaction; but for Severus they seem to have done the trick. 'Because the actions of this man were great and notable in a new prince', Machiavelli writes, 'I want to show briefly how well he knew how to use the persons [*la persona*] of the fox and the lion, whose natures I say

---

[21] Recalling how French parlements kept both great and people within bounds. Note that Machiavelli calls the people and soldiers 'orders' (*ordini*) when they are kept within their proper limits; otherwise they are 'humours' (*umori*) or partisan 'parts' (*parte*) that wreak havoc when unregulated.

above are necessary for a prince to imitate'. Severus, he recounts, rose through army ranks to become emperor by means of specious pretexts, dissembling, and bullying—skilfully combining the ways of an 'astute' fox and a fearsome lion. After inducing the Senate to elect him emperor 'out of fear', he overcame further difficulties by using open attacks (lion) in the east, deception and false accusations (fox) in the west. He thus was 'not hated by the army', on the one side, while on the other 'his very great reputation always defended him from the hatred that the people could have conceived for him because of his rapacity [*rapine*]'. Machiavelli calls a spade a spade here, making no effort to camouflage Severus' crimes; he openly calls him a criminal in the *Discourses*.[22] After all, though we have heard repeatedly that to avoid popular hatred princes must avoid rapacity, at this stage in Rome's decline the people's feelings scarcely mattered; Severus' terrifying reputation and the army's reverence were enough to defend him.

The next three emperors in Machiavelli's account, however, did become hated or contemptible, and were killed by conspirators. Severus' son Caracalla (who succeeded his father in reality as well as in Machiavelli's virtue-ranked order) was a hard military man of 'most excellent parts that made him marvellous in the sight of the people and pleasing to the soldiers'. But soon his 'ferocity and cruelty were so great and so unheard of [*inaudita*]', leading him to 'put to death a great part of the people of Rome and all the people of Alexandria, that he became most hateful to all the world'. Feared even by his own soldiers, 'he was killed by a centurion in the midst of his army'. The good Marcus' son Commodus had a 'cruel and bestial spirit' that made him rapacious toward the people and indulgent toward the soldiers. The latter despised him for his laxness, and he was killed in a conspiracy of his own disgruntled inner circle. Maximinus, chronologically the last of Machiavelli's ten emperors but seventh on his list, also became hated through his cruelties and ferocity, and was killed by 'his own army'. Since the remaining three emperors were 'altogether contemptible' and thus 'immediately eliminated', Machiavelli declares them unworthy of discussion.

Such is the ordinary and natural course of the extraordinary disease of tyranny. At the beginning there is still some room for reverence, order, even justice. But the fever soon burns these out of the city, impeding the efforts of virtuous men, leaving only fear, then hatred, and finally nothing but contempt. The Roman Empire endured for centuries. But what a way to live: with nothing but contemptible emperors who lived in constant fear for their lives, and stifled, stupefied, and contemptible peoples.[23]

And what a relief for princely readers when Machiavelli returns to 'our times': when princes 'have less of this difficulty of satisfying the soldiers by extraordinary means in their governments [*governi*]'. The armies held such

---

[22] *D* I.10. [23] See *D* I.10 on the dire and lingering legacy of Rome's empire.

sway in Rome because it needed them to hold its highly contested empire over far-flung provinces. These armies were 'entrenched in the government and administration of provinces', making it 'necessary to satisfy the soldiers rather than the people', since 'the soldiers could do more than the people'. Now, however, 'it is necessary for all princes except the Turk and the Sultan'—undisguised despotisms—'to satisfy the people rather than the soldiers, because the people can do more than the soldiers'.[24] Machiavelli's depressing imperial genealogy has left no doubt as to the dreadful power of the soldiers to make or destroy princes. Should modern princes fear that 'in our times' the people can do as much, or even more?

HAPPY ENDS

'Whoever considers the discourse written above', Machiavelli concludes, will see that the cause of ruin for the majority of emperors discussed was 'either hatred or disdain' (*disprezzo*). They will also 'know whence it arises that, though some of them proceeded in one mode and some in the contrary mode', in each mode, 'one of them came to a happy end and the others to unhappy ends [*felice . . . infelice fine*]'. The two happy cases were evidently those of Marcus and Severus. All the others were killed in conspiracies; these two alone survived.

But if Machiavelli's 'happy' men enjoy private good fortune and success for a time, they seldom do lasting political good, and deserve no praise for their happiness. For Marcus Aurelius, the Stoic philosopher who loved justice and hated cruelty, avoiding conspiracy would have been an insufficient condition for happiness, which depends on virtue. His end may have been happy by the standard of brute survival, but not if he hoped to return Rome to a more virtuous path. For all his success in keeping the people and the soldiers in check, Marcus still left the empire to his 'bestial' and licentious son Commodus, who promptly tore his father's decent legacy to shreds. Since he operated within a deeply corrupt form of rule, moreover, Marcus stood little chance of reaching the *Prince*'s highest standards of political *virtù*. However one might hope that a single forceful and well-intentioned ruler like Marcus might be able to reverse widespread corruption, 'there cannot', as Machiavelli would write in the *Discourses*, 'be one man of such long life as to have enough time to inure to good a city that has been inured to bad for a long time'; as soon as such a man is dead, the city returns to its bad old habits.[25]

---

[24] Then follows a cheeky comparison between the sultan's state and that of the Christian pontificate, suggesting that both share tyrannical features and lack of respect for the people.
[25] *D* I.17.

For his part, Severus followed fortune more than *virtú* by indulging the soldiers' corrupt humours, thus aggravating the disease to a point where no later emperor could even try to cure it. However happy his personal end, his wider legacy was neither happy nor virtuous. Machiavelli makes this clear in the *Discourses*, in a chapter that echoes many themes of the *Prince*, chapter 19. Having noted that most of the 'criminal' emperors died violently, Machiavelli then points out that 'if there was any criminal among those who died ordinarily, such as Severus, it arose from his very great fortune and *virtú*, two things that accompany few men'. Severus may have died 'ordinarily', but he was still a criminal, with a species of *virtú* that wins a certain kind of admiration but falls far short of that needed to elicit the highest praise. While the better class of emperors tried to reorder a 'kingdom' in the corrupt conditions of post-republic Rome, the criminal class, including Severus, tried to found a 'tyranny'. And though Severus was 'rare' in avoiding 'extraordinary' death by conspiracy, he deserves no praise for this, since it was due to 'his very great fortune' and a deficient kind of *virtú*.[26]

Our chapter ends, nonetheless, with an intriguing suggestion. 'A new prince in a new principality', Machiavelli writes, 'cannot imitate the actions of Marcus, nor again is it necessary to follow those of Severus'. Instead, 'he should take from Severus those parts necessary to found his state and from Marcus those which are fitting and glorious to conserve [*conservare*] a state that is already stabilized and firm [*stabilito e fermo*]'. This seems to suggest that a new prince should 'found' his state by indulging the soldiers' cruel and rapacious appetites, deceiving political colleagues, and using military threats against the Senate. Once supreme power is his, he should turn around and 'conserve' his state by treating the soldiers and people even-handedly, checking the former's excessive desires to injure the latter.

Here, again, we have a superficially clever argument for pragmatic flexibility. After all, the *Prince* has taught us that it's easier to acquire with fortunate and criminal modes, but easier to maintain with virtuous ordering—so why not start with the one, then leap to the other? Readers should have learned, however, that it is exceedingly hard to make this leap, especially if one's modes of acquiring were criminal. Machiavelli explains the difficulty in the *Discourses*:

> Because the reordering of a city for a political way of life presupposes a good man, and becoming prince of a republic by violence presupposes a bad man, one will find that it very rarely happens that someone good wants to become prince by bad ways, even though his end be good, and that someone wicked, having become prince, wishes to work well, and that it *will ever occur to his mind to use well the authority he has acquired badly*.[27]

If readers are still unsure why this should be so, they may consider the examples provided in chapter 19. Severus, who rose to power by deception

---

[26] *D* I.10. [27] *D* I.18. Italics added.

and crimes, then held the people in thrall by 'somehow' keeping them astonished and stupefied. Marcus was modest, loved justice, an enemy of cruelty, humane and kind, and was held in reverence for these virtues. It seems most unlikely that anyone who becomes prince by using the first methods could find it in his nature to switch to the second. Once a prince has indulged the soldiers on the way up the ladder, the attempt to reverse this mode once in power would almost certainly make the soldiers hate and despise him, as chapter 17 said would have happened to Caesar had he lived. If his initial support comes from troops who love him for his indulgence towards them and his crimes against others, it is all the more dangerous to try to control these violent supporters later; they may rip him apart.

Note, moreover, that Machiavelli does not say that new princes should 'acquire' by using parts of Severus' modes, but 'found' with them. It seems rather doubtful, however, that Severus' modes can 'found' a 'state' in Machiavelli's implicitly normative sense of both words. Neither fortune nor criminal modes can really 'found' states at all; they can throw up scaffolding that soon collapses. If we take the *Prince*'s general standards rather than particular statements as our guide, the argument for founding by Severus' modes and conserving by Marcus' looks fallacious and unrealistic. After reflecting on the chapter's end, we are left with a simple choice between fundamentally opposed modes of founding and conserving. Mirroring the end of chapter 19 on the same subject, the *Discourses* Book I, chapter 10, ends by explaining the high stakes—beyond mere happiness—of such a choice to those who consider imitating Rome's emperors:

> In sum, those to whom the heavens give such an opportunity may consider that two ways have been placed before them: one that makes them live secure and after death renders them glorious; the other that makes them live in continual anxieties and after death leaves them a sempiternal infamy.[28]

---

[28] *D* I.10.

Prudence and trust

20

Trusting one's own subjects

Whether fortresses and many other things that are made and done by princes every day are useful or useless

Descending from empire, our discussion now turns to six methods princes use to defend themselves: (1) disarm subjects, (2) keep subject towns divided, (3) nourish enmities against themselves, (4) gain to themselves those who had been suspect at the beginning of their states, (5) build fortresses, and (6) knock down and destroy them. Machiavelli argues that all but (4) and (6) are mostly useless.

DISARMING SUBJECTS

While 'some princes have disarmed their subjects', Machiavelli asserts, new princes 'never' do this. On the contrary, whenever a new prince 'has found them unarmed, he has always armed them'. As a statement of fact, this is questionable, but the exaggeration underlines the overpowering reasons why princes should never disarm. For when subjects are armed, Machiavelli tells them yet again, 'those arms become yours; those whom you suspected become faithful', while those who were already faithful 'remain so; and from subjects they are made into your partisans [*sudditi/partigiani*]'. Given all these advantages, it sounds as if new princes have no rational choice but to arm their unarmed subjects.

Having surveyed the advantages of keeping subjects armed, Machiavelli turns to the dangers of disarming them. 'When you disarm them', he points out, 'you begin to offend them; you show that you distrust them either for cowardice [*viltà*] or for lack of faith [*poca fede*], both of which opinions generate hatred against you.' This argument seems designed to unsettle those in a new *principato*—such as the returning Medici—who rushed to disarm former citizens, making them more like subjects than *cittadini*. They perhaps imagined that by stripping citizens/subjects of arms, they would reduce any threat of popular resistance to their new government. On the contrary, Machiavelli tells them, you intensify the threat by offending the general populace and making them hate you; and even disarmed subjects have the power to threaten princes. By disarming Florentines, it seems, the new Medici princes have gone against every reasonable policy.

The question of how much trust a prince should invest in others lies at the heart of Machiavelli's warnings. Earlier chapters contained contradictory statements about trust. On the one hand, chapter 18 declared that since men in general are 'ungrateful, fickle, pretenders and dissemblers', and so on, they cannot be trusted. The *Prince*'s main arguments for particular military and political 'orders', however, consistently stressed that firm foundations depend on measures that build trust between princes and peoples. Here, again, Machiavelli reminds us that while entrusting one's subjects with defence creates bonds of obligation that are a prince's best security, depriving them of arms also deprives princes of their salutary effects.

Machiavelli notes, however, that 'all subjects cannot be armed'. Does this mean that princes need only 'benefit' those who are, since these pose the greatest potential threat to his power? 'If those whom you arm are benefited', Machiavelli tells them, 'one can act with more security toward the others.' Some princes might take this to mean that the unarmed others' views are of little account. But Machiavelli's further remarks suggest that they would be wrong. On the contrary, the prince's security toward these 'others' results precisely from *their* reasoned judgement that armed subjects deserve special benefits. For if 'the difference of treatment' (*diversità del procedure*) makes those who are armed obligated (*obligati*) to you, 'the others excuse you, judging it necessary that those who have more danger and more obligation deserve more [*più merito*]'. Since reasonable subjects accept reasonable inequalities in the benefits they receive—believing that unequal burdens deserve unequal benefits— princes need not arm or benefit all subjects equally, or worry that this kind of differential treatment will be seen as unfair.

When, however, 'a prince acquires a new state that is added as a member to his old one', there seem no good reasons to trust them. In this case 'it is necessary to disarm that state, except for those who were your partisans in acquiring'. On second thoughts, not even these one-time supporters should be trusted. They too must be rendered 'soft [*molli*] and effeminate . . . so that the arms of all your state are only with your own soldiers, who live next to you in your old state'.

Perhaps Machiavelli is convinced that the 'modes' for securing princes on their home turf are diametrically opposed to those that secure them abroad. Or perhaps he is testing what princes have absorbed from their earlier reading. Enough was said before to make them reflect that so long as 'new states' are disarmed in this way—with even friendly 'partisans' treated with deep suspicion after a conquest—they can never become part of a prince's 'own' state or arms. Their subjects remain very much 'others', and thus a source of persistent insecurity. If some readers overlooked this general warning, they should ask themselves whether rendering people 'soft and effeminate' is ever a good strategy for optimizing a prince's strength, rather than a waste of potential *virtú*.

KEEP SUBJECT TOWNS DIVIDED

A second method used by princes in hope of defending themselves is to keep subject towns divided. 'Our ancients', Machiavelli declares, 'and those who were esteemed wise, used to say that it was necessary to hold Pistoia with parties [*parte*]', in the manner already discussed in chapter 17, 'and Pisa with fortresses [*fortezze*].' In Pistoia and other subject cities, Florentines 'nourished differences' (*differenzie*) to 'possess them more easily'.

How useful is this method? At first, Machiavelli says it depends on circumstances. It 'would have been good' in times 'when Italy was in balance in a certain mode', presumably as he described it in chapter 11; but 'I do not believe that one could give it today as a precept [*precetto*]'. Then he offers a more sweeping, indeed absolute, judgement: 'For I do not believe that divisions ever do any good.' The 'ever' here baldly contradicts the initial, relative-to-circumstances claim that divide-and-rule 'would have been good' in other times. Both cannot be true; the second, absolute judgement must override the initial relativist argument. This is confirmed by Machiavelli's equally absolute explanation: 'when the enemy approaches, of necessity divided cities are immediately lost', since 'the weaker party'—usually the one that is kept weaker by the prince's deliberate policy—'always joins the external forces' to fight against the prince who keeps them weak, making it impossible for the other party to rule. He concludes that 'such modes, therefore, argue for weakness in the prince'. In a 'vigorous [*gagliardo*] principality such divisions are never permitted', for they only profit princes in peacetime, but show their fallaciousness (*fallacia*) when war comes.

The reason weaker parties 'always' join the enemy is that they have been treated differently from the stronger party in ways they consider offensive or unmerited. In the discussion of armed and unarmed subjects, the unarmed 'excused' differential benefits as reasonable because they understood that armed subjects assumed heavier 'obligations'. By contrast, we now have a policy where the only reason for inequalities between stronger and weaker subjects is the prince's desire to dominate both. Both discussions deal with *differenzie* among subjects. But the first kind of difference enhanced the prince's security because less-benefited subjects regarded it as reasonable. The second threatens that security, because it creates a division that the weaker party regards as arbitrarily benefiting the stronger and the prince.

A further inference can be drawn about when it is useful to treat different subjects differently. In order to 'hold' subjects securely, princes need to satisfy them that any inequalities in treatment are transparently *merited* by services rendered by some to all, not generated for a prince's private advantage or some other arbitrary cause. Since unarmed subjects judge—or should judge—that their armed compatriots deserve greater benefits because their labours benefit everyone, they see this kind of inequality as a source of their common bond of obligation with armed subjects and the prince, rather than as a source of division. Differences based on partisan hatred have the opposite effect, especially when a prince foments them for his own apparent advantage.

Traditionally, questions of merited and unmerited differences in treatment fall under the heading of justice—a topic so far muted in the *Prince*, if not entirely absent. The word *giustizia* has only made one appearance so far, in chapter 19 when Marcus and a few other emperors were described as 'lovers of justice'. Machiavelli has, however, frequently discussed appropriate punishments, distributions of public goods and rewards, and conditions for keeping or breaking promises. He may not have used the word justice, but the classical topics of justice are omnipresent in the *Prince*, and what philosophers called punitive, distributive, and promissory justice are major themes of the book's second half.[1]

NOURISH ENMITIES AGAINST YOURSELF

If the first two methods of defence are utterly useless, some princes might feel encouraged by Machiavelli's initial remarks on a third. Princes, he observes, 'become great when they overcome difficulties made for them and opposition made to them'. Thus 'fortune, especially when she wants to make a new prince great', often helps him out, knowing that a new prince needs to do impressive things to increase his reputation. Fortune accordingly 'makes enemies arise for him and makes them undertake enterprises [*imprese*] against them', so that in overcoming these obstacles he can 'climb higher [*salire più alto*] on the ladder that his enemies have brought for him'. Seeing this happen over and over, 'many judge [*molti iudicano*] that a wise prince, when he has the opportunity for it, should astutely [*con astuzia*] nourish some enmity so that when he has crushed it, his greatness [*grandezza*] emerges the more from it'. The warning signals fairly jump off the page. This method should appeal to princes who still haven't grasped the risks of relying on fortune to climb ever 'higher', who pursue greatness and reputation at any cost, who take what 'many

---

[1] His other works speak frequently, and very interestingly, of justice and injustice; see *ME* chap. 8.

judge' wise as a guide for their actions, and who confuse 'astuteness'—code for cunning opportunism—with prudence.

GAIN TO YOURSELF THOSE WHO WERE
SUSPECT AT THE BEGINNING

At last we come to a useful method: princes should gain to themselves men who were held suspect 'at the beginning of their states'. Paradoxically, by investing trust in people who appeared untrustworthy, princes render them more reliable than others who were never suspect in the first place. The thinking behind this is that men who know that a new prince mistrusts them 'are all the more forced to serve him faithfully as they know it is more necessary for them to cancel out with deeds the sinister opinion one has taken of them'. Eager to demonstrate their new-found loyalty, such former enemies are more useful than men whom the prince never doubted; for the latter, 'while serving him with too much security, neglect his affairs'.

Machiavelli's arguments for this useful method read like a thinly veiled appeal to his Medici addressees, who indeed held him in great suspicion at the beginning of their principality. Here we seem to have one of the *Prince*'s most personal moments, where the author addresses specific princely readers and gives them reasons to trust him. Princes 'who have newly taken a state through internal support' should, Machiavelli insists, 'consider well what cause moved those who supported them to support them', since an analysis of different men's motives can help them to judge their trustworthiness. Some people may have backed the new prince because they were 'not content with the former state'. But once in power, the prince has 'trouble and great difficulty' keeping these people friendly, because 'it is impossible for him to make them content'. The thought here seems to be that different men tend to operate in different general 'modes' according to nature and habit—an idea spelled out in chapter 25. The ingrained modes of some men incline them to 'discontent' under any government, and presumably make them more eager for conspiracy than those of opposite, more temperate modes. If someone is prepared at one time to support a coup to overthrow a legitimate government, as Medici supporters did in 1512, they might do the same again if the new government disappoints their expectations. Men of less restless, unquiet, conspiratorial disposition therefore make more reliable friends, even if they opposed the new princes at first.

Without spelling out these implicit criticisms of certain Medici partisans, Machiavelli implies that men like him have the steadier kind of temperament that would bring great *utilità* to the new rulers. Princes are wrong to hold in high suspicion men who faithfully served their opponents in the previous

government. They should judge others' trustworthiness by their general character, not their particular loyalties. Malcontents are always malcontents, while
men of good faith can be trusted no matter whom they serve, as Machiavelli had
already insisted in a letter to Vettori—the same letter which announced that he
had 'composed a short study, *De principatibus*', which he wanted to present to
'these Medici princes' in hope that they might 'begin to engage my services':

> There should be no doubt about my word; for, since I have always kept it, I should
> not start learning how to break it now. Whoever has been honest and faithful for
> forty-three years, as I have, is unable to change his nature; my poverty is witness
> to my loyalty and honesty.[2]

BUILD FORTRESSES

Fortresses are the fifth item on Machiavelli's list of useful or useless methods of
defence, and the only one mentioned in the chapter's title. He approaches this
subject more tentatively than the others, noting that 'it has been the custom of
princes, so as to hold their states more securely, to build fortresses that would
be a bit and bridle [*la briglia e il freno*] for those who might have designs
against them', and to provide 'a secure refuge from sudden attack'.

How effective are fortresses in providing the hoped-for security? At first,
Machiavelli seems ambivalent. 'I praise this mode', he declares, 'because it has
been used since antiquity.' By Machiavelli's own standards, this is a pretty
poor reason for praise. While his *Prince*, *Art of War*, and *Discourses* all pick
out some ancient 'modes and orders' for praise and imitation, they urge
readers to recognize the shortcomings of others: 'Men always praise ancient
times', Machiavelli declares in the *Discourses*, 'but not always reasonably.'[3] It is
thus unsurprising that his modern examples—no ancient ones are given—call
the utility of fortresses into question. The duke of Urbino, Machiavelli notes
approvingly, after returning to his dominion 'from which Cesare Borgia had
expelled him . . . razed all the fortresses in that province to their foundations
[*funditus*]; and he judged', apparently with good reason, 'that without them he
would with greater difficulty lose his state again.'[4]

Going beyond recent examples to general reasoning, Machiavelli starts with
an according-to-circumstances maxim. 'Fortresses', he states, are thus 'useful
or not according to the times, and if they do well for you in one regard, they
hurt you in another.' When their qualities are described this way, fortresses
begin to sound worryingly similar to fortune, which also helps you in some

---

[2] Machiavelli to Vettori, 10 December 1513, *MF* 265.   [3] *D* II.Pref.
[4] A reminder that Borgia's expulsions didn't last long, and that unlike more virtuous princes,
he did rely on fortresses.

respects but hurts you in others. Like fortune, the utility of fortresses varies with the 'times'. 'In our times', Machiavelli observes, they 'have not been seen to bring profit to any prince, unless to the Countess of Forlì' in her famously stubborn resistance to several attackers.[5] But as soon as 'the times' turned against her in more important respects, fortresses failed to save her state, which lacked the stable foundations of virtuous defences.

What would have constituted such foundations, and saved her more surely than fortresses? Both 'then and before', Machiavelli tells readers, 'it would have been more secure for her not to be hated by the people than to have had fortresses'. It turns out 'the best fortress there is' is metaphorical rather than physical: 'not to be hated by the people', since 'if the people hold you in hatred fortresses do not save you'.

Fortresses not only do little good when a prince lacks popular support. They actually defeat their own defensive purposes by showing how little a prince trusts his own people, making him more hated. Thus Francesco Sforza, for all his *virtù*, made a cardinal error when he built fortresses in Milan—a policy, Machiavelli opines, that 'will bring more war to the Sforza house than any other disorder of that state'. In choosing his methods of defence, then, each prince should ask himself what or whom he fears most. 'The prince who has more fear of the people than of foreigners [*forestieri*] ought', Machiavelli writes, 'to make fortresses; but the one who has more fear of foreigners than the people, ought to omit them.' Any prince who has read the *Prince* should understand that if he has reason to fear the people, he must have failed to build the good *ordini* needed to remove this fear. 'I shall praise whoever makes fortresses and whoever does not', Machiavelli concludes in arch-ambiguous mode, 'and I shall blame anyone who, trusting [*fidandosi*] in fortresses, thinks little of being hated by the people.' This leaves us with the sixth and last method listed at the outset, whose utility now speaks for itself: knock fortresses down and destroy them.

---

[5] Caterina Sforza, with whom Machiavelli had rather fraught negotiations early in his political career. See *FH* VIII.34.

21

Gaining trust from allies

What a prince should do to be held outstanding

While the title promises to teach princes how to keep up their reputation,[1] the chapter also considers the importance of trust as a foundation of security—this time, how to gain it from one's external allies. Together with military defence, foreign policy had been one of Machiavelli's main fields of expertise when he was Secretary to the Florentine republic. Since he says rather little about foreign relations or alliances elsewhere in the *Prince*, the present chapter is thus of great interest. It begins in a heavily cynical tone, seeming to praise examples of contemporary princes who achieved *grandezza* by deceptions and extreme cruelty. The rest of the discourse moves in a very different direction.

GREAT AND RARE ENTERPRISES

'Nothing', Machiavelli begins, 'makes a prince so much esteemed [*stimare*] as to carry on great enterprises [*grande imprese*] and to give rare examples of himself'. At the present time 'we have', Machiavelli tells us in chatty mode, Spain's king Ferdinand. We encountered him briefly at the end of chapter 18, as the unnamed 'a certain prince of present times' who 'never preaches anything but peace and faith, and is very hostile to both'.

Here Machiavelli names Ferdinand and praises his exploits to the skies. 'If you consider his actions', Machiavelli declares grandly, 'you will find them all very great and some of them extraordinary [*grandissima e qualcuna estraordinaria*]'. Firstly, he attacked Granada, and 'that enterprise was the foundation of his state'. Ferdinand's main device was distraction: by constantly launching wars on different fronts, he kept the barons of Castile, who might otherwise have opposed his policies, too preoccupied to stop him. He sustained his armies 'with money from the Church and the people'—who were heavily

---

[1] Although the Latin word translated here as 'outstanding' is the ambiguously remarkable-or-excessive *egregius*; see chap. 19.

taxed—and was able 'with that long war to lay a foundation for his military, which later brought him honour'.

Plunging headlong into even 'greater enterprises, always making use of religion', Ferdinand 'turned to an act of pious cruelty [*una pietosa crudeltà*],[2] expelling the Marranos'—Spain's converted Jews and Moslems—'from his kingdom and despoiling it of them. Nor', Machiavelli adds in a sudden, damning shift of tone, 'could there be an example more wretched [*miserabile*] and rare than this.'[3] Great and rare examples, it seems, are as often as miserable as they are glorious. Then the busy Ferdinand attacked Africa 'under the same cloak', made his campaign in Italy to reclaim Naples from the French, and more recently attacked France in 1512. And 'so he has always done and ordered great things, which have always kept the minds of his subjects in suspense and admiration [*sospesi e ammirati*] and occupied with their outcome'.

This breathless narration of Ferdinand's multiple enterprises is packed with ironic praise, expressed through both negatively coded words and wry descriptions of his deeds. However impressive the initial achievements, princely readers should know by now that constant energetic motion cannot produce firm foundations for any state. Machiavelli makes this argument about Ferdinand in his 1513–14 letters to Vettori who, in a bid to get Machiavelli employment after his fall from grace, showed them to the Medici Pope Leo X's advisers as evidence of Machiavelli's invaluable skills as a foreign policy analyst.[4] The letters leave no doubt that he saw the king as anything but a model of princely *virtú*. Ferdinand, he writes, 'has always been the prime mover of all the confusions [*confusioni*] in Christendom, ever since he came into Italy'.[5]

Machiavelli's analyses of Ferdinand's mobile 'modes' is fascinating for the light it sheds on his general criteria for prudent or imprudent action. His key point is that the skills needed to win impressive victories, or avoid defeat for a time, should not be confused with genuine prudence. Prudent actions should, first of all, have clear *ends* of a certain kind: not short-term victories, but lasting orders. Ferdinand's actions, in Machiavelli's opinion, had no such aims. The king, Machiavelli observes,

> has not tried to foresee the outcome: for his aim is not so much this, that, or the other victory, as to win reputation among his various peoples and to keep them hanging with his multifarious activities. Therefore, he has always started things spiritedly [*animoso*], later giving him that end which chance [*sorte*] places before him or which necessity teaches him.

---

[2] Or 'merciful cruelty', playing on the ambiguity in *pietoso* noted in chap. 17. Either way, the term is bitterly ironic.

[3] In 1501–2.

[4] See Najemy (1993) for sensitive, detailed readings of the entire Machiavelli–Vettori correspondence.

[5] Machiavelli to Vettori, 16 April 1514, *MF* 283.

This is exactly what Machiavelli says about Ferdinand in the present chapter of the *Prince*, except that here he purports to praise as useful that which in his letters he exposed as aimless posturing. Vettori wondered whether Ferdinand's hyperactivity might conceal some carefully thought-out strategy. Machiavelli judges that it merely throws dust in people's eyes. 'One mode for holding on to new states', he observes, 'is to arouse great expectations of oneself, always keeping men's minds busy with trying to figure out the aim of one's decisions and one's new ventures.' If some think that by keeping everyone on edge Ferdinand shows himself master of the situation, Machiavelli crushes that opinion underfoot as well. The king acts in this high-risk way, he insists, not out of well-founded confidence but from weakness, unreasonable expectations of gain, and underestimations of his rivals.[6]

A second sign of prudence is to avoid taking unnecessary risks. In Machiavelli's view, Ferdinand's recent adventures 'unnecessarily endangered all his states—always a reckless course of action for any man', for no worthy or even determinate ends. There was no objective, pressing necessity for Ferdinand's constant wars. On the contrary, there were other far better options that he ignored. At one stage, his rivals' freedom of action was so limited that 'Spain could have been either the mediator of a stable [*ferma*] peace or the architect of a secure accord [*accordo securo*] for himself'. Nevertheless, Ferdinand 'left out all those alternatives and chose war, even though he might fear that in one decisive battle his entire territory might go'.[7]

The first two elements of prudence depend on a third: foresight, based on an ability to form realistic expectations of how others will react to one's movements in the long run. Ferdinand thought only of how to bewilder and stupefy enemies, allies, and subjects alike. He evidently failed to consider that all his deceptions, violations of faith, and unnecessary aggression would come home to bite him before long. At some point he would need reliable friends as much as everyone else; and then his potential allies would 'remember more about old wrongs' he has done them 'than recent favours' aimed at luring them on side. Machiavelli saw no 'security for Spain' resulting from Ferdinand's latest manoeuvres between France, the Swiss, and the pope. 'So unless ... they all destroy one another, each one might turn against the cause of all their evil'— that is, Ferdinand—'because we believe that his snares are well-known and that they have begun generating hatred and loathing in the minds of his friends as well as his enemies.'[8]

So much for the great foundations thrown up by Ferdinand's wars. On the contrary, Machiavelli tells Vettori, the vast expense of these wars was rapidly

[6] Machiavelli to Vettori, 29 April 1513, *MF* 235.
[7] Machiavelli to Vettori, 29 April 1513, *MF* 232.
[8] Machiavelli to Vettori, 29 April 1513, *MF* 233–5. He adds with regret, rather than 'Machiavellian' sang-froid: 'No one these days has any regard for promises or commitments.'

undermining the king's power-base. 'I have learned from a well-placed person', he writes, 'that the king's exchequer is bare and there are no means for replenishing it and that the king's army consisted only of conscripts who, moreover, were starting to disobey him.' He concludes unambiguously that the king 'may have understood matters badly and brought them to a worse conclusion'.[9]

Back in the *Prince*, Machiavelli continues to speak in awestruck tones of princes who give 'rare examples' of themselves in internal government, 'similar to those that are told of Messer Bernabò [Visconti] da Milano'. Machiavelli's contemporaries knew Messer Bernabò well as a war-mongering, unpopular prince, whose most famous action did indeed constitute a 'rare' example that increased his reputation in some sense. On being excommunicated, Bernabò arrested the pope's envoys and refused to release them until they had eaten the parchment, seal, and silk cord that comprised his excommunication orders. Neither this nor his other 'great' actions did much for his or his state's security.[10]

THE PERILS OF NEUTRALITY

Then the tone shifts again, and we read that 'a prince is also esteemed when he is a true friend and a true enemy; that is, when without any hesitation [*respetto*] he discloses himself in support of someone against another'. This is a very different sort of reason to esteem a prince: one that concerns his demonstrated commitments to others rather than 'great' or 'rare' appearances.

Far from arguing that prudent princes should be able to change sides according to their present advantage, Machiavelli comes out with a robust argument against this kind of pragmatic flexibility. When two powers (*potente*) close to you get into conflict, he argues, it is *always* advantageous to take clear sides and stick with your chosen ally through defeat as well as victory. This general rule holds, moreover, regardless of whether 'you have to fear the winner' or have no reason to fear either warring party.[11] In the first case, some might think it more prudent to stay neutral and avoid the winner's reprisals. But they would be wrong to think that only winners can harm them; offended losers can do so too. Thus if you stay neutral 'you will always be the prey of

---

[9] Machiavelli to Vettori, 29 April 1513, *MF* 234.

[10] His constant wars, despotic ways, and heavy taxes made him hated by the Milanese. He was deposed and poisoned by his nephew, as reported in *FH* I.27; compare *D* II.13.

[11] Compare Machiavelli's letter to Vettori, 20 December 1514, *MF* 303: neutrality 'has always been an extremely destructive policy because it is certain to lose'.

whoever wins, to the pleasure and satisfaction of the one who was defeated', leaving 'no reason, nor anything, to defend you or give you refuge'.

Machiavelli asks readers to reflect on questions of reciprocity and fair exchange that might reasonably be raised about neutrals. From the perspective of both winners and losers, the basic problem with third-party neutrality is that it suggests a lack of reciprocity: why should anyone help or protect you when you avoided helping them in their hour of need? 'For whoever wins does not want suspect friends who may not help him in adversity'; in other words, don't expect much from the winner if you gave him little reason to trust your allegiance when he asked for it. And 'whoever loses does not give you refuge, since you did not want to share his fortune with arms in hand'. External powers, especially those from whom a prince sometimes seeks help himself, have good reason to expect firm commitments in return, and not to worry that you might back out or change sides as the winds of fortune command. By remaining neutral you seem either lukewarm or suspect in your allegiances, something victor and loser will remember when you come asking for favours later.

Machiavelli uses an example from Livy to illuminate these reflections. In 192 BC the Greek Achaeans, long-time allies of the Romans, were asked by the Syrian king Antiochus to remain neutral in his conflict with Rome. A Roman legate dissuaded the Achaeans—then under Philopoemen's leadership—from taking that course, arguing that if they remained neutral they would fall prey to the victor.[12] From this example Machiavelli derives a rule of thumb for identifying true friends and enemies: 'it will always happen that the one who is not friendly will seek your neutrality', while 'he who is friendly to you will ask that you declare yourself with arms'.

The Roman–Achaean example has an important connection to the foreign policy context in which Machiavelli developed his views on neutrality. The same example appears in a letter where Machiavelli sought to advise the new Medici pope about alliances. Here as elsewhere in the *Prince*, the Italians are loosely identified with Philopoemen's Achaeans, a league of Greek peoples who sought to defend themselves from much stronger foreign powers by seeking further union with other Greeks. The friendly yet threatening Romans are associated here with the contemporary French. Machiavelli argued that, like the Achaeans, the Italians led by the pope should avoid 'a neutral way' in the wars between Spain, France, and the Swiss, and take firm sides with the tried and tested power: France. They should do this regardless of temporary setbacks, and despite the undoubted inconveniences of any alliance with such strong powers.[13]

Having said that 'irresolute princes' opt for neutrality 'in order to escape present dangers', Machiavelli now adds a new argument for making transparent commitments. 'When the prince discloses himself boldly in support of one

---

[12] Quote in Latin from *LH* XXXV.49.   [13] See chap. 3.

side', he not only avoids harm, but gains positive benefits. For if the one he supported wins, the winner has 'an obligation [*obligo*] to you and has a contract of love [*contratto lo amore*] for you; and men are never so indecent [*disonesto*] as to crush you with so great an example of ingratitude'. If the one he backed loses, he still benefits. For that power is still a power who will give you 'refuge'; 'he helps you while he can, and you become the companion [*compagno*] of a fortune that can revive'.

This argument about the long-term benefits of firm commitments speaks strongly against the view that prudence in external affairs lies in preserving extreme flexibility. Machiavelli says, on the contrary, that it consists in a demonstrated willingness to take risks on behalf of others, thereby creating obligations that bind them to you over time. Obligations are based on reasons for reciprocity that both parties find good. By itself love is a less reliable bond in politics, but love based on good reasons for reciprocity can help underwrite a kind of 'contract' that holds, so long as those reasons hold. If you sometimes find yourself on the losing side by virtue of your commitments, this is a price worth paying for a bond with such enduring utility.

Here yet again, this time with allies instead of subjects, Machiavelli stresses the advantages of trust and the excellent prospects one has of establishing reliable obligations by demonstrating one's own reliability. This message is unsettling for princes who believed chapter 18's remarks about the low value of good faith and the general untrustworthiness of men. Machiavelli now says, on the contrary, that you can often, if not always, expect minimal decency and gratitude from others. So when you declare your fidelity to men and give them reason to trust it, they in turn generally do what's needed to earn your trust. If this weren't true—if one should assume that men in general are ungrateful and dishonest—then clearly it wouldn't be prudent to take sides. Far from arguing that princes should place little trust in others, especially in external relations, Machiavelli suggests that lax fidelity is an utterly useless 'mode'. It is unrealistic to think that you can secure yourself by mistrusting everyone else and honouring your commitments only when it suits you.

NEUTRALITY AND JUSTICE

And the un-cynical remarks multiply on this theme. 'Then too', Machiavelli adds, 'victories are never so clear that the winner does not have to have some respect, especially for justice [*le vittorie non sono mai sí stiette che el vincitore non abbia ad avere qualche respetto, e massime alla iustizia*].'

This is the second use of the word 'justice' in the *Prince*. The reference here is to promissory justice, or the justice of keeping one's commitments. Machiavelli's point is one he has made before in several different contexts. The victor in any particular war or political struggle never has total control over the outcome. Strong losers can always try again, or become still stronger and reverse what seemed a stable victory. But even the weakest of losers can find ways to cause trouble for victors—siding with foreign enemies in future conflicts, or fomenting whatever resistance they can among themselves. Losers are more likely to challenge a victory if its terms are not seen as just, while allies who consider that they did not get due 'respect' from the victor will abandon them. Other people's reasonable reactions, as we've learned many times before, matter for your own lasting success; if you offend or injure them, they tend to try to harm you or to curtail your power. A victor therefore does well to treat both losers and allies with some respect, instead of adding injustice to their losses; otherwise losers or injured former allies will find some future opportunity to harm him. A prince who has taken sides with a victor can reasonably expect, then, that a reasonable victor will not turn against him after victory, but will honour the two-way obligations created by the prince's commitment.

The argument that men are not so indecent as to show ingratitude is based on a judgement about the partial goodness in human nature. The argument that they also 'have to have some respect, especially for justice' is a judgement about their rationality—their ability to reason well about the consequences of failing to show respect for others' interests, which justice requires. A reasonable victor will realize that respect for others is advantageous for him; that is, that *justice is expedient*. Machiavelli does not quite spell this out, but he comes close in this sentence. Elsewhere in the *Prince* he has said that it is always harmful for a prince to 'offend' anyone but a few on first taking power, or to 'injure' people by rapacity, cruelty, or violence. He may not have called these actions 'unjust', but clearly that is what they are, by his own standards: actions that are wrong because they harm others without sufficient reason. Machiavelli usually expresses his disapproval of them by saying that they threaten a prince's security or undermine the foundations of his *stato*. But the fact that the actions have these disadvantages for princes doesn't mean that they aren't also unjust. On the contrary, perhaps they harm princes *because* they are unjust—because to harm others' interests unreasonably is always harmful to whoever commits it, as well as to its victims.

In the second case where you don't have to fear either party, neutrality is clearly a less dangerous option than in the first case, since neither winner nor loser has the power to harm you. But if the costs of neutrality are lower, Machiavelli argues that great benefits may be gained from taking sides. Indeed, the very fact that you have less to lose and more to gain means 'so much the greater is the prudence of joining sides'.

INESCAPABLE INCONVENIENCES

Machiavelli's argument for taking sides 'when one has to fear' both parties assumes that you have good reason to trust your chosen ally to recognize and fulfil his obligations to you. But while Machiavelli suggests that it is generally prudent to do so, he now touches on an instance where you may have reason to mistrust a stronger ally: namely, when he wants your help in order to attack others without good cause. A prince, he states, 'must beware never to associate with someone more powerful than himself so as to offend others'. A party's ends should be taken into account when you consider whether or not to join them, apparently because their ends tell you quite a lot about their general modes of action, and thus about how they are likely to treat you. An ally who launches offensive wars—where *offendere* is close to injury, and thus to injustice—can't be trusted to respect your claims on him after victory. 'For when you win, you are left his prisoner': prudent princes 'should avoid as much as they can being at the discretion of others'.

Self-interest, again, coincides with the prudence of avoiding offence to others, and hence with justice. Unfortunately, previous commitments or some other necessity may force you to fight an offensive war with an ally. When this cannot be avoided, you should join 'for the reasons given above' against neutrality, while bearing in mind Machiavelli's latest warnings about trusting allies who offend others.

These warnings remind princes that whether in internal or external affairs, politics is the art of choosing among imperfect options. Even the strongest princes and states have to deal with 'inconveniences' posed by the existence of other people and states with their diverse desires, humours, and ambitions. Because of these constant challenges, 'nor should any state believe that it can always adopt safe courses [*partiti sicuri*]; on the contrary, it should think it has to take them all as doubtful [*dubi*]'. Leaders must be prepared to take risks no matter which side they choose in wars.

Yet this does not mean that they should be as indifferent to risks as Spain's short-sighted King Ferdinand. They can be prepared for risks, yet pick their risks carefully after examining all options. 'For in the order of things [*nell' ordine delle cosa*]', Machiavelli writes, 'it is found that one never seeks to avoid one inconvenience without running into another'; but 'prudence consists in knowing how to recognize the qualities of inconveniences, and in picking the less bad as good'. On this view, even weak states can improve their security by picking the right inconveniences to grapple with, and dealing with them virtuously. By the same token, the powerful can shoot themselves in the foot by failing to pick prudently, often in the belief that their present strength makes them completely secure.

Several general precepts of prudence emerge from this discussion:

- It is more prudent to have committed allies than always to be on the winning side.
- Firm obligations are more important for safety than infinite flexibility.

- Most people recognize the value of decency (*onestà*) and good faith; if you show yourself worthy of trust, they will be less inclined to take advantage of you. Generally speaking, if not in every particular case, good faith and loyalty pay rich dividends.

- One's own reflective advantage tends to coincide with doing what others consider just, or at least not unjust or offensive. When you act prudently out of self-interest, you end up acting in ways that respect justice, even if you weren't motivated by a concern to respect others.

HOW PRINCES CAN INSPIRE THEIR CITIZENS AND GAIN ESTEEM

The chapter ends with a quaintly archaic-sounding mini-lecture, reminiscent of the moderating caveats in several other recent chapters. A prince should

> show himself [*mostrarsi*] a lover of the virtues, giving recognition to virtuous men, and he should honour those who are excellent in an art [*arte*]. Next, he should inspire his citizens [*cittadini*] to follow their pursuits quietly [*quietamente esercitare li esercizi loro*], in trade and in agriculture and in every other pursuit of men, so that one person does not fear to adorn his possessions for fear that they may be taken away from him, and another to open up a trade for fear of taxes. But he should prepare rewards for whoever wants to do these things, and for anyone who thinks up any way of expanding [*ampliare*] his city or his state.

The call to recognize virtue, honour excellence, reward what amplifies the public good, respect individuals' private property and choice of pursuits, and avoid arbitrary actions that intimidate citizens, sounds suspiciously like an old-fashioned concern for justice.[14] Leaving to each what is rightly his own is among the most primitive and uncontested definitions of justice; honouring virtues and rewarding good works are essential parts of distributive justice. In ancient literature, these most basic forms of justice are routinely violated by tyrants, who tend to seize others' property and reward undeserving, servile men while holding worthy, self-motivated, free-spirited men in suspicion. According to Aristotle, tyrants who voluntarily reverse these injustices—which in fact threaten their own safety—improve their own prospects of survival.[15]

What, for Machiavelli, is the point of taking these steps toward justice? Do they help a prince to improve his reputation by satisfying subjects without,

---

[14] Various forms of what is usually called justice were touched on in previous chapters: distributive (chap. 16), punitive (chap. 17), promissory (chap. 18). The present chapter has mentioned all these forms of justice: punitive early on, when discussing 'extraordinary' actions; promissory at length in the middle; distributive at the end.

[15] *AP* V.ix.10–20.

however, granting them too much power? Or do princes who follow this archaic advice do much more than make themselves 'esteemed', satisfying subjects in such a way that they retain—or recover—some of the powers appropriate for citizens?

The same ambiguity is found in an ancient text that Machiavelli seems directly to paraphrase here. In Xenophon's dialogue *Hiero*, the poet Simonides outlines various measures that would help the tyrant to relieve his anxieties about untrustworthy subjects. He will win gratitude and esteem by 'teaching the people what things are best, and dispensing praise and honour' to those who merit it. By rewarding citizens from all walks of life, Hiero will improve his standing with the populace while strengthening the state. He should therefore reward farmers and villagers for improving cultivation, and merchants whose diligence in business attracts others to commercial activities that enrich the tyrant's realms and attest to his power. Indeed, 'once it became clear in every field of activity that any good suggestion will not go unrewarded, many will be encouraged to activities that look to the good'.[16]

Like Machiavelli with his prince, Simonides urges these measures only for the sake of the tyrant's own interests, saying nothing about justice. Up to the end of the dialogue, the poet-adviser's only openly stated concerns are the tyrant's personal pleasure, reputation, and safety. Tyrants are prickly, self-centred types, unlikely to be moved by appeals to the interests of others, and liable to be angered by direct criticisms. But if the tyrant adopts policies that relieve subjects' fears of rapacity, arbitrary taxation, and interference with their private labours, indeed rewarding the latter, he will simultaneously serve their best interests and his own. A tyrant who adopts all the apparently modest reforms Simonides suggests can escape his vexations while still satisfying his desire for glory—if not his appetite for unlimited power. By apparently echoing 'the treatise Xenophon makes *Of Tyranny*', as Machiavelli described the *Hiero* in the *Discourses*, he may have been hinting that his *Prince* had similar moderating aims.[17]

But perhaps Simonides' aims—and Machiavelli's—are more far-reaching than they appear. By luring Hiero to face up to the great difficulties he must endure as tyrant, Simonides prepares the ground for a bloodless revolution-from-above. His strategy is subtle. On the surface, at least, he questions the tyrant's methods, not his ends. But the proposed reforms aim to relieve Hiero's burdens by redefining his personal advantage in the light of a key fact: namely, that a tyrant's own security, happiness, and glory depend on his subjects' well-being. In seeking his own true security and power instead of chasing an illusion of self-sufficiency, Hiero will inadvertently benefit his subjects as well, by establishing a well-ordered polity—one that respects *their* desires for security, freedom in their productive labours, and transparent judicial authority.

---

[16] *XH* ix.2–11.   [17] *D* II.2.

Simonides' most important advice, like Machiavelli's in the *Prince*, concerns a tyrant's defences. If Hiero wants to become less hated and more secure, he should stop depending so much on the mercenaries who serve as his personal bodyguard. So long as he mistrusts his subjects, he's obliged to keep them disarmed and has to rely on foreigners to defend him and fight his wars. But if he starts to treat subjects as trusted friends, his own people might come to play a greater part in defending their ruler and his territories, making him safer at home and from foreign attacks. Simonides couches this rather radical proposal for a civilian-militia element in a tyrant's defences in deceptively modest terms. At first he says merely that if Hiero's mercenaries were used to defend the wider community as well as the tyrant personally, citizens would feel less cut off from the ruler. Then, without announcing the quiet shift, Simonides moves from discussing mercenaries as chief protectors of both tyrant and subjects to treating them as mere supplements to a *predominantly* citizen force, now describing a standing force of citizens as the tyrant's own best defence. For 'which will make you appear more terrible to the enemy', he asks, 'to dazzle all beholders with your own glittering armies, or to present the whole of your people [*tês poleôs holês*] in their own goodly armour?'[18]

In form and content, Simonides' argument that the tyrant should trust his own citizens with military arms clearly chimes with the *Prince*'s similar arguments. Further, the quiet shift in Machiavelli's passage and elsewhere from subjects (*sudditi*) to citizens (*cittadini*) seems a clear borrowing from Xenophon's Simonides. Up to the last pages, both poet and tyrant speak only of the latter's 'subjects' (*archomenoi*). But at the end, especially when advising Hiero to share his defences with others in the community, Simonides begins to refer to these others as 'citizens' (*politois*) or 'allies' (*summachoi*). Both terms are more suited to people who are treated in the respectful ways he now says Hiero should treat them, and who because of his changes in policy have become friends and comrades who now 'fight for your good [*sois agathois*] as if it were their own'.[19] In the *Prince* too, Machiavelli's shifts from speaking of subjects to citizens signal that a prince who seeks strong foundations should consider adopting modes of government that treat people more like free and active participants in a well-ordered *vivere civile* than subjects of a prince's will.

The chapter's last lines at first sound more like old-fashioned, top-down methods of princely control. 'And because every city is divided into guilds [*arte*] or into clans [*tribi*]', it concludes, the prince 'should take account of those communities [*università*], meet with them sometimes, and make himself an example of humanity and munificence', while 'always holding firm [*ferma*] the majesty of his dignity nonetheless.' On a conservative reading, this simply says that the prince should sometimes deign to come down to the level of the

---

[18] *XH* xi.3.   [19] *XH* xi.12–14.

people, as suggested in the *Prince*'s Dedication, discussing their concerns while never letting them forget his superior rank.

A more subversive reading is suggested if we compare these lines with a very similar one from Xenophon's *Hiero*. 'All cities (*poleis*)', Simonides tells the tyrant, 'are divided into tribes (*phulas*), wards, or other parts, each with its own ruler (*archontes*)'; and it is in the tyrant's best interest to recognize these distinct entities and encourage fruitful competition between them.[20] The key point in both texts is the same: namely, that every well-ordered city has separate parts that are best left intact, not eliminated or subjected to a tyrant or prince's dominating will. There are good and harmful divisions in cities and these are among the good ones, since unlike partisan divisions, they arise from good orders and are regulated by them in ways that benefit the whole city. More subtly than Simonides, Machiavelli hints at the wisdom of decentralized orders that leave considerable freedom to a city's distinct parts. While these communities may consult the prince on certain matters and look to him as an example of 'humanity and munificence', they also have clear corporate identities and powers of their own that set limits on the prince's power.

A prince who respects these limits will resemble French kings whose powers were constrained by the *parlements* more than less-accountable monarchs like Spain's Ferdinand—who, as Machiavelli told us early in the chapter, used the distractions of war to gain 'reputation and empire [*imperio*]' over the barons of Castile 'which they did not perceive'. In the former case, a prince's majesty and dignity stem from his exemplary qualities and more limited role as arbiter in the disputes among a city's parts, not from his superior power *per se*. It is noteworthy that in the *Discourses* Machiavelli considers *maestà* in this sense, and even a certain regal power, or *potesta regia*, as valuable elements of any well-ordered government, including republics.[21] Indeed, in parallel with the paragraph's avoidance of the word 'subjects' in favour of 'citizens' and 'people', it ceases to refer to the prince as 'prince' after the first sentence, simply saying 'he'. This might be a more limited kind of princely office than control-seeking monarchs might desire. But if they willingly scale back their ambitions and cede more power to their people, they will gain a far firmer kind of esteem than those who pursue excessive control through *astuzia* or violence.

---

[20] *XH* ix.5–6.   [21] *D* I.2.7, I.18.5.

22

Trustworthy ministers

Of those whom princes have as secretaries

HOW TO JUDGE A PRINCE'S BRAIN

After numerous chapters that brought princes down to the lowly perspective of the people, this one seems to return to a somewhat loftier one. It concerns the prince's relations with those who help him govern: his ministers. The choice of ministers *(la elezione de' ministri)*, Machiavelli writes, speaks volumes about the one who chose them. Indeed, 'the first conjecture that is to be made of the brain [*cervello*] of a lord is to see the men he has around him'. When 'they are capable and faithful [*sufficiente e fedeli*]' he will always get a reputation for wisdom, since it seems that he has been wise enough to recognize capable men and 'maintain them as faithful'. If a prince's ministers lack these two essential qualities, capability and fidelity, one can 'always' judge him unfavourably, 'because the first error he makes, he makes in this choice'.

Note that the dominant perspective of this discussion is not that of a prince picking out those to serve him, but that of non-princes who are invited to judge a prince's brain by his choices. Never before in the *Prince* has Machiavelli set up such a clear standpoint from which non-princes can evaluate the prudence of princes. Fortunately for the latter, he offers no examples of their bad choices, but only one of a well-chosen minister. 'There was none who knew Messer Antonio da Venafro as minister of Pandolfo Petrucci, prince of Siena', Machiavelli declares, 'who did not judge Pandolfo to be a most worthy [*valentissimo*] man, since he had Antonio as his minister.'[1]

It's unclear whether this judgement of Pandolfo was altogether sound. After all, it is really Messer Antonio who was known to be most worthy, whereas

---

[1] Petrucci was a rather brutal 'prince' who died in 1512; Machiavelli calls him 'tyrant' in *D* III.6. Machiavelli knew Antonio Venafro in his diplomatic years, perhaps as a friend.

whatever might be 'known' about the true qualities of his master is left out here.[2] This raises the question: can the prudence shown in a prince's choice of ministers ever be of the highest *virtuoso* quality, or does even the best choice show only a lesser kind of prudence? If one's 'first conjecture' about princes like Pandolfo is based on the prudence of his ministers, further distinctions bring him down a peg, suggesting that he may not deserve to be considered 'most' worthy. For

> since there are three kinds of brains [*tre generazione cervelli*], one that under-
> stands [*intende*] by itself, another that discerns what others understand, the third
> that understands neither by itself nor through others; the first is most excellent,
> the second excellent, and the third useless—it follows, therefore, of necessity that
> if Pandolfo was not in the first rank, he was in the second.[3]

Princes who acquire a reputation for great wisdom based only on their choice of ministers, then, may not fully deserve it. While some of them may also 'understand by themselves', others—probably most of them, like most men in general—only discern 'what others understand'.

But if we can't, after all, conclude that a prince himself is most worthy merely because he has most worthy ministers, we can draw inferences about his 'brain' by scrutinizing his more specific judgements. Machiavelli now suggests that anyone who has to rely on others to administer policies needs to be a good judge of the quality of *actions*, as much as of the quality, of men. 'For every time that someone has the judgement to recognize [*iudizio di conoscere*] the good or the evil that someone does or says', this kind of judgement is sufficient for keeping ministers in line. If a prince knows 'the good deeds and the bad of his minister and exalts [*esalta*] the one and corrects [*corregge*] the other', and otherwise leaves him to 'invent' various actions, 'the minister cannot hope to deceive him and remain good himself'. These valuable capacities—knowledge of how to distinguish good from bad actions, and the ability to apply it as a check on ministers—may, Machiavelli implies, be found in brains of the second rank as well as in first-rate ones. But a prince who exercises them plays a far more active role in shaping policies than one who, taking his minister's good personal qualities for granted, seldom scrutinizes the quality of his actions.

Machiavelli's reflections thus suggest that there are more and less prudent sorts of second-ranking brain. The inferior one 'discerns what others understand' in the sense that it 'hearkens to the wise' and willingly does what wiser authorities

---

[2] Machiavelli slyly suggests a comparison between Pandolfo and Borgia by calling the former *valentissimo*, recalling the popular nickname Duke Valentino. Both, Machiavelli implies, relied on second-hand prudence.

[3] The quote about three kinds of brain comes from Livy, *LH* XXII.29 (the same number book as the present chap. 22). An earlier source is Aristotle *ANE* I.iv.7–8, quoting the poet Hesiod's *Works and Days*, lines 293–7.

propose. Better-quality leaders recognize good and bad for themselves, and take responsibility for checking bad actions and 'exalting' the good, instead of assuming that good ministers will always act well. Those who rely heavily on the wisdom of others lean toward the 'modes' of fortune, leaving too much discretion to ministers and trusting too little in their own *virtuoso* judgement. The others trust their own judgement enough to oversee ministers' actions, since they are performed on the authority of the prince; but they also trust first-rate ministers to 'invent' policies within these constraints.

HOW TO TEST MINISTERS

So far, Machiavelli has discussed two distinct modes in which a prince or any other leader should deal with his ministers. The first seemed prudent enough, but on closer scrutiny turned out to be deficient because it entrusted too much to ministers. The second was better because it trusted ministers to devise policies and strategies, but upheld the prince's authority to limit the bad in these and reward the good.

Turning now to the question of 'how a prince can know his minister', Machiavelli gives us a third, very different perspective on the theme of trust. Whereas the second advised princes to judge ministers' actions according to their *general* goodness and badness, this one treats the prince's *private* advantage as the sole basis for judgement. 'When you see a minister thinking more of himself than of you, and in all actions looking for something useful to himself', we now read, 'one so made will never be a good minister.' So far, fair enough: a purely self-serving minister can't be trusted. But the reasons that follow are more questionable. 'Never [*mai*] will you be able to trust [*fidare*] him', Machiavelli declares, 'because he who has someone's state [*lo stato di uno*, lit. 'the state of one'] in his hands should never think of himself but always of the prince.' What's more, 'he should never remember anything that does not pertain to the prince'. This, we are told, is 'a mode that never fails'.

That is a suspiciously large number of 'nevers' in one sentence. Together with the exaggerated 'always' (*sempre*) in the claim that a minister should 'never think of himself but always of the prince', the wording creates a strong impression of unrealistic expectations about what a prince can control. Here he expects somehow to read the very *thoughts* of his ministers, and to monitor what they *remember* as well as their actions. He confidently asserts that this is a foolproof mode for judging who can be trusted. This control-hungry speaker needs to be reminded of the last chapter's argument that when you need others' help, you have to live with certain inconveniences—including the inconvenient fact that others have their own thoughts and purposes. There *is* no completely foolproof way to test a minister's trustworthiness, or anyone else's. The desire to find one smacks of a tyrant's megalomania and paranoia.[4]

The chapter's discussion is structured not as a univocal argument, then, but as a discourse that canvasses three different modes of dealing with ministers. The first (I) placed too much trust in ministers' judgement and too little in the prince's. The third (III) trusts ministers too little, seeking excessive control over their thoughts as well as their actions. The second (II) mode seems the most prudent: it shows a realistic awareness that even the best ministers may err, and makes the prince responsible for keeping their actions on a good path, yet doesn't try to get inside their very heads.

How, then, should the prince 'think of the minister so as to keep him good'? Machiavelli seems to raise this issue only as a counterpart of the third mode. But whereas its aspiration to know and control the thoughts of ministers was a hallmark of tyranny, the measures now proposed echo Xenophon/Simonides' and Aristotle's advice on how tyrants can make themselves less hated—and perhaps less tyrannical. Princes can keep a minister good by 'honouring him, making him rich, obligating him to himself' and 'sharing [*participandogli*] honours and burdens with him'. This list of measures might sound trite, but it dovetails with the *Prince*'s recurring argument that the best way to ensure that anyone is trustworthy—whether one's ministers, subject/citizens, or allies—is to benefit them in ways that 'obligate' them to you. A prince who fails to do this finds himself depending more on these 'others' than they depend on him. By adequately benefiting them, he makes their dependence mutual; a well-treated minister 'sees that he cannot stand without the prince'.

Of course, by sharing honours and burdens with other top-flight men who help him govern, the prince must give up any aspirations to be the *only* great man in his state. He must be confident enough to share that honour with others, and not mind that his own powers are scaled back when he shares the burdens of government.

Machiavelli sells this self-limiting mode to princes by arguing that it helps them to contain the ambitions of ministers. By lavishing 'so many honours' and so much wealth on the latter, they will not desire more, while the burdens of responsibility they have in the state will make ministers 'fear changes [*mutazioni*]'—that is, disorderly upheavals or conspiracies. Nevertheless, the same measures that curb the excessive ambitions of ministers also curb those of princes. The salutary effect of this reciprocal limiting is to increase trust between the different parts of a government. For when 'ministers and princes in relation to ministers are so constituted, they can trust [*confidare*] one another; when it is otherwise', however, 'the end [*fine*] is always damaging either for one or the other'.

---

[4] As depicted in *XH* and *AP* V.ix.1–9.

It is in the prince's best interests, then, to share authority to make and implement key policies, as well as to give his people their share in defending the state. When these powers are shared instead of being controlled by one man, each part of the government keeps the others within its limits, to the advantage of the whole. Princes who recognize these implications might also start to draw more self-critical conclusions. With Machiavelli's help—but not taking this on his authority, since he never spells it out—they might discern the disadvantages of *any* government based on the supremacy of one, whether that one is called prince or lord or king or tyrant. On the other hand, there are great advantages in governments that give the people their share of authority, and another share to the few whose first-rate brains qualify them to serve as ministers, and a further share to a 'prince' who oversees, consults, and rewards but does not invent or control everything in the state. Machiavelli's *Discourses* recommend this well-mixed form of government as 'firmer and stabler' (*più fermo e più stabile*) than any other. If the *Prince* never examines its merits directly, it offers plenty of arguments that speak indirectly in its favour.

23

Why princes need the truth

In what mode flatterers are to be avoided

HOW TO SEEK THE TRUTH WITHOUT BECOMING CONTEMPTIBLE

A particularly insidious threat to princes arises from a common 'error': that of falling prey to the flatterers who infest princely courts. Machiavelli calls flattery a plague (*peste*), a fast-spreading and lethal disease that princes avoid 'with difficulty, if they are not very prudent or do not choose well'.

What makes flattery so harmful? By giving princes an inflated sense of their own qualities and powers, it encourages them to take risks or pursue ambitions that far exceed their capacities.[1] Most men are vulnerable to flattery, for men generally 'take such pleasure in their own affairs and so deceive themselves there that they defend themselves with difficulty against this plague'. New princes, however, are more susceptible than most. Even before flatterers get to work on them, they tend to be exceptionally ambitious men with an exaggerated sense of their own worth. Such men are easy targets for sycophants who—whether for their own advantage or out of malice toward the powerful—like to puff great men up in order to watch them come crashing down.

From the outset, Machiavelli seems pessimistic about any prince's chances of warding off flattery. It's bad enough that the psychology of new princes, and the upbringing of some hereditary ones, make them believe that they are stronger, wiser, and more deserving of glory than others. To make matters

---

[1] Ancient writers often discuss problems of free speech and criticism of the powerful under the more innocent heading of 'flattery'; for example, see Plutarch, 'Flatterer'. Aristotle describes the flatterer as a sham admirer or friend in *AR* XI.18: friends tell one the truth, while flatterers deceive. Elsewhere he associates flattery with tyranny, writing that anyone who speaks the truth to a tyrant 'meets his pride with pride and shows a free spirit', and thereby 'robs tyranny of its superiority and position of mastery.' *AP* IV.iv.5, V.ix.6–7.

worse, the only measures that princes can take against flattery carry risks of their own. For 'in trying to defend oneself from it, one risks the danger of becoming contemptible'. On the one hand, (I) 'there is no other way to guard oneself from flattery unless men understand that they do not offend you in telling you the truth [*il vero*]'. To avoid fatal errors of judgement, a prince needs others to tell him the truth, even when it is displeasing; truth is necessary for good defences. To stay safe, a prince must not object to being criticized, corrected, warned about his shortcomings or unreasonable desires, or restrained if he tries to achieve what is beyond his powers. A prince who can't stomach such harsh truths will be in trouble—and people will not tell him the truth as they see it if they are afraid of offending him. Yet if he seeks the fullest possible truth about himself and his state, he risks becoming contemptible, since (II) 'when everyone can tell you the truth' about your own limitations, 'they lack reverence [*reverenza*] for you'.

This puts princes in a terrible bind. They must risk either falling for flattery by going with (II), or becoming despised by using the only means (I) that can ward it off. To express the dilemma in more general terms, both truth and reverence are, it seems, important for a prince's defence. But the conditions needed to get the fullest possible truth—an environment where no one fears that in telling the truth as he sees it, he will offend the prince—are incompatible with the conditions for reverence. According to the view hinted at in (II) and elaborated in what follows, conditions for reverence are found where the prince has tight control over the process of truth-acquisition. Is there a way, then, to get as much truth as a prince needs to avoid self-deception, and at the same time to demonstrate that he is in full control of the truth-telling process?

Luckily for princes, Machiavelli offers them an alternative 'mode' (III) that aims to avoid the inconveniences of the first two. 'A prudent prince must hold to a third mode', in which procedures for acquiring truth are subject to three conditions. Firstly, the prince must choose 'wise men in his state'. Secondly, 'only to these should he give freedom to speak the truth to him', and thirdly, they should speak 'of those things only that he asks about and nothing else'. This third mode strikes a compromise between Modes I and II by seeking a more limited kind of truth, thereby keeping the process of truth-telling under the prince's rigorous control. Mode III says: choose wise men, but control what they can say; give them freedom to speak the truth, but only in answering your questions.

This looks like a clever solution that satisfies the prince's need for the truth *and* his desire for reverence, since he holds tight control over those who hear the truth and how and when. If some readers have misgivings, wondering whether the truth obtained in this highly constrained mode is sufficient for good defences, the ensuing remarks might appease them. Having said that advisers should speak 'of nothing else' than what the prince asks, Machiavelli now says that 'he should ask them about everything and listen to their opinions', and only then 'decide by himself, in his own mode'. Moreover, 'with these councils [*consigli*] and with each member of them he should behave in such a mode that everyone knows that the more freely [*liberamente*] he speaks, the more he will be accepted'. So it seems that there might be room for a reasonably open exchange of views that might benefit the prince. But then there are other constraints: apart from these chosen counsellors, the prince 'should not want to hear anyone', and 'he should move directly to the thing that was decided and be obstinate in his deliberations [*deliberazioni*]'.

The guidelines for managing Mode III get even more complicated two paragraphs on, where Machiavelli re-describes its mix of freedom/truth and control/reverence from a slightly different angle. On the side of control, a prince 'should always take counsel, but when he wants, and not when others want it; on the contrary, he should discourage everyone from counselling him about anything unless he asks it of them'. On the side of freedom/truth, 'he should be a very broad questioner [*largo domandatore*], and then, in regard to the things he asked about, a patient listener to the truth'. Indeed, 'he should become upset when he learns that anyone has any hesitation to speak it to him'.

All these elaborate guidelines, delivered in an unusually stern prescriptive tone for the *Prince*, place quite a burden on princes to get the balance between freedom/truth and control/reverence just right. A prince who finds it easy to follow Machiavelli's requirements, let alone to implement them, must be very prudent indeed. He must be able to choose a handful of advisers who are independent enough to tell him the truth without fear, yet restrained enough to answer only what he asks and say no more. He must have the judgement to ask good questions of them, so that they tell him all he *needs* to know without saying anything he doesn't *want* to know. He must have enough patience and respect to listen to advisers, and enough independence and strength of mind to make key decisions on his own and stick 'obstinately' to them.

THE TROUBLE WITH THIRD MODES

Princes who trust themselves to strike this balance will conclude that they can have it both ways: they can get all the truth they need while still controlling who, how, and when it gets conveyed. Others might still have misgivings. Is it realistic to expect princes to pull off such a difficult balancing act, and to extract all the truth they need in the process? It's disconcerting that Machiavelli, who is usually so partial to simple 'modes' based on bottom-line truths, gives us one in Mode I—saying there that 'there is no other way'—then proceeds to recommend a convoluted, repetitive set of guidelines in Mode III. If we stop to think about how these guidelines might be implemented in practice, moreover, it becomes doubtful that he can seriously be recommending them.

From the perspective of the lucky advisers chosen to operate in Mode III, the mix of high demands and tight constraints it imposes on their truth-telling looks like a veritable minefield. On the one hand, a prince expects them to speak freely and without 'hesitation' (*respetto*), on pain of making him 'upset' (*turbarsene*)—a strong word, implying disturbance and disquiet—with them. On the other, they are to speak *only* when the prince asks and to tell him no more, no less than what he wants to know. On the one hand, freedom of speech for the chosen few, who should feel very free indeed; on the other, constant fear of saying too much or too little or the wrong things, lest the prince become upset. This hardly sounds like a promising strategy for extracting useful truths. If advisers speaking under these conditions 'hesitate' to tell the whole truth as they see it, who could blame them?

From the prince's perspective, Mode III's guidelines are both excruciatingly hard to apply and unlikely to extract the less convenient truths needed to protect the state. Imprudent princes may not recognize either problem. When Machiavelli says 'men take such pleasure in their own affairs and so deceive themselves' that they fall into unseen dangers, he of course has princes in mind above other men. More prudent princes, by contrast, know that they are prone to error. They know that an inflated view of one's own capabilities and virtues can encourage dangerous miscalculations and overreaching, leaving princes underprepared and poorly defended. Whatever helps a prince to avoid such self-deceptions should have a very high value for him. The truth is what does this. A prudent prince will thus want to be told the truth not only how and when it pleases him, but even when it is painful to hear, or when it comes at inconvenient times from unchosen sources.

Machiavelli's apparent preference for Mode III looks ever more unlikely when we consider his generally critical views on attempts to combine opposing modes. Recall that Mode I aims at truth, and requires extensive freedom of expression to get it; Mode II aims at reverence, and calls for extensive constraints on that freedom imposed by the prince as he sees fit. There may be some way to combine the ends of truth and reverence, but the means proposed here seem contradictory: you cannot have *both* extensive freedom of expression *and* extensive constraints on expression imposed by one man's personal judgement. Yet that is what Machiavelli's 'third mode' demands. It has all the hallmarks of what the *Discourses* call an unsustainable 'middle way', a *via del mezzo*. Machiavelli's middle ways try to combine two fundamentally opposed modes or courses of action: reliance on fortune and *virtú*, firmness with variation, caution with audacity, moderation and respect with total control. The results are always unstable, and eventually fall to the less virtuous side.[2]

---

[2] See *D* I.6.23, I.26.62. Machiavelli reserves his praise for Roman modes for cases where these 'fled from the middle way and turned to extremes'.

Machiavelli's third mode of avoiding flattery tries to satisfy both the need any stable order has for truth, and the prince's desire for a kind of reverence that makes it hard to satisfy that need.[3] In the end the prince's desires dominate the truth-seeking process, reducing the truth to whatever the prince is willing to hear.

If a prince's security lies in getting as full and timely an account of the truth as possible, then surely a prudent prince will value truth more than the kind of reverence that requires him to control so many facets of truth-acquisition. He would do well, some might think, to shed his fear that inconvenient truths and frank criticisms must undermine his authority. By allowing the desire for reverence to limit a prince's access to useful truths, Mode III lets the plague of flattery in through the back door while claiming to guard against it.

THE PRUDENCE OF THE PRINCE ALONE

As an example of imprudent flattery management, Machiavelli cites the German emperor Maximilian. His 'man' Father Luca—speaking, it seems, without much reverence for his master—'told how he did not take counsel from anyone', and yet 'never did anything in his own mode'. Clearly, taking no one's advice leads not to virtuous independence, but to hapless dependence on fortune. 'For the emperor is a secretive man who does not communicate his plans to anyone, nor seek their views'; but once he puts them into action, others discover his plans and begin to contradict them. At this point, being 'a facile [*facile*] person'—code for variable and fortune-dependent—Maximilian is easily 'dissuaded' from his course. 'From this it arises', Machiavelli declares, 'that the things he does on one day he destroys on another, that no one ever understands what he wants or plans to do, and that one cannot found oneself on his decisions'. Such conduct exemplifies the type of prince criticized in the previous paragraph: one who 'changes often because of the variability of views [*variazione de' pareri*], from which a low estimation of him arises'.[4]

Maximilian makes two errors. When making plans—the time when a prince most needs others' counsel—he consults no one. Once they are in motion, when it is too late to change without high costs, he listens too much. The example shows why it's important for princes to consult good advisers early

---

[3] The whole chapter's awkward repetitions, tangled reasoning, and nervous back-tracking hilariously mimic the control-hungry prince's attempts to justify his unreasonable desire for control when he knows, at some level, that it will stifle the useful truth.

[4] An example of 'variation' producing contempt; recall chap. 19.

on and not wait until after their private decisions are being implemented. It shows nothing about the need to combine truth/freedom with reverence/ control. If anything, it underscores the importance of having free exchanges of views at an early stage, and thus the dangers of unreasonable concerns about control.

Then, mimicking what tends to happen with 'third ways', the chapter veers sharply toward extreme controlling mode. It is wrong, we now hear, to think that anything but the prince's nature is responsible for prudent policies in his state. For there is 'a general rule that never fails', recalling the last chapter's similarly suspicious—and fallible—'mode that never fails' in getting to know what goes on in ministers' minds. This is that a prince 'who is not wise by himself' will not be 'counselled well unless indeed by chance he should submit himself to one alone to govern him in anything, who is a very prudent man'. We might conclude that princes should search high and low for such a *uomo prudentissimo*. Instead this option is immediately rejected, 'because that governor would in a short time take away his state'.

This would seem to speak in favour of having more than one adviser. But this option is flawed too, since 'by taking counsel from more than one, a prince who is not wise by himself will never have united counsel, nor know by himself how to unite them'. His counsellors will think too much of their own interests, while the not-wise prince 'will not know how to correct them or understand them'.

Any advisers, then, are problematic for any prince who is not already 'wise by himself'. A single prudent one will take away his state; several counsellors produce disunity. A 'wise' (*savi*) prince, of course, will be better equipped to deal with these challenges, since he will not need a single supremely prudent counsellor and will know how to 'unite' the advice of several. But if he is 'wise by himself', it's not clear why he needs advisers. Surely his sufficient wisdom means that their role may be reduced, if not eliminated altogether. 'So one concludes', we read at the chapter's end, 'that good counsel, from wherever it comes, must arise from the prudence of the prince, and not the prudence of the prince from good counsel.'

The question, then, is whether *any* prince is so prudent about all the important matters of state, so knowledgeable about internal and external affairs, so immune to deception and flattery, that he can 'be wise by himself' and require only limited counsel as per Mode III. Can any really prudent prince trust himself to have this kind of wisdom? And if someone does trust himself this much, does he deserve to be trusted by others? The truly wise know their limitations. They know that deciding how to govern and defend a state is a vast and difficult task that no one man, however prudent, can accomplish alone. Princes who don't realize this flatter themselves about their own abilities, and stand in particularly urgent need of the hard truth.

TRUTH BEFORE REVERENCE: THE FIRST
MODE REVISITED

This takes us back to Mode I's simple bottom line: 'there is *no other way* to guard oneself against flattery unless men understand that they do not offend you'. Perhaps, after all, the only guard against flattery is the truth, and the truth given without fear. Fearlessness and transparency might seem threatening to the prince who values others' reverence more than he values the truth. But perhaps he has his priorities wrong, since the fullest possible truth is a better guarantee of his security.

Are princely desires for reverence, or something like it, wholly misplaced? As usual in the *Prince*, the answer depends on what one means by 'reverence'. Machiavelli uses the word in different ways here and in other works. In its more positive sense it means respect for someone's superior authority, age, or wisdom, and is often associated with reasonable religious awe and morals. In its negative sense, *reverenza* is associated with inaccessible ideals, or with unreasonable or superstitious fear.[5] Respect for any leader's authority undoubtedly helps to uphold good orders. But Modes (II) and (III) wanted more: they identified reverence with the kind of deference that depends on a prince keeping tight control over many aspects of truth-seeking. The desire for this kind of reverence tends to impede the search for necessary truths about the prince and his state.

The wonderful irony is that in writing this chapter, and indeed the whole *Prince*, Machiavelli is brazenly violating all the rules he sets out under Mode III for ensuring that princes are treated with reverence in the second sense. In advising princes not to heed unsolicited advice, he offers precisely what he tells them to ignore. For no prince—certainly not his Medici addressees—had asked for Machiavelli's views on truth-telling or anything else. As we saw in chapter 21, after being released from prison in 1513, he sent numerous letters packed with foreign policy advice to his friend Vettori, who did his best to convey Machiavelli's unsolicited thoughts to the Medici pope. If Machiavelli really thought that princes should give freedom to speak the truth only to a few chosen men, he blithely ignored this precept. He did so more than ever in writing the *Prince*, and especially in this chapter, where pronouncements about what princes 'should' or 'must' do are rife. Machiavelli heightens the irony by adopting an uncharacteristically imperious tone when telling princes that they should only take counsel on their own terms. An incorrigible teller of the truth as he saw it, Machiavelli was most alert to both the advantages and the inconveniences of truth for men in power. The entire *Prince* is a masterpiece of dissimulated yet devastatingly honest truth-telling—the ultimate antidote to the flattery that drives princes to their ruin.

---

[5] For example, see *D* I.36.

Redemption

24

Stop blaming others

Why the princes of Italy have lost their states

THE *VIRTÚ* OF NEW PRINCES

Chapters 24–6 sum up the *Prince*'s main lessons and exhort princes to follow them. Chapter 24 gives a crisp explanation of why recent Italian princes have failed to hold their states. Firstly, their military orders were deficient: they had a 'common defect as to arms'. Secondly, they failed to ward off internal threats, either having the enmity of the people or not knowing 'how to secure themselves against the great'. If recent Italian princes had 'observed prudently' 'the things written above' in Machiavelli's book, they would have avoided these lethal shortcomings.

Yet a prince who wants to learn how to keep his state needs not just to read the *Prince*, but to read it prudently, shunning the allure of quick or easy options and promises of *grandezza*. He must decide which of the diverse, often contradictory 'things written above' will 'make a new prince appear ancient [*parere antico*] and immediately render him more secure and firm [*rendono subito più sicuro e più fermo*] in his state than if he had grown ancient in it'.

Some princes will be content with mere appearances of antiquity, and be attracted by the promise of 'immediate' results. Others will realize that though ancient, venerable, or great appearances can seize people's imaginations for a time, people only stick with you through thick and thin when they judge that your government deserves their support. 'For', Machiavelli writes, 'a new prince is observed much more in his actions than a hereditary one', and when his actions 'are recognized as virtuous [*conosciute virtuose*], they take hold [*pigliono*] of men much more and obligate them much more than ancient blood.' The idea here isn't just that a new prince has the chance to establish firmer control over his state than hereditary princes, who have to muddle through with customary orders they did not create. It confirms that the obligations that help make a state strong are produced by people's reasoned judgements about the quality of a leader's actions, never by deception or manipulation.

Since the *Prince*'s middle chapters, obligations have emerged as an essential component of any state's foundations. In chapters 10 and 12 Machiavelli told us that reciprocal obligations between the prince and his people are needed to constitute strong military arms. In chapter 21 he underlined the need for firm obligations between princes and their external allies. Now we find that the firmest obligations are founded on independent judgements about the quality of a prince's actions. It follows that the safety he derives from deserving—and continuing to deserve—their good judgement is far more lasting than the fleeting or false security generated by many of the other 'modes' of action discussed in the *Prince*.

So while at one level Machiavelli stresses the advantages of individual *virtú* over 'ancient blood', not just any kind of new prince will be more secure than any hereditary one. On the contrary, the whole *Prince* has stressed that new princes face special difficulties that can only be overcome with exceptional—though not 'extraordinary'—*virtú*. It may be true that 'men are much more taken [*piú presi*] by present things than by past ones' and will thus 'take up every defence on behalf of a new prince'. Yet they will only do this if 'they find good in the present', and if the prince 'is not lacking in other things as regards himself'.

Until now, the 'new' in 'new princes' simply described how their rule was acquired: either it was not hereditary, or it was acquired by gift or conquest over peoples outside one's native country. But Machiavelli's detailed advice has infused the words *principe nuovo* with a normatively charged new sense. From now on we can speak of two kinds of new prince: one whose newness consists merely in his mode of acquisition, the other who renews and improves the whole office of prince by following the *Prince*'s best advice. Machiavelli clearly has only the second in mind when he says that a new prince will win 'the double glory [*duplicate gloria*] of having made the beginning of a new principality', on the one hand, and of 'having adorned and consolidated [*ornatolo e corroboratolo*] it with good laws, good arms, good friends, and good examples', on the other. Like the poet Simonides in the *Hiero*, Machiavelli has taught his prince how to turn his principality into a form of government about as far from a top-down, controlling monarchy as it can get while still being called a *principato*.

A few readers might even doubt whether a prince who 'observes prudently' all the advice in the *Prince* will still be a prince in anything but official status. His powers will be limited, and widely shared with subjects or citizens—whatever one now wants to call them. This kind of new prince radically transforms the very idea of principality. His main accomplishment is not personal *grandezza* but good laws (*buone legge*) that make for good arms and good friends, and set good examples to other princes who follow his path.

MACEDONIANS, GREEKS, AND ITALIANS

Many princes, of course, will not have detected this message. Machiavelli's artful ambiguity has constantly tempted readers with two very different images of princely *virtú*. One is a dominating quality whose possessors seek to gain control by the fastest, most impressive-looking routes. Its most outstanding character-istic is 'spiritedness', or greatness of *animo*. The other is a more respectful quality whose possessors seek to found secure and lasting orders. This aim obliges them to recognize the limits of their personal power, and therefore willingly to share military and political power with subjects, citizens, or allies.

The present chapter's sole ancient example invites readers to consider what either kind of *virtuoso* prince might do if he faced the same plight as recent, *virtú*-deficient Italian princes. Like Italians in Machiavelli's day, Philip V of Macedon—not the father of the famous Alexander, 'but the one who was defeated by [the Roman] Titus Quintius'—found himself up against much greater foreign powers. He 'did not have much of a state' by comparison with 'the greatness of the Romans and of Greece, who attacked him', any more than the king of Naples or the duke of Milan, who had recently lost their states, had against Spain, France, or the Swiss. Nevertheless, Philip 'kept up a war against them for many years' because 'he was a military man and knew how to get along with [*intrattenere*] the people and secure himself against the great'.

This suggests that Philip avoided the two grave defects of Italian princes. Being 'a military man', he presumably had sufficient arms, though Machiavelli doesn't tell us how they were organized. And he managed internal opposition, both securing himself against the great and 'knowing how' to get on with the people, presumably avoiding their enmity. By exercising his military and people-managing skills, Philip emerged from all his wars against far stronger powers beaten but not crushed. For 'if at the end he lost dominion [*dominio*] over several cities, his kingdom [*regno*] nonetheless remained to him'.

Philip was not a 'new' prince in his means of acquiring principality, but one who inherited it. He is presented here as an example with special relevance for Italians 'who, having been born prince', lost their *stati* through their lack of prudence. But if Philip is a model of *virtú* for contemporary Italians, which kind of *virtú* does he exemplify, and how praiseworthy is it?

On a straight reading uninformed by ancient sources, the example seems to tell new Italian princes not to give up hope in their inevitable struggles against the greater powers encroaching on them. If they are military men like Philip and handle their own subjects well, they have a decent chance of clinging on to a chunk of power in their core territories and reigning there as monarchs. They may have to scale back their more grandiose imperial ambitions, but they will still be princes in Naples, Milan, or Florence.

More disturbingly, Machiavelli introduces Philip as 'the one who was defeated' by the Romans—not a very promising first glimpse of our hero.

The *Prince* does not, of course, measure success or *virtú* only by victories in war; as chapter 21 pointed out, those who lose some wars can always recover from defeat and win others, if they are virtuous. The test of *virtú* isn't how great an empire you have, or whether you win every war, but whether you *choose* to scale back your empire and military aims as Francesco Sforza did in chapter 7, recognizing the advantages of self-restraint—or are *forced* to do so by others.[1] Machiavelli's brief description of Philip says that he 'lost' his dominions involuntarily. If so, we may wonder whether these losses resulted from his lack of prudence rather than from bad luck. If recent princes of Naples and Milan 'may not accuse fortune' for losing their states altogether, then could Philip blame fortune for losing a great part of his?

Readers who consult Polybius and Livy, who described Philip's wars with Romans and Greeks, may reach one of two conclusions: either Machiavelli is seriously recommending the bad behaviour 'his' ancients describe at length, or his praise for Philip is ironic. Philip might have been a 'military man', but the *Prince* has described all sorts of military men, not all of them shimmering examples of *virtú*. According to Livy, some of Philip's key military preparations were downright slovenly. He describes the 'general slackness and negligence in the Macedonian army', which resembled more a 'disorderly rabble' than a proper military.[2] Machiavelli himself casts a critical light on Philip's military virtues in the *Discourses*, where he recounts an episode in which Philip misjudged his Roman adversaries' intentions and, wanting to avoid a battle, 'put himself with his army on the summit of a mountain . . . judging that the Romans would not dare to go to meet him'. When they did dare, he had to flee ignominiously with his troops.[3] If the *Prince* presents Philip as an example of princes who 'have enough nerve [*tanto nervo*] to put an army into the field', the *Discourses* expose the irony. Philip *did* put an army out there, and his state was 'not lost' altogether. But had he not tried recklessly to confront the much stronger Romans on his own, he might have lost even less.

Machiavelli's claim that Philip 'knew how to get along with' the people is positively comical when set alongside Livy's account, which describes Philip's use of crude populist ploys to get popular support against the great. Far from succeeding, the buffoonish king even manages to get these old tricks wrong. On one public occasion he removed his 'diadem and purple and other marks of royalty' to please the populace, then proceeded to sully this theatrical show of humility with his libidinous and criminal behaviour toward subjects' wives and children.[4] Readers of Machiavelli's original text may already have detected an ironic reference to this un-virtuous conduct. While *sapeva intrattenere il populo* tends to be translated as 'knew how to get on with' or 'deal with' the

---

[1] See chap. 19 and *D* II.27–8 on the dangers of men not knowing 'how to put limits to their hopes'.
[2] *LH* XXIV.40.   [3] *D* III.10.   [4] *LH* XXVII.31.

people, *intrattenere* more often means to entertain, divert, distract, or indulge in the way that popularity-seeking leaders do *en route* to tyranny.[5]

If Philip handled his army and people in this manner, violating Machiavelli's detailed advice on how to order armies and avoid popular hatred, how did he manage to hold his kingdom? On consulting ancient sources, the claim that he *did* hold it looks laughable. Philip lost much more than a few cities in his dominions. He kept his kingdom, for what it was worth, only on sufferance of Rome and its allies, who henceforth controlled most of Macedonian foreign policy. Despite his apparent praise, Machiavelli's subtle choice of words signals his own critical views of this quasi-subjection to foreigners. Philip did not 'maintain', or even hold, his rump kingdom by his own active efforts. His kingdom merely 'remained to him' (*rimase*), suggesting a passive, unwilled result.

Italians who noticed these ironies would perhaps come to see Philip less as a positive role model than as a cautionary example of errors to be avoided. According to Polybius and Livy, Philip's seminal failings included one discussed in the last two chapters of the *Prince*: the failure to choose good ministers and take good advice. The young prince had a promising start under the tutelage of good advisers such as Aratus, whose wisdom helped Philip to become a model of openness and good faith, adored by all the Greeks. But excessive ambition later got the better of him, making him lose allies at home and abroad, so that he was forced to defend Macedon in lonely isolation. His key error, according to Polybius, was his failure to keep faith with either allies or adversaries, rejecting Aratus' prudent advice that good faith is a polity's best defence.

These actions flagrantly violate the *Prince*'s teachings in chapter 21 about the need to show oneself a reliable ally, and in chapter 22 about heeding the counsel of the wise. Having set out on this path, Philip went quickly from bad to worse: becoming a cruel tyrant at home, transgressing the laws of war abroad, and betraying fellow Greeks who, like himself, were struggling to ward off threats from Rome and other foreign powers. His unscrupulous policies brought him little private joy, and destroyed any chance of cooperation among Greek states to prevent them all from falling under Roman dominion—as they soon would.

Machiavelli has already told us something about the sad fate of the Greeks in chapters 3–5. They fought back hard against Roman encroachments, but since they also fought each other, their efforts proved ineffectual. Philip's methods look like a fine example of the *wrong* way for weak states to deal with pressures from stronger powers—alienating potential allies through bad faith, thus being forced to fight alone for the hollow trappings of royalty. The root of Philip's errors, now replicated by Italian princes, was his insistence on fighting the Romans and other foreign powers on his own. Recklessly making enemies of

---

[5] Recall chap. 3, where Romans 'indulged' (*intrattenuti*) the Achaeans and Aetolians by making alliances against Philip's Macedonia—before taking advantage of their allies.

the rest of Greece, he squandered his youthful pan-Hellenic popularity instead of using it to build better common defences against non-Greeks.

The *Prince* has frequently suggested parallels between the disunited, fratricidal Greek cities that fell under Roman control in ancient times and the similar plight of contemporary Italian states. Together with the Syracusan Hiero, who struck up 'new friendships' with other Greeks, Machiavelli's better Greek models are the Achaeans who, led by Philopoemen, tried to unify formerly hostile Greek cities in a single defensive league. Philip obstinately resisted such cooperative projects, preferring his own reckless brand of unilateralism. When Machiavelli says that he 'did not have much of a state' compared with 'the greatness of the Romans and *of Greece*', he suggests that at this stage the Greeks, though divided and lacking the imperial *grandezza* of the Romans, still might have built a *stato* of sufficient greatness to avoid crushing conquest.[6] Mavericks like Macedonia—and Nabis' Sparta in the same period—made this impossible, and Philip's chastening by the Romans proved a first step toward the subjugation of all Greece.

In Machiavelli's times, fortune-hunting, go-it-alone states like Venice posed similar obstacles to Italian cooperation. If Italian princes in their separate states imitated Philip's actions, they stood a good chance of ending up as he did, with their 'kingdoms' reduced to puppet states under Spanish or French or imperial dominion. This indeed happened to Florence a few decades after Machiavelli wrote the *Prince*.[7]

PICK YOURSELF UP

Machiavelli's damning conclusions prepare the way for the next two chapters' central argument: namely, that Italians and no one else are responsible for their own losses and future redemption. Italian princes above all are to blame for losing their states. Machiavelli mentions 'the king of Naples, the duke of Milan, and others'.[8] 'These princes of ours', he proclaims with bitter contempt, especially those 'who have been in their principalities for many years, may not accuse fortune when they have lost them afterward, but their own indolence [*ignavia*].'

In concrete terms, those who 'accuse fortune' tend to blame the foreign powers who took their states from them, instead of asking what measures they themselves might have taken to avoid this outcome. Machiavelli has little time

---

[6] Polybius, Livy, and Plutarch are all intrigued by the question of how better Greek military and political cooperation might have averted Roman conquest.

[7] Florence fell under *de facto* papal and imperial control after a bitter civil war that broke out soon after Machiavelli's death. Republican forces were defeated in 1530, and the Medici were made hereditary dukes of the Habsburg Empire.

[8] Naples became part of the Spanish Empire after being taken from France in 1503. In 1500 Milan fell under French then Swiss control, and later came under the Spanish Empire in 1535.

for this kind of complaint. Blaming others for one's failures is typical of those who depend more on fortune than on their own *virtú*. They take the easy road to princely heights, confident that the faster and higher they go the safer they must be—then accuse fortune, foreigners, and everything but themselves when they fall. Alternative paths and different modes were always open to Italy's fallen princes, yet they did not take them. For Machiavelli, this is like saying that they *chose* to rely on the same fortune that they blame when things go badly.[9] 'For one should never fall', he declares:

> in the belief that you can find someone to pick you up [*ti ricolga*]. Whether it happens or not, it is not security for you, because that defence was base and did not depend on you. And those defences alone are good, are certain [*certe*], and are lasting [*durabili*], that depend on you yourself [*da te proprio*, or 'on your own'] and on your *virtú*.

The worst princes are those who expect 'that their peoples, disgusted by the insolence of the victors, would call them back', as if peoples are too dim to realize that their princes' 'indolence' would harm them again. Here Machiavelli touches a painful Florentine nerve. In 1494 Piero de' Medici, the father of the *Prince*'s dedicatee Lorenzo and brother of Pope Leo X, had done more or less what this passage describes. Lacking sufficient 'arms' of his own to confront the vast French army marching through Italy, Piero had opened Florence's gates to the French and ceded control over key cities in Florentine dominions to Charles VIII. This move so enraged Florentines that Piero was forced to 'flee' into exile. Piero and his family still hoped that the people, 'disgusted by the insolence' of the French, would call them back. Instead, many Florentines hailed the French incursion as a gift that liberated Florentines from a corrupt home-grown dynasty. Until they returned from exile in 1512, the Medici still hoped that someone else—the French, the papacy, or the Spanish who did eventually assist their return—would 'pick them up'. Having been restored to unofficial principality with the help of foreign arms, they promptly dissolved Florence's militia, in the belief that armed citizens posed an internal threat to their government. The 'new' Medici-led Florence now relied more than ever on mercenaries and foreign auxiliaries for its defence.

With his direct, informal 'you', Machiavelli seems to look his addressees in the eye and issue a challenge: have you younger Medici princes learned anything from the experience of your older relatives? Will you have enough *virtú* to restore Florentine defences that depend on yourselves and your own people? If so, they would have to build a truly new *principato*—and ultimately reform themselves out of their princely status.[10]

---

[9] He treats such petulant accusations ironically in the Dedication by blaming fortune for his own sorry plight, and when he blames fortune for Cesare Borgia's sudden fall in chap. 7.

[10] As recommended in the *Discursus*.

25

How to deal with fortune

How much fortune can do in human affairs, and in what mode it may be opposed

How much can any human being, whether prince or not, expect to do against the apparently arbitrary power of fortune? The *Prince* has addressed this question from various angles. Yet we still lack a single, straight answer, since the book has presented two contradictory perspectives on fortune's powers. On the one hand, Machiavelli urges readers never to put themselves into fortune's hands, but to rely solely on their own defences and *virtú*. On the other, he has sometimes told princes to let fortune take the lead, to 'change as the winds of fortune and variations of things command' (chapter 18). And he has proffered a recent example of fortune's power to destroy even princes who do, or seem to do, all they can to stand on their own: Cesare Borgia, who lost his *principato* through 'an extraordinary and extreme malignity of fortune' (chapter 7).

If readers hope that chapter 25 might now pull these conflicting strands together in a unified account of fortune's powers, they'll be disappointed. Machiavelli still presents bafflingly diverse perspectives on the power of fortune and 'modes' for dealing with it. The main ones may be called Building/Caution (I) and Variation/Impetuosity (II) modes. Building and varying are the main *means* used to 'oppose' fortune. Caution [*rispetto*, also meaning 'respect'] and impetuosity [*impetuosità*] are the chief *qualities* needed to operate each mode.[1]

The chapter does not explain their relationship. It simply confronts readers with a choice. If they see no deep logical or practical inconsistencies between the two modes, they may try to confront fortune's power by combining them: shifting modes as circumstances require, or building cautiously at first but resorting to impetuous 'variation' if precautions fail. If readers doubt that the two modes can fruitfully be combined, they may pick one as the more prudent way to manage fortune's destructive potential, and reject the other.

---

[1] As we'll see, Machiavelli does not say that varying calls for 'flexibility' as an operating quality, though this chapter is often read in this way.

IS ONE'S FORTUNE EVER DESERVED?

The *Prince* has treated fortune as a power that gives or takes desired goods regardless of a person's qualities or actions. It thus appears to be an amoral power, utterly indifferent to merit and hence to justice, since justice gives and takes according to merit. When someone receives benefits that he did not earn, we call this good fortune; when he suffers undeserved harm, we call it bad.

On the other hand, though Machiavelli often speaks of fortune in abstract terms, he also describes fortune's power in terms of concrete means of gaining or losing power that have little to do with merit. Demystified in this way, fortune may after all have some connection to desert. When someone gains by means of others' arms or weakness rather than his own forces, by bribes and favours instead of his own merits, we doubt that he deserved his good fortune. But when the same person loses those unearned goods, we consider his bad fortune deserved or just.

In the *Prince* so far, 'bad' fortune has usually befallen princes who, if their actions are scrutinized, didn't really deserve the power or reputation they later lost; they deserved their bad fortune in so far as they relied on unreliable gifts, bribes, favours, and weaknesses to gain power when better means were available. It thus makes little sense to say that they 'lost through fortune', since they really lost because of their own bad choices. By the same token, if someone suffers despite his good choices, we can reasonably see him as a victim of bad fortune. But if those choices help him to thrive, it makes little sense to attribute his thriving to good fortune rather than to his own prudence or *virtù*.

Machiavelli's attempts to define fortune's powers in concrete, rational terms therefore take issue with two one-sided accounts of those powers: fatalistic accounts that deny human agents any power to regulate fortune's vicissitudes, and all-controlling accounts that deny fortune any role in human affairs. The most reasonable view of fortune, Machiavelli suggests, leaves room for human agency—but also acknowledges its limits.

Some *virtù*-blind factors do influence human actions, however well considered. No one can calculate every consequence of his actions in advance, or foresee every obstacle that might impede them. To acknowledge the power of fortune in this sense is simply to recognize the 'natural and ordinary' limits of human control.

FORTUNE, GOD, AND OUR OWN RESPONSIBILITY

This balanced estimation of fortune's powers underpins Machiavelli's first mode of 'opposing' it. He famously compares fortune to an unreasoning, unfeeling natural force impervious to all human entreaties or manipulations. 'I liken her', he writes, to one of those ruinous rivers which, when they become enraged, flood the plains, ruin the trees and the buildings, lift the ground from this part, dropping it in another; everyone flees before them, everyone yields to their impetus [*all' impeto*] without being able to hinder them in any part.

Many who take this view of fortune 'have held and hold the opinion that the things of the world are governed [*governate*] in such a mode, by fortune and by God, that men cannot correct them with their prudence'.

Are fortune and God similar kinds of power? Yes and no. The powers of both God and fortune exceed human powers to control them completely, and move in ways that we cannot entirely grasp. But unlike fortune, God's power is just, used to distribute good and bad to those who deserve either. Sometimes Machiavelli suggests that God, as the far higher power, unleashes fortune's blind force so that it can wreak havoc with human beings whose badness or indolence deserves a good deluge.[2] When this happens, the original command to flood a corrupt city or province was God's, and therefore just. But along the way, fortune's ravages may harm people who don't personally deserve such a pounding—including individuals who did their best to restore *virtú* to their cities, but were over-powered by rampant corruption. Machiavelli often characterizes himself as such an individual in his post-1512 letters and poems, and in the Dedication of the *Prince*. If there is a touch of self-mocking irony in his bewailing 'the great and continuous malignity' of his fortunes, he could reasonably explain his fall from grace in terms of Florence's collective bad fortune—the result of its weak civil *virtú*—in failing to defend its republic against a princely coup.

Did Machiavelli therefore have reason to accuse fortune, or even God, for his plight? The larger question is whether it *ever* makes sense to blame fortune or God for one's woes, even if they aren't self-inflicted. It might make sense if we conceive of fortune or God as powers that take a direct interest in every human individual, expecting them to help us in weak moments and reward us for good conduct. But Machiavelli sees neither power in such personal terms. His *fortuna* is indifferent to merit and ruthless toward the weak. And while his God sometimes commands 'the heavens' (*il cieli*) or fortune to punish or warn, it is presumptuous to expect him to show concern for every individual's fate in the wider cosmos under his control.[3] While Machiavelli and other virtuous victims may well *attribute* their sufferings to fortune and perhaps to God, then, it would be almost as unreasonable for them to *blame* these powers as it is for the un-virtuous princes discussed in chapter 24.

The difference between attributing and blaming is crucial. Italian princes are wrong to blame fortune since their own lack of *virtú* was responsible for

---

[2] In his 'The Ass' (Asino) III.80–119, Machiavelli describes blind fortune as an element in a cosmos ruled by God through the 'heavens'. A similar cosmology can be seen in the *Discourses* and these last chapters of the *Prince*.

[3] See chap. 26.

opening the floodgates—but also because it makes no sense to blame a morally blind power that owes you nothing. Virtuous people who suffer as a result of their princes' or fellow citizens' failings may accuse them, but not fortune, for the same reason. Both virtuous and *virtú*-deficient victims of fortune can reasonably *attribute* their troubles to it. But the ultimate test of their *virtú* is whether, while recognizing that powers beyond their control have thwarted their hopes, they still take full responsibility for their responses to bad fortune. Do they bemoan their fate and wait for someone else to pick them up—or pick themselves up and do what they can to carry on their virtuous labours? Italian princes and Cesare Borgia did the former. In writing the *Prince*, Machiavelli tried to do the latter, devising virtuous orders through writing when he was prevented from building them in practice.

BUILDING/CAUTION MODE I: FREE WILL

But if fortune is so ruthless, perhaps even unleashed by God, what's the point of trying to resist it at all? Many hold the opinion, Machiavelli observes, that men 'have no remedy' against fortune's caprices. 'On account of this', he writes, 'they might judge that one need not sweat [*insudare*] much over things, but let oneself be governed by chance [*sorte*]', a word that evokes even more randomness than *fortuna*. Machiavelli confesses that he has sometimes been tempted by this kind of fatalism. When he has pondered the 'great variations [*variazione grande*] of things that have been seen and are seen every day', especially in his own turbulent times, 'I have been in some part inclined to their opinion'.

In the end, however, he has decided that while fortune may sometimes exhibit terrifying powers, human beings have powers of their own that can limit its worst effects. For 'it is not as if men, when times are quiet, could not provide' against fortune's floods 'with dykes and dams in such a mode that when they rise later, either they go by a canal or their impetus is neither so harmful nor so licentious [*dannoso/licenzioso*]'. Human beings cannot extinguish fortune's power over their affairs. But they can do a good deal to deflect its harms and contain its worst 'licentious'—that is, disordering—movements.

In other words, people always have a choice about how to respond to fortune's powers. They can hand more power to fortune than they need to—because they don't realize that they can manage its effects by their own intelligence and hard work, or because they hope to gain great power or other goods with fortune's help. Or they can seize the initiative and build their own fortune-governing orders. *Virtú* is the highest expression of this human power to choose even when facing great obstacles.

The power that makes *virtú* possible Machiavelli calls free will or free choice (*libero arbitrio*).[4] So while Machiavelli sympathizes with the 'many' who see the upheavals of his times as evidence of fortune's omnipotence,

> Nonetheless, so that our free will not be eliminated, I judge that it might be true that fortune is arbiter [*arbitria*] of half our actions, but also that she leaves the other half, or close to it, for us to govern.

Machiavelli doesn't say why he wants to avoid eliminating 'our free will', but two reasons can be inferred from what he says elsewhere. Firstly, if we human beings had no choice in how to respond to fortune, necessity, or other factors beyond our control, there would be little reason to praise or blame our actions. And as he says in chapter 26, Machiavelli is determined that we should be able to claim our share of glory as well as blame.

Secondly, fortune's powers are too random and obscure to be measured precisely. Since it is impossible to know exactly how much power fortune has over us, we may reasonably assume that there is *some* margin for the exercise of choice. As Machiavelli put it in the *Discourses*, men 'should never give up' their own small residue of power, even if they knew it was less than half of fortune's. 'For, since they do not know [fortune's] end and it proceeds by oblique and unknown ways, they have always to hope', and thus never abandon themselves to fatalism 'in whatever fortune and in whatever travail they may find themselves.'[5] However minuscule our powers of choice, it would be irresponsible—and un-virtuous—not to use them as well as we can.

So Machiavelli's first answer to the chapter title's question 'how much power does fortune have?' is that fortune can do a lot—but so can we. As for the other titular question, 'how to oppose it?', our free will gives us a choice of very different modes. One option, discussed at the end of the chapter, is ferociously confrontational: to meet fortune's impetus with equal violence, dominating or cajoling her into submission. Machiavelli's Mode I outlines a very different approach: it presupposes that fortune can be 'regulated' but never dominated completely.[6] On this view, it is as unreasonable to suppose that you can master the uncontrollable factors in life as to think that you are powerless to limit their bad effects. Human free will is not an unlimited power. In relation to fortune or necessity, it is only a power to respond more or less prudently to 'variations' or other pressures beyond our control.

To build effective dykes and dams calls for the most praiseworthy of the many admirable qualities people call *virtú*: industry, foresight, awareness of one's own limitations as well as of one's powers—and above all capacities to impose firm orders on natural or disordered conditions. The last quality is especially import-ant, since it distinguishes Mode (I) from other fortune-opposing strategies

---

[4] Literally free arbitration or choice. Machiavelli's usual word for 'will' is *volontà*.
[5] *D* II.29.
[6] *D* II.29 again: 'men can second fortune but not oppose it, weave its warp but not break it'.

discussed in the chapter. Fortune, Machiavelli points out, 'demonstrates her power where virtue has not been ordered [*ordinata*] to resist her [*a resisterle*], and therefore turns her impetus where she knows that dams and dykes have not been made to hold her'. The entire *Prince* has shown why Italy urgently needs builders who know how to do this kind of 'ordering'. It needs them far more than princes who show great energy, spirit, or ambition, but are clueless about how to make lasting orders. If, Machiavelli declares, 'you consider Italy, which is the seat of these variations' that have disordered recent times, 'you will see a country without dams and without any dyke. If it had been dyked by suitable *virtú*, like Germany, Spain, and France'—apparently referring here to these countries' having their own military 'arms'—'either this flood would not have brought the great variations that it has, or it would not have come here.'

VARIATION/IMPETUOSITY MODE II: VARY ONE'S MODES WITH THE TIMES

According to Mode I, then, fortune's power to hurt us depends on how well we use *our* powers to order and restrain it. Machiavelli has clearly identified this mode with *virtú* at its best, and described it as the mode needed to rescue Italy from imminent ruin. 'And I want this to be enough to have said', he writes, 'about opposing fortune in general.'

But this is not the end of Machiavelli's general discussion at all. As if imitating fortune itself, the discussion suddenly takes an unexpected turn, introducing a host of doubts about Mode I's sufficiency. Now 'restricting myself more to particulars (*a' particulari*)', Machiavelli launches into lengthy, complex ruminations on the arbitrariness of fortune. He starts with observations about how much power 'one sees' fortune exert over men, especially in taking away good things and causing ruin. If one judges by what 'one sees', it seems that a person's chosen or habitual modes of action have little influence on his success or failure. When pursuing their desired ends, some people proceed with caution (*rispetto*), art (*arte*), and patience (*pazienza*); others with impetuosity (here *impeto*, the same word used to describe fortune's floods), violence (*violenzia*), and 'the contrary' of patience. Yet 'one sees' that men who work in different modes attain their desired ends. 'One sees' that of two men working in the same mode, one attains his end while the other does not. And 'one sees a given prince be happy [*felicitare*] today and come to ruin tomorrow without having seen him change his nature or any quality'.

If particular modes of action don't explain success or failure, what does? Why are two people 'equally happy with two different methods [*studi*], one being cautious [*rispettivo*], the other impetuous [*impetuoso*]'? Machiavelli offers an explanation: 'This arises from nothing other than the quality of the times that they conform to or not in their procedure.' If this is right, then a person's choice of mode is less important than 'the times'—that is, human conditions and events beyond any individual's control—for producing 'happy' ends. If the times 'vary'—if new governments come in or wars break out or general corruption deepens—they can overturn an individual's or state's fortunes overnight. 'On this', Machiavelli says:

> depends the variability of the good [*la variazione del bene*], for if one governs himself with caution and patience, and the times and affairs turn in such a way that his government is good, he comes out happy; but if the times and affairs change, he is ruined because he does not change his mode of proceeding.

All this points to the need for a completely different mode for dealing with fortune than the first one. Instead of sticking with Building Mode I, Machiavelli now suggests that it might be unwise to restrict oneself to a single habitual mode or set of qualities when confronting fortune's extremely potent effects. To hedge one's bets, it is better for a man to 'change his mode' and even his nature: 'for if he would change his nature [*si mutassi natura*] with the times and with affairs, his fortune would not change'. Instead of opposing fortune or 'the times', one should adapt to their whims. For 'I believe further', Machiavelli declares, 'that he is happy who adapts [*riscontra*] his mode of proceeding to the qualities of the times; and similarly, he is unhappy [*infelice*] whose procedure is discordant with the times'.

As for the qualities that help people to change modes and natures at every turn, we are now told that it is better to be impetuous than cautious (or respectful). The cautious/*respettivo* man 'comes to ruin' because he doesn't know how to change his modes or his nature; though 'if he would change his nature with times and with affairs, his fortune would not change'. The impetuous man finds this easier—and has other charms that help him to win *fortuna* over to his side, as we'll see shortly.

How can this mode be squared with Machiavelli's Building/Cautious Mode I, which he has already linked to *virtù* and Italian redemption? Perhaps we should build precautionary dykes and dams as suggested by (I), but be prepared in particular circumstances to change our modes and act impetuously when the times call for variation. After all, Mode I isn't infallible. Pragmatic flexibility might help us to avoid even more of fortune's downturns—perhaps even to make greater gains when we find her in a more generous mood.

But if Machiavelli thinks the two modes should be combined, he doesn't say how. And a moment's reflection suggests that Modes I and II must work at cross-purposes. If you devote your energies to building firm orders that make you independent of fortune, you need to defend and reinforce them continuously. If you adapt your modes and nature to fortune's whims, you make yourself dependent on her, and will find it hard to uphold any orders you build. One kind of action or the other, adaptive varying or self-ordering, must be a more adequate manifestation of *virtú*. Both modes cannot be equally virtuous, since they call for directly antithetical qualities. Either caution/ *rispetto*—here identified with art and patience—are virtuous and impetuosity—identified with violence and impatience—is not, or vice versa. One cannot have it both ways.

CAN IT BE VIRTUOUS TO CHANGE WITH FORTUNE?

Machiavelli explicitly aligns Mode I with *virtú* and redemptive possibilities. What about Mode II? The kind of hyper-pragmatic flexibility described here is sometimes taken to be the pinnacle of Machiavellian virtuosity. But Machiavelli never even comes close to identifying this kind of 'variability' with *virtú*. On the contrary, his second mode for dealing with fortune is clearly related to the more general mode of relying on 'fortune and the arms of others', rather than on *virtú*. Throughout the *Prince, variazione* is identified with fortune's destabilizing oscillations. In chapter 18, a variable person was one who follows fortune's commands; in chapter 19, variability topped the list of qualities that win contempt. As soon as a prince grants fortune the power to force him out of his habitual modes, he gives up any chance of managing events with his own intelligence and forethought. One who varies with fortune's moods neither opposes nor manages her, but puts her firmly in the driver's seat.

Since *fortuna* is variable, it seems reasonable to infer that the *virtuoso* way to escape dependence on it is to impose orders that are firm and unvarying, so that they can 'govern' fortune's changes and caprices. And indeed, the *Prince*'s final chapter will call for a redeemer of Italy who, far from being a master of flexibility, is 'prudent and virtuous enough' to 'introduce a form [*forma*] that would bring honour to him and good to the generality of men there'—one based on 'orders and laws' that fortune cannot overturn because they have been 'well founded'. Elsewhere, Machiavelli stresses that he shows more *virtú* who has less need to change because of circumstances or the 'times', and who steers his own steady path through whatever trials fortune may throw in his way.

Why then are some people tempted to veer off a straightforwardly virtue-building path toward variation? As we've seen before, this tends to happen when people have unrealistic ends or expectations. When they expect uninterrupted success or seek continuous 'happiness', they confuse occasional setbacks with 'ruin'. People who have more realistic expectations and limited ends are unlikely to be drawn to the Variation Mode. If someone should point out that cautious building doesn't always bring success, the *virtuoso* response is: of course it doesn't. Even the most prudent builder must expect setbacks, even serious difficulties or outright defeats. But he won't see every defeat as ruinous, knowing that he can always recover if he is patient, industrious, and disciplined.

The argument for varying modes looks most convincing when we don't look too closely at the *apparently* similar results produced by different modes. Machiavelli made this point in a famous 1506 letter where he outlined the arguments for 'varying' with fortune that later appear in the *Prince*.[7] These arguments, he says, seem wise from 'the perspective of the many'—though not from the 'prudent' perspective of his correspondent. The many 'see the ends, not the means, of things'; and on seeing that the same end can be reached by different means, they conclude that no mode of action is always better than the other, but that it is good to use whatever means one can to one's ends. But those who judge from this perspective fail to ask whether the results attained through different modes are of equally good quality. It's true that Hannibal's cruelty and Scipio's mercy both won many victories, and that different Roman emperors stayed in power by opposite modes. But beyond the end of 'victory', or 'holding power', their modes produced very different results. Hannibal's so-called cruelty—perhaps more properly called severity—kept his armies well ordered; Scipio's 'mercy' corrupted his and Rome's. Some resilient emperors won glory, others infamy. Opposing modes may attain the same generic ends. But they have very different effects on the quality of one's orders, and the quality of praise or blame one deserves for them.

CAN ONE VARY ONE'S MODES OR NATURE?

Machiavelli wraps up his case for the Variation Mode with highly equivocal remarks about whether, after all, it is possible or desirable to change one's modes or nature with fortune's winds. On the one hand, someone 'who governs himself with caution and patience' is ruined if times change and he does not change his mode. On the other, Machiavelli now says that this kind of change is *impossible*. 'No man may be found so prudent as to know how to accommodate himself to this', either 'because he cannot deviate from what nature inclines him to', or 'because, when one has always prospered by walking on one path, he cannot be persuaded to depart from it'. An ideally prudent man, *if* he could be found, would be able to deviate from his *natura*— a word that may refer to deeply ingrained habits as well as inborn tendencies— and would realize that what worked for him in the past cannot always work. But Machiavelli says that *no* man can be found so prudent as to change his nature; changing one's nature is beyond what ordinary human prudence can effect. He had already written in his 1506 letter that:

---

[7] Machiavelli to Giovan Battista Soderini, 13–21 September 1506, *MF* 134–6.

truly, anyone wise enough to adapt to and understand the times and the pattern of events would always have good fortune or would always keep himself from bad fortune; and it would come to be true that the wise man could command the stars and the Fates. But such wise men cannot be found [*non si truova*]: in the first place, men are short-sighted; in the second place, they are unable to command their own natures; thus it follows that Fortune is variable [*varia*], commanding men and keeping them under her yoke.[8]

His poem 'On Fortune', probably written a few years later, expressed the same view:

> since you cannot change your character [*persona*] nor give up the orders [*l'ordin*] that heaven endows you with, in the midst of your journey [*fortuna*] abandons you.
> ... a man who could leap from wheel to wheel would always be happy and blessed [*felice e beato*],
> but because to attain this is denied by the occult [*occulta*] *virtú* that rules us, our condition changes with her course.[9]

Even if some rare man were found who could vary his nature with the times, it's unclear that he could produce lasting benefits for anyone, including himself. A man who constantly changes his basic habits and modes seems unlikely to contribute to stable orders. Nor could others readily trust someone, especially a political leader, who seems to lack a settled temperament or mode of action. As Machiavelli wrote to Vettori, people have reason to trust a man who has always shown consistency and integrity of character.[10] They can't be expected to rest much faith in one who changes his modes whenever his popularity ratings sink, or when his state is threatened from inside or out.

It might be better, then, to place *rispettivo*/cautious people at the helm of state. Since such people do not know how to switch to impetuosity mode, their fortunes may sometimes change with the times. But variable fortunes aren't necessarily 'ruinous' for such people, who care more about building lasting orders than about winning every contest.

In the *Discourses* Machiavelli does consider one circumstance in which alternating modes can contribute to stable orders. Since different modes or temperaments may benefit a city at different times, good political orders allow for well-regulated changes in leadership so that the people best able to tackle current problems can take office.[11] Machiavelli sees this kind of well-ordered

---

[8] Machiavelli to Giovan Battista Soderini, 13–21 September 1506, *MF* 134–6 (translation modified). He also writes: 'I believe that just as Nature has created men with different faces, so she has created them with different intellects and imaginations. As a result, each man behaves according to his own intellect and imagination ...'.

[9] *Di Fortuna*, lines 112–19. Dante uses the phrase 'occult virtue' in *Purgatorio* XXX. Compare *D* III.9.240.

[10] See chap. 20.

[11] See *D* III.9. This doesn't alter Machiavelli's judgement that it is neither possible nor desirable for individuals to vary their natural modes with the times. The shift from caution to

'varying' as one of the chief advantages republics have over principalities: whereas the latter have to make do with one man in all circumstances, republics frequently change personnel to place more cautious or impetuous men in leading positions, as 'the times' require.[12] Princes who insist on carrying the burdens of government and defence by themselves are liable to feel pressed to vary their modes, and their very nature—although, as the variable and impetuous voice sheepishly admits, no man prudent enough to do this 'can be found'.

FROM VARIATION AND IMPETUOSITY TO VIOLENCE

Constant variation, then, doesn't solve the problem of imperfect security. It just hands more power to fortune. And as we've seen before, people who give up their own powers to choose and build firm orders end up relying on vastly inferior methods. Not knowing how to regulate fortune's variations, they try to dominate it with violence.

The last part of the chapter dramatically mimics this impetuous, fortune-dependent mentality. It shows how, if you pursue the logic of Mode II about the need to vary your modes and nature, you soon end up abandoning cautious *rispetto* altogether in favour of pure *impetuosità*. As with all combined or 'middle way' modes, Mode II can't be held for long in the middle, but tends toward the less virtuous extreme. Instead of oscillating between caution/ art/patience and impetuosity/violence/impatience, Machiavelli—or his volatile speaker—now decides that:

> it is better to be impetuous than cautious, because fortune is a woman, and it is necessary, if one wants to hold her down, to beat her and strike her down [*batterla e urtarla*]. And one sees that she lets herself be won more by the impetuous than by those who proceed coldly [*freddamente*]. And so always, like a woman, she is the friend of the young, because they are less cautious, more ferocious [*feroci*], and command her with more audacity [*audacia*].

Perhaps this unequivocally impetuous approach is better than the wavering Variation Mode. It certainly sounds less passive, less anxious, and clear-headedly assertive. Is this, then, the more virtuous way to 'oppose' fortune—by means of vigorous self-assertion and seduction?

---

impetuosity here is political, not individual; and it is achieved 'ordinarily' by the republic's established orders, not extraordinarily with a view to 'varying' those orders themselves.

[12] Compare chap. 12. Caution (or respect), too, may be excessive; see *D* III.36. But in the *Discourses*, Machiavelli suggests that it is generally better to have men in high political or military office who err on the side of *rispetto* than that of impetuosity; see *ME* 177–9.

Not if an awareness of one's own limits is an essential part of *virtú*. The image of fortune as a woman easily 'held down' by hard-man violence makes conquest sound too easy. It is a far cry from Mode I's image of fortune as a ruinous river—an insensate force of nature, blind to who you are and what you do, susceptible to regulation but not to manipulation. Now fortune is pictured as an anthropomorphic power open to negotiation and seduction, and capable of being dominated. From the perspective of Mode I, this sounds like naïve wishful thinking. Virtuous people avoid over-assertive as well as fatalistic responses to necessities brought by shifts of fortune. The over-assertive respond with violent confrontation, in the belief that they show *virtú* by conquering fortune. Brute ruthless energy, however, cannot found lasting orders.

For all its woman-beating bravado, moreover, this extreme impetuosity mode hands far more power to fortune than Mode I, and even more than the mixed Variation Mode. Those who believe that they should seduce 'her' with manly violence treat fortune as a valued partner and helpmate in their enterprises. This view implies that they *depend on* fortune's help. It may make sense to be aggressively impetuous *if* you rely on fortune because you lack the patience or prudence to build your own success. But since genuinely prudent people don't rely on fortune at all, they don't bother to court her.

Beating and striking are characteristic 'modes' of young men in a hurry.[13] The young think they can and should conquer fortune. They tend to be over-assertive because they don't know their own limits, or don't want to admit them. Their boundless energy and 'spirit' help them make great strides toward greatness, but seldom bring good, lasting results, and often wreak great havoc. They don't realize that fortune's friendship is a very mixed blessing indeed, since she is fickle, untrustworthy, and in time *always* turns against her favourites, however attractive they make themselves for her. In the passage calling for an aggressive approach to fortune, one can almost hear the voice of a self-assertive young man: impetuous Scipio rivalling the older, cautious Fabius Maximus in Rome, Alcibiades confronting the cautious Nicias in Athens, Cyrus, Alexander the Great, Cesare Borgia. The views it expresses clash head-on with those Machiavelli explicitly identifies with *virtú* at the beginning of the chapter and throughout most of the *Prince*.[14]

If this doesn't suffice to alert readers to the irony in Machiavelli's apparent endorsement of the Variation/Impetuosity Mode, his use of Pope Julius II as an exemplary practitioner of that mode should make his views clearer. Julius'

---

[13] Compare *AR* 1389a and Plato, *Laws* III 691.

[14] In the Dedications of the *Prince*, *Discourses*, and *Art of War* Machiavelli presents himself as an experienced older mentor seeking to educate younger princes or future political leaders. In general, he stresses a preference for older, more experienced men in high office; his *Discursus* (p. 108) makes 45 the minimum age for his highest magistracies.

previous appearances in the *Prince* have been less than stellar. Machiavelli has cited him as a model of anti-*virtù*: he used corrupt modes of 'accumulating money' to get ahead in the Church, unthinkingly 'thrust himself entirely into the hands of a foreigner', and made numerous 'bad choices' in foreign policy.[15] Here, again, Machiavelli suggests that Julius 'succeeded' by flukes of fortune in spite of his methods, not because of them—confirming the view that **one can't judge *virtù* by asking only whether a person attained whatever ends he happened to have, but also by asking whether those ends brought his state lasting order and himself lasting glory.** Julius 'found the times and affairs so much in conformity to' his impetuous modes that 'he always achieved a happy end'. But his happiness depended solely on the times and fortune, which allowed him to take advantage of other princes' rivalries and weaknesses, not at all on *virtù*. 'If times had come', Machiavelli notes, 'when he needed to proceed with caution, his ruin would have followed: he would never have deviated from those modes to which nature inclined him'. Only 'the brevity of his life'—another fluke of fortune—'did not allow him to feel the contrary', bad effects of fortune's shifts.

Machiavelli claims to cite Julius' example to illustrate how the Variation Mode can work. In fact, it confirms that it is unworkable—as the chapter's confusingly varied ruminations already suggested. The example also fails to prove that impetuosity is generally better than caution. If we take seriously Machiavelli's claims that Mode I is the more virtuous way to deal with fortune, the opposite must be true. Looking back at the whole chapter, its chameleon-like arguments—first for firm building, then for variability, then for violent impetuosity—seem to simulate the variations of fortune itself.

---

[15] See chaps 11, 13; compare *D* III.9.240 on Piero Soderini and Pope Julius.

26

Redeem yourselves

Exhortation to seize Italy and to free her from the barbarians

WHO CAN SAVE ITALY?

The final chapter's title exhorts someone to take or seize Italy and liberate her from the *barbari*. These tasks should fall to 'someone so prudent and virtuous as to introduce a form [*forma*] that would bring honour to him and good to the generality' of Italians. This suggests that seizing and liberating involve far more than just throwing out the foreigners. Whoever undertakes to do these things should know how to introduce a 'form', a word with close affinities to 'order', to Italy. This form or order should not just benefit him, but bring good to Italians generally. And it should bring honour (*onore*) to him, not merely a reputation for greatness.

The times are ripe, Machiavelli declares, for a new prince to take on these worthy tasks. But what kind of new prince could perform them, and in what mode? As chapter 24 pointed out, 'new prince' may mean simply a prince who acquires power by means other than birth or inheritance. The entire book, however, has described a very different kind of *principe nuovo*, or *nuovo principe*:[1] one who undertakes all the reforms Machiavelli has proposed, and thereby builds a new model of principality, whose basic modes and orders are different from those of other princes past or present. Most princes' chief ends are personal self-preservation and greatness, which make them depend heavily on fortune. A prince who follows Machiavelli's advice will seek to preserve the safety and good order of the entire *stato*, above all by making Italy's peoples their own defenders—ends that can only be realized by virtuous modes.

Some princely readers, more attracted by the impetuous mode evoked so dramatically in chapter 25, will discount this second possibility. The idea of

---

[1] Note the shift from one to the other in the chapter's opening lines.

retaking Italy by patiently building good orders for her defence has little appeal for them. They would rather seize Italy by themselves and give the foreigners who now hold her a good beating, inspired by the examples of 'most excellent' ancient men presented in chapter 6 and recalled again here. Moses, Cyrus, Theseus: in these men, they think, one sees real *virtú*.

But can any modern prince honestly claim to have Moses' prophetic powers or one-to-one rapport with God? And could any Italian leader in Machiavelli's times seriously hope to command the loyalties or military resources needed to expel foreigners single-handedly, let alone force mutually hostile Italians into unity? The *Prince* has shown why such go-it-alone 'modes' are childish fantasies. Common defensive orders built with patience, art, and respect for the independent wishes of various Italian peoples: this is the more realistic and *virtuoso* way to go.

One ancient prince who expanded by military force was Romulus, who founded a great Italian city and empire. But by making Rome a monarchy and constantly attacking its neighbours, he came to represent an ambiguous legacy: one that established some orders suited to a free republic, and others more suited to tyranny.[2] Romulus is missing from Machiavelli's list of virtuous (Moses), great-spirited (Cyrus), and excellent (Theseus) men in this final chapter. Leo Strauss suggests that the omission silently answers the question of whether Italians should imitate Rome in their modes of seizing Italy.[3] But as chapter 6 indicated, Rome had very different modes, personified by two different legendary founders: the bellicose, insatiably conquest-hungry, tyranny-prone Romulus, and Aeneas, who as a poorly armed refugee was compelled by harsh necessity to use more moderate modes, building voluntary partnerships with the peoples he encountered instead of raping and bludgeoning them into submission. By dropping Romulus from his list, Machiavelli seems to dissociate modern Italy from Rome's problematic militaristic-imperial legacy—but not from its better traditions of building a voluntary 'empire' by means of 'partners and confederates'.

So there is much more in the *Prince*'s final oration than heated rhetoric aimed at inflaming Italians against 'barbarian' invaders. The passage exhorting Italians to take heart from the examples of Moses, Cyrus, and Theseus is one of the *Prince*'s most uplifting moments, but also a deeply ambiguous one. 'It was necessary', Machiavelli tells us, 'for anyone wanting to see the *virtú* of Moses', the greatness of spirit of Cyrus, or the excellence of Theseus that their peoples be enslaved, oppressed, and dispersed. But was their peoples' misery a golden opportunity for these men to rescue them—or an opportunity to show their extraordinary individual prowess and increase their own power at others' expense? Might Italians do better to emulate the more modest, human-sized *virtú* of Hiero, who worked hard to reorder Syracuse and improve her relations with other Greek cities, and that of Philopoemen, who tried—not as a

---

[2] See chap. 6.   [3] Strauss (1958), 69.

monarch but as an 'ordinarily' appointed leader—to build a confederation of Greek city-states capable of withstanding Roman encroachments?

Whatever we make of these ancient examples, there is an almost excruciating irony in Machiavelli's statement that 'to know the *virtú* of an Italian spirit' it was necessary for Italy to 'be reduced' to its present pathetic condition. If Italy is at present 'more enslaved than the Hebrews, more servile [*serva*] than the Persians, more dispersed than the Athenians', this was not the work of an unjust necessity or predatory foreigners. It is their own fault that Italians are 'without a head, without order, beaten, despoiled, torn, pillaged, and having endured ruin of every sort [*sanza capo, sanza ordine, battuta, spogliata, lacera, corsa, e avessi supportato d'ogni sorte ruina*]'. The rhythm of Machiavelli's prose ruthlessly drums in this shameful appraisal. While arousing Italians to fight back against humiliation, it also warns them that much hard work is needed to make an Italian *virtú* rise from the ashes. The hardest servitude to break, after all, is the kind you unthinkingly impose on yourself.

CAN GOD HELP?

The short answer: he could if he wanted to, as the scriptures say he helped Moses and his Hebrews. But Italians shouldn't expect the same treatment. Unfortunately, they kept hoping for divine aid, either direct or through a God-sent saviour, while failing to examine their own errors or acting to correct them. Machiavelli had deplored these tendencies in his earlier poems; the *Prince*'s next lines gently mock them. 'And though up to now', he intones solemnly, 'a certain glimmer [*spiraculo*] has shone in someone who could judge that he had been ordered by God for her redemption [*ordinate da Dio per sua redenzione*]', sadly 'later it was seen that in the highest course of his actions, he was repulsed by fortune.'

Most scholars have thought that this 'someone' was Cesare Borgia, who like this nameless man flew 'high' in chapter 7 before fortune abandoned him at his zenith. Machiavelli's *Decennale* had already described his soaring flights on the back of his father's fortune. Cesare—though not necessarily Machiavelli—'could judge' that God appointed him Italy's redeemer because his father, the pope, God's chief emissary on earth, wanted him to dominate Italy. The description also recalls another man with excellent divine connections mentioned earlier, in chapter 6: the friar, Girolamo Savonarola, who 'was ruined in his new orders as soon as the multitude began not to believe in them'. Machiavelli leaves it to readers to recall the various men in recent times who claimed, or had grounds for claiming, that they were 'ordered by God' to save Italy. Whoever they were, however high they soared, they all failed in the end, defeated by fortune.

Does this mean that random fortune trumps even God? No: it merely means that they were wrong to 'judge' that God had appointed them to save Italy.

Perhaps Machiavelli refrains from naming his fortune-repulsed 'someone' because his particular identity is beside the point. The essential point is that *any* individual who imagines that he has been appointed by God to save a country tends to confuse his temporary good fortune with divine orders. Thinking that he is 'ordered by God', he never grasps how much ordering he would need to do *by himself* if Italy is to be saved. His own and his compatriots' longing for orders imposed by God is a symptom of their sickness, of their deficient *virtú*. The central message of the entire *Prince* has been that self-reliance is your only reliable security. Again, this is not to downplay God's powers. It only suggests that if God wants human beings to act virtuously, as Machiavelli thinks any God worth worshipping must, he will want them to pick themselves up instead of running to him whenever things go wrong.

This is the *virtuoso* perspective on Italy's failed, nameless redeemer. The converse, far more usual perspective is that he failed only because of an extremely bad fortune. Those who take this view still hope that another extraordinary healer will crop up to cure Italy of 'her sores that have festered now for a long time'—this time, at last, one whom both fortune and God will bear aloft to a happy end. 'One may see', Machiavelli declares with more than a touch of melodrama, how Italy 'prays to God to send her someone to redeem her from these barbarous cruelties and insults.' This pathetic image has ambivalent effects. Read in dead earnest, it might fill a potential saviour's heart with pity and inspire him to attack the source of Italy's ills. Read against the background of Machiavelli's usual cool analyses and scepticism about divinely ordered saviours, it alerts readers that what follows should also be taken with a pinch of salt.

Italy, he says, appears 'ready and disposed to follow a banner', if only someone would take it up. What kind of banner he does not say: the kind used to rally Machiavelli's civilian troops before they were disbanded, or a more spiritual kind? Perhaps both, if his new prince can combine them virtuously. And perhaps Machiavelli has found one who, with the right advisers, might do this. For the first time since the Dedication, he addresses the Medici directly. At present, he declares, one can 'see' no one in whom Italians 'can hope for more than in your illustrious house'. With its 'fortune and *virtú*, favoured by God and by the Church of which it is now prince' thanks to Giovanni de Medici's recent appointment as Pope Leo X, the house of Medici 'can put itself at the head of this redemption [*capo di questa redenzione*]'.

Note the warnings intermingled in this flattering appeal. 'Fortune and *virtú*' is always an unstable, if not tainted, combination; it would be far better to redeem Italy by *virtú* alone. And to put oneself at the head of such a great enterprise is less safe than to be put there by others.[4] Machiavelli throws in

---

[4] As noted in chap. 6 about Hiero.

other tests of Medici *virtú*. To make oneself head 'is not very difficult if you summon up the actions and lives of those named above' and keep as your aim 'the orders of those whom I have put forth'—but *which* actions and orders does he mean? Although Moses, Cyrus, and Theseus 'were rare and marvellous [*rari e maraviglioso*], nonetheless they were men' who had 'less opportunity than the present': is this an exhortation to imitate these flawed heroes without further ado, or a reminder that merely human redeemers need to work within the narrow bounds of merely human *virtú*?

Or did the Medici, whose house was now headed by the pope himself, have the rare advantage of God's support? Here, Machiavelli proclaims, 'may be seen extraordinary things without example, brought about by God': the sea has opened, a cloud escorts you, the stone pours forth water, the skies rain manna; 'everything has concurred in your greatness'. All these miracles promised success to Moses as he led his people toward the Promised Land.[5] Perhaps the Medici return to Florence, followed by the election of a Medici pope, could be interpreted as similar hopeful signs from God. Yet even if God has encouraged them this far, they should expect no further help: 'the remainder you must do yourself'. Machiavelli's God 'does not want to do everything, so as not to take free will from us and that part of the glory that falls to us'. If the new Medici princes hope to set themselves at the head of Italy's redemption, they had better learn more about what genuine *virtú* requires.

With or without God's active support, at least the Medici seemed to have justice on their side. 'Here', Machiavelli declares, 'is great justice [*iustizia grande*]: "for war is just to whom it is necessary, and arms are pious when there is no hope but in arms [*iustum enim est bellum quibus necessarium et pia arma ubi nulla nisi in armis spes est*]".' With this quote from Livy, Machiavelli seems to give his redeemers permission to set aside moral scruples while they fight their necessary wars for Italy.[6]

Or does he? In Livy's original, the words occur in a speech delivered by a military leader of the Samnites, an Italian people who were unjustly harassed— and eventually beaten into submission—by their empire-hungry Roman neighbours. The speaker calls on the gods for help in war, but only after explaining that the Samnites have tried every other legal and political expedient to get the Romans off their backs. Could present-day Italians say the same—that they had tried all virtuous options to contain their more powerful neighbours? Popes Alexander and Julius, who both put themselves at the head of great plans to save Italy from foreign 'barbarians', certainly could not. In the context of an exhortation to the present pope's family, the reference to 'pious' arms brings to mind the numerous counterproductive wars launched by Pope Leo's

---

[5] Compare the *Decennale* I, line 112 on Florentines waiting, mouths pathetically agape, 'for someone from France' to bring them manna in the desert.

[6] *LH* IX.i.

predecessors, who used their supposedly pious and God-given arms to fight wars for no discernible necessity or justice.

Read in this light, Machiavelli's use of Livy is scathingly ironic. By recalling a virtuous ancient argument for necessary war, it exposes how modern Christian leaders—indeed the highest princes of Christendom, the popes—have repeatedly abused the good words piety, necessity, and justice for their own impious ends.[7] If the Medici hoped to use the papacy to better ends, they would do well to think more carefully than their predecessors about what necessity and justice demand.

GOOD HUMAN ORDERS

While Machiavelli's ironies tend to be most biting when he writes about the Church and papacy, his closing address to the Medici is not wholly satirical. If any Medici 'prince', whether secular or papal, were virtuous enough to decode the *Prince*'s subtler message, he might become the kind of reforming new prince Machiavelli hopes for: one who would reform Florence along more republican lines, restore her militia, and use the Church's authority to spearhead a collaborative Italian defensive policy. But he could only hope to succeed if he relied more on the actions Machiavelli has described as virtuous, and less on fortune or God.

This becomes clearer in the chapter's next part, which again deplores Italian's sorry lack of military *virtú* (*virtú militare*). The root of the problem is not bad luck, God's deafness to Italian pleas, even a lack of military talents in Italy. The problem is the lack of good orders that can discipline these talents, organize them under clear command structures, and motivate them for committed defence. And behind this is the further problem that no one, so far, has known how to do all this. Italy has had plenty of brave, energetic, spirited military commanders; but valour, energy, and spirit cannot save Italy without knowledge of how to make good orders. Throughout the *Prince*, Machiavelli has mimicked everyday language in calling *both* the first set of qualities *and* knowledge of ordering *virtú*. But only the second kind of *virtú* can get Italy out of its present mess, and merit highest praise. 'Nothing brings so much honour to a man rising newly [*nuovo surga*]', Machiavelli writes, 'as the new laws and the new orders found [*trovati*] by him.'

If the reference to a new man 'surging' forth encourages eager fortune-hunters, the claim that honour comes from new laws and orders calls for caution, *rispetto*, and art. The orders that bring honour are military, but also political and legal, since military deficiencies are inseparable from these wider

---

[7] Machiavelli uses the same quote in a similarly ironic way in *D* III.12 and *FH* V.8.

deficiencies. 'When these things have been founded well and have greatness in them', Machiavelli writes, 'they make him revered and admirable [*reverendo e mirabile*].' Significantly, the greatness resides in the works, not their maker. Before, the words 'greatness' and 'reputation' were usually hyperbolic, linked to excessive ambitions pursued more by appearances than by good orders. Now Machiavelli implies that such orders confer true greatness and well-deserved reputation on a new prince.

Fortunately for the fortunate and virtuous Medici, there is now someone who does know how to build better orders for Italy, and who is at their disposal. Machiavelli has this knowledge. Yet like many earlier political philosophers who wished to heal their countries' self-inflicted wounds, he lacks the power to put it into practice, as he would later write in his *Discursus*:

> no man is so much exalted by any act of his as are those men who have with laws and with institutions [*constituti*] reformed [*reformati*] republics and kingdoms... And so much has this glory been esteemed by men seeking nothing other than glory that when unable to form a republic in reality [*in atto*], they have done it in writing [*in iscritto*], as Aristotle, Plato, and many others, who have wished to show the world that if they have not founded a civil life [*fondare un vivere civile*], as did Solon and Lycurgus, they have failed not through ignorance but through their impotence for putting it into practice.[8]

In a last attempt to persuade the Medici that his solutions are highly practical as well as philosophical, he claims to have identified specific weaknesses in the Spanish and Swiss militaries, and explains how his new military orders for Italy will improve on them. The gist of his proposals is that carefully calibrated, man-made orders and discipline are everything. As the chapter and book draw toward an end, there is no impetuosity, variation, or God in sight.

Italy's problems, Machiavelli insists, stem 'from the weakness in the head'—in the princes at the pinnacle of her various states, and in the great who support them. Her best hope of recovering *virtú* can be found in its 'limbs' (*membra*), where 'there is great *virtú*'. Does this imply that Italy's redemption depends on its people, as well as on finding 'someone'—a prince, or perhaps Machiavelli—who knows how to make orders and laws capable of ordering their defences? Indirectly, Machiavelli has been saying this throughout the *Prince*: the people are a prince's and Italy's best arms, when they are well ordered.

THE BARBARIANS AND US

Evoking poor Italia's suffering 'from these floods from outside', her people's 'thirst for revenge', plaintive tears, eagerness to obey her long-awaited

---

[8] *Discursus* 113–14.

redeemer [*redentore*], our book's final paragraph summons 'your illustrious house' to 'take up this task with the spirit [*animo*] and hope in which such just enterprises are taken up'. Under the Medici banner, 'this fatherland (*patria*)' of Italy 'may be ennobled' and the poet Petrarch's lines come true:

> *Virtú* will take up arms against fury (*contro a furore*),
> and make the battle short,
> because the ancient valour (*valore*) in Italian hearts
> is not yet dead.[9]

By opposing *virtú* to fury, Petrarch suggests—as Machiavelli does in the *Prince*—that the foreign mercenaries who were already ravaging Italy brought nothing but disorder, which a better-ordered Italian *virtú* must correct.[10] Like Machiavelli, Petrarch longed for an end to Italy's fratricidal wars, and blamed her rulers for bringing in 'so many foreign swords'—those of hired mercenaries. When Machiavelli declares that 'this barbarian domination stinks [*puzza questo barbaro dominio*] to everyone', he echoes the great poet's sentiments, and Petrarch's use of the harsh word 'barbarian' to describe foreign mercenaries. More ironically, as contemporary readers would have realized, Machiavelli also echoes recent papal rhetoric. When proclaiming his intentions to throw foreign powers out of Italy by force of arms, the impetuous and fortunate Pope Julius II had raised the battle-cry '*fuori i barbari*'—'out with the barbarians!', although he himself frequently invited foreign troops into the peninsula when it served his own purposes.[11]

Otherwise, and unlike Petrarch's poetic letter, the *Prince* avoids xenophobic statements.[12] In the *Discourses*, Machiavelli defines a prince as a 'barbarian' who is 'a destroyer of countries and a waster of all the civilizations of men'.[13] Such men show no respect for limits or for human orders. Mercenaries are barbaric in these respects. But so were many popes and Italian princes whose pursuit of greatness, reputation, and false glory was destroying every last hope of order in Italy, even as they claimed to defend her from the *barbari*. Italy needed new dykes and dams to hold back outsiders—but also to restrain its home-grown barbarians, including those 'gatekeepers of Paradise'[14] puffed up by belief in their own divine grace.

---

[9] Petrarch, *Italia Mia* (*c.* 1344/2004a).

[10] Petrarch's letter ends with a call for peace. His reference to 'ancient' Italian valour evokes Rome in its days of glory—when it was a republic.

[11] In 1510, after dissolving the League of Cambrai he formed with Spain and France against Venice. Julius' warlike behaviour was widely criticized at the time; he was nicknamed *Il Papa Terribile* and *Il Papa Guerriero* (the Warrior Pope).

[12] Petrarch denounces the backward Germans, deceitful Bavarians, and others.

[13] *D* II.2.

[14] As Julius II is called in *Decennale* I, lines 460–1. With wonderful irony, the *Florentine Histories* begins with the 'barbarian' invasions of Rome—except that Machiavelli avoids the word, and describes Rome's attackers as rational and well ordered, in pointed contrast to the decadent Romans, who brought their woes on themselves.

Conclusion

Gli regni i quali dipendono solo dalla virtú d'uno uomo, sono poco durabili, perché quella virtú manca con la vita di quello... Non è, adunque, la salute di una republica o d'uno regno avere uno principe che prudentemente governi mentre vive, ma uno che l'ordini in modo che, morendo ancora, la si mantenga.

Kingdoms that rely solely on the virtú of one man are not long-lasting, since upon his death that virtú is gone... The health of a republic or a kingdom therefore does not lie in having a prince who governs prudently while alive, but rather in having one who orders it in such a way that it maintains itself upon his death.

(*Discourses* 1.11)

THE 'BOOK OF REPUBLICANS'

The *Prince* presented in these pages is indeed 'the book of republicans', as Rousseau called it in 1762.[1] The reasons for this judgement are, however, far from self-evident. Early on, Machiavelli declares that his work will 'leave out' republics. Unlike the *Discourses*, it expresses no overt preference for republics, presents no detailed analysis of their foundations or institutions, and offers no ringing endorsement of the republican ideals of universal freedom, shared authority, or the rule of law. In fact, many of the boldest assertions in the *Prince* run directly counter to these ideals.

Yet in various indirect ways, the book shows why well-ordered republics are *always* better than principalities at maintaining states. Most obviously, they establish and maintain better defences because they can draw forces from highly motivated citizens, regulate armies and captains by public laws, and prevent good military orders from being weakened or dismantled by the whims of a monarch (chapters 10, 12–13). More subtly, and often under the pretext of a narrower concern to improve princely defences, Machiavelli

---

[1] Rousseau (1964/1762), III.6.

smuggles in a host of far-reaching proposals for political reform, all tending more toward a republic than a principality. For his militia project cannot be bought alone. It is part of a package deal that includes many laws, institutions, and policies that call for a wide sharing of power, and for strict limits on princely authority.

Thus in trying to sell princes better arms, the *Prince* also tries, ever so discreetly, to make them buy republican orders. It does this not by tricking unwary princely readers into acting against their own interests, but by suggesting that to move toward more republic-friendly 'modes' *is* in every prince's best interests. Readers who add up all the reforms Machiavelli suggests, scattered throughout different chapters and often presented as low-key asides, will get the message: that prince is most secure who can trust his own subjects. And to trust his subjects, he needs to treat them more like citizens. He needs, that is, to reduce the gap Machiavelli noted in his Dedication between the *altezza* of princes and peoples below. This is prudent because peoples—armed or unarmed—have great power to do good when their basic needs and reasonable desires are addressed, and equally great power to do harm when they are not.

The possibility that Machiavelli wanted to embed a veiled pro-republican message in the *Prince* fits more comfortably with his past and later writings than with the view that, longing to return to politics, he wrote a thoroughly pro-monarchical book to please the Medici. In the period when he wrote the *Prince*, Machiavelli had excellent reasons to play down his critical and pro-republican agenda.[2] And in the more relaxed climate of 1520, some seven years after he wrote the *Prince*, he did more straightforwardly in his *Discursus* what the *Prince* does from behind a prince-friendly mask: he advised the Medici to transform their own *stato* into a *vera repubblica*, a true republic, instead of trying to mix princely practices with republican appearances.

The reforms he proposes here are designed to ensure that all classes of citizen have their fair share of political power, that magistrates are given authority by willing citizens, and that the laws treat every citizen equally. Above all, 'Your Holinesses'—Pope Leo X and Cardinal Giulio de' Medici— must realize that the most important class in a republic is not the patricians but the 'generality of citizens', who must be satisfied in any government that hopes to last beyond a generation or two. Ingeniously, Machiavelli even maps out a way for leading Medici to transform their quasi-princedom into a republic without jeopardizing their or their friends' safety. In their own lifetimes they may continue to rule as monarchs, but must make provisions for a peaceful transition to a broad-based republic on their passing.[3] There are good reasons to suspect that Machiavelli diagnosed similar problems in the

---

[2] See Introduction and the remarks on simulation below.
[3] *Discursus* 113–14.

new Medici *stato* when he wrote the *Prince*, and that he favoured a similar solution: the voluntary self-conversion of the Medici from *de facto* princes into the 'orderers' of a firm republican constitution, defended by a citizen militia.

HOW TO REFORM A CORRUPT STATE

Machiavelli assiduously maintains the fiction that his *Prince* is an advice book for 'princes' in the monarchical sense: one-man rulers for life whose relatives or chosen successors may inherit the *principato*. But the work's examples and discussions underscore the difficulties that plague this kind of prince, while stressing the advantages that accrue to those who transform their principality so that the 'name' of prince acquires a new meaning. In the *Discourses*, the ancient role model for this alternative type of *principe* is a Roman: not the city's legendary founder Romulus—recalling that Aeneas is another possible founder for Machiavelli—but the *re*-founder then consul Lucius Junius Brutus, who expelled the last kings from Rome. In reordering the city as a republic, Brutus and his colleagues prudently retained a 'kingly power' in the consulate. But they ordered that there should be two consuls at any time instead of one, set strict limits on the terms of consular tenure, and subordinated consular powers to Senatorial and popular scrutiny.

These might sound like minor variations on Romulus' mixed monarchical–Senatorial foundations. Yet by subordinating kingly power to the laws and public councils, and checking the powers of one leading man with the equal authority of another, Brutus' far-sighted reordering rescued Rome from the chronic instability it experienced under Romulus' excessively princely institutions.[4] The resulting, better-ordered republic was one where not one but 'infinite most virtuous princes' could be found to serve the public at any given time; where it was judged appropriate 'that the plebs have hope of gaining the consulate'; and where consequently even humble men knew that their offspring 'could, by their virtue, become princes'.[5] If Brutus' reforms appear less 'great' than Romulus' original founding, Machiavelli implies that they and not Romulus' orders were responsible for the Roman state's longevity and *virtú*. By eliminating monarchy while preserving strong leadership, Brutus and his collaborators provided a secure and free life for four centuries of Romans—something Romulus' quasi-princely, quasi-republican orders could not have done.

In Machiavelli's own times, the unstably mixed Medici *stato* described in his *Discursus* bore an uncanny resemblance to Romulus' degenerating mixed monarchy a few generations after its founder's death. The cure for Rome

---

[4] Chap. 6; *ME* 418–24. [5] *D* I.20, I.60, II.2.

was not a new incarnation of Romulus. It was a less extraordinary and far more glorious sort of 'orderer': one who like Brutus would introduce strict new limits on any individual's or party's power, and rigorous new laws punishing serious crimes against the state—laws applied without exception even to the friends and family of men in power, as Brutus applied the death penalty to his sons who conspired against the new republic.[6] This kind of justly severe, self-limiting *ordinatore*, not a mover and shaker of superhuman energy, wisdom, and morality-free ruthlessness, is what Machiavelli seeks for Florence in the *Discursus*. It is the kind of re-orderer represented in the *Prince* by the 'lesser' example of Hiero, who used tough yet transparent and *ordinario* means to overhaul Syracuse's government and defences; and by the even more understated Philopoemen, who used intelligent reflection and continuous deliberation with 'friends' to work toward the unification and defence of the Greeks. The *Prince* tries to find leaders for Italy who understand the value of such low-key *virtuoso* methods, and who are able to resist the lure of personal *grandezza* in favour of long-term results.

Machiavelli presents Junius Brutus as a master of virtuous 'simulation' (*simulazione*) as well as a *virtuoso* reformer. 'There was never anyone so prudent or esteemed so wise', we read in the *Discourses*, 'than Junius Brutus deserves to be held in his simulation of stupidity [*stultizia*]'. If 'one cause that induced him to such simulation . . . was to be able to live more securely', another was 'to be less observed and to have more occasion [*commodità*] for oppressing the kings and freeing his own fatherland whenever opportunity [*occasione*] would be given him'. While Machiavelli deems it 'less dangerous and more honourable' to declare war openly, not all 'who are discontented with a prince' are strong enough to do this. They have instead to simulate a desire to please that prince, 'following his pleasures and taking delight in all those things they see him delighting in'.[7] Machiavelli's *Prince* is a prime example of this kind of hidden intellectual warfare on princes. Like Brutus, the book expresses well-camouflaged desires to free the author's fatherland and 'oppress' princes—not by plotting to murder them and their supporters, but by establishing public laws that eliminate monarchical powers and severely punish anyone who tries to reintroduce them.

The *Discourses*' remarks on political simulation recall Machiavelli's own precarious position when he wrote the *Prince*. Some people, he observes, say that 'with princes one should not wish to stand so close that their ruin includes you, nor so far that you would not be in time to rise above their ruin when they are being ruined'. (Note the unquestioned assumption that princes must eventually be ruined.) This 'middle way', Machiavelli recognizes, 'would be

---

[6] Machiavelli praises this as an act of statesmanlike impartiality and judicious *severità*—a word of very high praise—in *D* I.16 and III.3.
[7] *D* III.2.

the truest if it could be observed'. But 'because I believe that it is impossible' to keep to middle ways, any man 'notable for his quality' must either stay far away from princes or 'bind oneself to them'. The following passage may tell us more about Machiavelli's purposes in writing the *Prince* than anything he felt safe enough to write in a letter:

> Nor is it enough to say: 'I do not care for anything, I do not desire either honours or useful things; I wish to live quietly and without quarrel!'—for these excuses are heard and not accepted. Nor can men who have quality choose to stand back even when they choose it truly and without any ambition, because it is not believed of them; so if they wish to stand on their own, they are not allowed to by others. Thus one must play the crazy man [*fare il pazzo*] like Brutus, and make oneself very much mad, praising, speaking, seeing, doing things against your intent so as to please the prince.

While doing all this, however, 'one' must never stop working like Brutus to 'recover freedom'.[8]

SELF-ELIMINATING PRINCES

The most *virtuoso* prince is thus one who makes himself redundant *qua* prince in the usual monarchical sense. Voluntary self-elimination is the most logical means of achieving a reflectively prudent prince's ends: to secure his 'own arms' beyond his own lifetime, so that they serve his country well for as long as humanly possible.[9] This, not huge gains made for a prince's own sake in his short lifespan, is what wins true glory in the annals of posterity. If princes set no limits on their own authority but constantly extend it, they leave a legacy of grave disorders that often last for centuries. If like Romulus they do limit their own monarchical powers, but not enough to prevent their abuse, their good orders soon become tainted with bad.

At the heart of Machiavelli's *Prince* is the argument that the *armi proprie* of any prince who wants to establish stable rule in and beyond his own lifetime are constituted by the steady, willing commitment of the people he governs.[10] This commitment can only be secured if the prince makes himself into an accountable office-holder subject to public laws, and if the people are ordered under laws that they regard as their own. A prince who fails to recognize this risks alienating himself from the popular body of the polity, which would then cease to constitute 'his own' united arms. Princely rule defeats itself unless it

---

[8] *D* III.2.
[9] Compare Neville's (1681) reading of Machiavelli and his comparisons with Plato.
[10] On the importance of willing as a condition for stable orders, see *ME* 255–62.

transcends itself. As Machiavelli notes in the *Florentine Histories*, 'a city based on good laws and good orders has no necessity, as have others, for the *virtú* of a single man to maintain it'—and all other cities lack good *ordini*.[11]

Although Machiavelli asserts that he will omit speaking of republics in the *Prince*, the *idea* of a republic is never far from the surface in his 'little work on principalities'. A comparison between its Dedication and that of the *Discourses* shows the complementary relationship between the two books. The *Discourses* start by saluting men who are not princes but deserve to be. It goes on to show how polities should be ordered so that all those who deserve to be princes may share in the honours and labours of *principato*—that is, of political leadership—within a well-ordered republic. 'Princes' here are leading men who take turns in elective office, not individuals who seize, inherit, or buy their way into power and are loath to share it. The *Prince* is dedicated to the latter type of prince. But it tells him from the outset that he and other princes need to supplement their lofty perspective with the understanding of ordinary men, and goes on to show that princes make themselves stronger by taking greater account of their subjects' reasonable desires for safety, a decent living, public respect, and freedom. By denying that princes can fully grasp their own 'nature' and responsibilities without consulting men of humble status, Machiavelli puts princes and ordinary men on a par with respect to knowledge in matters of governing, and challenges princes to rethink their desires to dominate peoples or cities.

ARE PRINCES EVER NECESSARY? THE ANCIENT TOPOS OF ONE-MAN ORDERERS

A number of scholars have begun to place a fresh, welcome emphasis on republican themes in the *Prince*.[12] While our interpretations agree on many points, mine diverges on a fundamental issue. Other scholars argue that while Machiavelli strongly favours republics over principalities, he holds that princes—or assertive prince-like figures—are needed in two sets of circumstances: to found new republics, and to purge corruption in failing states and restore strong, well-ordered polities.[13] Early in the *Discourses* we read that 'it never or rarely happens that any republic or a kingdom is ordered well from the beginning or reformed altogether anew . . . unless it is ordered by one

---

[11] *FH* IV.1.146.

[12] For example, Stacey (2007), McCormick (2011, 2012), Viroli (2013), and Skinner (2013).

[13] Scholars differ on the question of whether Machiavelli thinks such princes should establish or restore a republic, or whether any form of government will do so as long as it provides security against outside threats.

individual [*da uno*]'.[14] This seems to imply that the *Discourses'* usual reasons for preferring the well-ordered government of many over the rule of one don't apply when new cities are being founded, or in corrupt times when they must be reformed anew. In such conditions, an *ordinatore's* good ends justify his use of 'extraordinary' or extra-legal means, including those set out in the *Prince*. On this view, the 'modes' needed to found and reform republics may be utterly different from those needed to maintain them in good health.[15] Some kinds of prince, at least, are a necessary antidote to defects in republics.

I have argued, by contrast, that the *same* modes—those Machiavelli associates with order-producing *virtù*—are needed to found, reform, and maintain any type of state. Moreover, the most virtuous modes always involve collaboration, not extraordinary individuals acting alone. The *Prince* presents many examples of extraordinarily self-assertive founders and 'innovators' whose new *ordini* proved problematic. In some cases, they created such difficulties for themselves or their states that *other* refounders or reformers were needed to purge the corrupt elements introduced in the name of founding, reform, or redemption. Romulus made many orders conducive to a republic, but also founded Rome as a monarchy that soon deteriorated into tyranny; the city's good orders were saved only by the republican reforms of Junius Brutus and his colleagues. Cyrus redeemed the Persians from Mede oppression, but went on to build a despotic new state complete with new élites composed of his intimate friends, whom he set far above the mass of people in their wealth and political power.[16]

When we scrutinize the careful wording of Machiavelli's 'praise' for modern one-man innovators who promised to save Florentines and Italians from their tribulations, it turns out to be mingled with sardonically sceptical undertones. Pope Julius vowed to purge Italy of its foreign barbarians and restore its long-tarnished glory; yet look at the poor, prostrate Italia he left for future would-be redeemers to dredge out of the mire. The Medici and Savonarola in Florence offered their rival brands of redemption. Throngs of citizens who should have known better rushed to embrace one or the other, hoping in vain for some great man or prophet to 'pick them up'. The *Prince* reminds readers of all these exhilarating princely promises—and their sorry results.

Why, then, do the *Discourses* declare that republics are never or seldom 'ordered well' without the ordering genius of one man? And how are such orderer-reformers related to Machiavelli's princes? While some scholars tend to

---

[14] *D* I.9.

[15] What modes scholars think are needed to maintain Machiavelli's republics depends in part on what kind of republic they think he preferred: one dominated by the popular 'part' which must sometimes use extraordinary, violent means to rein in the 'great' (see McCormick 2012), or one based on the rule of law rather than any one section of the population. I defend the latter view in *ME* chap. 7.

[16] *XC* VII–VIII.

identify the *Discourses'* one-man founder or orderer/*ordinatore* with the extraordinary 'princes' discussed in the *Prince*, Machiavelli never refers to the former as princes. The nomenclature is important because, as we saw in chapter 1, 'princes' for Machiavelli always go hand in hand with a particular type of *stato*—one fundamentally opposed to republics. A *principe* who single-handedly founds or reforms a republic is thus a contradiction in terms, unless he also reforms himself out of a principality, as Machiavelli urged the Medici to do in 1520.

Nonetheless, the *Discourses'* apparent demand for a one-man *ordinatore* poses one of that work's deepest puzzles. There, as in the *Prince*, Machiavelli repeatedly stresses the risks of unlimited power for *any* individual, however exceptional or prudent or virtuous. His anthropology is both non-idealistic and egalitarian: it suggests that unless they are checked by self-discipline and the laws, *all* human beings are prone to do bad as well as good, and vulnerable to temptations of excessive power and to the self-flattering deception that they benefit others while seeking to aggrandize themselves.[17] It is hard to conceive how the Machiavelli who advanced such a problematic view of human nature could have thought that there were rare and wonderful exceptions—almost superhuman men who may be trusted to act prudently at every turn; who always choose the best means to the best ends when performing the most arduous tasks of founding, defending, and running a state; whose ambitions and self-confidence need no restraining; and who indeed may find it necessary to transgress all legal and moral restraints in the name of universal liberation. If this is the conviction that links Machiavelli's *Discourses* and *Prince*, it presents nothing short of a mind-boggling paradox.

There is, however, an ancient solution that was familiar to Machiavelli's humanist contemporaries, but overlooked by most readers today. The *Discourses'* assertions about the need for extraordinary one-man founders or reformers echo a well-known topos of ancient thought. The theme was a favourite among writers who were concerned about the rise of charismatic leaders who sought to assume princely powers in ancient Greek democracies or the Roman republic. It enjoyed a revival when Julius Caesar persuaded the Roman Senate to give him the powers of dictator for life, promising the people that he would use this extraordinary authority to restore sound republican orders. At the time, critics such as Cicero evoked the Greek motif of the ideal one-man founder to warn fellow citizens *against* encouraging one-man rule. In his dialogue the *Republic*, Cicero has the main interlocutor set out the traditional, sceptical Roman view of one-man founders:

> Cato used to say that our constitution was superior to those of other States on account of the fact that almost every one of these other commonwealths had been established by one man, the author of their laws and institutions; for example,

[17] See *ME* chap. 5.

Minos in Crete, Lycurgus in Sparta . . . On the other hand our own republic [*res publica*] was based upon the genius, not of one man, but of many; it was founded, not in one generation, but in a long period of several centuries and many ages of men. For, said [Cato], there never has lived a man possessed of so great genius that nothing could escape him, nor could the combined powers of all the men living at one time possibly make all necessary provisions for the future without the aid of actual experience and the test of time.

Cicero argues that though the superiority of Rome's constitution was due to many men not one, it was easily *ruined* by the actions of one alone.[18]

A more subtly dialectical use of the one-man ruler topos occurs in Plato's dialogues the *Statesman* and *Laws*. The pattern is the same in both works: the rule of one outstandingly wise man is presented as an ideal, examined from different angles, and eventually modified to fit better with human limitations.[19] In the *Statesman*, the dialogue's participants agree that government by a wise individual or a few would be their 'first choice'. But further discussion shows that this ideal is unsuitable for cities where flawed human beings, not omniscient gods, are responsible for government. If statesmanship depended on the wisdom of one man or minority, citizens would often be subject to the arbitrary whims of men who claim to have superior expertise. But even the best human experts err: they imagine that their knowledge of good and bad is more secure than it is, and misjudge the best means for achieving what they deem to be good.

By a process of elimination, the interlocutors find that they are left with a 'second-best' strategy: one that 'imitates' the ideal of one man ruling with expertise by retaining the rule of one at the head, but giving sovereign authority to the laws rather than to any single individual. By treating laws and ancestral customs as the foundation of political knowledge, instead of depending on one or a few to provide the expertise of statesmanship, this 'second-best' choice avoids the pitfalls of arbitrary rule. The precept 'there must be nothing wiser than the laws' emerges as the central pillar of the knowledge 'of the statesman' and 'of statesmanship'. Thus 'when some ruler [*archôn*] acts neither according to laws nor according to customs, but pretends to act like the person with expert knowledge [*epistêmôn*], saying that after all one must do what is contrary to what is written down if it is best', such a person must be called a tyrant.[20]

The impatient participants in Plato's *Laws* start by considering how a city can establish 'as quickly [*tachista*] as possible' a political order 'that will enable

---

[18] Cicero, *Republic* II.110–13, 156–9.
[19] A classic case of ironic transformation; see 'Ironic Techniques' (6).
[20] Plato, *Statesman* 296a–301c; *ME* 432–7.

it to live a life of supreme happiness'.[21] They agree that there is 'no quicker or easier way to legislate than to follow the leadership' of one or a few supremely wise men. But what 'is difficult, and a very rare occurrence in history' is a situation in which prudent restraint and justice guide those who wield great power. The dialogue evokes the theme of a mythical golden age when, 'they say, such a paragon did exist, but he is certainly unheard of today'.

The terminus of these reflections is that the rule of law must be set over even the wisest of men. Retreating from the call for a dictator able to establish a 'supremely happy' city, the main interlocutor now says that any man who nurtures the arrogant belief that he 'can play the leader to others' with no need for laws to guide him has been deserted by God and right reason. Although 'many people think he cuts a fine figure', before long, he 'brings himself, his home and state to rack and ruin'.[22] Machiavelli issues similar, direct warnings against the *hubris* of one-man rulers in his early poems 'On Fortune' and 'Ambition'—and less direct ones in the *Prince* and *Discourses*.[23]

In the latter work, Machiavelli's approach to the pipe dream of one-man orderers has much in common with Plato's dialectical treatments. After declaring in the *Discourses* I.9 that 'it never or rarely happens that any republic or a kingdom is ordered well from the beginning or reformed altogether anew . . . unless it is ordered by one individual', Machiavelli goes on in several further chapters to consider whether the one-man ideal is realistic. His most reflective arguments agree with Plato, Cicero, and other ancient writers that neither founding nor reordering is best done by 'one alone'. Even if one man using 'extreme force' could restore a corrupt city to some semblance of goodness, 'as soon as such a one is dead', Machiavelli observes, the city will revert to its former bad habits. This happened in Thebes, 'which could hold the forms [*forma*] of a republic and its empire through the virtue of Epaminondas while he lived, but returned to its first disorders when he was dead'. The cause of this is clear: 'there cannot', Machiavelli avers, 'be one man of such long life as to have enough time to inure to good a city that has been inured to bad for a long time'. Until extraordinary individuals become immortal, the ambition to reform corrupt people single-handedly and 'at a stroke' is doomed to fail.[24]

---

[21] Plato, *Laws* 710b–712a. The words 'quickly' and 'easily' are repeated many times in the discussion, and linked to the 'good fortune' (*eutuchês*) of finding an ideal one-man ruler—a possibility quietly ruled out by the discussion's end. See 'Coded Words' on Machiavelli's similar uses.

[22] Plato, *Laws* 714a–716b.

[23] See chap. 7. Guicciardini (*GD* I.12–13, II.94–5) makes a similar dialectical use of the one-man ruler topos. Early on, his *Dialogues'* key speaker says that since it seems evident to any man on the street that the rule of one good man is better than any other form of government, the present discussion will start with this opinion, and examine it from various angles. By the end of the dialogue, the opinion has not been explicitly refuted; but many reasons have been given to suspect that the naïve ideal of one-man rule invariably fails in its promise.

[24] *D* I.17.

As for founding, it is true that the *Discourses* seem to argue that Romulus was justified in killing his brother Remus so that he could order Rome alone. No 'wise understanding', Machiavelli declares, will 'ever reprove anyone for any extraordinary action that he uses to order a kingdom or constitute a republic. It is very suitable [*conveniente*]', he goes on, 'that when the deed accuses him, the effect excuses him; and when the effect is good, as was that of Romulus, it will always excuse the deed'.

But again, this is only the start of further reflections on this extreme consequentialist precept, not Machiavelli's final position. His further ruminations raise a very serious problem with the initial assertion that effects or ends always justify the means.[25] How can one-man orderers who use violent means be trusted to use authority virtuously, not ambitiously? After all, Machiavelli points out, the 'reordering of a city for a political way of life presupposes a good man'. But 'becoming a prince of a republic by violence presupposes a bad man'. Thus 'it very rarely happens that someone good wishes to become prince by bad ways, even though his end be good'. It is also almost impossible 'that someone wicked, having become prince, wishes to work well, and that it will ever occur to his mind to use well the authority that he has acquired badly'.[26] The more one examines the implications of unrestrained one-man ordering, the less reasonable it appears that people should entrust their political fate to one man alone—however wise he may seem, and however desperately they seek quick-fix, authoritarian solutions to their problems.[27]

Further remarks in the *Discourses* warn mere mortals against thinking that they can get away with doing what Romulus and other extraordinary ancient founders reputedly did. When one examines the rare examples of men who are said to have pulled off extraordinary deeds, they often turn out to be less prudent or praiseworthy than admirers claim. Like their ancient sources, Machiavelli's treatments of ancient founders in the *Discourses* are finely discriminating and often critical, not idealistic.[28] Since his aim is to unsettle popular heroic ideals without attacking them—so that people come to recognize the flaws in their heroes for themselves—his discussions of such examples are ambiguous, mixing high praise with subtle questions about whether their

---

[25] See *ME* chap. 9 for a fuller discussion of Machiavelli's consequentialism.

[26] *D* I.18.

[27] Compare Spinoza's (1958/1677, VI.4–7, VII.1) similarly dialectical consideration of the one-man ruler topos: although 'experience seems to teach that it makes for peace and harmony if all power is vested in one man', reflection shows that 'it is slavery, not peace, that is furthered by the transfer of all power to one man'; and further, 'those who believe that one man *can* hold the supreme right of a commonwealth by himself are greatly mistaken'. According to Spinoza, both Machiavelli and Plato argued that 'right is determined by power', yet 'the power of one man is far too small to bear so great a burden'. Further, 'if everything depended on the inconstant will of one man, nothing would be stable'.

[28] See *ME* chap. 11.

deeds deserve unqualified praise, and whether ordinary mortals can hope to imitate them.

Both the *Prince* and the *Discourses* invoke the ancient theme of rare and most excellent one-man orderers to get readers to reconsider its superficial attractions. In the real world as Machiavelli depicts it, there are no super-human men, no individuals ancient or modern who can be trusted to pull off feats of selfless founding or reordering that save the rest of us the trouble of thinking about how to maintain a safe, stable, or free polity. There are only ordinary human beings who have to learn to work together, within and across their separate cities, finding ways to accommodate each other's reasonable desires. God will not pick them up, and neither will some preternaturally wise redeemer. When he sheds his ironic mask in his *Discursus*, Machiavelli urges the Medici to lead Florence out of her long corruption not by imitating Romulus or Cyrus, and not by 'extraordinary' means of violence against the great or the cunning use of political spin, but by returning to the transparent, legal methods needed to found a 'true republic'. Florence's redemption depended not on the marvellous good fortune of finding some single, *virtuoso* saviour to drag her and Italy out of the ashes, but on the ordinary commitment of *many* Florentines and Italians to the hard collaborative work of reordering their cities and their common fatherland. Princes who willingly hand over power to the many will win great glory for their prudent recognition that stable orders cannot depend on any one man or dynasty alone.

Like Plato and other ancient writers, Machiavelli sees the longing for one-man saviours as natural in times of great stress and upheaval. These desires are so perennial that people recur to them time and again when they are worn down by conflict, fearful of the future, weighed down with self-doubt—or when they are too lazy, impatient, or divided to work toward more realistic solutions. It is, as the *Discourses* say, 'almost impossible' to find men who can pull off one-man redemptive acts. But it is very, very easy to find ambitious men willing to try, in all times and places.

This is why Machiavelli and his ancients return so often to the theme of one-man orderers.[29] It is of the utmost importance to him, as it was to his ancient writers, that people should reason for themselves about why princely 'remedies' are always unstable. It is not enough that they should see particular examples as pernicious but make exceptions for other one-man rulers, saying that these conditions or that individual will *not* fall prey to weakness or *hubris*. The Florentines spurned many tyrants and princes, yet they embraced—at least for a time—the Medici and Savonarola. People must grasp the reasons

---

[29] Spinoza (1958/1677, V.7, XVII.6) argues that if Machiavelli 'describes at great length' the means used by 'a prince whose sole motive is lust for despotic power', he must have had 'some good purpose, as we must believe of so wise a man'; and one of these was to warn a free people against 'entrusting its welfare entirely to one man'.

why *no* human individual who is released from strict legal constraints should be trusted to order well. Otherwise they will remain susceptible to appeals by *some* individuals who claim to be different from the rest.

MACHIAVELLIAN DISSIMULATION

Unlike some scholars, then, I do not see the *Prince* as a book of mainly positive *exempla* to be imitated, but as a work that presents a handful of positive examples among a host of problematic and prophylactic ones.[30] In this respect, Machiavelli's book resembles the cautionary type of 'handbook for princes' mentioned in the Introduction: those like Xenophon's *Cyropaedia* and a number of Plutarch's *Lives* and essays that seem to praise their subjects, but ironically suggest that some of their widely admired qualities and policies tended to destroy good orders. These works challenge readers to spot what's wrong with their apparently glowing pictures of successful statesmen, as I've suggested Machiavelli provokes readers to ask whether his accounts of ancient and modern princes furnish reliable models for imitation. They have to rely on their own judgement as much as on what Machiavelli as author tells them, and search for a few powerful grains of truth among many misleading assertions.

Their familiarity with Plutarch, Xenophon, and other masters of ironic dissimulation may help explain why readers such as Gentili, Bacon, Neville, Spinoza, and Rousseau rejected the view of Machiavelli's *Prince* as an amoral treatise for princes. Machiavelli himself frankly admitted that he practised dissimulation. 'For a long time', he wrote to Guicciardini in 1521, 'I have not said what I believed, nor do I ever believe what I say, and if indeed I do happen to tell the truth, I hide it among so many lies that it is hard to find'. He describes himself here as 'a doctor of this art' of lying while telling the truth.[31]

Machiavelli's correspondence often mentions his own use of signs (*cenni*), codes (*cifre*), and other techniques of dissimulative writing in his political works and plays.[32] While he sometimes states that political constraints forced him to write in this way, his letters also point to a different, more constructive reason to dissimulate: to teach people 'the way to hell' so that they may learn to avoid it. His writing often mimics the unreflective or corrupt judgements or naïve hopes of salvation that lead people to embrace self-destructive policies, and thus unwittingly to create their own political hell. By seeming to endorse these opinions while 'letting drop' arguments that hint at their shortcomings,

---

[30] Thanks to John McCormick for helping me clarify this difference between my reading and his, as well as those of other scholars.
[31] Machiavelli to Guicciardini, 17 May 1521, *MF* 336–7.
[32] See Introduction, n.34.

Machiavelli challenges readers to spot the errors for themselves—ensuring that they work harder to avoid them in future.

In the *Prince*, Machiavelli goes to considerable lengths to camouflage his arguments for republics among an array of elaborate, much more conspicuous arguments for various princely 'modes' of government. But if pro-princely arguments dominate the text and command greater attention, they are far weaker in quality than the lower-register arguments for preferring republics. The challenge for readers is to see through the *Prince's* carefully constructed sophistic appearances to the less striking, more powerfully reasoned undercurrents.

If they approach the book not as a treatise that sets out rules for getting and keeping power, but as a series of *discorsi* designed to exercise their intellectual and practical judgement, readers are more likely to notice Machiavelli's teasing provocations toward independent thinking. Inconsistencies among the book's precepts press readers to examine the quality of the reasons presented for one or the other. Words of high praise grate against accounts of unsuccessful or disorder-creating deeds. Textbook rhetorical fallacies invite readers to spot and arm themselves against old demagogues' tricks—or fall into their traps. The *Prince* not only offers constructive political proposals; it also conveys these general lessons—to both political leaders and ordinary citizens—on how to recognize and resist dangerously seductive arguments for lowering moral standards in politics.

Appearances notwithstanding, the *Prince* does not teach politicians to practise the kind of political 'realism' that aims to maximize power before concerning oneself with ideals such as universal freedom or impartial justice. On the contrary, it repeatedly shows that respect for other people's freedom and a concern for justice are bedrocks of lasting power and security. Nor do the book's strongest arguments defend the pragmatically amoral view that while it's generally good to respect other people's desires for security, freedom, and transparent dealings, sometimes these considerations have to be set aside or compromised for expediency's sake. On the contrary, the *Prince* insists that states remain weak and vulnerable so long as they lack orders founded on reciprocal trust between leaders and citizens/subjects, and between states and their external allies—a trust that cannot be sustained if leaders often 'vary' their policies and commitments in hope of gaining an impossibly absolute security or an advantage over others. In the *Prince* as in Machiavelli's other works, freedom and justice are not unworldly ideals but basic elements of any *virtuoso* order. They underwrite both personal and collective safety: it is necessary to observe them if one wants to remain safe, or build secure political foundations. Neither princes nor anyone else can ignore them without putting themselves and their states at risk, no matter what the circumstances.

If anything, Machiavelli thought his Italian and Florentine contemporaries suffered from too much pragmatism, not too little: they adjusted too easily to the plummeting standards of conduct set by unscrupulous princes and popes. His *Prince* mirrors the amorality of his times, but does not recommend it as sound practice. Machiavelli holds up a mirror to show his contemporaries their true qualities—the 'effectual reality' of their self-destructive actions— behind all their professions of piety, decency, and prudence. Few teachings are more necessary for political leaders and citizens in every time and place, or more pertinent to human beings' ongoing struggles to construct and maintain a decent quality of life.

Bibliography and further reading

Primary sources

Machiavelli
Citations in original from:
Machiavelli, Niccolò. 1997–2005. *Opere*, vols 1–3. Torino: Einaudi-Gallimard.
Main citations in English from:
——2003. *The Art of War*. Trans. ed. Christopher Lynch. Chicago: University of Chicago Press.
——1989. *The* [Golden] *Ass (Asino)*, in *Machiavelli: The Chief Works and Others* (3 vols), vol. 2. Trans. ed. Allan Gilbert. Durham, NC: Duke University Press, pp. 750–72.
——1989. *Decennali* I and II, in Gilbert, ed. *Machiavelli: The Chief Works*, vol. 3, pp. 1444–62.
——1989. 'Description of the Mode used by Duke Valentino in Killing Vitellozzo Vitelli, Oliverotto da Fermo, and others', in Gilbert, ed. *Machiavelli: The Chief Works*, vol. 1, pp. 163–9.
——1989. *A Discourse on Remodelling the Government of Florence*, in Gilbert, ed. *Machiavelli: The Chief Works*, vol. 1, pp. 101–15.
——1996. *Discourses on Livy*. Trans. Harvey C. Mansfield and Nathan Tarcov. Chicago: University of Chicago Press.
——1988. *Florentine Histories*. Trans. Laura F. Banfield and Harvey C. Mansfield. Princeton: Princeton University Press.
——1989. *The Life of Castruccio Castracani of Lucca*, in Gilbert, ed. *Machiavelli: The Chief Works*, vol. 2, pp. 533–60.
——1996. *Machiavelli and his Friends: Their Personal Correspondence*. Trans. ed. James B. Atkinson and David Sices. DeKalb, IL: University of Northern Illinois Press.
——1989. 'On the Method of Dealing with the Rebellious Peoples of the Valdechiana', in Gilbert, ed. *Machiavelli: The Chief Works*, vol. 1, pp. 161–2.
——1995. 'A Portrait of German Affairs' [*Ritracto delle cose della Magna*], in *The Prince and Other Political Writings*. Trans. ed. Stephen J. Milner. London: J.M. Dent, pp. 20–7.
——1998. *The Prince*, 2nd edn. Trans. intro. Harvey C. Mansfield. Chicago: University of Chicago Press.
——1989. *Tercets on Ambition (Dell'Ambizione)* and *Fortune (Di Fortuna)*, in Gilbert, ed. *Machiavelli: The Chief Works*, vol. 2, pp. 735–49.
——1989. 'Two Sonnets to Giuliano', in Gilbert, ed. *Machiavelli: The Chief Works*, vol. 2, pp. 1013–15.
Other translations cited or consulted:
——1990. *Der Fürst* (Parallel Italian/German text). Trans. ed. Philipp Rippel. Stuttgart: Reclam.
——1996. *Machiavel Oeuvres*. Trans. ed. Christian Bec. Paris: Éditions Robert Laffont.

——1961. *The Prince*. Trans. intro. George Bull. Harmondsworth: Penguin.

——1976. *The Prince*. Trans. intro. James B. Atkinson. Indianapolis/Cambridge: Hackett.

Other classical works

Aristotle. 1894. *Ethica Nicomachaea*. Oxford: Oxford University Press.

——1953. *Eudemian Ethics*. Trans. H. Rackham. Cambridge, MA: Loeb Classical Library, Harvard University Press.

——1957. *Rhetorica ad Alexandrum*. Trans. H. Rackham. Cambridge, MA: Loeb Classical Library, Harvard University Press.

——1990. *Politics*. Trans. H. Rackham. Cambridge, MA: Loeb Classical Library, Harvard University Press.

——1991. *On Rhetoric*. Trans. intro. George A. Kennedy. New York and Oxford: Oxford University Press.

Bacon, Francis. 2001 [1605]. *The Advancement of Learning*. New York: Random House.

——1985 [1597–1625]. *The Essays*. Ed. intro. John Pitcher. Harmondsworth: Penguin.

Cicero, Marcus Tullius. 2000. *On the Republic and On the Laws*. Trans. Clinton Walker Keyes. Cambridge, MA: Loeb Classical Library, Harvard University Press.

——2005. *On Duties [De Officiis]*. Trans. Walter Miller. Cambridge, MA: Loeb Classical Library, Harvard University Press.

Dante, Alighieri. 1991. *La Divina Commedia*. Ed. Giuseppe Villaroel, revised commentary, Guido Davico Bonini and Carla Poma. Milan: Mondadori.

Fichte, Johann Gottlieb. 1971 [1807]. 'Über Machiavelli', in *Fichtes Werke*, vol. 11. Ed. Immanuel Hermann Fichte. Berlin: Walter de Gruyter & Co., pp. 400–53.

Gentili, Alberico. 1924 [1594]. *De legationibus libri tres*, vols 1–2. Trans. Gordon Liang, ed. John Brown Scott. New York: Oxford University Press.

Guicciardini, Francesco. 1932. *Dialogo e discorsi del reggimento di firenze*. Ed. Roberto Palmarocchi. Bari: Giuseppe Laterza e Figli.

——1949. *Ricordi*. Trans. Ninian Hill Thomson. New York: S. F. Vanni.

——1969. *The History of Italy*. Trans. ed. Sidney Alexander. Princeton: Princeton University Press.

——1994. *Dialogue on the Government of Florence*. Trans. ed. Alison Brown. Cambridge: Cambridge University Press.

Hegel, G. W. F. 1999 [1800–1802]. 'Die Verfassung Deutschlands', in *Werke: Frühe Schriften*, vol. 1. Frankfurt: Suhrkamp, pp. 451–620.

Herodotus. 1922. *The Persian Wars* (4 vols). Trans. A. D. Godley. Cambridge, MA: Loeb Classical Library, Harvard University Press.

Hobbes, Thomas. 1996 [1652]. *Leviathan*. Ed. Richard Tuck. Cambridge: Cambridge University Press.

——1998 [1642]. *On the Citizen [De Cive]*. Ed. Richard Tuck and Michael Silverthorne. Cambridge: Cambridge University Press.

Isocrates. 1928. 'To Nicocles', vol. 1. Cambridge, MA: Loeb Classical Library, Harvard University Press.

Justin, Marcus Junianus. 1853. *Epitome of the* Philippic History of *Pompeius Trogus*. Trans. Rev. John Selby Watson. London: Henry G. Bohn.

Livy, Titus. 2000–2002. *History of Rome [Ab Urbe Condita]*, vols 1–30. Cambridge, MA: Loeb Classical Library, Harvard University Press.

Macaulay, Thomas Babington. 1910. 'Machiavelli', in *English Essays: Sidney to Macaulay*. The Harvard Classics vol. 27. New York: P. F. Collier.

Neville, Henry. 1681. *Plato Redivivus: or, a dialogue concerning government*. London: Printed for S. I. and Sold by R. Dew.

———1691. *Nicholas Machiavel's Letter to Zenobius Buondelmontius, in Vindication of his Writings*. London: s.n.

Nifo, Agostino. 2008 [1523]. *De Regnandi Peritia* (Latin and French parallel). Trans. ed. Paul Larivaille. Paris: Les Belles Lettres.

Petrarch, Francesco. 2004a [*c*. 1344]. *Canzoniere*. Ed. Marco Santagata. Milan: Mondadori.

———2004b. *De Viris Illustribus*. Ed. Silvano Ferrone. Firenze: Le Lettere.

Plato. 1991. *Sämtliche Werke*, vols 1–10 (Greek and German parallel). Based on trans. by Friedrich Schleiermacher. Frankfurt: Insel Verlag.

———1997a. *Complete Works*. Ed. intro. John M. Cooper. Indianapolis and Cambridge: Hackett.

Plutarch. 1998–2002. *Lives*, vols 1–11. Cambridge, MA: Loeb Classical Library, Harvard University Press.

———2000–2005. *Moralia*, vols 1–13. Cambridge, MA: Loeb Classical Library, Harvard University Press.

Pole, Reginald. 1997 [1536]. 'Apology'. Selections in Jill Kraye, ed. *Cambridge Translations*, vol. 2, Cambridge: Cambridge University Press, pp. 274–86.

Polybius, 2001–2003. *The Histories*, vols 1–6. Trans. W. R. Paton. Cambridge, MA: Loeb Classical Library, Harvard University Press.

Rousseau, Jean-Jacques. 1964 [1762]. 'Du contrat social', in *Oeuvres complètes*, vol. 3, pp. 348–470.

Sallust, Gaius Crispus. 1921. 'Jugurthine Wars', in *Works*. Trans. J. C. Rolfe. Cambridge, MA: Loeb Classical Library, Harvard University Press.

———2007. *Bellum Catiline* (The War with Catiline). Trans. ed. J. T. Ramsay. Oxford: Oxford University Press.

Seneca, Lucius Annaeus. 1928a. 'De Clementia' [Of Clemency], in *Moral Essays*, vol. 1. Trans. John W. Basore. Cambridge, MA: Loeb Classical Library, Harvard University Press.

———1928b. 'De Beneficiis' [On Benefits], in *Moral Essays*, vol. 3. Trans. John W. Basore. Cambridge, Mass: Loeb Classical Library, Harvard University Press.

Spinoza, Benedict de. 1958 [1677]. 'Tractatus Politicus', in *The Political Works*. Trans. ed. A. G. Wernham. Oxford: Clarendon Press.

———2007 [1669–1670]. *Tractatus theologico-politicus*. Ed. Jonathan Israel, trans. Michael Silverstone and Jonathan Israel. Cambridge: Cambridge University Press.

Tacitus, Cornelius. 1979. *Works*, vol. 1. Cambridge, MA: Loeb Classical Library, Harvard University Press.

Thucydides. 1991. *Historiae*, vols 1–2. Ed. Henry Stuart Jones. Oxford: Clarendon Press.

———2003. *History of the Peloponnesian War*, vols 1–4. Cambridge, MA: Loeb Classical Library, Harvard University Press.

Xenophon. 2000. 'Hiero' and 'Lacedaemonians', in *Scripta Minora*. Trans. E. C. Marchant. Cambridge, MA: Loeb Classical Library, Harvard University Press, pp. 1–57, 136–89.

Xenophon. 2000–2001. *Cyropaedia*, Books 1–8. Trans. Walter Miller. Cambridge, MA: Loeb Classical Library, Harvard University Press.

Other sources

Acton, Lord. 2005 [1907]. 'Introduction to L. A. Burd's Edition of *Il Principe* by Machiavelli', in *The History of Freedom and other Essays*. New York: Cosimo Inc., pp. 212–31.

Alvarez, Leo Paul de. 1999. *The Machiavellian Enterprise*. DeKalb: Northern Illinois University Press.

Anglo, Sydney. 2005. *Machiavelli: The First Century. Studies in Enthusiasm, Hostility, and Irrelevance*. Oxford: Oxford University Press.

Ascoli, Albert Russell, and Kahn, Victoria (eds). 1993. *Machiavelli and the Discourse of Literature*. Ithaca, NY: Cornell University Press.

Ascoli, Albert Russell and Capodivacca, Angela Matilde. 2010. 'Machiavelli and Poetry', in John M. Najemy, ed. *Cambridge Companion to Machiavelli*, pp. 190–205.

Baron, Hans. 1955. *Humanistic and Political Literature in Florence and Venice at the Beginning of the Quattrocento*. Cambridge, MA: Harvard University Press.

——1968. *From Petrarch to Leonardo Bruni: Studies in Humanist and Political Literature*. Chicago: University of Chicago Press.

——1988. *In Search of Florentine Civic Humanism*. Princeton: Princeton University Press.

Benner, Erica. 2009. *Machiavelli's Ethics*. Princeton: Princeton University Press.

Berlin, Isaiah. 1981 [1958]. 'The Originality of Machiavelli', in *Against the Current: Essays in the History of Ideas*. Oxford: Oxford University Press, pp. 25–79.

Bock, Gisela, Quentin Skinner, and Maurizio Viroli (eds). 1990. *Machiavelli and Republicanism*. Cambridge: Cambridge University Press.

Booth, Wayne C. 1975. *A Rhetoric of Irony*. Chicago: University of Chicago Press.

Brown, Alison. 2000. 'Demasking Renaissance republicanism', in James Hankins, ed. *Renaissance Civic Humanism*, pp. 179–99.

Carlier, Pierre. 2010. 'The Idea of Imperial Monarchy in Xenophon's *Cyropaedia*', in Vivienne Gray, ed. *Xenophon*, pp. 327–66.

Chabod, Federico. 1960. *Machiavelli and the Renaissance*. Trans. David Moore, intro. A. P. d'Entrèves. London: Bowes and Bowes.

Coby, J. Patrick. 1999. *Machiavelli's Romans: Liberty and Greatness in the* Discourses on Livy. Lanham, MD: Lexington Books.

Connell, William J. and Zorzi, Andrea (eds). 2000. *Florentine Tuscany: Structures and Practices of Power*. Cambridge: Cambridge University Press.

Crick, Bernard. 1970. 'Introduction. So Many Machiavellis', in *Machiavelli: The Discourses*. Harmondsworth: Penguin.

Danner, Richard. 1985. *Patterns of Irony in the Fables of La Fontaine*. Cincinnati: Ohio University Press.

De Grazia, Sebastian. 1989. *Machiavelli in Hell*. Princeton: Princeton University Press.

Desideri, P. 1995. 'Plutarco e Machiavelli', in I. Gallo and B. Scardigli (eds) *Teoria e prassi politica nelle opere di Plutarco*, pp. 107–22.

Dietz, Mary. 1986. 'Trapping the Prince: Machiavelli and the Politics of Deception', *American Political Science Review* 80, no. 3, pp. 777–99.

Duncan, Douglas. 1978. *Ben Jonson and the Lucianic tradition.* Cambridge: Cambridge University Press.

Fachard, Denis. 2013. *Teatro di Machiavelli.* Rome: Carocci Editore.

Feldman, Louis H. 2007. *Philo's Portrayal of Moses in the Context of Ancient Judaism.* Notre Dame: University of Notre Dame Press.

Gallo, I. and Scardigli, B. (eds). 1995. *Teoria e prassi politica nelle opere di Plutarco.* Naples: Atti del V Convegno plutarcheo, Certosa di pontignano, 7–9 June 1993.

Garin, Eugenio. 1965. *Italian Humanism: Philosophy and Civic Life in the Renaissance.* Trans. Peter Munz. Oxford: Oxford University Press.

——1972. *Portraits from the Quattrocento.* Trans. Victor and Elizabeth Velen. New York: Harper & Row.

——1993. *Machiavelli fra politica e storia.* Torino: Einaudi.

——1994. *La cultura filosofica del rinascimento italiano.* Florence: Sansoni Editore.

Garver, Eugene. 1987. *Machiavelli and the History of Prudence.* Madison: University of Wisconsin Press.

Gilbert, Alan. 1938. *Machiavelli's Prince and its Forerunners: the Prince as a Typical Book de Regimine Principum.* Durham, NC: Duke University Press.

Gilbert, Felix. 1977. *History, Choice and Commitment.* Cambridge, MA: The Belknap Press.

Giorgini, Giovanni. 2008. 'The Place of the Tyrant in Machiavelli's Political Thought and the Literary Genre of the *Prince*', *History of Political Thought* XXIX, no. 2, pp. 230–56.

Godorecci, Barbara. 1993. *After Machiavelli: 'Re-writing' and the 'Hermeneutic Attitude'.* West Lafayette, IN: Purdue University Press.

Grafton, Anthony. 1988. 'The Availability of Ancient Works', in Charles B. Schmitt and Quentin Skinner (eds) *The Cambridge History of Renaissance Philosophy.* Cambridge: Cambridge University Press, pp. 765–91.

Grant, Ruth W. 1997. *Hypocrisy and Integrity: Machiavelli, Rousseau, and the Ethics of Politics.* Chicago: University of Chicago Press.

Gray, Vivienne (ed.) 2010. *Xenophon:* Oxford Readings. Oxford: Oxford University Press.

Guarini, Elena Fasano. 1990. 'Machiavelli and the crisis of the Italian republics', in Gisela Bock, et al. (eds) *Machiavelli and Republicanism*, pp. 17–40.

Hankins, James (ed.) 2000. *Renaissance Civic Humanism.* Cambridge: Cambridge University Press.

Hexter, J. H. 1956. 'Seyssel, Machiavelli and Polybius IV: The Mystery of the Missing Translation', *Studies in the Renaissance* 3, pp. 75–96.

Höffe, Otfried (ed.) 2012. *Niccolò Machiavelli: Der Fürst.* Berlin: Akademie Verlag.

Hörnqvist, Mikael. 2004. *Machiavelli and Empire.* Cambridge: Cambridge University Press.

Hutcheon, Linda. 1995. *Irony's Edge.* London: Routledge.

Kahn, Victoria. 1994. *Machiavellian Rhetoric: From Counter-Reformation to Milton.* Princeton: Princeton University Press.

Knox, Dilwyn. 1989. *Ironia: Medieval and Renaissance Ideas on Irony.* Leiden: E. J. Brill.

Knox, Norman. 1961. *The Word Irony and its Context, 1500–1755.* Durham, NC: Duke University Press.

Kraye, Jill (ed.) 1997. *Cambridge Translations of Renaissance Philosophical Texts*, vols 1 and 2. Cambridge: Cambridge University Press.

Langton, John. 1987. 'Machiavelli's Paradox: trapping or teaching the Prince', *American Political Science Review* 81, no. 4, pp. 1277–88.

McCormick, John. 2011. *Machiavellian Democracy*. Cambridge: Cambridge University Press.

——2012. 'Subdue the Senate: Machiavelli's "Way of Freedom" or Path to Tyranny?', *Political Theory* 40, pp. 714–35.

McDonnell, Myles. 2006. *Roman Manliness: 'Virtus' and the Roman Republic*. Cambridge: Cambridge University Press.

Major, Rafael. 2007. 'A New Argument for Morality: Machiavelli and the Ancients', *Political Science Quarterly* 60, pp. 171–9.

Mansfield, Harvey C. 1979. *Machiavelli's New Modes and Orders: A Study of the Discourses on Livy*. Chicago: University of Chicago Press.

——1998. *Machiavelli's Virtue*, 2nd edn. Chicago: University of Chicago Press.

Martinez, Ronald L. 2010. 'Comedian, Tragedian: Machiavelli and traditions of Renaissance theater', in John A. Najemy, ed. *Cambridge Companion*, pp. 206–22.

Mattingly, Garrett. 1958. 'Machiavelli's Prince: Political Science or Political Satire?', *American Scholar* 27, pp. 482–91.

Meinecke, Friedrich. 1998 [1925]. *The Doctrine of Raison d'État and Its Place in Modern History* [Die Idee der Staatsräson in der neueren Geschichte]. Ed. intro. Werner Stark. New Brunswick: Transaction Publishers.

Muecke, D. C. 1970. *Irony*. London: Methuen.

——1982. *Irony and the Ironic*. London: Methuen.

Najemy, John M. 1990. 'The controversy surrounding Machiavelli's service to the republic', in Gisela Bock, et al. (eds) *Machiavelli and Republicanism*, pp. 101–17.

——1993. *Between Friends: Discourses of Power and Desire in the Machiavelli–Vettori Letters of 1513–1515*. Princeton: Princeton University Press.

——2006. *A History of Florence, 1200–1575*. Oxford: Blackwell.

——(ed.) 2010. *The Cambridge Companion to Machiavelli*. Cambridge: Cambridge University Press.

O'Gorman, Ellen. 2000. *Irony and Misreading in the Annals of Tacitus*. Cambridge: Cambridge University Press.

O'Hara, James. 2007. *Inconsistency in Roman Epic: Studies in Catullus, Lucretius, Vergil, Ovid and Lucan*. Cambridge: Cambridge University Press.

Parel, A. J. 1993. 'The Question of Machiavelli's Modernity', in Tom Sorell, ed. *The Rise of Modern Philosophy: The Tension between the New and Traditional Philosophies from Machiavelli to Leibniz*. Oxford: Clarendon Press, pp. 253–72.

Patterson, Annabel. 1987. *Pastoral and Ideology: Virgil to Valery*. Berkeley and Los Angeles: University of California Press.

Philp, Mark. 2007. *Political Conduct*. Cambridge, MA: Harvard University Press.

Plamenatz, John. 2012. *Machiavelli, Hobbes, and Rousseau*. Ed. Mark Philp and Zbigniew Pelczynski. Oxford: Oxford University Press.

Pocock, J. G. A. 1975. *The Machiavellian Moment: Florentine Political Thought and the Atlantic Republican Tradition*. Princeton: Princeton University Press.

——1985. 'Machiavelli in the Liberal Cosmos', *Political Theory* 13, no. 4, pp. 559–74.

Poppi, Antonino. 1988. 'Fate, fortune, providence, and human freedom', in *The Cambridge History of Renaissance Philosophy*, pp. 641–67.

Quillen, Carol Everhart. 1998. *Rereading the Renaissance: Petrarch, Augustine and the Language of Humanism*. Ann Arbor: University of Michigan Press.

Radif, Ludovica. 2010. *Le Maschere di Machiavelli*. Genova: Ennepilibri.

Rahe, Paul. 2000. 'Situating Machiavelli', in James Hankins, ed. *Renaissance Civic Republicanism*, pp. 270–308.

Ridolfi, Roberto. 1963. *The Life of Niccolò Machiavelli*. Trans. Cecil Grayson. Chicago: University of Chicago Press.

Rubinstein, Nicolai. 1990. 'Machiavelli and Florentine republican experience', in Gisela Bock, et al. (eds) *Machiavelli and Republicanism*, pp. 3–16.

Sancisi-Weerdenburg, Heleen. 1990. 'Cyrus in Italy: from Dante to Machiavelli', in *Achaemenid History, V: The Roots of the European Tradition*. Ed. H. Sancisi-Weerdenburg and J. W. Drijvers. Leiden: Nederlands instituut voor het nabije oosten.

Sasso, Gennaro. 1958. *Niccolò Machiavelli: Studio del suo pensiero politico*. Naples: Istituto italiano per gli studi storici.

——1987–1997. *Machiavelli e gli antichi e altri saggi*, 4 vols. Milan: R. Ricciardi.

Schmitt, Charles B. and Quentin Skinner (eds). 1988. *The Cambridge History of Renaissance Philosophy*. Cambridge: Cambridge University Press.

Schofield, Malcolm. 1999. *Saving the City: Philosopher-Kings and other Classical Paradigms*. London: Routledge.

Sedgewick, G. G. 1965. *Of Irony: Especially in Drama*. Toronto: Toronto University Press.

Siegel, Jerrold E. 1968. *Rhetoric and Philosophy in Renaissance Humanism: the Union of Eloquence and Wisdom, Petrarch to Valla*. Princeton: Princeton University Press.

Skinner, Quentin. 1978. *The Foundations of Modern Political Thought*, vol. 1: *The Renaissance*. Cambridge: Cambridge University Press.

——1981. *Machiavelli*. Oxford: Oxford University Press.

——1988. 'Political Philosophy', in Charles B. Schmitt and Quentin Skinner (eds) *The Cambridge History of Renaissance Philosophy*. Cambridge: Cambridge University Press, pp. 387–452.

——2002. *Visions of Politics*, vol. 2: *Renaissance Virtues*. Cambridge: Cambridge University Press.

——2013. 'How Machiavellian was Machiavelli?', public lecture delivered at Princeton, 7 February.

Sorensen, Roy. 2005. *A Brief History of the Paradox: Philosophy and the Labyrinths of the Mind*. Oxford: Oxford University Press.

Stacey, Peter. 2007. *Roman Monarchy and the Renaissance Prince*. Cambridge: Cambridge University Press.

Strauss, Leo. 1952. *Persecution and the Art of Writing*. Chicago: University of Chicago Press.

——1958. *Thoughts on Machiavelli*. Chicago: University of Chicago Press.

——1987. 'Machiavelli', in Leo Strauss and Joseph Cropsey (eds) *History of Political Philosophy*, 3rd edn. Chicago: University of Chicago Press, pp. 296–317.

Sullivan, Vickie. 2004. *Machiavelli, Hobbes, and the Formation of a Liberal Republicanism in England*. Cambridge: Cambridge University Press.

Tarcov, Nathan. 1982. 'Quentin Skinner's Method and Machiavelli's *Prince*', *Ethics* 92, pp. 692–709.

Tarcov, Nathan. 2008. 'Freedom, Republics, and Peoples in Machiavelli's Prince', in Richard L. Velkley, ed. *Freedom and the Human Person*. Washington, DC: Catholic University of America Press, pp. 122–42.

Thomson, J. A. K. 1927. *Irony: An Historical Introduction*. Cambridge, MA: Harvard University Press.

Triantafillis, Constantino. 1875. *Niccolò Machiavelli e gli scrittori greci*. Venice: Tipografia del Giornale 'Il tempo'.

Viroli, Maurizio. 1990. 'Machiavelli and the republican idea of politics', in Gisela Bock, et al. (eds) *Machiavelli and Republicanism*, pp. 143–71.

——1998. *Machiavelli*. Oxford: Oxford University Press.

——2001. *Niccolò's Smile: A Biography of Machiavelli*. Trans. Anthony Shugaar. London: I. B. Tauris.

——2013. 'The Prince as Redeemer', unpublished paper delivered at Machiavelli Workshop, Princeton, 8 February.

Vlastos, Gregory. 1991. *Socrates: Ironist and Moral Philosopher*. Cambridge: Cambridge University Press.

Walker, Henry John. 1995. *Theseus and Athens*. Oxford: Oxford University Press.

Watkins, Renée Neu (ed. trans.) 1978. *Humanism and Liberty: Writings on Freedom from Fifteenth-Century Florence*. Charleston: University of South Carolina Press.

Whitfield, J. H. 1969. *Discourses on Machiavelli*. Cambridge: W. Heffer & Sons.

Whitmarsh, Tim. 2001. *Greek Literature and the Roman Empire*. Oxford: Oxford University Press.

Worcester, David. 1940. *The Art of Satire*. Cambridge, MA: Harvard University Press.

Index